Eastern Europe

BOOKS BY
PHYLLIS MÉRAS

Eastern Europe:
A Traveler's Companion

Mermaids of Chenonceaux

Castles, Keeps, and Leprechauns

The New Carry-Out Cuisine

A Yankee Way with Wood

First Spring: A Martha's Vineyard Journal

Eastern Europe

A TRAVELER'S COMPANION

Phyllis Méras

HOUGHTON MIFFLIN COMPANY / BOSTON / 1991

Library of Congress Cataloging-in-Publication Data

Méras, Phyllis.
Eastern Europe : a traveler's companion / Phyllis Méras
p.   cm.
Includes index.
ISBN 0-395-55871-9
1. Europe, Eastern — Description and travel — 1981–   2. Méras,
Phyllis — Journeys — Europe, Eastern.   I. Title.
DJK19.M47   1991
914.704 — dc20   91-17894
CIP

Printed in the United States of America

AGM 10 9 8 7 6 5 4 3 2 1

In memory of

THOMAS H. COCROFT

1917–1989

Acknowledgments

I am grateful to many for their aid and support in the prepara-
tion of this book — in particular to Alan Kerr, Nancy Luede-
man, Cynthia Meisner, Dorothy Pieniadz and Heinrich Repke,
Jeff Smith, and Frances Tenenbaum.

In addition, this work would have been impossible without the
research assistance of Alexandru Budisteanu, Dinu Giurescu,
Victoria London, the Romanian Library, the Romanian National
Tourist Office, and Hanna Suliteanu; Lajos Csaszi, Frank Dobo,
Yvette Eastman, Ilonka Fischer, the late Eugene Fodor, Mary
Gluck, Andrea Hlacs, Suzanne Sekey, and Ildiko Henni of Ibusz;
Borša Hlinecka, Jana Krismanova, Henry Kucera, Tatyna Mc-
Auley, Jeanne Nemcova, Melanie and Ctibor Rybár, Jiři Šetlik of
the Czechoslovakian Embassy, Cihak Travel in Berwyn, Illinois,
and Čedok; Marek Borchert, Magda Paszciewicz, Edward Pien-
iadz, the Polish National Tourist Office, Hania and Tom Swick
and Wegiel Tours in Springfield, Massachusetts; Linda Bullard,
Nevard and Gary Dahayan, Cynthia Vakareliyska, and Maxim
Starkov and Anna Droumov of Balkan Holidays in New York;
Irma Bauman, Tom Bross, Karla Carl, Gabi Feyeler, Peter Janz,
Cindy and Seymour Pearlman, Christa Petrak, Hildegarde and
Klaus Ruof, Lisa and Donald Shanor, Hermann Sprenger, and
Helga Brenner-Kahn and Hedy Wuerz of the German National
Tourist Office.

I am indebted also to Helen Aruda, Joan Bloom of Hill and
Knowlton, Inc., Mikki Catanzaro, Linda Clapp, Lynn Chaput,
Joyce Dauley, Paula Del Bonis, Brian Dickinson, Urs Dur of the
House of Travel in Newburyport, Massachusetts, Mary Jane Ert-

man, Odette Fodor of KLM Royal Dutch Airlines, Phyllis Ellen Funke, Globe Travel of Washington, D.C., Ruth Gottlieb, Channing Gray, Lucille Hoshabjian of Lufthansa German Airlines, Joram Kagan of Unitours in New York City, Koch Travel of New York City, Andrew J. Lazarus and Eurailpass, Gerhard Markus of the Austrian National Tourist Office, Bedford Pace of the British Tourist Authority, Ursula and John Parry, Chèle Reekie, Larry Ryan of Roma Ryan Books and Prints of Belfast, Northern Ireland, Edwin Safford, Philip Terzian, Alan Tucker, John E. Wallace, Henny Wenkart, and Robert Whitcomb.

I have also made extensive use of the Boston Public Library, the Providence Public Library, the Wellesley College Library, the West Tisbury Public Library, and Book Den East in Oak Bluffs, Massachusetts.

CONTENTS

INTRODUCTION

For the last year, I have been exploring Eastern Europe, visiting the painted monasteries of northern Romania and of Bulgaria; Czechoslovakia with incomparable Prague; proud Poland with its soaring Tatra Mountains; the Hungarian capital of Budapest glittering on both sides of the Danube; cultural Weimar and Dresden in what was East Germany. For forty years, Western travelers have rarely ventured into these lands, put off by the Communist complexity that was required to cross their borders. And so these have remained countries much as they were at the end of the Second World War. For good or bad, until 1989, they have been largely untouched by commercialism. With Walkmen, cassette players, VCRs, and cars costly and in short supply, there has been a dependence on old-fashioned pleasures — afternoons in the parks and at zoos, evenings at concerts, Sundays shared with family and close friends. Sea, mountain, and lake resorts have received a fair complement of tourists from Eastern countries and facilities to care for them have, in those areas, been erected. But elsewhere, in picturesque villages and towns — even in some major cities of Eastern Europe — accommodations and other amenities that help to make travel enjoyable are often not of a quality that tourists from the West have come to expect. So travel in the East does remain an exploration — an adventure. It is not, however, an inexpensive adventure. With the opening of the East to the West and the opportunity now for Easterners to go to the West — if they have hard cash to spend there — prices have risen. Eager to obtain as much Western currency as they can, shopkeepers, hoteliers, and restaurateurs have been raising their prices and asking payment for their products and services in Western (generally United States) currency.

As for the quality of products and services supplied, they vary greatly from country to country and community to community. In general, it is the smaller communities that, to the best of their ability, are most hospitable. But forty years of communism have not fostered either initiative or enthusiasm among workers, and the visitor to the East is still likely to find lethargic waiters in restaurants and impatient clerks and excessive rigamarole at hotel reception desks, banks, airports, and train stations, as well as bored salespeople in shops. Museums and similar cultural attractions may or may not be open at the times signs say they should be. Whim and dinnertime play a very important part in museum and tourist office hours. The best restaurants, the churches, and the castles you most want to see often are closed indefinitely for renovations.

Travel in the East can also be arduous. In most areas, though roads are good and traffic light, the thoroughfares are single-lane. As of this writing, gas stations in many Eastern nations are widely spaced and gas not always available without a wait. No independent traveler should consider driving without a map locating gas stations. Rail service, with old equipment, tends to be slow, but negotiations are under way with the railroads of Western Europe that should soon streamline rail travel in the East. Though air service into the East is now frequent, local air service within the East Bloc countries is limited.

As in much of the West, pollution has adversely affected some of the landscape. There has been no money for emission controls for cars or industry. Fumes have blackened and eaten at the facades of historic sandstone buildings. Rivers and streams have died from chemical effluents.

On the other hand, there are incalculable treasures of art and architecture in the East and warm and welcoming people to meet, even if language is a problem. The traveler still can go for miles through untouched farmland and forest.

Less industrialized, as most of it is, than the West, the East still offers interesting handicrafts. In Bulgaria, Hungary, and Romania, good, simple peasant pottery can still be bought from the country artisan at his front door. Bright weaving, fine embroidery, wood carving, and copies of ancient icons are also to be found in Bulgaria and Romania, and Romanian floral-design rugs are known the world around.

In Hungary, in addition to pottery and embroidery, there is exquisite lace, delicate Herend porcelain, exotic Zsolnay porcelain, dolls that are charmingly dressed in local costume, and colorfully painted wooden eggs.

Hand-knitted woolens, at a fraction of the cost of hand-knits in America, are sold in the villages of the Polish Tatras, along with painted wooden eggs, wood carvings of varying quality, and costumed dolls. In the jewelry shops of Warsaw and along the Baltic, golden amber is the souvenir item for which to be on the lookout.

Czechoslovakia is renowned for its Bohemian glass and wooden toys; more industrialized eastern Germany for Meissen china, art books, old prints and engravings, and fur.

Up to now, travelers to the East principally have arrived on group tours, and government tourist offices (and new private ones) are better equipped to guide and assist groups than independent travelers (who may, for example, find restaurants fully booked by tour groups, and street names and museum hours changed in the new East). But the courageous independent tourist who is challenged rather than put off by inefficiencies and bureaucratic nonsense will not only find that Eastern European nations are culturally, sociologically, and politically rewarding (democracy, after all, is being reborn in the East), but that the very inefficiencies — once the frustration has passed — can be amusing.

What follows is a very personal selection of sites to see in the East. Although those included have been selected primarily because of cultural, historic, or scenic significance, their accessibility and the quality of tourist facilities in their neighborhoods has also been considered.

Phyllis Méras
March 1991

Bulgaria

Romania

Danube River

Golden Sands

Varna

Veliko Tŭrnovo

Balkan Mountains

Sofia

Valley of the Roses

Sunny Beach

Black Sea

Sredna Gora

Plovdiv

Rila Monastery

Bachkovo Monastery

Rhodope Mountains

Turkey

Yugoslavia

Greece

$\mathcal{B}$ulgaria is the land of the poet Orpheus, who charmed not only men but beasts with his lyre and his songs. It is the land of the Valley of the Roses that produces 70 percent of the attar of roses the world's perfumers use. Bulgaria was ancient Thrace, conquered by Philip II of Macedon and his son, Alexander the Great, in the fourth century B.C. Lying on the eastern end of the Balkan peninsula, where Europe meets Asia, it is both Eastern and Western in outlook. (Like the Turks, the Bulgarians nod "no" and shake their heads "yes.") Homer and Herodotus, Thucydides and Xenophon wrote about Thrace. Spartacus, leader of the slave revolt against the Romans, was a Thracian.

Bulgaria's Balkan Mountains, for which the peninsula is named, are mighty and snow-capped. Mightier still is the Rila range, where the fortified monastery-church of Rila, founded in the tenth century, has been designated a World Cultural Heritage by UNESCO. And Bulgaria's Black Sea coast of sloping golden sands is studded with up-to-date resorts (probably the most up-to-date of any Eastern European country's).

Bulgaria is where yogurt was invented, and the bacillus that turns fresh milk into yogurt is named *Lactobacillus bulgaricus*. Fruits and vegetables grow here in abundance — purple eggplants and crimson tomatoes, refreshing cucumbers, fat strawberries and purple plums. Thrace was the land of the cult of Dionysus, god of wine, and the wines of today's Bulgaria delight its visitors.

The Thracians whom the ancient poets and historians describe were a tribal people occupying the land between the Danube River and the Aegean Sea. They were farmers, shepherds, and accomplished goldsmiths. Indeed, they were accomplished in so many respects that Herodotus believed they would have been the greatest among the ancient nations had they been able to organize under one leader. Trading with the Greeks, they exchanged many ideas, but they could not, apparently, accept the idea of a single ruler. Fighting among themselves rather than uniting against foreign invaders, they were absorbed into the Macedonian Empire.

From then on, the history of Bulgaria is a story of conquests.

After the Macedonians, the Romans came, and when that empire was divided into East and West in the fourth century, the lands that are today's Bulgaria fell under Eastern — Byzantine — rule. There, the language and culture were Greek; the religion, Christian.

The next invaders were the Slavs, but they soon settled down peaceably to be farmers — until, in the seventh century, the horse-riding Bulgars (relatives of today's Finns) galloped down from between the Ural Mountains and the Volga on their fleet horses. Named, some say, for the skins they wore that came from the *bulga*, an animal of Central Asia, they were fierce fighters ruled by khans. Soon they had vanquished the Slavs, intermingled and intermarried with them; in 681, Byzantium was forced to recognize the existence of the First Bulgarian kingdom on the Balkan peninsula and to pay tribute annually to it.

But that was not enough for Khan Krum the Terrible. While extending his territory, he killed the Byzantine emperor and cut off his head, which he had silver-lined and, thereafter, used as a drinking cup.

In the ninth century the Bulgars' Boris I was frightened into converting to Christianity when a monk painted a picture of the horrors of Hell on his palace walls. Meanwhile, disciples of the two Greek missionary brothers, Cyril and Methodius (Cyril or one of his followers is said to have devised the Cyrillic alphabet to translate the Bible from Greek to Slavonic for the common man), were welcomed here. (It wasn't until several years later, the Bulgarians proudly point out, that the Cyrillic alphabet reached Russia, which also employs it.)

Though Byzantium and Bulgaria now shared the same religion, relations did not improve. They came to a bloody end in 1014 when the Byzantine emperor Basil II, "the Bulgar Killer," defeated a force of Bulgarian soldiers and blinded his 15,000 prisoners. One man in every hundred was left with one eye so he could lead the others back to their king, who was so shocked when he saw them, it is said, that he was dead of despair within three days.

Four years later, Bulgaria was under the rule of the Byzantine Empire again and remained so for more than a century and a half. During this time the Byzantine style in architecture and art that has remained in Bulgaria ever since was introduced.

Not until 1185 was there an independent Bulgaria once more. That was when two boyar (noble) brothers, Petŭr and Asen, led a successful revolt against their imperial overlords and established the Second Bulgarian Kingdom. It lasted till 1396 (a highlight was the coronation of a swineherd as tsar). But when it was weakened by infighting among nobles, the Turks invaded. Bulgaria's king was forced to take an oath of fealty to the Turkish sultan while his sister was carried off to the sultan's harem.

For the next five centuries, Turkey ruled Bulgaria. Muslim colonists occupied the rich lands and forced the Bulgarian Christian peasants to do their bidding. Although the Islamic faith was not "imposed," it was to the advantage of Bulgarians to convert so they would have the same rights as the Turkish settlers in their land, and many did. Bulgarian culture was in danger of disappearing entirely.

But at the beginning of the nineteenth century, almost miraculously, a National Revival got under way. It was spurred by an account of the lives of Bulgarian saints and kings written by a monk, and by the memoirs of a bishop who brokenheartedly wrote of the disintegration of Bulgaria under the Turks. The resultant enthusiasm for things Bulgarian led to movements in art and architecture that account for some of the finest buildings standing in this country. In place of the fortresslike homes of the Turkish period (*see* Arbanasi), the Bulgarian middle class adopted the symmetry, curves, and columned porticoes of the Baroque and Byzantine styles, but proudly added their own colorful decoration and fine wood carving.

For the younger generation, this was not enough. They looked for independence from Turkish rule, and an underground began working toward it. But an uprising in 1876 was put down with such repression — 15,000 massacred and 58 villages destroyed, with women and children who had taken refuge in a church in one village hacked to pieces or burned to death — that all Europe spoke of the "Turkish atrocities." Oscar Wilde, Garibaldi, Dostoevski, England's Prime Minister William Gladstone, Turgenev, and Victor Hugo all called on the peoples of the world to do something about such cruelty.

The Russians did. They declared war on Turkey in 1877 and, joined by Bulgarian and Romanian forces, arrived almost at the gates of Constantinople to force the Turks to recognize an independent Bulgaria. It looked at last as if Bulgaria had a future.

But the superpowers of Europe, fearful of Russian influence in the Balkans, didn't want it that way. The peace that the Turks had agreed to, giving three fifths of the Balkan peninsula to Balkan peoples, was quashed in the face of threats from Western powers, and Turkey got back much of what it had lost. That done, the great powers arranged for the election of a German prince, Alexander of Battenberg (of the line that would become England's Mountbatten family), as constitutional monarch of the new Bulgaria.

In the years between then and World War I, two more German princes occupied the Bulgarian throne. There were wars with Turkey, then with the other Balkan states over land acquisition. When Bulgaria lost, it joined World War I on the side of its German-born ruler. By the war's end, Bulgaria had lost both men and lands and was paying heavy reparations for having chosen the loser's side.

Discontent in these postwar years led to virtual civil war. A Communist uprising ended in thousands dead and the Communist party banned. More unrest led to the dictatorship of Boris III in 1935. As World War II began, Adolf Hitler, eager to have access to Yugoslavia and Greece through Bulgaria, promised Bulgaria land if it would join the Axis side, and Bulgaria did.

But in 1944, after its old friends the Russians had crossed the Danube into their land, the Bulgarians quickly rallied to their side, and two years later the Russians saw to it that a People's

Republic was established. Bulgaria has been a People's Republic ever since, though in 1989 Todor Zhivkov, its long-time rigid Communist dictator, was ousted; free elections were held in the spring of 1990.

Today one tends to think of Bulgaria in terms of hard-line communism or of Balkan intrigue. (Boris III died mysteriously, some said of poison, when he returned from Berlin in 1943 after having committed his country to the Nazi cause. Bulgarians were linked to the 1961 plot to kill the pope. A Bulgarian journalist, outspoken against the rulers of his nation, died in London in the 1960s after having been pricked with a poison umbrella on a London bridge.) But the visitor forgets this stuff of spy thrillers as well as the miseries Bulgaria has suffered when standing here in a still mountain pass, watching a river tumble over gray rocks, listening in an oak wood to the song of birds, or looking, bedazzled, at the craftsmanship that created a fourth century B.C. Thracian goblet.

SOFIA

Most visitors agree that Sofia's location is this Bulgarian capital's prime attraction. Above it rises wooded Mount Vitosha with its rivers, waterfalls, and soaring peaks. More than 3,000 different plants grow in the mountain forests. The air is crisp and clear. In less than an hour, you can be far outside the city in beech woods beside a bubbling stream, in a thirteenth-century monastery garden, or schussing on a pristine ski slope.

Sofia itself is largely a city of wide boulevards and squares, pleasant but not especially interesting parks, and enormous Socialist Realism–style buildings. Exploring, however, one can happen on more old-fashioned, jumbled places with an air of the East.

In the fifth century B.C., Sofia was the Thracian city of Serdika. When the Romans conquered Thrace, they made it the capital. Then the hordes of Attila the Hun set it on fire in the fifth century A.D. Justinian rebuilt it and, as part of the refurbishment, had the

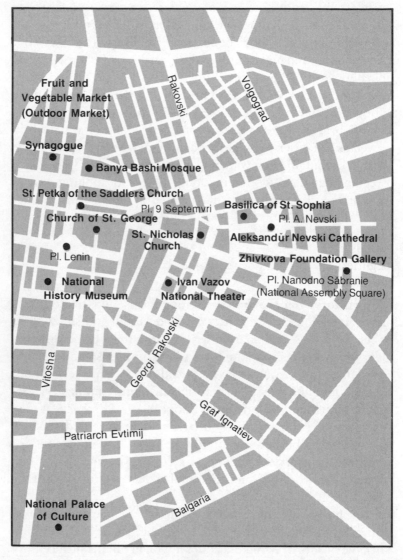

SOFIA

Basilica of St. Sofia built, from which it takes its name. "Sofia" means wisdom.

Later centuries saw Sofia suffering as the rest of Bulgaria suffered — from invasion after invasion, so that most of what you see today was erected after 1878 when Sofia became the capital of the Third Bulgarian Kingdom. The principal sites follow.

Aleksandŭr Nevski Cathedral (Hram-pametnik Aleksandŭr Nevski), ploshtad Aleksandŭr Nevski: This five-aisled basilica, the largest on the Balkan peninsula, was built with such care and in so grand a style that it took thirty years to complete. Begun in 1882, it was erected in gratitude to Russia's Tsar Alexander II and the 200,000 Russian soldiers who died freeing Bulgaria from the Turks in 1878. Alexander Nevsky was the tsar's patron saint who had defeated the Swedes attacking Russia in the thirteenth century. The Russian architect who designed the cathedral, A. N. Pomerantsev, was also the architect for what is now Moscow's sprawling galleried GUM department store. Marble from Brazil, Morocco, and Italy was used in the basilica; in 1960 eighteen pounds of gold leaf were donated by the Soviet Union to create its glittering central golden dome. Everything in the cathedral is enormous and overpowering. God with a white beard looks down from the central dome; a fresco of the Last Supper is above the altar and a warning Last Judgment is at the door. The combining of Russian and Bulgarian elements was tactfully done: the central iconostasis is Russian; on the left as you face the altar is Bulgaria's patron saint, Boris I, who introduced Christianity; on the right are the Slavic patron saints, Cyril and Methodius (the Cyrillic alphabet was named for Cyril, one of whose students devised it). Mosaics and frescoes are used in the decoration and both Russian and Bulgarian artists painted the frescoes, mostly of the life of Christ. To the right of the altar as you face it is the throne of Boris III, Bulgaria's World War II king. The alabaster lions with onyx eyes before it symbolize the power of the king. Although Boris made himself all-powerful by establishing a dictatorship, he died of unexplained causes after returning from a 1943 visit with Hitler. Some speculate that he was poisoned when he refused to send Bulgaria's Jews to concentration camps, giving the country's 50,000 Jews time to escape. Local stories have it that his death was predicted by Bulgaria's blind prognosticator, Vanga, to whom Bulgarians still go to ask about their future (having slept the night before with sugar cubes under their pillows so that she can read them). The cathedral is particularly notable for its choir, which can be heard on Saturdays at the 6:00 P.M. service, at midnight on Easter Eve, and, occasionally, when it is making the recordings that are sold where the candles are sold in the entrance to the church.

The **Museum of Icons** (Muzeyat na Ikoni) in the cathedral crypt, an annex of the **National Art Gallery,** is a magnificent collection of icons of many centuries from all over Bulgaria. Of particular interest are the icon of Nessebar, the fourteenth-century processional icon of Poganovo with the pensive faces of the Virgin and St. John the Evangelist on one side and on the other a vision in blue of the prophet Ezekiel and a seventeenth-century icon of St. George on a horse. It is open from 10:30 A.M. to 6:30 P.M., except Tuesday.

Banya Bashi Mosque, bulevard Georgi Dimitrov: This 1576 mosque with its striking minaret is one of the few Turkish monuments still standing here. It continues to be a working mosque but has been undergoing repairs for some time.

Basilica of St. Sophia (Sv. Sofia), ploshtad Aleksandŭr Nevski: This triple-naved red-brick church, reconstructed in 1930, stands on the foundations of the basilica that Justinian built in the sixth century. It is as simple in style and decoration as the cathedral is ornate and combines the architecture of East and West by having round Romanesque arches on a structure that otherwise is Byzantine. Even before Justinian, however, there were churches here, and a mosaic of trees and flowers from one of these predecessors may be seen.

During the centuries of Ottoman rule, St. Sophia's was transformed into a mosque, but after it was damaged in earthquakes in 1818 and 1858 (with the minaret destroyed in 1818) the Turks heeded the warnings and ceased to use it. Outside is the Tomb of the Unknown Soldier.

Central Market (Halite), bulevard Georgi Dimitrov: This

Grand National Revival–style covered market built in 1911 is now undergoing reconstruction.

Church of St. George (Tsŭrkvata Sv. Georgi), ploshtad Sveta Nedelya: In the courtyard just outside the Hotel Sheraton are the remains of this fourth-century red-brick rotunda that is only rarely open to the public, for it is undergoing restoration. No one is certain what occupied this site originally. Some speculate it may have been a Roman bath; others a pagan temple. The belief is that in the fourth century, the emperor Constantine, known to have an affection for Serdika, as Sofia was then called, toyed with making it his capital (he chose Constantinople instead), and transformed the Roman structure into a Christian church. In Turkish days, of course, it became a mosque. A minaret was erected and its frescoes covered with black paint.

Fruit and Vegetable Market (Pazar), ulitsa Georgi Kirkov: For the devotee of outdoor markets, this one with its lines of stalls can be a colorful place, but it is wise to keep your hand on your wallet in the crowds of buyers and sellers of bright bouquets and newly sheared wool. In this part of the city, a Gypsy with a dancing bear on a leash may be doing some entertaining.

Ivan Vazov National Theater (Narodniyat Teatŭr Ivan Vazov), ulitsa Vasil Levski 5: This striking red-and-gold neoclassical building with its white columns was designed by two Viennese architects and opened with much fanfare in 1908. But in 1923, a fire that started on the stage and spread with great rapidity destroyed all but the facade of the building. A German architect was employed for the reconstruction, which was finished in 1929. But World War II bombing destroyed much of the theater again. In 1973 it was rebuilt and boasts a National Revival Baroque interior in more or less the fashion of the 1908 original. It is named for the nineteenth-century writer Ivan Vazov, famous for his account of life under the Turks, *Under the Yoke,* and the founder of the Bulgarian classical literature movement. After his death, his admirers wanted to bury him in the Basilica of St. Sophia, but in agreement with his wish to lie where he would still be among working, living people, they buried him outside in the square.

National History Museum (Natsionalniyat Istoricheski Muzei), bulevard Vitosha 2: The original fourth or third century B.C. Thracian gold Panagyurishte treasure is here and should not be missed. Consisting of eight gleaming drinking horns fashioned with stag and billy-goat heads and a dish decorated with a design of acorns and the heads of blacks, this twelve-pound golden treasure was found by accident in 1949 by peasants digging clay for bricks. It has since traveled the world as an example of the exquisite workmanship in gold of the ancient Thracians. Also of interest are the Bronze Age Vulchitran treasure, objects from the fourth-century Varna necropolis, and a copy of the ninth-century glazed-tile icon of St. Theodore Stratilatus, unusual because no one knows how the painting of the twenty tiles was done. Folk costumes are also displayed. If possible, arrange a day in advance at the ticket desk for an English-speaking guide. (This will require determination as few of the ticket sellers know English, but appreciation of what you are seeing is greatly enhanced by information about it.) The museum is open from 10:30 A.M. to 6:30 P.M., except on Monday, when it is closed, and Friday, when its opening time is 2:30 P.M.

National Palace of Culture (Narodniyat Dvorets na Kulturata), ploshtad Baba Nedelya: The only reason to see this 1981 complex of shops, theater, discotheque, restaurant, bowling alley, and fountains is because it is so immense and because so many Bulgarian young people frequent it. If they speak English (and university students are likely to), they often go out of their way to be warm and welcoming to foreigners. Outside, the colossal 1,300 Years Monument celebrates Bulgaria's founding in 681.

St. Nicholas or the Russian Church (Tsŭrkvata Sv. Nikola), bulevard Ruski: This charming little church with its rich interior was built for Russian diplomats in Sofia in 1912 because one of them was nervous about worshipping in a Bulgarian Orthodox rather than a Russian Orthodox church. It remains particularly popular with intellectuals.

St. Petka of the Saddlers Church (Tsŭrkvata Sv. Petka Samardzhiyska), ploshtad Sveta Nedelya: From the fourteenth century till after World War II, this inconspicuous little church built for the Saddlers Guild continued to hold services. Since it was constructed after the Turkish invasion, it had to be restrained in size and shape and in no way could its exterior challenge a mosque. It was, therefore, built low to be below the main Turkish settlement. But in its fifteenth- to seventeenth-century interior frescoes, you can see the pent-up longing for freedom.

Synagogue (Synagoga), ulitsa Eharh Iozif: Situated behind the Central Market, this enormous green-domed synagogue was built in 1909 after the design of Vienna's Sephardic synagogue, which was destroyed in World War II. In its day, it could welcome 1,170 worshippers and is the largest Sephardic (Spanish) Jewish synagogue in Europe. For some years now, however, it has been undergoing restoration and services are held in a small anteroom whose walls are decorated with gifts from Jewish communities around the world. The custodian will sometimes let visitors inside the synagogue, but as yet there is little to see.

Gallery of the International Foundation of Sts. Cyril and Methodius (Galeriyata Zname na Mira), ploshtad Aleksandŭr Nevski: There is much fine art in this former nineteenth-century printing house turned art gallery. French works in the collection put together by Bulgarian dentist Kostadin Delchev, whose home is in France, include works by Renoir, Matisse, Rouault, Delacroix, Pascin. There is a Henry Moore sculpture that was a gift from the artist.

THE OUTSKIRTS OF SOFIA

Boyana Church (Boyanskala Tsurkva), ulitsa Belite Brezi, Boyana: The medieval frescoes in this beautifully situated fifteenth-century church that looks down on Sofia and across to the wooded Balkan mountain range are simple and charming. Originally, the church that now stands in a quiet garden was part of a boyar's large fortified property. The first church here, domed, with a two-armed Greek cross, was added onto in 1250 by Sevastokrator Kaloyan, who ruled over the Sofia area and for whom the finest of the frescoes were painted. (He and his wife, Desilava, are portrayed offering a model of the church to God.) A man known simply as the Master of Boyana was the artist for the 240 extraordinarily realistic portraits in the Life of Christ series — extraordinary, because this was a period when stylization was expected in religious art. The people painted are young and vigorous and though their expressions are often sorrowful or meditative, each face has its own individuality. The boy, Jesus, in the Temple with the Elders is a typical, round-faced ten-year-old. The food on the Bulgarian checked tablecloth that has been spread for the Last Supper is typical Bulgarian peasant food — radishes, bread, and garlic — and those eating it are dressed in medieval Bulgarian garb. Interestingly, these frescoes predate the Italian Renaissance master Giotto, who is generally credited with being the first to inject life and compassion into Western art. Other paintings are of the Disciples, the Life of the Virgin, and St. Nicholas. (The last are painted by a different unknown master.)

Unfortunately, preservation of the frescoes from the humidity has long been a problem, and visitors' breathing has contributed to it so that now restoration work is being done on the church itself and tourists can only see copies of the original frescoes, which are housed in a small museum on the church grounds. It seems unlikely in the future that the church itself will be opened to any but art historians with special permission. Museum hours are from 8:45 A.M. to 5:00 P.M., Monday through Friday.

Dragalevtsi Monastery, Dragalevtsi: The fourteenth-century church in a beech wood is all that remains of the original monastery, the oldest in Bulgaria, that stood here. There are fifteenth- and seventeenth-century frescoes to see — the former considerably better than the latter and including portraits of the donor and his family and of the ancient philosophers marching to Heaven.

This monastery is particularly notable for having often sheltered Vasil Levski, Bulgaria's underground fighter against the Turks, who, betrayed, was tortured and hanged in Sofia in 1873.

A monk provided shelter here for him and carried messages to his headquarters in Sofia. The monastery is open from 10:00 A.M. to 5:00 P.M., Monday through Friday.

For hikers wishing to climb the highest peak of Mount Vitosha, Cherni Vrah (the Black Peak), Dragalevtsi is the perfect starting place. And for skiers, there are an increasing number of facilities at nearby Aleko.

THE BALKAN MOUNTAINS

In ancient times, a young Thracian warrior, Hem, fell in love with Rhodope, a lovely neighbor. He was soon calling her Hera as a pet name, after the queen of the gods, and she was calling him Zeus, after the king. But the gods did not take kindly to having their names used frivolously by mortals. In their anger, they hurled Hem across the northern part of what is today's Bulgaria and Rhodope into the south, turning him into the wooded Balkan Mountains and his beloved into the Rhodope range.

In Ottoman days, when rich plains land was taken away from Christian Bulgarians and given to Turks, many of the Bulgarians moved into Hem's mountains — the Balkan mountain range — for they were a reasonable place to live. They were not too high (Botov, the highest peak, is only 7,480 feet); they provided good pastureland for cows and sheep, and near the bottom they were forested with useful beech, oak, and fruit trees. As a result, the Balkan Mountains became one of the most populated parts of Bulgaria.

But even before the days of the Turks, these rounded green mountains with their hideaways had attracted settlers. Pliska was the capital of the First Bulgarian Kingdom. Later Preslav took its place. Then Veliko Tŭrnovo was built as capital of the Second Kingdom. In the quiet mountain valleys, where the only sounds were wind, birds, and sheep bells, monasteries were constructed.

Of course, battles were fought here, too. It was in a narrow pass near Pliska that Khan Krum fought, killed, and beheaded the emperor of Byzantium in 811. At Shipka Pass in 1877, 6,000 Russians and Bulgarians successfully held off a force of 27,000 Turks, thereby leading the way to Bulgaria's freedom from Turkish rule. The main sites of these Balkan Mountains and the valley below them follow.

ARBANASI

This fortified village with its stone houses surrounded by high walls, its churches hidden in the hillsides, was founded by Albanians fleeing the Turks in the fifteenth century. But it owes its richness — its spacious, splendidly decorated houses — to those same Turks; in the sixteenth century, Sultan Suleiman the Magnificent gave the village and the surrounding countryside to one of his sons-in-law. As a result, it received special treatment. The residents of Arbanasi were able to prosper as businessmen and traders. The villages were allowed to remain, and the churches, too, went untouched as long as they didn't advertise their presence with bell towers or steeples. In the seventeenth century, Arbanasi prospered; indeed, it was so prosperous that it was frequently attacked by Turkish brigands. In 1798, they set it on fire and destroyed much of it. Nevertheless, there are thirty-six houses preserved here as national monuments and several are open to the public. Among them is the **Konstantsalieva House** (Kŭshtata na Konstantsaliev), built after the 1798 fire.

Owned by the grandmother of the sultan, its ground floor was constructed of stone, as protection against marauders and earthquakes. Around the house is a high stone wall with heavy, nail-studded wooden doors to stop the entry of brigands, and there are hidden escape doors. The wooden second story living quarters are spacious, opulent, and very Oriental.

Bright-colored carpets and cushions cover the sleeping and sitting benches along the walls. Floors are tiled. Fireplaces are so arranged as to provide even heat. In addition to quarters for everyday living, there is a merchant's office and a confinement room where the new mother and her baby were tended for forty days after the infant's birth.

Several other restored houses, notable in particular for their carved ceilings, are open to the public — except on Monday and from noon to 2:00 P.M. — on guided tours that you can join as you enter the village.

Tours also take visitors inside the seventeenth-century **Church of the Nativity** (Tsŭrkvata Rožhdestvo Hristovo), concealed in a hillside, with an interior decorated with brilliantly colored restored frescoes, some said to date back to the sixteenth century. Some 3,500 figures are painted here, including the Greek philosophers and the forebears of Christ. There are four other churches here that may sometimes be visited and two monasteries — the **Monastery of St. Nicholas** (Mónastiryat Sv. Nikola) and the **Monastery of the Holy Virgin** (Bogoroditsa).

BOZHENTSI

This white-and-brown community of one hundred houses with fifteen residents is distinctly a museum-village nowadays, but that doesn't detract from its prettiness. In summer wild geraniums and buttercups brighten the grass and golden acacia flowers dangle over the doorways. Its well-maintained houses have second stories jutting out over the first. For aficionados of peasant architecture, Bozhentsi, an architectural preserve that remains as it was in the second half of the nineteenth century, will surely be of interest; for travelers with more general interests, less so. It is named, so the story goes, for its founder, the widow of a boyar from the nearby city of Veliko Tŭrnovo.

After the Turks took over the Second Kingdom capital and killed her husband, Bozhana is said to have fled here with her sons, following her flocks of sheep that liked the thick green grass and the freshwater springs. In time, others ousted from the city by the Turks joined her. They began selling wool and, noting the way the bees took to the acacia blossoms, producing honey. Between the wool, beeswax, and honey, the embroidery the villagers liked to do, and metalwork, Bozhentsi in the mid-nineteenth century was a prosperous as well as a pretty community. Today, there are sometimes-open souvenir shops and a restaurant, but an hour's stroll through the village should satisfy most travelers.

ETŬRA

Five miles south of Gabrovo on the road to Shipka Pass, potters, wheelwrights, carvers, bakers, and gold and coppersmiths do their tasks in this outdoor bazaar-museum. Many of the houses in which they work are genuine National Revival houses that were brought here and set along little Sivek Brook to make this a National Revival outdoor museum, or they were constructed on the site following old pictures and plans. Souvenir shops sell the articles — from copper bells to sheepskin coats — that the craftsmen make. An old-fashioned water mill provides the power for timber cutting for the village. There's strong Turkish coffee to drink at the café, barley-sugar roosters at the confectioner's, *simiti* — glazed chick-pea flour buns — to try at the bakery, and grilled sausages and kebabs at the restaurants.

LOVECH

The old town here is notable for its covered bridge over the River Osŭm, designed in 1874 by architect Kolyo Ficheto, but the bridge crossing the river today is a 1982 reconstruction. Inside are gift shops and café–ice cream parlors. Were it not that it is the main foot route to Varosha, the old town, the bridge would not be worth spending much time to see, but across the river, with a sheer gray cliff backdrop, are the red-roofed white houses of Lovech on winding cobblestoned streets and the restored ruins of the Roman fortress of Melta.

In the old city square, vendors offer wild geranium bouquets and paper tubes full of sunflower seeds to snack on. There are scales to check weights of passersby — for a price. On the narrow streets of Varosha, roses peek invitingly over high stone walls. Grapes climb arbors. Diligent knitters ply their needles outside front doors. *Chardaki* — balconies — extend out over the streets and the little enclosed courtyards. From the fortress itself, where an enormous statue of Vasil Levski stands, is a fine view of the birch-edged river cutting its way through rock, the whitewashed houses with garret windows like giants' eyes peering out from the roofs.

There is a **Levski Museum** (Muzeyat na Vasil Levski) here, outlining (in Bulgarian) his life; this revolutionary leader carried on many of his underground activities against the Turks here, and it was near here, in the village of Kukrina, that he was betrayed in 1873.

The unearthing of the remains of a Socialist-period concentration camp near here where 2,000 are said to have been interned and forced to do hard labor in the stone quarries, and where virtually all of them died, has put Lovech recently in a bad light. Still, old Lovech's charms (even if much of what was old has been restored or reconstructed) cannot be denied. While Bozhentsi is strictly a museum village, Lovech lives.

MADARA

Carved high up in the cliffside here, eight miles east of Shumen, is the Madara Horseman spearing a lion, with his greyhound following behind. Its origins remain mysterious, for there is Greek as well as early Bulgarian writing on the rock. Some speculate that the carving in some way records the debt of fifth-century Khan Tervel to the Roman emperor Justinian. Others believe that it is meant to show the power of the khan against his enemy, Byzantium — symbolized by the lion — followed by his loyal people the dog and is one of a series of rock carvings an early khan had ordered. Unfortunately, the wind and rain of centuries have seriously eroded the carving, and it is not easy to see. Sundown is probably the best time for viewing. Nearby are the remains of a fourteenth-century monastery whose cells were cut into the rock and a small museum of Thracian and Roman artifacts as well as caves that suggest that centuries ago they, too, were inhabited.

SHIPKA PASS

Like gold-wrapped candy kisses, the domes of the turn-of-the-century **Memorial Church** shine above ash, oak, and birch trees in this mountain pass. Here, 6,000 Russian soldiers and Bulgarian volunteers managed to hold off 27,000 Turks in August 1877, which led to the defeat of the Ottomans at nearby Kazan-lŭk and the end of their five centuries of rule in Bulgaria. The bells that toll so melodiously here now were cast from bullets found in the pass after the battle. Because of those it honors, the church, like the Russian Church and the Aleksandŭr Nevski Cathedral in Sofia, is in Russian-Byzantine style.

TROYAN

Built in 1835, after several earlier monasteries on the site had been destroyed, the colorful Troyan Monastery here is entirely a work of the National Revival period. It is best known for the frescoes by Bulgaria's greatest fresco painter, Zahari Zograf. Painted from 1847 to 1849, the frescoes are remarkable because, for the first time, ordinary people, the monks who lived here and the artist himself, are realistically painted along with the always accepted saints and biblical figures. Also of interest are the icons done by Dimitŭr Zograf, Zahari's brother, and the wooden iconostasis.

In the museum are memorabilia of Vasil Levski, the hero in the nineteenth-century fight against the Turks. He had headquarters here and his activities were actively supported by the monks.

THE VALLEY OF THE ROSES

Nestled between the Balkans and the Sredna Gora range is Bulgaria's Valley of the Roses (Dolinata na Rozite), the source of 70 percent or more of the attar of roses the world's perfumers use for their most delicate fragrances. The mountains that rise like cresting waves along both sides of the valley are the guardians of these precious fragrant flowers, with the higher Balkans protecting them from the cold winds of the north and the low Sredna Gora virtually inviting the warm winds from the south. By far the best time for a visit here is early June, for there is a colorful Rose Festival then, usually the first week, with costumed rose pickers dancing, souvenir attar of roses being sold in pocket-sized wooden minarets, rose liqueur and rose-flavored Turkish delight for the tasting, and a Queen of the Roses crowned. But any time in late May or early June the roses — pink Kazanlŭk roses, red Damask roses, and white roses — will be coming into flower and perfuming the air. Though there are more than 10,000 varieties of roses in the world, only 200 of them produce the oil with long-lasting fragrance essential for fine perfumes, and these thrive here. A rose tree is at its best when it is about ten years old, but it can live for fifty years. For maximum strength, its flowers must be picked when they are fully open but before the morning sun has dried up any of the oil. To produce one pound of extract, 3,000 to 4,000 pounds of petals must be gathered. They then go into copper vats to be distilled, and the attar and rose water are the result. Unfortunately, though there is a small **Museum of Rose Production** in the rose fields, even if you find it open (which is unlikely) there is virtually nothing inside to see. There is also a research laboratory nearby, but it is not open to the public.

There are any number of tales of how roses came to be grown in this valley. One has it that a Bulgarian architect sent to Constantinople to build a palace for the sultan was offered anything he would like by the satisfied monarch. He requested the hand of the sultan's daughter. The enraged sultan ordered him immediately out of the land, but the lovely daughter sent a rose tree with him so he would always remember her. This tree was the first rose tree in the Valley of the Roses.

KAZANLŬK

In 1944, when an air raid shelter was being dug in a mound here, a fourth-century Thracian tomb was uncovered in this capital city of the Valley of the Roses. Although the brick tomb itself is not open to the public (for fear of damage to the wall frescoes by visitors' breathing), a replica has been created and is open to visitors. In the domed burial chamber, the burial feast of a man, either a ruler or an important military man, is depicted on walls that are stained Pompeian red. The dead man is seated at the feasting table, holding his wife's hand; coming toward them are musicians with instruments and servants offering gifts. On the passage walls leading to the burial chamber are friezes of battle scenes from the life of the deceased. The feast paintings, in particular, are done with great richness of color, sensitivity to the individuals being portrayed, and artistic dexterity, and are ranked among the world's finest examples of ancient art. The replica is open daily from 9:00 A.M. to noon and from 1:00 to 5:00 P.M.

A more probable story of the arrival of the first roses here is that they were brought from Damascus in Syria during the Crusades (hence the Damask name). In the 1830s a Turkish merchant was so impressed with the fragrance of these roses that he began extracting the attar and started a business that led to the exportation of attar of roses by the 1860s. Today, one ounce of attar of roses sells for between $280 and $300.

VELIKO TŬRNOVO

Clinging to the crags that rise above the River Yantra, this capital of the Second Bulgarian Kingdom of the Middle Ages is one of the country's most picturesque sites. It rises on three main hills: fortified Tsarevets; Trapezitsa, where the boyars lived; and Sveta Gora, then the center of a scholarly monastery, now a university site. The old houses of Tsarevets "huddle together like a flock of frightened sheep," according to Bulgaria's most prominent nineteenth-century literary figure, Ivan Vazov. Veliko Tŭrnovo's entry into Bulgarian history came in 1185 on the day of the consecration of the Church of St. Demetrius of Thessalonica, when the saint was said to have come here to help free the Bulgarians from Byzantine rule.

As the crowd assembled for the ceremony, two boyar brothers, Petŭr and Asen, announced their determination to be independent of Byzantium again (the Byzantines had taken over Bulgaria in 1018). Already in possession of the fortress whose restored walls still rise on Tsarevets Hill, the brothers were easily able to enlist the support of their fellow Bulgarians, and Petŭr was declared king. Two years later, Veliko Tŭrnovo became the Second

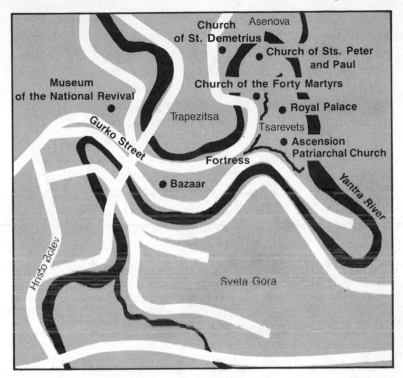

VELIKO TŬRNOVO

Kingdom's capital and remained such until 1396 and the arrival of the Ottomans. There is much to see here, but before embarking on a sightseeing tour, it would be wise to visit the Balkan tourist office at bulevard Vasil Levski 1 to see when churches and other sites are open. The historic, architectural, and religious sites of Veliko Tŭrnovo follow.

Ascension Patriarchal Church (Tsŭrkvata Uspenie Bogorodichno), Tsarevets Hill (Hŭlm Tsaravets): This church, which you reach up a long flight of stairs, is now completely restored and decorated with frescoes in Socialist Realist–Modern style. On a gray background, the largely black-and-white figures, with an occasional dash of red, depict the history of the Bulgarian nation. The artist selected to do the painting (his expressionistic style is distinctly controversial) was Teofan Sokarov, who appears in the work wearing a red hat.

Bazaar (Samovodskata Charshiya), ulitsa Rakovski: Coopers and wood carvers, weavers and potters work at old-time crafts here and sell them as souvenirs in what was once the bustling Samovodene market street. Today, however, the street lacks the bustle and excitement that are such essential parts of a bazaar and the hours the shops are open are uncertain.

Church of the Forty Martyrs (Tsŭrkvata na Chetiredesette Muchenitsi): On the western slope of Tsarevets on the riverbank in the Azenova quarter rises this thirteenth-century church built by Tsar Ivan Asen II. The bits of fresco that have survived here date, like the church itself, from 1230. Also of interest here are the pillars — one of them bearing a Greek inscription — but the church is something of a melange, for it was turned into a mosque by the Turks, then became a church again after the minaret fell (appropriately tossed down in a storm, the Bulgarians said, by the hand of God).

Church of St. Demetrius (Tsŭrkvata Sv. Dimitu), Azenova quarter: It was in this red-brick, striped medieval church, now restored, that Petŭr and Asen announced their plans for independence from Byzantium.

Church of Sts. Peter and Paul (Tsŭrkvata Sv. Petŭr i Pavel), at the foot of Tsaravets Hill: This thirteenth-century church's Bulgarian-style columns with vine leaves on the capitals is worth viewing by those with an architectural interest, as are the fourteenth- to sixteenth-century frescoes. The church, now a museum, is open irregularly, however.

Fortress (Momina Kreposta), Tsarevets Hill: At the northern end of the fortress Execution Rock juts out over the river. From it many were hurled to their deaths, including Patriarch Joachim III, accused of being a traitor in the thirteenth century, and the swineherd Ivailo, who served as tsar in 1277 after a peasant uprising and was overthrown two years later by boyar leaders.

At the southern end of the fortress is Baldwin's Tower. There, in the early days of the thirteenth century, Baldwin of Flanders, the first Latin emperor of Byzantium, after being captured by a Bulgarian tsar, was held prisoner until his death.

Gurko Street (ulitsa Gurko): Whitewashed houses with overhanging second stories and wrought-iron balconies filled with flowers are all a jumble along the river here — some in good condition, some in poor, but all invariably picturesque. Simply wandering the back streets of Veliko Tŭrnovo, above or below the main streets of Vasil Levski and Georgi Dimitrov, passing backyards where roosters strut and white-stockinged youngsters play, gives a good sense of contemporary Old Town Veliko Tŭrnovo. Along the main streets, smartly uniformed military cadets, often with daggers in their belts, are a common sight, for there is a military training school here. The cadets' presence gives a vigor and youthfulness to this city where, on a warm weekend evening, young people stroll or hungrily await pizzas at a kiosk.

House of the Little Monkey (Kŭshtata na Maymunkata), ulitsa Vŭstanicheska 14: Built in 1849 in National Revival style by the architect Kolyo Ficheto, the waffle-work brick living quarters of this house, with a carving of a grimacing man high over the door, rise over a ground-floor shop.

Inn of Hadji Nikola (Khanŭt na Khadzhi Nikola), ulitsa Rakovski 17: Once a caravansary, also designed by Ficheto, this is now a museum of the National Revival, open 9:00 A.M. to 4:00 P.M., except Monday.

Monastery of the Transfiguration (Preobrazhenskiyat Manastiri), near Sanividene: Spectacularly set below a sheer gray cliff but high above the River Yantra, this monastery complex had its origins in the fourteenth century but was largely destroyed in the nineteenth. The most interesting of the buildings here is the dome-shaped Bulgarian Baroque **Church of the Transfiguration** that is largely Ficheto's work, with frescoes by Zahari Zograf. Opposite the church the belfry rises. But for the non–architectural buff, probably the most impressive part of the visit is the site, at the end of a wooded road above the river valley down which storks from Egypt fly. Nineteenth-century patriots fighting the Turks had hiding places in caves (reached by removable ladders) above the monastery.

Museum of the National Revival Period (Muzeyat na Vŭzrazhdaneto), ulitsa Ivan Vazov: Originally constructed by Ficheto from 1872 to 1875, this charming blue-and-white building was the residence of the local Turkish ruler. It was destroyed by fire but was reconstructed from pictures of the original in 1908 and now houses a museum whose 250 icons are of interest. Obtaining information about them in English, however, is something of a problem.

Royal Palace (Tsarskiyat Dvorets): You can amble at will around these ruins; in the evening, you can watch the summertime sound and light shows presented here and admire the view of neighboring Sveta Gora.

Sarafina House (Kŭshtata na Sarafina), ulitsa Gurko: Built in National Revival style for the moneylender Dino Sarafina, the well-furnished interior is typical of the nineteenth-century merchant homes of the city. It is now open as a museum from 9:00 A.M. to noon and from 1:00 P.M. to 6:00 P.M., except Monday.

SREDNA GORA

The nineteenth-century revolt that toppled the Ottoman rule of Bulgaria began in the mountain pastures and beech forests of the Sredna Gora mountain range that cuts like a scimitar through central Bulgaria. After five centuries of oppression, on April 20, 1876, patriots captured the Turkish headquarters in Koprivshtitsa; using the blood of the Turks they had killed, they wrote to the inhabitants of the neighboring mountain towns begging them to join the revolt. As bands of Turks and Pomaks, the Muslim Bulgarians, ferociously attacked the patriots, they fled to the wooded hills and the mountain caves where most were later killed. It is for this, above all, that the rounded Sredna Gora are known.

KOPRIVSHTITSA
The gaily painted houses — sky blue, canary yellow, dusky rose — that line the cobblestoned lanes of this historic village make it, architecturally as well as historically, one of Bulgaria's most interesting towns. Often, window frames are in contrasting colors. Slender, engaging wooden columns mark the entryways of these

homes — special to Koprivshtitsa — of the National Revival period. At the time of the revolt against the Turks, this was a substantial town and many of its finer structures were merchants' homes with lovely hidden gardens. High stone-and-timber walls were built as a protection against the snows of winter.

For all its picturesqueness, the town remains, rather miraculously, a living community. Indeed, it is miraculous that it still stands at all — hotbed of intrigue that it was — but the rich landowners who had collaborated with the Turks during their occupation managed somehow to convince the oppressors to spare their little town.

The loveliest of the houses open to the public is the **Oslekov House** (Oslekovska Küshta) with cypress pillars holding up its charmingly decorated facade that has an Oriental look.

Also of interest are the **Debelyanov House** (Küshtata na Debelyanov) (if it is open), the birthplace of insurrectionist Todor Kableshkov, which is now a museum of the insurrection, but the museum captions are only in Bulgarian. It was when Turkish troops came to arrest Kableshkov — having learned that a revolution was in the making — that this revolution actually got under way.

Other fine houses of the National Revival style — usually on a museum ticket that allows entry to six — are the **Desyov, Garkov, Markov, Mishkov,** and **Topalov** mansions. They have the undulating yokelike facades of the National Revival style and characteristic cozy niches. Tickets may be purchased at the Tourist Information Office in the center of town.

But Koprivshtitsa existed long before the nineteenth-century revival. Its earliest inhabitants, in the fourteenth century, were shepherds and sheep dealers, and the wooden one-story **Pavlikyan** and **Vakarelski** houses are examples of these first habitations. In the first half of the nineteenth century, a larger house, generally with a second story and a stone wall, developed. That style may be seen in the **Benkovski House.** From the stairs behind it, where an equestrian statue of the hero-tailor Georgi Benkovski stands, is a spectacular view of Koprivshtitsa's valley and the surrounding Sredna Gora.

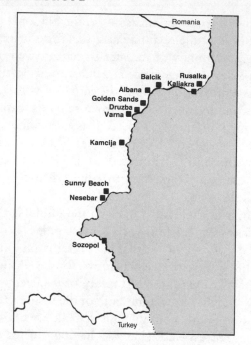

THE BLACK SEA COAST

It is said there is more sand per user on Bulgaria's Black Sea coast (Cherno More) than on any other beach in the world. And there are golden dunes, dramatic cliffs, and mountains; a shark-free, tide-free sea; mineral springs and woods, effulgent gardens, and ruins of antiquity. Foreigners are warmly welcomed here in up-to-date resorts with prices that are right (about $60 to $70 a night for a double).

Along this seacoast, Greeks and Romans, Venetians, Genoans, Bulgarians, and Turks have sailed and anchored, traded, fished, and fought for centuries. But tourism here is a relatively new development. Before World War II, this was largely a region of pristine dunes, seabirds, and the aquamarine sea. Off-putting to any extensive tourism then were the snakes — albeit harmless — who lived here.

Nikita Khrushchev apparently saw the tourist potential and urged Bulgaria to rid itself of the snakes. It did so with the assistance of hedgehogs, and in 1956, Golden Sands, the coast's first international resort, was opened. The major attractions of the Black Sea coast follow.

ALBENA

This is one of the coast's newer and most modern resorts, with thirty-four hotels, twenty-seven restaurants, and a five-mile-long beach. It is particularly popular with young people.

BALCHIK

In the 1930s, when this was Romania (from 1913 to 1940 Balchik belonged to Romania), Queen Marie built herself a villa — Tenka Yava, or Quiet Nest — here. Below her minaret-topped, Oriental-style villa are six levels of lovely gardens descending to the sea. The last one is cut short symbolically by a cliff and represents the child she had who died at two. Though the villa itself is now an artists' rest home, the gardens, with a silver well, ancient pillars from the king of Yugoslavia, thrones, and a minaret, as well as some 600 varieties of shrubs and flowers, are open to the public.

DRUZHBA

This is one of the quieter, cozier resorts of the coast, with a park of oak and cypress trees in the center and pleasant sandy coves. Its Swedish-built, 736-bed Grand Hotel Varna, a Bulgarian five-star hotel open year-round, attracts a sedate clientele.

GOLDEN SANDS (ZLATNI PYASŬTSI)

Along two miles of sand and dunes here, where the backdrop is a wood of oak and linden trees, are 81 hotels, 128 restaurants, and many villas. Sporting equipment of all sorts is available for tourists. Nightlife is probably the liveliest in the country, and in summer there are cultural and folkloric festivals. Foreigners of all nations come here, but Golden Sands has long been especially popular with Germans. About two miles inland, the **Aladya Monastery** was cut into the rock in the thirteenth century.

KALYAKRA

This lovely red-brown headland rising 230 feet out of the blue-green sea is home to the hooded cormorant, pink starlings, and wild rock pigeons, among other unusual birds. There are remains of a Byzantine fortress from whose walls, it is said, forty Bulgarian maidens tied their hair together and threw themselves into the sea rather than be captured by the Turks. Today, you can sometimes see seals in the water.

KAMTCHIA

Of more interest than this riverbank resort is the **Longoza Reserve** upriver, rich in waterfowl, pelicans, and golden marsh grasses. To see the birds, you must hire a fishing boat with a guide and be up and out early.

NESEBĂR

On this rocky peninsula, the Greeks established a trading center in 513 B.C. that they called Mesembria. (Before then, in Thracian days, the little settlement here had been known as Menebria after a Thracian chief.) After the Greeks, the Romans and the Byzantines came, and the Byzantines built forty-two stone and red-brick churches, some of which still stand.

Foremost among them are the fourteenth-century **Church of the Pantokrator** (Tsŭrkvata na Pantokratora), with its brick-and-marble designs and turquoise tile inlays; the eleventh-century **Church of St. John the Baptist** (Tsŭrkvata na Sv. Ivan Krŭstitel), where there is an archeological museum; the eleventh-century **St. Stephen's Church** (Tsŭrkvata na Sv. Stefan), with lovely sixteenth-century murals; the **Church of the Archangels Michael and Gabriel** (Arahangelite Mihail i Ganabedl), notable for the patterning of its exterior and its blind niches; and the ruins of **St. John Aliturgetos** (Sv. Ivan Neosveteni), on the shore. According to legend, this church was so grand with its exterior embellishment of crosses and shells, fashioned of limestone and contrasting brick, that it was never deemed appropriate to consecrate it.

Below St. John Aliturgetos, steps lead down to the fishing port, where modern boats have replaced old-fashioned open ones. Many Nesebăr men still make their living from the sea.

The narrow cobblestoned streets here are lined with National Revival houses with gray stone ground floors and overhanging second stories of wood, and strolling in old Nesebăr, it is not hard to imagine that you are part of another century. Visitors can see an interior in the **Muskoyanin House** (Muskoyaninska Kŭshta) on ulitsa Yana Laskova, now an ethnographic museum. It is open from 9:00 A.M. to noon and from 2:00 to 6:00 P.M., except Monday.

RUSALKA

A Club Med here with beaches surrounded by rocks and a view of Cape Kalyakra has one of the prime sites on the coast.

SOZOPOL

This fishing port on its rocky peninsula was the flourishing Apollonia of the Greeks. Similar in charm to Nesebăr, but smaller and less of a tourist center (though it attracts artists), its nineteenth-century houses sit in pretty gardens with fishing nets drying outside. The church of greatest interest is the **Church of the Holy Virgin** (Tsŭrkvata Bogoroditsa), with a lovely iconostasis.

SUNNY BEACH (SLŬNCHER BRYAG)

With 112 hotels, able to accommodate 25,000 tourists, Sunny Beach (Slŭnchev Bryag), a duney resort south of Varna, is the largest on the Bulgarian Black Sea coast. There are amenities aplenty along its five miles of beach, and with child-care facilities for young children, it is a fine place for a family vacation — but it has little charm.

VARNA

The third largest city and the major seaport of Bulgaria is, understandably, a busy industrial place, but it also has considerable charm and architectural and historical monuments well worth viewing.

Originally a Thracian shepherds' settlement, it was taken by the Greeks in the sixth century B.C. and named Odessos. Later it became a fortified Roman city; then, in the seventh century A.D., it became Bulgarian and was rechristened Varna, "the Black One," because, some say, so many fisherman set out from here and never returned. But in the days of the Second Bulgarian Kingdom, it thrived, becoming so prosperous that the Turks wanted it, capturing it in 1393 and largely keeping it till the liberation of 1878. Before setting out on a visit, stop at a Balkan tourist office at bulevard Lenin 23 or ulitsa Tolbuhin 5 to double-check museum hours. Sites of principal interest follow.

Marine Gardens (Morska Gradina): Edging the waterfront, this treed garden has an aquarium, a dolphin pool, and the Naval Museum, along with its swimming beach.

Museum of Art and History (Muzeyat na Iskustvoto i Istoriyata), ulitsa Dimitur Blagoev 41: Exquisite golden objects dating back 4,500 years and discovered accidentally during the digging of a canal in 1972 are the major — and surely mind-boggling — displays in this former National Revival Girls High School building of 1898, transformed into a museum in 1982. There are 1,850 golden objects here, some simple, some superbly crafted. On a tiny earring is a figure of Hermes in a shell. A later Thracian bracelet takes the shape of a snake's head. There are also Greek and Roman items and notable icons. Unfortunately, no guide to the collection is available in English and arrangements for an English-speaking guide must be made in advance at the ticket desk. It is open from 10:00 A.M. to 5:00 P.M., except Monday.

Museum of the National Revival (Muzeyat na Narodnoto Vazrazhdane), ulitsa Yuli 27: Classrooms of the 1860s that include a spanking frame, photographs of Varna of that day, and a restored church interior are among the displays in this former church and school. It is open from 10:00 A.M. to 5:00 P.M., except Monday.

Naval Museum (Voenno-Morskiyat Muzeiy), bulevard Chervenoarmeyski 2: Since for so many centuries, Varna has been a major Black Sea port, the exhibits here are of some interest to visitors. Part of the museum, but requiring a separate ticket, is the hull of the Bulgarian vessel *Drashki,* which sank a Turkish cruiser offshore in 1912. The museum is open from 9:00 A.M. to 6:30 P.M., except Monday.

Roman Thermae, ulitsa Han Drum: Though not a great deal remains of the marble and mosaic that decorated these second century B.C. baths, much of what they decorated is still here — dressing rooms, rest rooms, and bathing rooms. Their extent suggests that this was once a monumental and elegant public bath. A guidebook in English is available. The baths are open from 10:00 A.M. to 6:00 P.M., except Monday.

Stone Forest (Probiti Kameni): Ten miles west of Varna is this curiosity — a virtual field of strangely shaped stones rising from the sand. Some are as much as seventeen feet high. They are generally believed to be the remains of a fifty-million-year-old underwater stalagmite formation. This was originally called Hammered Stone.

SOUTHERN BULGARIA

Southern Bulgaria is mountainous land — the land of the snow-capped Rila range, where Mount Musala, the highest peak in the Balkan peninsula, hovers among the clouds at 9,564 feet. This is also the land of the sawtoothed Pirin range, where, the ancient Thracians believed, Petrun, the god of thunder, dwelt and shook the mountain passes with his roaring.

Curving across south-central Bulgaria are the Rhodopes that cross into Greece. Here, according to the ancient myth, the musician Orpheus descended to Hades through a crack in the mountainside on his quest for his dead wife, Eurydice. Because he turned to look at her when he was forbidden to, she was lost to him forever and he took to walking nearby and singing and playing melancholy songs. He walked through the evergreen forests and lush valleys playing his lyre till the women of Thrace, whose advances he spurned, tore him apart and Zeus turned his lyre into a constellation among the stars.

In the Rhodopes, there are still lush valleys and towering

spruces, firs, and pines reflected in quiet lakes. Streams and waterfalls tumble. Tobacco that the Turks planted during their occupation grows in the valleys, and caravans of donkeys carry baskets of its leaves in harvesting season.

In little red-roofed white villages, Pomak women, the descendants of those Bulgarians who converted to Islam centuries ago, rest by the roadsides, all in black but for white head-scarves and vibrantly flowered aprons.

In these mountains of southern Bulgaria are some of its oldest and most remarkable attractions, listed below.

MELNIK

Melnik is the Turkish word for "sandy cliffs," and this little town is picturesquely set between wind-carved sandstone walls and sculptures as much as 400 feet high. Whitewashed stone houses with chimney pots like minarets stretch along both sides of a stream bed. Farmers sell the thick red wine (so thick, the vintners insist, that you can drink it from a handkerchief) at their front doors. Everyone has his own grapevine in Melnik, the vines tumbling down the sides of the houses so the occupants can pluck the grapes by just reaching out a window.

Though today its population is under 500, from 1205 to 1229 fortified Melnik was the regional capital of southwestern Bulgaria. At that time the well-to-do Greeks invited to settle here built fine houses, churches, and monasteries. The ruins of the **Boyar's House** that rise above Melnik's hotel are from this period. In the seventeenth and eighteenth centuries, Melnik prospered from its red wine and tobacco trade, and its population was sizable enough to support seventy churches. Reminders of this time which may be visited are the 1754 **Kordopoulov House** (Kordopulovska Kŭshta) on the edge of town, home of a wealthy wine merchant and splendidly decorated, and the 1815 **Pashev House** (Pashevskata Kŭshta), now the town museum, with beautifully carved wood in its interior. Although much of Melnik burned down during the Balkan Wars of the turn of the century, five National Revival period churches still stand, including the **Church of St. Anthony** (Tsŭrkvata Sv. Anton), the **Church of St.**

Nicholas (Tsŭrkvata Sv. Nikola), and the **Church of Sts. Peter and Paul** (Tsŭrkvata Sv. Petŭr i Pavel). All have fine frescoes, icons, and iconostases. The town museum is open from 8:00 A.M. to noon and from 1:00 to 6:00 P.M., Monday through Wednesday.

Melnik is a particular favorite with oenophiles, as well as artists and photographers, who come to capture the Melnik Pyramids, as its clifflike surroundings have come to be called, on canvas and film.

Visitors here should not restrict their explorations to the main street along the river gully but should climb up the back streets and go into the hills. Five miles away is the **Rozhen Monastery** (Rozhenskijat Manastir) in the village of the same name. Inside the **Church of the Birth of the Holy Virgin** (Tsŭrkvata Rozhcstvo Bogorodichno), there is a handsomely carved iconostasis and seventeenth- and eighteenth-century frescoes.

PLOVDIV

Today's second-largest Bulgarian city was known as Pulpudeva to the Thracians till Philip II of Macedon's weary horse, in 342, collapsed under him here at the edge of the Thracian plain. Since that was surely an omen, he built Philippolis on this site in his own honor. Later, the Romans renamed it Trimontium — the City on Three Hills. For five centuries, under Turkish rule, when it was known as Philibe, it suffered much devastation. But today it is a city of great charm — with souvenirs of these and other rulers of its hectic past and, above all, with elegant nineteenth-century museum houses of the National Revival period. For the most current information on opening hours of houses and museums, which change frequently, stop at the Balkantourist office at bulevard Moskva 34. Plovdiv's principal attractions follow.

Balbanov House (Balbanova Kŭshta), ulitsa Matanov 57: Decorated with swags and medallions and a roof like a water carrier's yoke, this National Revival house is now an art gallery.

Dzhumaya Mosque, ploshtad Stamboliiski: The enormous lead-covered domes and the diamond pattern on its minaret make this fifteenth-century brick-and-stone mosque especially handsome. Its interior, too, is worth a visit — if it is open.

Georgiadi House (Kŭshtnea na Georgyadi), ulitsa Starinna 1: Now the Museum of National Liberation, this richly decorated house was constructed by self-taught builder Hadji Georgi, whose name it bears, and is handsomely decorated inside and out. Its most recent visiting hours were from 9:30 A.M. to 12:30 P.M. and from 2:00 to 5:00 P.M. daily, except Tuesday.

Hindlian House (Kŭshtata na Hindlyan), ulitsa Matinov: The Armenian merchant Hindlian who built this grandly decorated pale blue structure between 1820 and 1826 did not — for all the loveliness of his home — have a life to envy. His first wife was

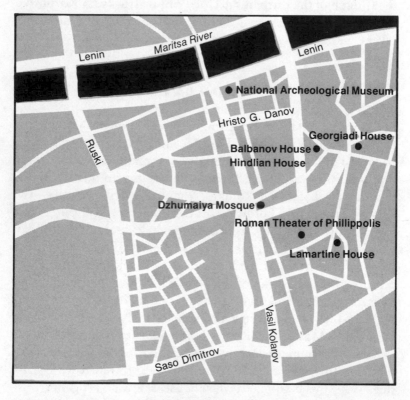

PLOVDIV

killed on their wedding day by a falling chandelier; his second died of the plague. But his house with its stenciled interior and exterior walls, its much-decorated Turkish baths, its richly painted and carved ceilings, and the marble tap in the reception room, through which rose water bubbled to perfume the air, must have given him some solace. And so, it appears, did his money. Constructed, like the other National Revival houses here, of timber, it apparently seemed unwise to keep money in such a flammable place, so a separate chapellike stucco structure was built as the house safe. Also, for safety's sake, the Hindlian House was connected with the Balbanov House next door, so, in time of danger, the families could flee from house to house. It is usually open from 9:00 A.M. to noon and from 2:00 to 5:00 P.M., except Monday.

House of Kouyoundjioglou (Kăshtata na Kuyundzhioglu), ulitsa Dr. Chomakov: Hadji Georgi built this twenty-room house with its pretty tree-shaded garden in 1847. Its first floor was occupied by his family; its second by his guests. The servants had a house of their own. Restored in 1950 after some years as a tobacco warehouse, it charms with its rich decoration both inside and out. Slender columns, an undulating roof, and yellow sprays and circles of leaves against a black background are highlights of its facade. Inside, around a central salon, bedrooms and drawing rooms are symmetrically arranged. Upstairs, darts and grasses are carved into the pine ceilings. There are friezes painted with sheaves of wheat and birds and flowers in vivid colors. On exhibit, too, are colorful Rhodope costumes, tools, musical instruments, and paintings. Of particular interest is a painting of the Plovdiv marketplace after the liberation from the Turks. It is open from 9:00 A.M. to noon and from 1:30 to 5:30 P.M. Tuesday through Thursday, and mornings only on Friday.

Imaret Mosque, ploshtad Saedineni: Since, in recent years, Bulgaria has been adopting a policy of forcing "assimilation" on its Turks, insisting that they take Bulgarian names and give up speaking Turkish in public, little effort has been made to restore such Turkish monuments as this magnificent 1444 mosque, with its zigzag exterior brickwork. It may or may not be open.

Lamartine House (Kŭshtata na Lamartin), ulitsa Khyaz Tsertelev 19: The nineteenth-century French poet Alphonse de Lamartine recovered here from cholera he had contracted in Constantinople, and there is a small museum honoring him. He called Plovdiv one of the most beautiful cities of the Orient. It is open Monday, Tuesday, and Wednesday from 5:00 to 6:00 P.M.

National Archeological Museum (Natsionalniyat Arheologicheski Muzei), ploshtad Saedineni: Anyone who has missed the Panagyurishte gold treasure in Sofia can view a copy of it here. In the basement there is also a fine collection of icons. It is open from 9:30 A.M. to 12:30 P.M. and from 2:00 to 6:00 P.M., except Monday.

Roman Stadium (Rimskiyat Stadion), ulitsa Stamboliiski: In this arena, during its second- and third-century heyday, charioteers and wrestlers performed for the thousands of spectators who could look down on the events from the surrounding hillsides. Today, this is the centerpiece of the **Stamboliyski Marketplace,** where transistor radios and modern Bulgarian pottery are sold side by side by young entrepreneurs. Plovdiv's pedestrian mall of golden and apricot houses, of shops and cafés (the ice cream for ice cream cones is carefully weighed out for each customer) begins here and ends at the enormous **Trimontium Square Hotel.**

Roman Theater of Philippolis, ploshtad Dzhunaya: In this restored second-century marble theater, classical plays are given in summer, and there is a fine view of the city of Plovdiv below.

BACHKOVO

Bachkovo Monastery (Băchovskijat Manastir), after Rila, is Bulgaria's largest monastery and, it, too, has been designated a UNESCO World Monument. And it, too, is situated with a backdrop of mountain peaks. Founded in 1083 by two brothers who were officers in the army of the Byzantine Empire in Europe, the site was selected because of its isolation. Its founders were Georgian, and it was to be inhabited by Georgian monks. But in 1344, when the Rhodopes became part of the Second Bulgarian Kingdom, Tsar Ivan Aleksandŭr, who donated significantly to the monastery, had Bulgarian monks installed. From the early period, only one building, the **Church of the Holy Trinity** (Tsŭrkvata Sv. Troitsa), still stands, with a full-length portrait of the tsar and of the monastery brother-founders on it.

You enter the cobblestoned courtyard through an impressive iron-studded door. Inside are oratories, chapels, and cloisters. Of particular interest are the recently restored colorful murals of the heads of the Greeks — Socrates, Plato, Aristotle, Pericles, Plutarch, Aristophanes, Diogenes, and Galen, as well as the heads of saints and martyrs.

Above the center doorway of the nineteenth-century **Church of St. Nicholas** (Tsŭrkvata Sv. Nikola) are frescoes of the master painter Zahari Zograf. In his painting of the Last Judgment he has included portraits, in 1840s clothes, of unpatriotic (or ruth-

1. A nineteenth-century mural by Zahari Zograf at the Bachkovo Monastery in the Rhodope Mountains.

less) merchants and known coquettes of Plovdiv. One of them is supposed to be a portrait of the fiancée who jilted him. The painter himself, the man with no beard, is portrayed in the upper left-hand corner.

Inside the church at the entrance to the **Archangels' Chapel** (Paraklisŭt na Arhangelite) is a silver icon of the Virgin said to have miraculous properties. The father of a blind girl, so the story goes, made the silver cover for the icon and when his daughter looked on it, her sight was restored. Three times in its history, however, the icon disappeared. Each time it was re- covered, but after the last disappearance, a monk of the monas- tery dreamed that it should be displayed at the top of three steps. The steps were built and the icon has not been removed since — except on the second Sunday after Easter, when it is taken to the mountains, where a Mass is said. It is returned in the evening. Bachkovo Monastery's art is some of the most significant of the National Revival period.

RILA

Rila Monastery (Rilskiyat Manastir): Seventy-five miles south of Sofia, at the end of a winding road through high rock walls with formations like giant animals waiting to pounce, this most-re- vered of all Bulgarian monasteries lies nestled in a soft green wood. Mountains rise all around it; below it the Rilska River races over a stony bed.

In the ninth century twenty-year-old Ivan Rilski — John of Rila — fled to this sylvan place seeking escape from the sordid- ness of the world. Finding a cave in the woods above this present monastery site, he took up the hermit life. Here he fed the ani- mals and the birds and prayed in the stillness to God. In time, like-minded men joined him, and they built the first monastery here about a mile and a half from the present site, where, today, you will find his tomb, the little **Church of St. Luke** (Tsŭrkvata na Sv. Luka), and the cave he inhabited. In the past, pilgrims were not deemed sinless enough to enter the monastery unless they had first passed the test of entering St. John's narrow cell. Those who could not bring themselves to enter it were sent away for a year to repent of their sins.

The first monastery here burned down. The next, of which eighty-foot-high **Hrelyo's Tower** still stands, was built by the boyar Stefan Dragovul-Hrelyo in 1335. But fellow boyars, jealous of honors he had been given by the emperor of Byzantium, threatened him and forced him to become a monk. Apparently, even that did not satisfy them, for he was strangled by one of them in his tower. An inscription on the tower reads, "Thy wife sobs and grieves, weeping bitterly, consumed by sorrow." But his fortified monastery remained, despite the Turkish conquest, until the nineteenth century, when it was destroyed by fire. Today's monastery, with its graceful arches, red-and-white and black-and-white checked and striped decoration, great courtyard, and green-and-gold domed church, was built between 1834 and 1860 in the days of the National Revival, largely by public donations both of money and craftsmanship. The bright frescoes that decorate it inside and out — portraits of the saints, tales from the Apocalypse — were done by the great nineteenth-century fresco painter Zahari Zograf. Also notable is the intricate gilded iconostasis of flowers, animals, and birds. The refectory should not be missed.

In 1961, a new museum wing, a UNESCO World Cultural Heritage, was added to hold manuscripts, books, icons, and pilgrims' gifts. In this fine collection is a cross with 1,500 figures carved so small that only a needle could be used in the carving by the monk Raphael, who, over the twelve years on which he worked at it, lost his sight.

SAMOKOV
It was in this mountain valley town that grew prosperous from its iron ore that Bulgaria's most famous National Revival artist, Zahari Zograf, was nurtured. Here his father, Hristo Dimitrov, after studies at Mount Athos and in Vienna, schooled him and his brother, Dimitŭr, in painting. From here he went out to adorn the walls of the monasteries of Bachkovo, Rila, and Troyan with

his colorful creations. Wood carving, too, was a specialty here, and the iconastasis of the main church at Rila is among its finest examples. The visitor to the **Samokov Historical Museum** will see memorabilia from Zograf's studio along with exhibits on the town's foundries. (In the seventeenth century, Samokov did much to supply the iron needs of the Ottoman Empire.) Other town sites of interest are the late-eighteenth-century **Metropolitan Church of the Holy Virgin** (Sv. Bogoroditsa) with its Samokov School wood carving; the richly decorated, elegant **Samokov Mosque** (Bajrakli Džamija); the **Turkish Fountain** (Geljama Češ-ima); and the **Beleu Church** (Bel'ovata Čarkva) on the outskirts of town, which has a naive 1869 School of Samokov painting of the Massacre of the Innocents.

SHIROKA LŬKA

This white village of 2,000 on the banks of the Vŭcha River is the site of the **School of Folk Instruments and Music** which, from

2. Bulgarian folk dancers.

time to time, offers performances. But even without them, it is a lovely Rhodope mountain community of tall houses with stone tile roofs climbing the mountainside, a square where old men sit in the sun, and the clean, clear river. The nineteenth-century National Revival–style architecture here is different from that elsewhere in the country. Since the topography does not allow houses to be spread out, they rise tall instead, often with upper stories jutting out over the lower ones.

GETTING THERE, SLEEPING, EATING, AND ENTERTAINMENT

The independent traveler to Bulgaria, like the independent traveler to any Eastern European country except Hungary, must have patience — but armed with it, there are many enjoyable excursions to be made. Prices remain lower than in other Eastern countries. The warm and sunny climate (on the Black Sea coast the sun shines an average of 240 days a year) means the shore is inviting and the water warm enough for swimming from May through October. And seacoast resort crowds are such that it is wise, if you are visiting the shore, to go in spring or fall.

In the same way that there is surely sun, there is invariably snow for skiers in the Rila Mountains in winter. Winter is a good time for musical attractions, too, and music is popular throughout Bulgaria. (*See* Entertainment under individual cities in this section.) In the spring, this "Garden of Europe," as it has been called, is aglow with apple and plum blossoms and thousands of acres of roses in the Valley of the Roses in May and June. In autumn, the fields are golden with grain and the elms, oaks, and beeches of the Sredna Gora blaze with color. Cars to facilitate independent travel may be rented in Sofia in advance through Hertz for prepayment in dollars.

Gas stations, generally twenty-five to thirty miles apart on the outskirts of towns and on main routes, are shown on maps that may be purchased in bookstores or at tourist offices. Both maps and destination road signs on main roads are printed in both the Latin and the Cyrillic alphabets. Main roads — usually paved and in good condition — are marked in red on maps. Secondary roads, often unpaved, are in yellow. Because there are few cars, driving for those accustomed to traffic is relatively easy, except on narrow, winding mountain roads.

Alternatively, there is rail service on the Bulgarian State Railways, but it is slow, and train destinations — even on railwaystation bulletin boards — are rarely given in anything but the Cyrillic alphabet.

There is also bus service between towns, but in general tickets must be bought an hour or more in advance at the terminal (Avtogara), and in remote communities where English is not spoken, finding the station or kiosk that sells tickets and making your destination clear will require patience, friendliness, and imagination.

Although Balkan Airlines, the Bulgarian national airline, does not fly to Sofia from the United States, Lufthansa and Swissair have New York to Sofia flights, with a change of planes in Frankfort or Zurich. Otherwise, connections with Bulgaria can be made from most European capitals. By rail, Sofia is on the international line from Belgrade and Istanbul. It is also accessible by rail from Athens and Bucharest. Visas are not necessary for visitors staying less than thirty days.

Street names and museum hours are constantly changing. In general, most museums are open Tuesday through Saturday from 9:00 A.M. to noon and from 2:00 to 5:00 P.M. Check with the local Balkantourist office for current museum hours.

Because it is a "garden" country with rich soil and good produce, food in Bulgaria — particularly in the growing months — tends to be more abundant and flavorful than in other Eastern

European countries. Cucumbers, strawberries, and tomatoes are delicious mainstays of the summer diet.

Bulgarian cuisine is, on the whole, a healthful one: a *shopska salata*, salad of chopped cucumber, tomato, onion, and red pepper sprinkled with crumbled sheep's cheese (*sirene*), served as a first course with most meals. (The Bulgarian accompaniment to it is plum brandy, *rakiya*, downed in a single swallow.) *Tarator*, a refreshing cold soup of yogurt, cucumber, garlic, sunflower oil, and walnuts, is another popular appetizer, as are pickled vegetables and *bob bob-chorba* — bean soup — sometimes called "monastery soup" because the monks prepared it for pilgrims. A tripe, garlic, and red pepper soup called *shkembe chorba* is also popular.

Grilled meats are frequently served in hotel restaurants, as are *gyuvech*, meats and vegetables slowly cooked in earthenware pots and served with poached eggs on top. Another egg dish likely to be on a luncheon menu is *sirene po shopski*, cheese, tomatoes, green peppers, and eggs baked in a casserole.

Bulgarian cooking has a good deal in common with Greek and Turkish cuisine. Charcoal-grilled kebabs served with a *pitka* — a hot fresh roll — and *chubritsa*, a mixture of salt and spices put on the table to dip your bread into, can be a tasty lunch. *Kavarma*, small pieces of meat, spring onions, and mushrooms cooked in a casserole, is likely to be on menus, as are *sarmi* — stuffed cabbage — and *kebabcheta* — grilled ground pork or veal rolls, highly spiced. *Banitsa* is a cheese- or spinach-filled pastry.

Yogurt, invented here, is served everywhere — for breakfast, lunch, and dinner. It is sometimes mixed with water in a thirst-quenching drink called *ayryan*.

For dessert, in any of the fruit seasons, there could be nothing better than fresh fat strawberries or raspberries, sweet plums or apricots, juicy grapes, pears or peaches. For those who prefer manmade sweets, there are *baklava* and *revane*, a nut pastry; *mlyako s oriz*, rice pudding; Turkish delight; and *saralia*, pancakes with walnuts and sweet syrup.

Bulgarian red wine is often extremely good. Mavrud, a dark red wine like claret that comes from the Rhodopes, is exceptional, as are Cabernet and Gamza. Unusual is the red wine of Melnik, so thick it can be poured through a handkerchief. Misket is a pleasantly scented wine made from the Muscat grape, Dimyat a popular pale dry white wine from the Black Sea, and Tamyanka another fragrant white wine. And there is rose liqueur to be sampled in the Valley of the Roses.

Restaurant service is slow, but, in general, there is less of a problem in getting a restaurant table without a reservation than in other Eastern European countries.

The two deluxe hotels in the capital city of Sofia, the Sheraton and the Vitosha New Otani, offer fine accommodations and serve good food in their dining rooms. On the coast and at mountain ski resorts, first-class accommodations tend to be new and good. Elsewhere, they can be poor. Nothing less than a Bulgarian first-class hotel should be sampled. Breakfast (bread, yogurt, cheese, ham, and coffee or tea) is generally included in the price. Bed and breakfast accommodations are also available through Balkantourist offices, but you must bear in mind that Bulgaria is a southern Central European country where bugs abound.

There follows, in alphabetical order by town, a list of better hotels and restaurants in major tourist sites. Because accommodations are in short supply, it is wise to make reservations considerably in advance of leaving the United States with Balkan Holidays at 41 East 42nd Street, New York, New York 10017, or with a travel agent whom that office recommends.

BOROVETS

HOTEL

Samokov. This is an up-to-date four-star mountain hotel in a spectacular Rila Mountain location. Including breakfast, the rate is $66 double.

GOLDEN SANDS (ZLATNI PYASŬTSI)

HOTELS

Ambassador (Tel. 85-53-60). Recently redecorated, this is a small (130-room) hotel in the woods near the beach.

International (Tel. 85-56-11). This is a four-star, 210-room hotel near the beach and the center of Golden Sands.

RESTAURANTS

Kosharata, on the edge of Golden Sands (Tel. 85-52-61). Mutton dishes are the specialty at this rustic restaurant.

Lovna Sreshta, near the Aladsha Monastery. Wild game is the culinary attraction here.

Mecha Polyana, in the woods above Golden Sands. Bulgarian entertainment and Bulgarian food are offered here.

Trifon Zarezan, on the Varna road (Tel. 85-50-36). Bulgarian cuisine is featured and accompanied by a folk show.

Vodenitsz, near the Diana Hotel (Tel. 85-53-77). There are lovely gardens here for dining on specialties like grilled chicken and freshly baked bread and pastries.

PAMPOROVO

HOTELS

Malina (Tel. 272). There are attractive chalets here for skiers.

Perelik (Tel. 376). This new hotel, with much blond wood in its interior decor, is superbly situated in the wooded Rila Mountains just below the ski slopes.

RESTAURANTS

Chevermeto (Tel. 326). This is a popular rustic restaurant serving fine country food. Its decor is that of a Rhodope Mountain dairy.

Malina. This is another rustic restaurant specializing in such dishes as stuffed peppers and spit-roasted lamb.

PLOVDIV

HOTELS

Hotel Trimontium, ulitsa Kapitan Raycho (Tel. 22-55-61). The location of this four-story, three-star hotel near the city's extensive pedestrian mall and the city park is convenient for tourists because it's near all major visitor sites.

Novotel Plovdiv, Zlatyu Boyardzhiev 2 (Tel. 55-58-92). Double-room prices in this modern five-star hotel above the River Maritsa and away from the city center are from $96 to $200 in season. There is a restaurant serving local cuisine, the **Evridika,** and an international restaurant, the **Benida,** here.

RESTAURANTS

Kambanata, Old Plovdiv (Tel. 26-06-65).

ENTERTAINMENT

There is a music festival in January and a chamber music festival in June and chance presentations at the Roman Stadium in summer.

TOURIST INFORMATION

Hotel Trimontium, ulitsa Kapitan Raycho (Tel. 22-55-61). Hotel Novotel Plovdiv, Zlatyu Boyardjiev 2 (Tel. 55-58-92).

SOFIA

HOTELS

Grand Hotel Sofia, ploshtad Narodno Sŭbranie (Tel. 87-88-71). This three-star, semicircular hotel edges part of the square where the National Assembly and the Bulgarian Academy of Sciences are located, and the Aleksandŭr Nevski Cathedral is also a near neighbor. The price range is comparable to the Novotel Europa.

Novotel Europa, bulevard Georgi Dimitrov 131 (Tel. 3-12-61). This Balkantourist hotel, built by the French Novotel chain, is situated near the central railroad station and not far from downtown. It specializes in catering to the business visitor to Sofia, and its room rates are about half those at the Sheraton.

Park Hotel Moskva, ulitsa Nezabravka 25 (Tel. 7-12-61). This three-star, high-rise hotel is just on the edge of a park — a pleasant but out-of-the-way location. Its **Panorama Restaurant** on the top floor takes full advantage of the park location, and the food is good.

Sheraton Sofia–Grand Hotel Balkan, ploshtad Sveta Nedelya

(Tel. 87-65-41). Situated in the heart of Sofia (with a Roman ruin that later became a mosque and still later a church in the courtyard), this is the ideal — but expensive — hotel for a short-term visitor. A single room, in season, is $190, a double $215. All tourist sites, airline offices, and shops are within walking distance, and there is good dining in the restaurants, which include the **Preslav,** where the cuisine is mostly French and a dinner with wine is about $50 a person, and the **Balkan,** where dinner is in the $25-a-person range. There is also a grill, a wine cellar serving Bulgarian dishes, and a Viennese patisserie. American credit cards are accepted.

Vitosha–New Otani Hotel, bulevard Anton Ivanov 100 (Tel. 62-41-51). This is a handsome hotel at the foot of Mount Vitosha — an attraction for skiers and hikers but not for all sightseers, as it is a fifteen-minute taxi ride and half-hour tram ride from the city center. There is, however, good dining in its top-floor **Musala Restaurant** ($50 per person) and local specialties and entertainment in its **Lozenets Restaurant.** There is also a Japanese restaurant and a grill. American credit cards are accepted. Room rates are slightly lower than at the Sheraton.

RESTAURANTS

In addition to hotel restaurants, there are a few (but not many) reasonably good places to eat in Sofia. For a country where, outside the capital, fine meals can be found, it's a pity there is not better dining.

Boyansko Hanche, Boyana District (Tel. 56-30-16). In the evening, a folklore show accompanies dinner.

Budapest, ulitsa Rakovski 145 (Tel. 87-37-50). Hungarian music is the accompaniment to the Hungarian fare that is served here.

Koprivshtitsa, bulevard Vitosha 3. Bulgarian specialties are accompanied by Bulgarian music at this popular tourist restaurant.

Krim, ulitsa Dobrudzha 2 (Tel. 87-01-31). This is a Russian restaurant, where, in the summer, there is dining in the garden.

Ropotamo, bulevard Lenin 63 (Tel. 72-25-16). This is a moderately priced, centrally located restaurant.

Rubin, ploshtad Sveta Nedelya (Tel. 87-20-86). This centrally located restaurant offers Bulgarian specialties in its main dining room and quicker, cheaper fare at its snack bar. A complete dinner here, with wine, is about $15 for one person.

Vodenicharska Mehana, in the Dragalevtsi district at the foot of Mount Vitosha (Tel. 65-50-88). Bulgarian specialties and a Bulgarian folklore show are offered at this out-of-town location.

ENTERTAINMENT

There is a November jazz festival, and opera and ballet are offered in the State Opera House off ploshtad Aleksandŭr Nevski. Operetta can be seen at the Stefan Makedonski Musical Theater on bulevard Volgograd 4, and there are concerts at the Bulgarian Concert Hall at ulitsa Benkovski 1 and at Slavyekov Hall. The chorus at the Aleksandŭr Nevski Cathedral is superb. The Central Puppet Theater (Sofiyskiyat Kuklen Teatŭr) at ulitsa Gurko 14 has entertainment of quality, and knowledge of the language is not a factor. Further information and tickets are available at the National Palace of Culture (Narodan Dvorets na Kultura — NDK) on ploshtad Baba Nedelya.

TOURIST INFORMATION

Interbalkan, ulitsa Sveta Sofia 4 (Tel. 83-11-35). Information is also available in major hotels.

STOLYKITE (Smolyan Region)

RESTAURANT

Vodenits, 7 kilometers west of Pamporovo. This folk-style, rustic restaurant serves hearty Bulgarian fare.

VARNA

HOTELS

Cherno More, bulevard Georgi Dimitrov 35 (Tel. 22-39-1). This is a 223-room, three-star hotel near the Marine Gardens. There is reasonably good food in the hotel restaurant.

Grand Hotel Varna, Druzhba Resort (Tel. 86-14-91). Prettily situated near woods and beach, this is a 736-room, Swedish-built hotel constructed in 1977. A deluxe hotel eight miles from Varna, it is one of the few Bulgarian Black Sea coast hotels that remains open year-round.

RESTAURANTS
Galata, ulitsa Druzki. Bulgarian food is offered here, but there may be a long wait to get it.
Starata Krusha, ulitsa Druzki. Local specialties are served, but — as everywhere in Varna — there are likely to be crowds of diners and it is wise to reserve space.

ENTERTAINMENT
This sunny beach resort has musical weeks.

TOURIST INFORMATION
Ulitsa Mussala 1 (Tel. 22-59-50).

VELIKO TŬRNOVO

HOTEL
Hotel Veliko Tŭrnovo, ulitsa Emil Popov 2 (Tel. 3-05-71). This is a small four-star hotel, basic and relatively inexpensive (under $100 a night for a double). The view of the city from the terrace of the **Tsaravets Restaurant,** where dining is done in season, is superb.

RESTAURANTS
Hotel Etar Restaurant, ulitsa Ivailo (Tel. 2-16-17). Kebabs are a good bet at this inexpensive hotel restaurant with its outstanding panoramic view.
Hotel Yantra Restaurant, ploshtad Velchova Zavera 1 (Tel. 3-02-91). The view is spectacular, though neither food nor service is particularly commendable.
Rodina, ulitsa Dimitrov 17. Recently renovated, this restaurant is in a picturesque National Revival house.

TOURIST INFORMATION
Hotel Veliko Tŭrnovo, ulitsa Emil Popov 2 (Tel. 35944).

Czechoslovakia

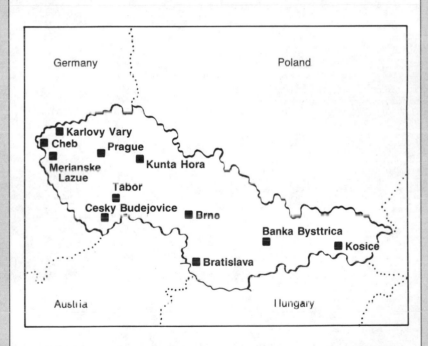

Germany

Poland

■ Karlovy Vary
■ Cheb
■ Prague
Merianske
Lazue
■ Kunta Hora
Tabor
■ Cesky Budejovice
■ Brno
Banka Bysttrica
■
■ Kosice
■ Bratislava

Austria

Hungary

$\mathcal{A}$lthough the country of Czechoslovakia was not created until 1918, the former provinces that are its components — Bohemia, Moravia, Silesia, and Slovakia — have been in existence a long time. Celtic tribes originally occupied this zigzag of land in the heart of Central Europe; one tribe, the Boi, is remembered in the name Bohemia. Germanic tribes drove out the Celts in the fourth century; in the sixth century, Slavs united to form the Great Moravian Empire. In the ninth century, its prince invited the Greek missionaries, Cyril and Methodius, to Christianize the country in the hope that then its Christian neighbors, the Germanic Franks, would leave it in peace.

In the tenth century the Great Moravian Empire crumbled and the Magyars took for themselves its southern Moravian and Slovakian portion. This forced the Czechs of the western Bohemian section to ally themselves with their Germanic neighbors.

In the ensuing two centuries, Bohemia became a kingdom in its own right — extending its lands as far as the Adriatic Sea and deep into today's Austria, ruling over Poland and eventually regaining Slovakia from Magyar Hungary. Meanwhile, the Germans were invited in as settlers to encourage trade.

The German-Czech, Czech-German antagonism that began then, and the cultural differences between Czechs and Slovaks that started with the tenth-century division of the Moravian Empire, have played an important role in twentieth-century Czechoslovakia, which indeed calls itself the Czech and Slovak Federal Republic.

Bohemia was united to the Holy Roman Empire in the fourteenth century with the marriage of one of its princesses to the son of the Holy Roman Emperor. The reign of their son Charles IV, king of the Germans and Holy Roman Emperors, was the Golden Age of Bohemian history.

In 1348, Charles established the University of Prague, the first university of Central Europe. Other accomplishments included the building of the "New Town" of Prague, enlarging the Cathedral, and starting the bridge that bears his name today. He tried (but did not succeed) in luring the Roman poet Petrarch to his capital to be a tutor to his son. (Petrarch wanted Charles to move the empire's capital to Rome.)

In these prosperous years, however, laxity in the Church developed — a laxity that was to result, in the fifteenth century, in the religious Hussite movement.

Jan Hus, though born of poor parents in South Bohemia, was sent to the University of Prague for his studies. He was ordained a priest in 1400 and made rector of the university and preacher in the city's Bethlehem Chapel two years later. Like Martin Luther, who came after him in Germany, he criticized the sale of indulgences as a way of paying for one's sins. Hus was excommunicated and in 1414 called to a meeting of the General Council of the Church at Constance to explain his views. He attended only after receiving assurances that he would not be harmed. But the promised safe conduct was not observed and he was burned at the stake, predicting, as he died, the coming of Martin Luther when he said, "Now you are burning a goose, but after me there will come a swan whom you will not be able to burn." (In Czech, *husa* means "goose.")

His excommunication aroused fury throughout Bohemia and resulted in the uniting of 452 nobles and knights as crusaders who swore to obey the word of God but defend the liberty of those who preached it. With their pledge Bohemia virtually became Europe's first Protestant nation.

For the next twenty years, the Hussites launched crusades against the Holy Roman Empire and the pope. In Prague, they hurled the city councilmen who had arrested Hussites from the Town Hall window, beginning a "defenestration" procedure for which they were to become notable. Though in 1434 the crusaders were defeated by a coalition of nobles and burghers, Jiří (George) of Poděbrady, who supported much of what they stood for, was selected to be king of Bohemian lands.

These were the days of Turkish advances into Central Europe. Jiří, fearful of Turkish power, united with the neighboring Christian nations against the Turks and designated Ladislaus of Poland his successor. In 1490, Ladislaus became king of Hungary, too. All went well, until his son died fighting the Turks and his kingdom fell. The crown went to his sister, wife of Ferdinand of Hapsburg, archduke of Austria. With Ferdinand's ascension to the Bohemian throne, the Hapsburgs became the rulers of most of central and southern Europe for the next 400 years.

Ferdinand's grandson, Rudolf II (a colorful eccentric who imported astronomers to his court, dabbled in alchemy, and collected art), briefly occupied the throne but was deposed in favor of his staunchly rigid Catholic brother Matthias. Persecution of the Protestant Hussites began. When the king's Roman Catholic counselors and Prague's Protestant Assembly met at the Prague Town Hall, the Hussites — again — hurled the offending Catholics out the window. No one was hurt (they are said to have been saved by falling into a dung heap), but the result was Europe's Thirty Years' War and the gloomiest of times in Bohemia.

Much of Catholic Europe — the Holy Roman Empire, Spain, Italy, Poland, Bavaria, and many German principalities — united against Protestant Bohemia, and the principality of Transylvania came to Bohemia's support. By the time the Thirty Years' War ended in 1648, more than 2 million people had been killed in Bohemia, most of them Protestant. Possession of a Protestant Bible or hymnal was a crime punishable by death, the estates of the Bohemian nobles were given to the supporters of the German emperor, and German Catholics were brought in to replace the murdered Czech Protestants. The Hapsburgs sought to "Germanize" the Czechs while the Magyars were enforcing their rule even more firmly over the Slovaks.

This repression of their Bohemian and Slovak heritage led to a rebirth of patriotism on the part of both peoples and increasing antagonism to the Hapsburgs, who now controlled them.

After the Austro-Hungarian Empire was created in 1867, an even grimmer time was in store for Czechs and Slovaks. Then

Hungary became independent of Austria in all but foreign affairs, and the Slavs of Hungary — though they represented a third of the population — were rigorously suppressed. Hungarian became the teaching language in Slovakian schools. Slovaks, who previously had gone to Bohemia for higher education, were forbidden to do so and Czechs were denied the right to travel in Slovakia. This was the state of affairs at the outbreak of World War I.

But in 1918, when the war ended, there was no longer an Austro-Hungarian Empire. There was, instead, a Czechoslovak Republic of Free Czech and Slovak Peoples. Inside this new republic were most of the industrial centers of the former Austro-Hungarian Empire and 3 million German-speaking people. And so, in 1938, after "annexing" Austria, Adolf Hitler invaded Czechoslovakia. Fearful of a second world war, Britain, France, and Italy did nothing to stop Hitler. Bohemia and Moravia became a German "protectorate," Slovakia an independent puppet state.

Because of this "protected" status and German plans to assimilate Bohemia and Moravia into the Third Reich, little damage was done to their cities and towns. Today's tourist, therefore, can see Prague much as it was in the Middle Ages and castles in the countryside still standing as stalwart as they did in the Renaissance.

Following the war, a coalition government came to power, but in 1948 the Communists took control. When the economy did not prosper, in early 1968 Communist party secretary Alexander Dubček tried to improve the country's lot with such reforms as releasing political prisoners, decentralizing some industries, and ending censorship. The Russians warned Dubček that he must repeal his reforms, and when he refused the U.S.S.R. and the Warsaw Pact forces invaded Czechoslovakia. The "Prague Spring" was over.

But in November 1989, when Poland, Hungary, and East Germany had revolted against communism, Czechoslovakia staged its quiet "Velvet Revolution" and in 1990 established a Czechoslovak Republic once again.

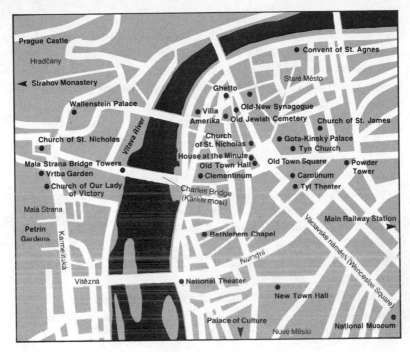

PRAGUE

Sometimes it is called Prague the Golden, sometimes Prague, the City of 100 Spires. It is compared with Florence and Rome in its beauty. Thomas Mann said it was one of the world's most magical cities; Goethe called it the prettiest gem in the stone crown of the world. Today's visitors from the West, seeing Prague for the first time, call it the Paris of Eastern Europe.

Virtually untouched by wars, its architecture is Romanesque and Gothic, Renaissance and Baroque and Rococo, Neoclassical and Empire and Art Nouveau. Light dances on its spacious squares, palace gardens, and the Vltava River that flows through it. Shadows lend mystery to narrow, winding streets and the toppled gravestones in the Jewish cemetery that dates back to the Middle Ages. On its highest hilltop, the towers of the Hradčany

Castle and the lacy Gothic spires of the Cathedral of St. Vitus reach toward the sky. Life-size Baroque saints look benignly (and sometimes sternly) down on the passersby and vendors on its fourteenth-century Charles Bridge.

Czechs are inclined to be self-contained, diligent people, but in these new days of freedom, there seems more swing in their stride, more exuberance, more "bohemianism" in the young milling, conversing, and playing guitars in the Old Town Square.

This city of 1.2 million people began, legend has it, when Libuše, its first queen, stood on a rock on the Vyšehrad side of the river, peered into the distance, and said she could see a city whose glory would reach to the stars. She bade her servants go into the forest there and look for a woodsman working at the threshold of his door. That threshold, she said, would be the site of her city and she would call it Praha from the Czech word for threshold.

There are four main sections of that city of interest to tourists today — the Old Town, the New Town, the Lesser Town, and Hradčany, where the castle stands.

THE OLD TOWN (STARÉ MĚSTO)

Old Town Square (Staroměstské náměstí): Beige, pink, and gray Renaissance palaces, green Baroque domes, and Gothic towers edge this gracious square which has as its centerpiece a monument to Jan Hus, the fifteenth-century Czech church reformer who was burned at the stake for his views. The highlight of the west side of the square is the **Old Town Hall** (Staroměstská radnice): Though much of the complex of fourteenth- to nineteenth-century buildings that comprise this town hall was destroyed at the very end of World War II, it has now been rebuilt. The Town Hall astronomical clockwork, also called a "sundial horologe," is a showstopper. Every hour on the hour its nineteenth-century figures emerge. They include a skeleton symbolizing Death who looks at his hourglass, then pulls a cord so that a procession of Apostles files by. Then a rooster crows and a turbaned Turk shakes his head as if to say he has no intention of giving up the land here in Central Europe which the Turks took.

The fifteenth-century designer of this astronomical clock was master clockmaker Hanuš of Růže. According to legend, he was blinded by Prague's town councilors for fear — so magnificent and applauded was his creation — that he would make another like it for another town. One day toward the end of his life, he asked a friend to lead him to his great creation. As the figure of Death tolled the hour, Hanuš thrust his hand into the clock's apparatus; the clock stopped, and it was centuries before a craftsman could be found who was skilled enough to make it work. (In World War II, the clock is said to have stopped again after a Nazi murder of hundreds of Praguers.)

In front of the Town Hall in 1621, twenty-seven Czech nobles and Prague officials were executed for their opposition to Hapsburg rule; the place of their beheading is marked in the pavement.

In the Town Hall's interior, the Gothic second floor is well worth seeing and guided tours are offered several times a day. It is wise to check their hours at a Čedok office.

3. A window decoration above Prague's Old Town Hall.

4. The Renaissance House at the Minute, part of the Old Town Hall complex, is decorated with sgraffito allegories of the virtues.

House at the Minute (Dům U minuty): This handsome Renaissance house next to the Town Hall was a pharmacy called "At the White Lion." It still has a stone lion decorating it and seventeenth-century sgraffiti of mythological and biblical scenes that include allegories of the virtues.

Church of Our Lady of Týn (Kostel Panny Marie před Týnem): This twin-towered Gothic church on the east side of the square with turrets surrounding the towers was built in 1365 and became the church of the followers of Jan Hus until 1621. After the Counter-Reformation, it became a Roman Catholic church. In the Hussites' church, the congregation shared Communion wine as well as wafers; when the Catholic Hapsburgs took over Our Lady of Týn, they melted down the Communion chalice on the facade and used the gold to make the Virgin that replaced the chalice.

Inside, buried beneath a red-marble tombstone, is the sixteenth-century Danish astronomer Tycho Brahe, who worked at the Bohemian court for Rudolf II. The church has been undergoing repairs for some time now, so entrance is only possible through the Týn School or from Celetna ulice 5.

Golz-Kinský Palace (Palác Goltz-Kinských): This mid-eighteenth-century palace by Baroque specialist K. I. Dientzenhofer that now houses the National Gallery's Czech, Slovak, and foreign print collection of works from the fifteenth to the twentieth centuries is also on the east side of the square. It is considered by many to be Prague's finest Baroque building. The palace is open from 10:00 A.M. to 6:00 P.M., except Monday.

Other structures of interest on the east side of the square are the **House at the Unicorn** (U jednorožce), with an early Renaissance portal and a Gothic arcaded ground floor, the gabled **Gothic Týn School** in Venetian Renaissance style, and the **House of the Bell** (Dům U zvonu), with a restored Gothic facade.

Church of St. Nicholas (Kostel sv. Mikuláše): This outstanding Baroque building constructed from 1732 to 1735 on the north side of the square was designed by K. I. Dientzenhofer and is notable for the interior frescoes on the cupola by the Bavarian artist Peter Assam and for the sculpture by Antonín Braun. It is, however, only open on Sundays. In the pseudo-Baroque building to the left, the nineteenth-century writer Franz Kafka was born.

The most significant structures of the Old Town outside the Old Town Square follow.

Bethlehem Chapel (Betlémská kaple), Betlémské náměstí: A peaked-roof 1950s reconstruction has been made of this chapel, where Jan Hus broke with precedent by preaching to his congregation in Czech rather than in Latin.

Carolinum (Karolinum), Železná ulice 9: This is the oldest building of Charles University, founded in 1348 by Charles IV, and is notable for a fine Gothic oriel window overlooking the street. Jan Hus was the outspoken rector of the university in 1402.

Charles Bridge (Karlův most): After Hradčany Castle, this Baroque bridge edged with more-than-life-sized statues of saints is Prague's most notable architectural structure. Started in the fourteenth-century reign of Charles IV by twenty-seven-year-old Peter Parléř, who was also the architect for St. Vitus Cathedral, the bridge was completed in the reign of Charles's son, Wenceslas IV. But the thirty statues here, inspired by the Ponte Sant' Angelo in Rome, were erected in the seventeenth and eighteenth centuries. The bridge's first statue was of St. John Nepomuk, said to have been hurled, bound and gagged, into the River Vltava on order of Wenceslas IV because as the queen's priest he had refused to reveal her confession to the jealous king. The legend (depicted in bronze at the foot of the statue along with the saint's execution) further recounts that the saint's body floated down the river for some time with five stars from the heavens hovering overhead. More recently, less romantic accounts of St. John's murder suggest that he had approved the appointment of an abbot Wenceslas did not wish approved. The statue is by M. Rauchmüller and Jan Brokoff.

Also of interest among the statues is the crucifix with the words "Holy, Holy, Holy" in Hebrew in a half halo near Jesus' head. It is said that an unknown Jewish heckler who mocked the figure had to pay for the carving of this Hebrew inscription in the seventeenth century by court order.

Artistically, of greatest merit is the statue of Christ on the Cross with blind St. Luitgarde — a figure filled with compassion — kissing his wounds. It is the work of Baroque sculptor M. B. Braun.

Pollution in the air has meant that many of the original statues have been removed and most of those that stand here today are copies. The originals are in the depository of the National and Municipal Museums.

With the Old Town Square and Wenceslas Square, Charles Bridge is surely the liveliest site in Old Prague. Blue-jeaned students strum guitars and sell souvenirs. Sunners bask here in fine weather. Strollers photograph the saints, the river below, and the towers of the city. And, as it has been for centuries, the bridge is a thoroughfare between the Old Town and the New Town that Charles IV also had constructed.

Church of St. James (Kostel sv. Jakuba), ulice Malá Šupartská: Founded in 1232, this church received its present Baroque look

between 1689 and 1702 and in the 1730s. The stucco reliefs on
the facade (not easy to see without craning your neck) are the
work of an Italian sculptor, Ottavio Mosto. The highlight of the
Baroque interior is the tomb of Václav Vratislav of Mitrovice,
once a lord chancellor of Bohemia, done by F. M. Brokoff after
the designs of the eighteenth-century Viennese architect J. B.
Fischer von Erlach.

Church of St. Martin in the Wall (Kostel sv. Martina ve zdil),
Martinská ulice: Originally a Romanesque building that was
part of the long-demolished old town walls, this church (now
Gothic) is notable for the fact that it was here that Communion
wine as well as wafers was first offered to a congregation of the
Roman Catholic Church in Europe.

Clam-Gallas Palace (Palác Clam Gallasův), Husova ulice: This
splendid eighteenth-century Baroque palace with enormous stone
giants by M. B. Braun beside the door was built for Jan Václav
Gallas following plans of the Viennese court architect, J. B.
Fischer von Erlach. In 1742, the palace passed into the hands of
Philip of Clam — hence its present name. It now houses the archives of the City of Prague.

Clementinum (Klementinum), at the foot of the Charles Bridge:
The Jesuits built this sprawling complex of buildings from 1653
to 1723 as part of the effort to bring Prague back into the Catholic fold. It consists of three churches, four courts, and three gardens. Today a government library is housed here.

Convent of St. Agnes (Klášter sv. Anežky), Anežská ulice: Built
by Wenceslas II in 1234, this large complex of religious buildings
is the oldest early Gothic structure in Bohemia. It was shut down,
however, under Joseph II and fell into disrepair, being used principally as a hostel for the poor. Now concerts are held here sometimes and nineteenth-century Czech art is exhibited.

Ghetto (Josefov): This Jewish ghetto dates back to the Middle
Ages. It exists today because, in his perverse way, Adolf Hitler
wanted a museum to the race he hoped to exterminate. (Of
50,000 Prague Jews, only about 10,000 survived.) It had its own
Town Hall, as well as its synagogues and cemetery. Almost all the

sites in the ghetto are part of the State Jewish Museum and are open from 9:00 A.M. to 4:30 P.M. daily except Saturday.

The first Jews are believed to have arrived in Prague in the tenth century. Some were traders from the east, some from the west. They settled in three parts of the city, but after a massacre by Crusaders in 1096, for safety's sake they gathered together in this area. They remained here, through good times and bad, till the nineteenth-century Hapsburg days of the reforming Holy Roman Emperor Franz Joseph II, when many of the area's dilapidated structures on narrow, winding streets were torn down and Prague's Jews allowed to live anywhere in the city.

The following ghetto buildings are still standing:

Ceremonial Hall (Mannice): The telling contents of this Neo-Romanesque structure beside the cemetery are children's drawings from the Terezin (Theresienstadt) concentration camp.

High Synagogue (Vysoká synagóga), Červená ulice. This square, high-windowed Renaissance structure, originally part of the Jewish Town Hall, now serves as a museum of Jewish contributions to the spiritual life of the community. Here, too, are some of the finest liturgical textiles in the world.

Jewish Town Hall (Židovská radnice), Maislova ulice: This handsome dust-pink building with its gold clock tower (one side of the clock has a face in Hebrew and its hands go counterclockwise) was designed in the second half of the sixteenth century by architect Panacius Roder. Its interior today contains offices of the Prague Jewish community. Of interest outside is the stucco Star of David with a Swedish cap inside it; like the banner in the Old-New Synagogue, it commemorates the Jewish role in the seventeenth-century defeat of the Swedes.

Klaus Synagogue (Klausova synagóga), Ulice U starého hřbitova: This seventeenth-century Baroque structure in the back of the Old Jewish Cemetery now is a museum of the old Prague ghetto and its inhabitants.

Maisel Synagogue (Maislova synagóga), Maislova ulice: The original of this synagogue was a sixteenth-century construction built as a family synagogue for Mordecaij Maisel, the mayor of Prague's Jewish community, but the neo-Gothic building standing today is a nineteenth-century creation. Today it houses a collection of stunning pieces of Jewish liturgical silver — candlesticks, menorahs, and wedding and holiday plates from 153 Jewish communities all over Bohemia and Moravia brought here by the Nazis in 1942 as they removed the residents of those communities.

Old Jewish Cemetery (Starý židovský hřbitov), Ulice U starého hřbitova: Founded in the first half of the fifteenth century, and enlarged in the sixteenth and eighteenth centuries, this shady corner of 12,000 gravestones holds 100,000 graves. Because of the centuries of burials it was necessary to cover old graves with new layers of earth and bury on top of the old graves. In some places, there are as many as twelve layers of burials, with the headstones, consequently, heaped together, forming the unusual contours of the cemetery. Piles of pebbles are often heaped before

5. The Old Jewish Cemetery in Prague has 12,000 gravestones dating from 1439 to 1787.

a tomb — a gift to the deceased. Stones rather than flowers were used for this purpose in the desert, since they would not only not be blown away by desert winds, but eventually would renew the sand.

The earliest tombstone here dates from 1439 and marks the grave of poet and scholar Abigdor Karo, whose elegy to the victims of a pogrom in 1289 is still read today. Carvings of plants and animals, symbolic of the name of the deceased (a wolf, a bear, a rose, a bird) or of his profession (medical instruments, a tailor's scissors) often decorate the headstones. A gravestone of particular interest is that of Rabbi Jehuda Löw ben Bezalel, the sixteenth-century leader of Prague's religious community, a friend and adviser to Rudolf II and the creator of the legendary Golem which he is said to have fashioned of clay and brought to life by putting a tablet with a magical Hebrew inscription on it into its mouth. It was created, so the story goes, to walk the Jewish quarter at night and protect inhabitants from anti-Semitic attacks. Because it needed neither food nor rest, the Golem did its tasks well. Each Sabbath day of rest, however, the rabbi dutifully removed the tablet from the Golem's mouth and it once again became simply a sculpture of lifeless clay. But one Friday, Rabbi Löw forgot to take the magic tablet from the Golem's mouth and it went mad, destroying whatever was in its path. Frantic members of the congregation came to the rabbi to tell him. Boldly, Rabbi Löw approached the wrathful creature he had made, reached into its snarling mouth, and removed the tablet. The Golem, nothing but clay again, crashed to the floor. Rabbi Löw never brought it back to life. The Golem (which actually has its origins in the Talmud) has been the subject of a nineteenth-century Czech novel and a play that is still performed.

Old-New Synagogue (Staronová synagóga), Červená ulice: Built in 1270, this early Gothic structure is the oldest functioning synagogue in Europe. It may have gotten its curious name because it replaced an earlier synagogue on this site or because its name was Nová (New) Synagogue until the seventeenth-century construction of another New Synagogue, at which time this early one acquired the Old-New name. Or it may be that its name comes from the Hebrew word for "on condition" and that this synagogue was built on condition that it be torn down when the Messiah had arrived and a new one had been built in the Holy Land.

Inside are Renaissance wooden pews, richly decorated chandeliers, and a banner presented to the Jews by king of Hungary and Holy Roman Emperor Ferdinand III in appreciation for their assistance in the defense of Prague against Sweden in 1648. In the small park outside is a statue of Moses.

Pinkas Synagogue (Pinkasova synagóga), Ulice U starého hřbitova: Built on the edge of the Old Jewish Cemetery in the fifteenth century on foundations dating back to the eleventh century, this can probably be called the oldest synagogue in the city. Originally late Gothic in style, it was redone in the late Renaissance and a women's gallery added in the seventeenth century. At the start of World War II it and the Old-New Synagogue were the leading synagogues of Prague. Now undergoing reconstruction, it has served since 1958 as a memorial to Czechoslovakia's 72,297 Jewish victims of Nazi oppression. The names of all those killed in the Holocaust, their dates of birth, and the dates of their deportation to concentration camps are inscribed on the walls.

Spanish Synagogue (Španělská synagóga), Dušní ulice: Once a synagogue for Sephardic Jews who fled the Spanish Inquisition, the Spanish Synagogue has been closed to the public for many years.

House of the Black Mother of God (Dům U Černé Matky Boží), Celetná ulice: This cubistic 1912 office building that gets its name from the black wood Baroque Madonna in a niche on the corner is one of three cubistic structures erected in Prague in the first part of this century. The others are now apartment buildings.

Paris Avenue (Pařížká třída): Art Nouveau buildings now housing fashionable shops and airline and travel offices line this rather elegant street that leads to the Ghetto.

People's House (Obecní dům hlavního města Prahy), Celetná ulice beside the Powder Tower: The Czech Republic was declared in this Art Nouveau building in 1918. Its interior, where there is now a café, a restaurant, and a cabaret, seems a little tired, its old-fashioned elegance notwithstanding; still it is interesting to see, for a whole generation of zealous, proud Czech artists expressing their Czech nationalism here helped in its design.

Powder Tower (Prašná brána), Náměstí Republiky: This soaring, richly decorated, neo-Gothic arched tower, erected in 1475 but given its neo-Gothic appearance in the nineteenth century, was part of the original defense system in the walls of old Prague. It got its name in the seventeenth century, when it was used as a storage place for gunpowder. In summer, fine views of the city can be seen from the top. In the days of the kingdom of Bohemia, it was the start of the Royal Route to Hradčany Castle.

Small Square (Malé náměstí): Though it is barely a stone's throw from the busy Old Town Square, this intimate little square with a Renaissance fountain caged in elaborate wrought iron seems a different world. Some of the houses around the square are in typical Renaissance style, with sgraffito decorations on the plaster; others are in restrained Empire style. The **Richter House** is neoclassical. Above many a door are signs signifying the craft or profession of an early owner — a white lion, a black horse. In a house that formerly stood here, Bohemia's Winter King — Frederick, Protestant son-in-law of James I of England — spent his last night on Czech soil after the defeat of the Protestants at the fateful Battle of the White Mountain in 1620.

You can wander tirelessly for hours in the narrow cobblestone streets like Karlova ulice and Husova ulice and the alleys off this little square, passing under arches, crossing courtyards. Look up at the elaborate facades and windows of the past. An especially charming portal is at the Renaissance **House at the Two Golden Bears** (Dům U dvou zlatých medvědů) on Kožná ulice.

Other streets of architectural interest are Melantrichova ulice, Michalská ulice, Celetná ulice. It was along Celetná ulice — the Royal Route — that Bohemia's kings and queens traveled across the Old Town Square and the Charles Bridge to Prague Castle on Coronation Day. A particularly handsome house on this route is the late Baroque **Hrzán Palace** (Bývalý Hrzánský palác) on Celetná ulice.

Smetana Museum (Muzeum Bedřicha Smetany), Novotného lávka 1: Photographs, programs, manuscripts, and scores relating to the life of nineteenth-century Czech-born composer Bedřich Smetana are housed in the old waterworks here near the Charles Bridge. The museum is open daily, except Tuesday, from 10:00 A.M. to 5:00 P.M.

Square of the Knights of the Cross (Křižovnické náměstí): This "gateway" to the Charles Bridge has a statue of fourteenth-century Charles IV, who began the bridge, in its center. Around the square stand **St. Saviour's** (Salvatora) **Baroque Church,** the Baroque **Church of the Crusader Knights** (Kostel sv. Františka Serafínského), and the **Old Town Bridge Tower** (Staroměstské mostecká věž). Of particular interest is the graceful, highly decorated tower, with its Gothic sculptures from the workshop of Peter Parléř, who designed the bridge. On top are statues of St. Adelbert and St. Procopius, the patron saints of Bohemia; in the middle a statue of St. Vitus, and, seated, are Charles IV and his son, Wenceslas IV, in whose lifetime the bridge was finished. After the 1621 execution of the loyal Czech nobles who resisted Hapsburg rule, their heads were mounted here.

Tyl Theater (Tylovo divadlo), Železná ulice 11: Mozart's *Don Giovanni* premiered in 1787 in this neoclassical theater now undergoing restoration.

Týnský dvůr-Ungelt, between Týnská ulička and Malá Stupartská: In this enclosed Renaissance courtyard, foreign tradesmen for centuries sold their wares and purchased local merchandise. The **Granovský Palace,** with an arcaded loggia that faces on it, is now undergoing restoration.

THE NEW TOWN (NOVÉ MĚSTO)
Its name notwithstanding, Prague's New Town is hardly new. Charles IV conceived of it in 1348 when Prague needed expanding. In those days, the separation between the two parts of the city was a moat and a wall. Today the separation is the broad and lively walking street, Na příkopě, built atop the old moat.

Though the New and Old Towns are not that different in age, they are surely different in spirit. The New Town is alive with theaters, shops, and wide malls. It was here that the gathering leading to the relatively smooth governmental change of November 1989 — called the Velvet Revolution — took place. It lacks the charm of the Old Town, but the New Town does have its sites to see. The most interesting are

Church of Our Lady of the Snows (Kostel Panny Marie Sněžné), Jungmannovo náměstí: Charles IV founded this church in the fourteenth century and there were plans to make it the tallest building in the city, but the Hussite Wars broke out and it was never completed. The outspoken preaching in this church led its angry Hussite congregation to throw the mayor and councilmen from the window of the New Town Hall in 1419. (*See* New Town Hall.)

Church of St. Cyril and St. Methodius (Kostel sv. Cyrila a Metoděje), Resslova ulice: This eighteenth-century Baroque church is among the many Baroque creations here designed by K. I. Dientzenhofer. But its place in contemporary history rests on the fact that in May 1942, after the assassination of Nazi Reich protector Reinhard Heydrich by Czech parachutists flown in from England, three of the parachutists and several other members of the Czech Resistance hid in the crypt here for a month before they were discovered and bloodily routed out by the SS. In retaliation for Heydrich's assassination, the little village of Lidice (*see* Lidice) on the outskirts of Prague was wiped out.

Main Railway Station (Hlavní [Wilsonovo] nádraží), Wilsonovo ulice: Though much of this Art Nouveau building has recently been modernized, the former ticket hall, adorned with coats of arms of the cities the railroad once served, is worth seeing.

National Museum (Národní muzeum), Václavské náměstí: The imposing neoclassical turn-of-the-century exterior of this museum is probably more interesting to foreign tourists than its dusty collection of plants and rocks, stuffed birds and animals, and Czech historical items. The interior staircase, ramp, and entry hall lined with statues are worth looking at. If you are caught in Prague on a rainy day and choose to visit, it is open daily except Tuesday from 9:00 A.M. to 4:00 P.M.

National Theater (Národní divadlo), Národní třída: Virtually on the eve of the opening of this grand neo-Renaissance theater in 1881, its interior was almost entirely destroyed by fire (Prague's firemen, it turned out, were all attending a funeral at the time). But the building was soon restored and now has been restored again. It is rich in turn-of-the-century art by the leading Czech painters and sculptors of that period.

New Town Hall (Novoměstská radnice), Karlovo náměstí: Founded in 1367 and built and rebuilt over the years, the latest (1905) restoration has returned this building famous in Czech history to its sixteenth-century appearance. In 1419 the Catholic mayor and several Catholic town councilors were thrown out a window of the hall by enraged Hussites after a stone had been hurled at them as they paraded by. This was Prague's first "defenestration," as such expressions of anger came to be called.

Villa America (Villa Amerika), Ke Karlovu: The Antonín Dvořák Museum of memorabilia of the nineteenth-century Czech composer of the *New World Symphony* is housed in this little Baroque villa. It is open from 10:00 A.M. to 5:00 P.M. daily except Monday.

Wenceslas Square (Václavské náměstí): The largest square in Prague, 179 feet wide and 2,230 feet long, has at one end an early-twentieth-century equestrian statue of tenth-century St. Wenceslas (the "Good King Wenceslas" of Christmas carol fame). There is plenty of room for protests around it, and it has seen its share of them. Though the square is a good place for people watching, there is little window-shopping to be done, for the buildings ranged along it are for the most part banks and restaurants, hotels and movie theaters. Once, Baroque houses lined it, then Art Nouveau, but now largely a mishmash of structures.

THE LESSER TOWN (MALÁ STRANA)

Set just below Hradčany on a hill is this second oldest section of Prague after the Old Town. It was founded in 1257 by King Přemysl Otakar II and enlarged by Charles IV. Because the Hapsburgs found it an attractive site they firmly entrenched themselves here after the Battle of the White Mountain in 1620, building richly embellished Baroque houses and palaces. The most important sites follow.

Church of Our Lady of Victory (Kostel Panny Marie Vítězné), Karmelitská ulice: The first Baroque building in Prague was constructed by German Lutherans in 1611–1613 but taken over by the Catholics only a few years later after the Hapsburg victory at the Battle of the White Mountain. Today its principal appeal to tourists is the wax figure of the Infant Jesus, made in Spain in the Renaissance and said to have miraculous powers. It is always kept beautifully dressed from a wardrobe of thirty-nine gowns. The church is open every day during services, which begin at 9:00 A.M., and on Sunday all day.

Church of St. Nicholas (Kostel sv. Mikuláše), Malostranské náměstí: The Jesuits built this stunning Baroque church to establish firmly the power of the Catholic Church in heretic Prague. It is the finest building, architectural historians concur, that Christoph Dientzenhofer and his son, K. I. Dientzenhofer, ever built and the most splendid Baroque church in all Prague. Though by Baroque standards the exterior is restrained, in the interior are curving balconies, concave niches, and a large dome supported by Corinthian columns. There is sinuous movement everywhere. Though the structural design shows the influence of Italian Baroque, the decoration — stucco painted and gilded to resemble white and colored marble and the large graceful statues — show the Bavarian influence. (The Dientzenhofer family of architects was originally Bavarian.) The ceiling fresco by Jan Lukas Kracker recounting incidents from the life of St. Nicholas is nearly a third of an acre in size, one of the largest frescoes in Europe. The church is open daily from 8:00 A.M. to 5:00 P.M.

House of the Three Ostriches (Dům U tří pštrosů), beside the Charles Bridge: This sixteenth-century Renaissance burgher's house, now an inn, has a seventeenth-century sgraffito decoration of feathers on it that suggests it once belonged to a supplier of feathers to the king.

Kampa Island (Kampa): This is a quiet getaway if you have a little time simply to stroll and explore this section of Prague. There are fine views of the river and the Charles Bridge and a number of handsome houses with Baroque and Rococo facades.

Malá Strana Bridge Towers (Malostranské mostecké věže), west end of the Charles Bridge: From the taller of these two towers there is a fine view of the Old Town, the Charles Bridge, and Hradčany Castle. The lower, twelfth-century tower was a part of the Judith Bridge that crossed the river here before the Charles Bridge. The tower is open only in the summer. The hours are from 10:00 A.M. to 5:30 P.M. daily.

Mozart Museum, Villa Betranka, Mozartava 15, Smichov: In this villa not far from the Malá Strana Cemetery, Wolfgang Amadeus Mozart twice stayed with his friends the music teacher Franz Dušek and his wife, Josepha, an opera singer for whom, they say here in Prague, Mozart wrote *Don Giovanni*. The harpsichord and the piano on which he composed on those visits — one in 1787, one in 1791 — are still in the villa, along with some musical scores and letters and a few locks of his hair kept as a souvenir by Josepha, whose lover he is said to have been. The villa-museum is furnished with eighteenth-century objects. It is open Tuesday through Friday from 2:00 P.M. to 5:00 P.M. and Saturday and Sunday from 10:00 A.M. to noon and 2:00 P.M. to 5:00 P.M., but it is wise to check the hours before visiting. On the left bank of the river, the villa can be easily reached by bus from the castle.

Neruda Street (Nerudova ulice): Originally, many of the houses along this street were Renaissance, but in the seventeenth century Baroque alterations were made. The street is particularly notable for its stucco signs, signifying the craft or profession of the owner. In Maria Teresa's time, this — not numbers — was the means of identifying houses. Interesting ones include Number 6 with two angels, Number 12 with three violins, Number 18 with St. John Nepomuk. At Number 47, the nineteenth-century Czech author and journalist Jan Neruda, for whom the street is named, lived for a time and wrote about the life of the area. The Chilean Nobel Prize–winning poet, Pablo Neruda, adopted his name.

Embassies along this street include the Romanian Embassy, which is housed in the Baroque Morzin Palace (Morzínský palác), whose door is supported by two monumental sculptures of Moors by F. M. Brokoff, and the Italian Embassy in the Thun-Hohenstein Palace (Thun-Hohenštejnský palác), where the door is decorated with two sculpted eagles with outstretched wings by M. B. Braun.

Our Lady Beneath the Chain (Kostel Panny Marie pod Řětězem), Lázeňská ulice: Founded in the twelfth century, this is the oldest church of the Malá Strana, with stern fourteenth-century towers and a fourteenth-century facade. The porch, by Charles Bridge architect Peter Parléř, is High Gothic.

Palace of the Grand Prior of the Knights of Malta (Palác Maltézského Velkopřevora), Velkopřevorské náměstí: One of the loveliest palaces of the Malá Strana, the Museum of Musical Instruments, where there are concerts in the gardens in summer, is now housed here. The museum is open daily in summer from 10:00 A.M. to 5:00 P.M.

Petřín Gardens (Petřínské sady): Once there was a forest here, then vineyards. A funicular from the First of May Bridge (Most 1. Máje), offering a fine view of the city en route, will bring you here. There is a 197-foot miniature of the Eiffel Tower to be seen, built for the Prague Jubilee Exhibition of 1891, an observatory popular with amateur astronomers, a labyrinth of mirrors that was also created for the 1891 Exhibition, a charming eighteenth-century wooden church moved here from the Carpathian Ukraine, and Villa Kinsky, which now houses the **Ethnographic Museum** that is now undergoing reconstruction.

Square of the Knights of Malta (Maltézské náměstí): Handsome palaces surround this square, whose centerpiece is an eighteenth-century statue of St. John the Baptist by F. M. Brokoff. It is all that remains of a fountain that once stood here. Of particular interest around it are the late Baroque Nostic Palace (Nostický palác), which is now the Dutch Embassy, and the Rococo Turba Palace (Palác Turbů), now the Japanese Embassy.

Tomášská Street (Tomášská ulice): All along this street are interesting stucco sculptures above the doors signifying the profession or craft of its owner. Of particular interest are the signs above Number 12, "The Golden Pretzel" (Dům U zlatého preclíku), and, after it, "The Golden Stag" (Dům U zlatého jelena), an eighteenth-century sculpture showing St. Hubert with a stag.

Vrtba Garden (Vrtbovský dům se zahradou), Karmelitská ulice: Though not very large, this lovely eighteenth-century terraced garden is a veritable museum of Baroque sculpture by M. B. Braun.

Wallenstein Palace (Valdštejnský palác), Valdštejnské náměstí: The grandest Baroque palace in Prague was built between 1624 and 1630. To make room for the enormous palace and its terraced gardens with their artificial cave, twenty-three houses, three gardens, and a brickworks were demolished on orders from the colorful Albrecht von Wallenstein. Wallenstein quit the Czech army when the Hapsburgs came to power and joined the army of Ferdinand II. He rose quickly through the ranks and soon had both a general's and a duke's title. In keeping with his titles, he wanted a palace of the greatest grandeur — one that would rival Prague Castle itself. The palace he created is largely Italian Renaissance in style, with a handsome loggia, though the facade and courtyard are Baroque. There are fine interior frescoes and in the chapel interesting scenes from the life of St. Wenceslas. The palace is not open to the public, except for a section where the **Pedagogic Museum** is located. The public may enter the garden in the summer.

Unfortunately, Wallenstein's greed was his undoing, and he had barely four years to enjoy the splendid surroundings he created here. Setting his sights on occupying the throne of Bohemia, Wallenstein entered into secret negotiations with Sweden. The emperor Ferdinand II learned of the plans and had him murdered. The palace gardens are filled with copies of bronze statues of gods and goddesses by Adrian de Vries. The gardens are open daily from May to September from 9:00 A.M. to 7:00 P.M.

The Castle District (Hradčany)

There is no more splendid castle complex in Europe than that of Prague Castle, whose green copper turrets and spires rise on their hill above this capital city. Set in what was once the small feudal town of Hradčany, the castle, with its courtyards, churches, and museums, is surely the high point of any visit to Prague. But the old town of Hradčany itself has more than its complement of attractions — churches, palaces, and convents that should not be missed either.

Hradčany Square (Hradčanské náměstí): Several palaces of interest are at the front of this square at the entrance to the castle. They include the sixteenth-century Rococo **Archbishop's Palace** beside the castle, open to the public only on Maundy Thursday, and the former Schwarzenberg Palace that today houses an outstanding **Museum of Military History** (Vojenské muzeum) covering 5,000 years of European wars. It is open Monday through Friday from 8:30 A.M. to 5:00 P.M. from November to March and daily except Monday from 9:30 A.M. to 4:30 P.M. April through October. Then there is the Baroque **Palace Toscana** (Toskánský palác), with the coat of arms of Tuscany on the facade, and the seventeenth-century **Martinic Palace** (Martinický palác), built in Renaissance style and notable for the sgraffito mythological and biblical stories scratched in plaster on its exte-

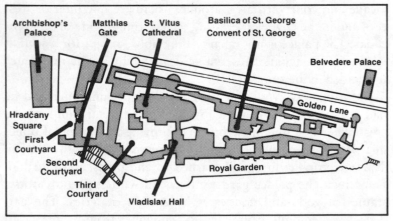

PRAGUE CASTLE

rior. Finally, the seventeenth-century **Sternberg Palace,** the principal building of the National Art Gallery (Národní galerie), includes works by such European masters as Seurat, Matisse, Utrillo, and Delacroix, among others. It is open from 10:00 A.M. to 6:00 P.M. daily except Monday.

Prague Castle (Pražský hrad): Though it was the legendary Bohemian queen Libuše, founder of Prague, who selected the site for this castle, ninth-century Bořivoj I, Bohemia's first Christian king, established the first church here and made this his governmental site. His grandson, Good King Wenceslas, a century later built a rotunda dedicated to St. Vitus where the towering Cathedral of St. Vitus rises now. But Wenceslas's rule was cut very short, for his younger brother Boleslav thought him too much of a peacemaker as king and had him murdered.

They like to tell you all this history at the castle, though nothing still stands from Wenceslas's day except the foundation of the rotunda, which can be viewed under St. Vitus Cathedral, for Czechs are proud of gentle Wenceslas, who was sainted for his martyrdom.

Sightseeing of the castle involves three courtyards. Outside the first an honor guard stands before eighteenth-century statues of giants dispatching enemies with daggers. These show the way (albeit somewhat uninvitingly) through the wrought-iron gate to the **First Courtyard** (První nádvoří), constructed in Maria Teresa's day and the most recent of the courtyards. Beyond it, the seventeenth-century **Matthias Gate** (Matyášova brána), an imposing Baroque arch, leads to the **Second Courtyard** (Druhé nádvoří). (The reception rooms of President Václav Havel are up a flight of steps to the right of the gate, but they are not open to the public.)

In the spacious but not especially decorative Second Courtyard, which also dates from Maria Teresa's day, are the **Holy Cross Chapel** (Kaple sv. Kříže) and the **Picture Gallery of Rudolf** (Rudolfova galerie). Among the items in the former (previously kept in the Cathedral Treasury) are the chain mail of King Wenceslas, the fifteenth-century sword of St. Stephen, and a large collection of precious relics from the days of Charles IV. In Rudolf's

Gallery (open from 10:00 A.M. to 6:00 P.M. daily except Monday) — formerly the stable for Rudolf II's Spanish horses — are works by Tintoretto, Titian, Veronese, and Rubens, among others. Seventeenth-century Rudolf II, patron of the Danish astronomer Tycho Brahe and the English alchemist Edward Kelley, was also a passionate collector of art, and before the Swedes carried off some of the collection to Stockholm after the Thirty Years' War and the Hapsburgs took more to Vienna, he owned Raphaels, Michelangelos, and Leonardos. Today there are only seventy paintings left (some were rediscovered in the 1950s in rooms so dark they had been overlooked).

Inside the **Third Courtyard** (Třetí nádvoří) the pinnacles of **St. Vitus Cathedral** (Katedrála sv. Víta) soar. With its lacelike towers, its lofty interior, pointed arches, and sweeping vaulting, it is Prague's Gothic masterpiece. Its construction was begun in 1344, in the days of John of Luxembourg. Matthias of Arras, who had been employed at the papal court at Avignon in France, was selected as its architect. It is patterned after the French cathedrals, with chapels around the choir. But Matthias died in 1352 and his place was taken by Peter Parler from Cologne (the Charles Bridge architect). The vaulting, particularly in the Sacristy and the Wenceslas Chapel, show his German influence. When Peter Parler died in 1399, his sons continued his work, but it was interrupted by the Hussite revolution. Altogether, between wars, rebellions, and the natural problems of building, it was 600 years before this cathedral was completed. The cathedral is open every day except Monday.

Outside the cathedral, note the latter-day (twentieth-century) sculptures of saints on the towers of the western facade and the portraits of the builders beside the rose window that recounts the creation of the world. Above the Golden Portal on the south facade, the work of Peter Parler, is a much restored fourteenth-century mosaic of the Last Judgment showing Charles IV and his fourth wife, Elizabeth of Pomerania, in the center. Above it to the left on the main tower gilded Renaissance grillwork gleams from a Gothic window.

Of particular interest inside is the **Chapel of St. Wenceslas,** which, at the time of its construction in the fourteenth century by Peter Parler, was the most sacred place in the cathedral and, indeed, in the whole castle complex. Amethysts, jasper, and agates set in gilded plaster gleam from around the frescoes depicting Christ's Passion and the life of St. Wenceslas. His helmet and chain mail as well as a statue of him are here.

Of interest in the gallery of the choir is the silver tomb of St. John Nepomuk, designed by Vienna's J. B. Fischer von Erlach, and in the royal crypt are the sarcophagi of Charles IV, his children and four wives, and of King Jiří Poděbrady, and Rudolf II, among others.

Powder Tower (Mihulka): Just outside the cathedral this fifteenth-century gunpowder storage tower is now open to the public as a small museum of Renaissance science and military history.

The Third Courtyard is also the site of the old **Royal Palace** (Královský palác). The first room of major interest is the late Gothic **Hall of Vladislav** (Vladislavský sál). Today the National Assembly meets in this vaulted room, with its shimmering chandeliers, but once in past centuries it was the site of coronation banquets and indoor tournaments. In Rudolf II's time, markets were held here and works of art sold.

Off this room is the **Bohemian Chancellery** (Česká kancelář). It was from a window in the little room off it, formerly the office of the imperial governor, that the Second Defenestration of Prague occurred, on May 23, 1618.

The Catholic Hapsburgs had announced that anti-Protestant Archduke Ferdinand was to occupy the Bohemian throne. A delegation of Bohemia's Protestant noblemen came here to meet with the Catholic counselors Ferdinand had appointed to discuss the religious issue. The Protestants insisted that Ferdinand abide by the guarantee of religious freedom for Protestants that had been issued by Rudolf II. They accused the counselors of being traitors manipulated by the Jesuits. After many harsh words, the enraged Protestants — in Prague tradition (*see* New Town Hall) — threw the counselors out the window toward the moat below. As it turned out, they landed in a dung heap with nothing but their pride injured. (The Catholics later called this a miracle.) But what followed was the Thirty Years' War.

Other rooms of interest in the Royal Palace are the **Council Chamber** (Síň Říšské dvorské rady), where portraits of the Hapsburgs hang; the **Chapel of All Saints** (Kaple všech svatých), most notable for its paintings from Rudolf's period, and the **Equestrian Staircase** (Jezdecké Schodiy), constructed in 1510, which horses and their riders would climb from the court below to reach the Hall of Vladislav for tournaments.

The earliest part of the Prague Castle complex is the Romanesque **Basilica of St. George** (Bazilika sv. Jiří), founded in 920 and the repository of the bones of Bohemia's first saint, St. Ludmila, grandmother of Wenceslas.

From the outside, it hardly has a Romanesque look, for the facade is golden-yellow Baroque, but a turn-of-the-century restoration returned the interior to its original state. In addition to the tomb of St. Ludmila that is the work of Peter Parler, the sculpture of St. Bridget in the crypt is notable. Snakes and lizards writhe in the figure's intestines — a Baroque portrayal of the transitory nature of life. (The statue is said to have been carved in the eighteenth century as penance for an act of violence done in church.) The Old Bohemian Art Collection of the National Gallery (Národní galerie–Sbírka starého českého umění) is housed in the adjoining tenth-century **Convent of St. George** and is open from 10:00 A.M. to 6:00 P.M., except Monday. Splendidly displayed, the medieval works here include several startlingly modern portraits of saints by Master Theodoric, who did 128 such paintings for Charles IV's castle at Karlštejn outside Prague (now undergoing restoration).

The principal sites outside the castle complex follow.

Belvedere Palace (Královský letohrádek), Mariánské hradby: This inviting summer palace was built in Renaissance style by Italian artists for Ferdinand I's wife, Anna, in the mid-sixteenth century. It is the setting today, from time to time, for art expositions, but it is now closed while it undergoes repairs. The fountain in the garden is notable for the music the water makes as it strikes the basin.

Černín Palace (Černínský palác), Loretánské náměstí: This massive building, the largest palace in Prague, was constructed in Italian Mannerist style by a Bohemian nobleman, Jan Humrecht Černín, the imperial envoy to Venice, in 1669. Because of its size — more than 490 feet long — the palace was the talk of Vienna and Leopold I came to have a look at it. Annoyed that a subject was building something so grand, the emperor made his displeasure known. Černín apologetically explained that it really wasn't a palace he was building — just a very big barn. Today the palace, which has a majestic staircase and exquisitely painted ceilings on the second floor, as well as lovely frescoes, is the Bureau of Foreign Affairs. The palace is not open to the public, but its gardens are open in the summer.

Golden Lane (Zlatá ulička): If you arrive here early in the day, this little lane of sixteenth-century houses built for the archer guardians of the castle is charming to see and to photograph. In the years after the archers, craftsmen lived here and, it is said, so did some of the alchemists whose activities Rudolf II fostered (the reason for the Golden Lane name). But once the sightseeing crowds have arrived, the lane is nothing but a mass of tourists crowding into the tiny houses that are now souvenir shops. Franz Kafka is said to have lived at Number 22.

Our Lady of Loreto (Loreta), Loretánské náměstí: This copy of the house in which the Virgin Mary learned that she would be the Mother of Jesus has stood here since 1631, when the money for its construction was given by Blessed Catherine of Lobkowicz, a wealthy and devout Czech aristocrat.

In the thirteenth century, when the Turks were invading the Holy Land, two monks are said to have moved the house of the Virgin, stone by stone, to Loreto in Italy, where it was reconstructed. The copy of that house was built here as a pilgrimage place by an Italian architect, Giovanni Battiste Orsi of Como. In addition to the Loreto house, with Renaissance reliefs on its walls, scenes from the life of the Virgin in silver inside, and a carved wooden Madonna with Christ in her arms, there are quiet cloisters and walkways, as well as the **Church of the Nativity** (Kostel Narození Páně) designed by the Bavarian Baroque architect K. I. Dientzenhofer, builder also of the Church of St. Nicholas in the Old Town.

The devout have made many offerings to the treasury here. They are on display upstairs in the cloister. Particularly beautiful are the Prague Sun Monstrance of 6,222 glittering diamonds made in 1699 in Vienna on order of Ludmilla Eva Františka, who gave all the stones from her wedding dress for this purpose. The Loreto is open daily from 9:00 A.M. to 1:00 P.M. and from 1:30 to 4:30 P.M.

The carillon of the Loreto is famous for the opening bars of the Marian Hymn, which peal from it every hour and have, it is said, for centuries. But they didn't always. Time was when they only struck the hours. The story goes that a poor widow living near the Loreto had the same number of children as there are bells. When the plague struck, one after the other she lost her children. Poor as she was, she had only enough coins to pay to have the bells toll as each child died. When the mother died, too, there were no coins left to pay for the ringing of her death knell, but the bells rang of their own accord and played the hymn that they have played ever since.

Strahov Monastery (Bývalý Strahovský klášter), Strahovské nádvoří: Founded in 1140 by Vladislav II, this monastery of the Premonstratensian order of white-clad monks continued to function, with only a few interruptions, until 1952. Though Hapsburg Emperor Joseph II closed down most monasteries and convents in the eighteenth century, he allowed this one to remain open because of its centuries-old library of Western Christian literature. For admirers of Baroque, the **Theological Hall** (Teologický sál) on the first floor, with its manuscript showcases, enormous globes by Franz Anton Maulpertsch, and magnificent ceiling frescoes framed in their graceful stucco frames, is particularly impressive. Impressive, too, is the **Philosophical Hall** (Filozofický sál) of Ignac Giovanni Palliardi, which also has ceilings frescoes. Today, there are about 900,000 books and illuminated manuscripts in the library, now the Museum of National Literature (Muzeum národního písemnictvi). The monastery is open to

the public daily, except Monday, from 9:00 A.M. to 4:30 P.M.
From the monastery garden there are fine views.

THE OUTSKIRTS OF PRAGUE

If your Czechoslovakian stay is short, but you would like to see
a few sites outside the capital city, there are a number worth a
visit within an hour or two of Prague, by car or tour bus. There
are more than 3,000 castles and châteaux set in commanding positions on the country's hilltops. The outskirts of Prague offer
green fields and forests, vineyards, orchards, and historic towns.
There are also, it must be said, unappealing industrial sites. A
selection of some of the most interesting sites follows.

CASTLE KARLŠTEJN

With ramparts, square towers, and steel gray turrets, this reconstructed fourteenth-century castle, the summer residence of
Charles IV, is straight out of a fairy-tale book. The interior, however, is undergoing restoration, and although guided tours are
offered, there is little of fairy-story quality inside.

A map of the Holy Roman Empire in Charles's day shows
that the empire stretched as far as today's Istanbul. There are
photographs of the castle's reconstruction, copies of paintings of
Charles's four wives, and odds and ends of furniture, including a
throne set below a window, so that those requesting an audience
with the king would be staring straight into the sun and unable
to look him in the eye. In the **Chapel of the Holy Cross** (Kaple sv.
Kříže), where the crown jewels were once kept, semiprecious
stones stud the walls and the gilded ceiling is decorated with
Venetian glass in the shape of stars. What is probably the largest
collection of Gothic paintings in the world is here, including the
lifelike saints of Master Theodoric, but as this book went to

press, leaks in the chapel were being repaired and the chapel was closed. Its opening is expected in 1992.

In the **Church of the Virgin Mary** in **St. Mary's Tower** (Mariánská věž) are frescoes of battles between devils and angels, and in the **Chapel of St. Catherine** (Kaple sv. Kateřiny) is a Madonna that was a gift from Charles V of France, but it will be a while before Karlštejn is ready to receive visitors. The castle is open to the public daily, except Monday, from 9:00 A.M. to 4:00 P.M. in March and April and October through December. It is open from 9:00 A.M. to 6:00 P.M. from May through September and closed from January 1 to February 28.

KONOPIŠTĚ CASTLE

The castle that belonged to the Austrian archduke Franz Ferdinand (whose assassination in a carriage with his wife in today's Sarajevo, Yugoslavia, when the town was part of the Austro-Hungarian Empire, was the spark that ignited the First World War) is a gloomy place. An insatiable hunter, Franz Ferdinand shot 300,000 animals in his lifetime, traveling much of the world on hunts. The horns, heads, and skins of many of these decorate the halls of his castle. There are bison and bear, fox and tiger heads, and birds of all sorts; antlers are in such close proximity to each other that they almost mesh. The archduke's lust for the hunt was so great that Franz Ferdinand reputedly once questioned his own bloodthirstiness, asking himself if Hapsburg inbreeding could have damaged his brain. Guides point out the white hare that he insisted on shooting shortly before his death — not heeding the warning that he who shot it would be dead within the year.

Constructed as a Gothic castle in the French mode in 1300, Konopiště was enlarged in the seventeenth century, when a Renaissance palace was added to it. In the eighteenth century, there were Baroque additions and a large park was landscaped. In 1887, the archduke had the castle converted into a distinctly turn-of-the-century palace filled with heavy, late-nineteenth-century furniture and busy floral wallpaper (in those places empty of heads and antlers). Most visitors' feelings of sympathy for

Franz Ferdinand are likely to disappear in the face of the mementos of slaughter here.

Of considerable interest, however, is the arms and armor collection. To gain entry to the castle, you must take guided tours — one for the archduke's quarters, another for the weapons museum. If you must choose one or the other (the combination takes about an hour and a half), the eighteenth- and nineteenth-century weapons display — one of the best in Europe — is much more interesting. The collection includes armor for six-year-olds, a powder horn made from a crab claw, the contents of a harem tent (a gift to the archduke on his travels), cannon the Swedes used in the Thirty Years' War, and a rare group of statuettes of St. George killing the dragon. During World War II, SS troops occupied the castle. It was much richer in contents, it is said, before their stay.

Outside, the palace rose garden and park are worth a visit if the weather is good. Konopiště is open daily, except Monday, from 9:00 A.M. to noon and 1:00 to 6:00 P.M. from May through August, until 5:00 in September, and until 4:00 the rest of the year.

KUTNÁ HORA

Rich in silver deposits in the Middle Ages (they are said to have built Prague), this seat of the Royal Mint was the most important town in Bohemia after Prague and today still has much of the medieval architecture that was created then. Its most outstanding structure, and one of Czechoslovakia's finest examples of Bohemian High Gothic architecture, is the **Cathedral of St. Barbara** (Chrám sv. Barbory), built between the fourteenth and sixteenth centuries. The interior of the five-aisled structure soars to stellar and geometric ribbed vaults. Two large windows with delicate tracery make the interior light. The cathedral, appropriately dedicated in this mining community to Barbara, the patron saint of miners, is open from 9:00 A.M. to 5:00 P.M.

The medieval **Church of St. James** (Kostel sv. Jakuba), with its tall steeple, is another building worth looking at here. So, too, is the oldest house in town, the **Stone House** (Kamenný dům), built in 1480 in late Gothic style, and the **Italian Court** (Vlašský dvůr), which adjoins the Church of St. James. In 1300 it was the Royal Mint. Its name comes from the fact that skilled Italian miners were invited here to extract the silver. But at the turn of the fourteenth century, the Italian Court was redesigned as a royal palace for Wenceslas IV. In the **Knight's Hall** (Rytířský sál), there is a handsome Gothic ceiling and fifteenth-century frescoes. It is now a building housing municipal offices.

LIDICE

The Nazis' ruthless destruction of this little industrial village of 104 houses and 500 inhabitants on the night of June 9, 1942, left the civilized world aghast.

Because two sons of the village had fled to England, been trained by the Royal Air Force, and were believed to have assisted in the assassination of the Nazi "Protector of Bohemia," Reinhard Heydrich, and because a Nazi collaborator had made Lidice suspect, this entire village was razed. All of its men, from age fifteen to eighty-four, were shot, its women and children sent to concentration camps, and its infants given to German storm troopers to adopt. The following day, the village was burned to the ground and the ashes buried.

Today, Lidice stands again — a quiet little place, as it was then, of red-roofed stucco houses above green fields. Miners of Birmingham, England, were in the forefront of those who contributed money to help in its reconstruction.

In the **Garden of Friendship and Peace** that marks the site of the original village, roses grow, given by hundreds of countries. A fountain plays. A cedar grove marks the burial place of Lidice's dead. In a small museum, tapes in many languages recount the harrowing events of that June night, and pictures, passports, identity cards, and ration coupons are a poignant memorial to the dead. In the museum's reception area, a survivor of that horrifying night is an employee. The museum is open from 8:00 A.M. to 4:00 P.M. from October through March and until 5:00 P.M. from April through September. The grounds are open daily throughout the year.

SOUTHERN BOHEMIA

Southern Bohemia is a pretty countryside of woods, fields, ponds, and rounded hills of green and of quiet towns with enormous market squares. It is rich in history for it was in the little village of Husinec that the fourteenth-century reform theologian Jan Hus was born (he got his name from the village, not the other way around). In Tábor his followers labored and planned their revolutionary strategies.

Bordering Germany and resembling it topographically, southern Bohemia has attracted German settlers for centuries. Much of its architecture is German in character, and more than half of its population at the outbreak of World War II was of Germanic origin. This was the reason, Adolf Hitler said, as he embarked on World War II, that he was claiming southern Bohemia for the Third Reich. Many of its more interesting sites are only a day's trip from Prague. Its most outstanding attractions follow.

ČESKÉ BUDĚJOVICE

The capital of southern Bohemia has one of the largest market squares (náměstí) in all Europe. Eighteenth-century arcaded houses surround it. A Baroque fountain with Samson carved on it stands in the center. There is a Baroque **Town Hall,** with dragon gargoyles and allegorical figures of Prudence, Wisdom, Courage, and Justice on the facade. The sixteenth-century **Black Tower** (Černá věž), when it is open, affords a fine view of the square and the town. During the Thirty Years' War, the **Church of St. Nicholas** (Kostel sv. Mikuláše), next to the Black Tower, seemed far enough away from Prague to provide a safe hiding place for the crown jewels, which were kept in a strong room constructed in one of its chapels.

Europe's first horse-drawn railway ran from here to Linz in upper Austria from 1827 to 1832, and a small section has been preserved as a national monument. České Budějovice is also the home of the original Budweiser (Budvar) beer.

Hluboká Castle, north of České Budějovice: You might think you were in Gothic England looking up at this crenelated castle above the River Vltava, and that is exactly what you are supposed to think. Though somewhere deep inside is the masonry of the thirteenth-century Gothic structure that stood here, there have been many reconstructions over the years. Once Hluboká had a Renaissance look; later it was Baroque. In 1661 it became the property of the wealthy Schwarzenberg family, German nobles in Hapsburg employ, whose lands included 800 square miles of Bohemia. It was they who rebuilt the castle from 1841 to 1871, giving it its present Windsor-like design. Now a state property, the castle is a museum of fine china and Delftware, Flemish tapestries, Bohemian and Venetian glass, ebony furniture, and art that generations of Schwarzenbergs collected. The castle setting is an English-style hunting park, and the castle has a courtyard above which sculpted deer heads with antlers hang. The Hluboká stable is now an art gallery. The castle, gallery, and park are open to the public (the palace only from November to March), but it would be wise to check the hours in advance with Čedok in České Budějovice.

Český Krumlov

Medieval arcades and sgraffito-etched Renaissance facades in apricot, beige, and pea-green shades; rust-red, pink, and golden Baroque buildings surround this cobblestoned square with a **Plague Monument** (Morovy sloup) in its center. As you explore the square, side streets, and the winding River Vltava that separates the Old Town from the towering castle, look up to see a hatter's hat painted above a Renaissance door, peer around corners through arcaded towers and through the Gothic **Budějovicka Gate** (Budějovická bróna) that is part of the sixteenth-century fortifications. The lofty-towered **Krumlov Castle** itself — reached by crossing the meandering river and climbing a hill — is this country's second grandest castle after Prague's. As it stands today, it is largely sixteenth-century Renaissance in style, though it began as a thirteenth-century fortress and part of the castle of that period still stands. There are 300 rooms (some of which may be visited), a Baroque theater, a **Hall of Masks** (Maškarní sál) with realistic murals of masked faces, and an open air theater. A ghost called the White Lady, an unhappy princess married to a cruel lord in the Middle Ages, can be seen walking the ramparts when danger is in the air, it is said. Krumlov Castle for centuries was the home of the powerful and imperious Rožemberk family, one of the most powerful families in this region and one it was best not to contend with.

Once summoned by messenger to appear before the Prague law courts, the Rožemberks are said to have forced the messenger to eat the paper on which his message was written and then to have driven him from the castle grounds with dogs. The Rožemberk coat of arms was a five-petaled rose, which is frequently seen in the castle. Later, the castle passed into Schwarzenberg hands (*see* Hluboká Castle). The castle itself is open only from April through October, but its gardens and courtyards are accessible at almost any time. It is best to check castle hours with Čedok in Český Krumlov, but they are generally 10:00 A.M. to 6:00 P.M., except Monday.

6. Arcades like these are characteristic of Czech towns from the Renaissance to the neoclassical period.

TÁBOR

Had King Wenceslas IV, the son of Charles IV, been a better king, this town that turned all Bohemia — and much of Europe — topsy-turvy in the fifteenth century might never have come into being. But Wenceslas was a spendthrift, a drinker, and womanizer; when he had been drinking, he tended to give away his estates to rich and powerful noblemen. As they acquired more land, the nobles became more imperious. They treated the poor cruelly, and the poor, hearing sermons on goodness in church but seeing few acts of goodness in real life, became less acquiescent to the orders of the aristocracy and more questioning of the tenets of the Church. When one of its priests, Jan Hus, began to preach social and religious liberty for Czechs and openly questioned the selling of indulgences for remission of sins, ordinary people listened attentively. And when Hus was burned at the stake by Catholic authorities, the poor took up arms against the Church.

Led by one-eyed soldier-farmer Jan Žižka, the poor established this town in 1420 on the principle of communal sharing and named it after the biblical Mount Tabor, where the Israelites were victorious in a fierce battle against the oppressive Canaanites. It was to be the center of their religion and the center of their defense, and they planned to use it as a base for military forays. They began to build a fortress and laid out their streets around the square in such a crooked way that attackers would have trouble finding their way around. To this day, the streets of Tábor remain — for the outsider — a maze.

Today's visitor comes here because of Tábor's historical significance and to see the handsome **Town Square** (Žižkovo náměstí) that honors Žižka by its name and with his statue. Edging the square are Gothic and early Renaissance houses with stepped gables in reasonable, if not the best of repair. (Other fine houses with ornamental gables are on Prague Street [Pražská ulice].) There is a restored neo-Gothic **Town Hall** (Radnice) that contains a **Museum of the Hussite Movement** (Muzeum husitského knutí), but it is still under restoration. From it extend underground passages, long closed, that were constructed for use in time of attack. The late Gothic **Convent Church** (Kostel Conventi) on the marketplace is also of interest.

Though Tábor was captured by Catholic Hapsburg forces in 1621, Catholicism never took hold.

WESTERN BOHEMIA

Above all, western Bohemia is renowned for its waters — the spa waters of Františkovy Lázně (Franzensbad), Karlovy Vary (in German, Carlsbad), and Mariánské Lázně (Marienbad) — and for the strong dark beer of Plzeň (Pilsen). Though Plzeň is, today, a dingy industrial city with little to recommend it to a tourist, western Bohemia's spas were fostered and favored as sites for holidays and health during the Communist regime. Though they have lost some of the grandeur of their most famous days, their wooded settings, parks, and gardens are exquisite and their nineteenth-century columned promenades full of charm.

FRANTIŠKOVY LÁZNĚ
The least well known of the spa towns is perhaps the most charming. It is distinctly sedate, its yellow buildings frosted with extravagant dollops of white, its restful gardens and tree-shaded streets seemingly untouched by time. There is virtually no modern architectural intrusion. Though its curative mineral waters were mentioned in the sixteenth century by Paracelsus, the health spa itself was not started until the end of the eighteenth century and was named for the emperor Francis I. Most of its buildings are in Empire style. Spa guests drink the waters, bathe in them, inhale steam from them, or take mudbaths. The waters are said to be good for any number of ailments, including gynecological and circulatory problems.

KARLOVY VARY (CARLSBAD)
Charles IV is credited with discovering the beneficial waters of this spa in 1347, when the stag he was pursuing leapt from a rock into the Sprudel, the oldest of the twelve hot springs here.

Charles named the spa for himself, and it has prospered ever since.

Set below the wooded hills in the Teplá River Valley, it has, over the centuries, attracted the creative and the harried of many nations — composers Brahms, Liszt, and Dvořák; writers Gogol, Tolstoi, and Turgenev; Russia's Peter the Great; Austria's Empress Maria Teresa; Germany's Karl Marx, and Prussia's Bismarck.

Along both sides of the river are hotels, shops selling crystal, and colonnaded promenades with bubbling fountains from which guests "taking a cure" fill their flowered, long-handled porcelain drinking cups (the handle serves as a straw). The waters of Karlovy Vary are said to be best for digestive problems. The newest modernistic, ugly colonnade (Vřídelní Kolonáda Jurije Gagarina), made of steel and Bulgarian marble, with a hot

7. Drinking the water at Karlovy Vary.

water geyser in it, bears the name of Soviet cosmonaut Yuri Gagarin, who came here twice in the 1960s. There is an old-fashioned grace to such turn-of-the-century colonnades as the Greek Revival First Colonnade of Czechoslovak-Soviet Friendship, formerly the Mill Colonnade. Often there is an orchestra playing for strollers and water imbibers to watch.

Older sites are the square castle tower that replaced Charles's hunting lodge in 1608 and now is Baroque in character and the **Church of Mary Magdalene** (Kostel Máří Magdalény), built by Prague's Baroque genius, K. I. Dientzenhofer, in the eighteenth century. The **Grand Hotel Pupp,** built in 1893, is at the end of town and worth a visit. Now being refurbished after years when it was known as the Grand Hotel Moskva and was a quite ordinary hotel, it is being returned to its former elegance. It is notable for its handsome stained-glass ceiling and an impressive white-and-gold concert hall.

Not the least of the attractions here are the walks into the hills above town and the views they afford of the neighboring countryside.

MARIÁNSKÉ LÁZNĚ

This spa set among wooded hills was opened to the public in 1818 and began to attract guests like Edward VII of England, Gogol, Turgenev, Gorki, Rudyard Kipling, Mark Twain, Richard Wagner, and Johann Wolfgang von Goethe. Here the seventy-three-year-old Goethe fell in love with seventeen-year-old Ulrike Von Levetzow and sought her hand. When her mother discreetly moved the family to Carlsbad, Goethe wrote his "Elegy of Marienbad" ("Marienbader Elegie"), one of the most passionate love poems he ever wrote.

Though there are lovely parks and gardens (Goethe called Václav Skalník, who designed the gardens, "the poet of gardens"), modern development is, sadly, destroying the late-nineteenth-century tranquillity that made this such an attractive place. As this book went to press, a boxlike modern structure was in the process of being erected on the hill near the winding old **Maxim Gorki Colonnade** (Kolonáda Maxima Gorkého) with its iron columns that is the centerpiece of Mariánské Lázně. (Another newcomer here is a musical fountain at one end of the colonnade.) In the summer, there is a music festival. In winter, the hills lend themselves to tobogganers and skiers.

Because of its popularity among both English and Russians, English and Russian churches were constructed and still stand, but the **English Church** is in a state of dilapidation. The altar of the **Russian Church** is said to be the longest piece of porcelain in the world. There is a spa museum that contains memorabilia of Goethe's stays and a display of the tin boxes in which Oblaten (Karlovarské oplatky) — the crisp wafers that have been a spa specialty for generations — used to be sold, but the museum is hardly extensive or imaginative. There are fine walks through the neighboring pine forests to splendid views of the hills and mountains. The water here, considered good for kidney, respiratory, and skin problems, among others, comes from a spring at the nearby **Teplá Monastery** (Klášter Teplá). The spa's name honors the Virgin Mary.

CHEB

This recently restored medieval town is one of the most perfectly preserved of its kind in all Europe, but the visitor should not expect it to be big. It is very small, and the sites of most interest are the Gothic, Renaissance, and beautifully decorated Baroque burghers' houses around the statue of Roland, a medieval sign of independence, in the market square. A knight gazes down from a bright-yellow facade, the gold heads of two of Maria Teresa's young sons from another. Many of these houses around the square were originally Gothic shops and are half-timbered. In a now Baroque building behind them, today a museum, Albrecht von Wallenstein (*see* Prague, the Lesser Town, Wallenstein Palace), the colorful and ambitious Thirty Years' War general, was murdered by his soldiers in 1634 on order of Ferdinand II, who believed that Wallenstein sought his throne. Massive, with its thirteenth-century dark wood staircase, its ceiling painted with bulls' blood, and pieces of Wallenstein's own furniture, it is not hard to imagine Wallenstein struck from behind as he peered out the window and dreamed of the successes that seemed just ahead of him. The museum is open daily, except Monday, from 10:00 A.M. to 4:30 P.M. There is also a Baroque **New Town Hall** (Novoměstská radnice) on the square. Other sites worth seeing are the Gothic **Church of St. Nicholas** (Kostel sv. Mikuláše) with its Romanesque portal behind the museum and the remains of the Romanesque fort that Holy Roman Emperor Frederick Barbarossa built in the twelfth century. The fort is open daily, except Monday, from 10:00 A.M. to 4:30 P.M. from April to October.

MORAVIA

East of Bohemia stretch the untrammeled hills, the vineyards, the corn, sugar beet, and golden rape fields of Moravia. The Morava River and its tributaries form verdant valleys in central Moravia. In the south are Czechoslovakia's best wines while the north — formerly Silesia — is the coal mining and industrial land bordering Poland and Germany. Moravia has forests of spruce, pine, and fir and whitewashed villages with wine cellars in backyards. Jolly vintners grow their grapes and make their wine as second jobs. Folk art is important here, and Czechoslovakia's largest folk festival is held in the summer in Strážnice.

Moravia's attractions are more subtle than those of either Bohemia or mountainous Slovakia to the south, but they should not be overlooked when journeying from one to the other.

BRNO
This capital of the southern Moravian region is Czechoslovakia's third largest city. Primarily industrial and the site of international trade fairs in February, April, and September, its historical and cultural sites may seem hard to find, and Brno is not worth going out of your way to visit. But if you are passing through, notorious **Špilberk,** a Gothic castle built in the thirteenth century and later turned into a Baroque fortress with an underground prison, is open, in some sections, to visitors. In the nineteenth century, opponents of the Hapsburgs were imprisoned here, and many

died. In World War II, thousands of prisoners of the Nazis were kept here and many of them, too, perished.

On Petrov Hill, opposite Špilberk, rises the Gothic **Cathedral of Sts. Peter and Paul** (Katedrála sv. Petra a Pavla), with the remains of a Romanesque church inside. In 1645, when the Swedes were besieging the city, their weary general is supposed to have said that if they had not succeeded in taking the city by noon on a given day, he would withdraw his troops. Somehow, word of his intention reached the cathedral. An hour before noon, as the Swedish troops were readying to scale the city walls, the cathedral bells rang out twelve times. The general, as he had promised, retired his troops.

In the **Capuchin Monastery** (Kapucínský klášter and church on Kapucínské náměstí, a gruesome sight is the crypt, containing mummies of monks and important citizens of Brno who died before 1784.

At náměstí 25, února, is the former marketplace. It has a handsome **Trinity Column** (Sloup sv. Trojice) and a fountain designed by Vienna's J. B. Fischer von Erlach in 1695. For years, carp was sold from the waters of the fountain at Christmastime. All around it are Baroque facades including that of the former Dietrichstein Palace (Ditrichštejnský palác), now the **Moravian Museum**, which served as Russian army headquarters before the Battle of Austerlitz, which took place about eighteen miles away, in 1805. The body of the designer of the palace, Moritz Grimm, is one of those preserved in the monastery crypt.

The thirteenth-century **Old Town Hall** (Stará radnice) — a combination of Gothic, Baroque, and Renaissance structures — has an exceptional late Gothic pinnacled portico, behind which are the symbols of the city — a stuffed crocodile (equated with the dragon that was once said to terrorize the city) and a bewitched wheel that, legend has it, was made with the aid of the devil.

Brno's **Villa Tugendhat** at Černopolní 45 is one of its more impressive modern structures, designed by Ludwig Mies van der Rohe in 1932.

In the fourteenth-century **Augustinian Monastery** (Augustínský klášter), now a museum in the old quarter of Brno, Gregor Johann Mendel, in the nineteenth century, grew peas in the garden and developed the Mendelian theory of heredity.

SLAVKOV U BRNA (AUSTERLITZ)

In the green countryside just west of Austerlitz is a memorial garden and a chapel dedicated to the thousands who died in 1805 at the Battle of Austerlitz when Napoleon defeated the combined armies of Russia and Austria. The Baroque castle in town is a museum of Napoleon's life. It is open Tuesday to Sunday from 10:00 A.M. to 4:30 P.M. from April to November.

HUSTOPEČE

Vineyards surround this little white town of 5,500, and grapes grow in front yards. It is exceptional only in that there are 150 public places here serving wine. If you can manage to communicate with a local vintner, he will be happy to take you into his wine cellar and show off his product. Sauvignon is generally considered the best of Moravian wines.

TELČ

Here, in one of the best-preserved old towns of Czechoslovakia, the rectangular market square is edged with arcaded structures. Gothic, Renaissance, and Baroque houses with richly decorated gables have been preserved and the castle that began as a fourteenth-century Gothic structure and is now in Renaissance style has the loveliest interior — with carved and painted ceilings and frescoes — of any Moravian castle.

ROŽNOV POD RADHOŠTĚM

This open air museum of Wallachian farmhouses brightly decorated inside and out and set on the outskirts of town is one place the aficionados of folk art can get their fill. Too often, the genuine lived-in old village houses and farmhouses of Czechoslovakia have been replaced with their modern characterless equivalent. This is one of the few places in the country where the hand-fashioned, hand-painted houses of the past can still be seen.

SLOVAKIA

Slovakia provides Czechoslovakia with its lavender Tatra Mountain peaks and hiking and skiing trails; its still, green forests; bubbling streams; haystacks like miniature, peak-roofed houses. It is the Czechoslovakia for the outdoorsman. For one thousand years, from the tenth century till 1918, though its people were Slavs, Slovakia was part of Hungary, and Hungarians, Slovaks, and Germans for centuries have been part of the population mix here. The Hungarians forced the Hungarian language and culture upon the Slovaks and "kept them in their place" for a long time.

But Slovaks are welcoming people — eager to please, eager to savor life, proud of the beauty of their countryside. Unfortunately, until after World War II, Slovakia was the poorest part of Czechoslovakia. Though grapes grow on the slopes of the Little Carpathian Mountains, this is not a rich land. Or at least it was not till the postwar years, when industry moved in. Now, at the foot of lovely mountain peaks, smokestacks rise and networks of silver pipelines are everywhere. Industry has improved the economy here, but not the landscape.

Still, the beauty of the High Tatras that mark the border with Poland cannot be denied, nor can that of the Vrátna Dolina Valley with its pastures, woods, waterfalls, and sheer rocks.

BANSKÁ BYSTRICA

This splendidly situated capital of the central Slovakian region, prosperous in medieval times because of rich gold and silver mines, offers outstanding fifteenth- and sixteenth-century Gothic burghers' houses, set beside handsome patrician houses and the little wooden-balconied homes of the miners. The Kremnica Mountain range as well as the Great Tatra, the Lower Tatra, and the Slovak Ore mountains surround it, and it sits on a river bend. Its contemporary fame, however, is due to the valiant Slovak National Uprising against the Nazi occupiers in August 1944. Many plaques and monuments memorialize the Slovak patriots who died here.

BRATISLAVA

Many of the historic sites and architectural attractions of this sprawling, prosperous industrial city — Czechoslovakia's second largest city — that is the Slovak capital are hard to find — lost, as they are, among modern, uninteresting structures and equally uninspired roadways, but that is surely not the case with its castle. The Romans first had a watch post here above the Danube. In the eleventh century, a fortified castle was constructed on the site to protect the Hungarian kingdom. In the twelfth century Holy Roman Emperor Frederick Barbarossa took control of the castle. In the fifteenth century, it achieved its real fame when King Sigismund ordered construction of a fortified Gothic castle here. When the Turks invaded Buda in 1541, this castle became the seat of the Hungarian government. In sixteenth-century Hapsburg days, it was rebuilt in Renaissance style. In Napoleonic days, it is said that the Little Emperor watched the counterattack of the Russian and Polish armies after the Battle of Austerlitz from this site. But in Napoleonic times, a fire largely destroyed it. For 150 years, it remained in a state of disrepair, until 1953, when the renovation that still continues got under way. The interior is not extraordinary. It is the castle's commanding site and presence above the Danube that should not be missed. Of interest in the narrow alleys and winding streets in the Old Town is the fifteenth-century burgomaster's house that became the town hall and is now a municipal museum and the **Primate's Palace** (Primacionální palác), with its **Hall of Mirrors** in which Napoleon signed a peace treaty with Francis I of Austria after the Battle of Austerlitz. There is also **Michael's Gate** (Michalská brána). This gate and tower are all that remain of the city's early fortifications. In St. Martin's Cathedral (Dom Sv. Martina), nine Hungarian kings and eight queens were crowned.

It was in Bratislava that Maria Teresa, desperately seeking the support of Hungary to save the Austro-Hugarian Empire from an attacking Prussia, was heralded by the city's noblemen. Drawing their sabers near today's **Mirbach Palace** (Mirbachov palác) between Bridge and Gorki streets, they raised them to her as a pledge of their support and marched to Castle Hill.

ČIČMANY
Though a fire in 1923 destroyed many of the fine old wooden cottages in this village in central Slovakia, some still remain, with white geometric designs on chocolate-brown walls.

KOŠICE
Košice is a sprawling industrial city with a major steelworks. It is of interest because of the considerable number of Gypsies here and because of a number of historic structures. Most impressive of all is the Gothic **Cathedral of St. Elizabeth** (Katedrála sv. Alžbety), begun in 1380 but not completed until 1508. Some of its interior decoration by Viennese artists is exceptionally fine, and buried on the left side of the nave is Prince Ferenc Rákóczi, Transylvanian hero in the eighteenth-century fight against the Hapsburgs. Also of interest here are the turn-of-the-century **State Theater** (Státne divadlo), the Rococo former **Town Hall** (Radnice) that is now a theater, the early-eighteenth-century **Plague Column** (Morový sloup), the Košice **Gold Treasure** of fifteenth- to eighteenth-century items (many of the coins were accidentally discovered in the 1930s), and the ghastly medieval torture chambers of **Miklušová väznica** (two sixteenth-century houses on ulice Pri Miklušovej väznici 10). To enter the torture chambers, however, you must request the keys at the Zoology Museum in the Katuva Bastion. Bear in mind that most Košice museums are closed Sunday afternoon and Monday.

LEVOČA
This neatly arranged medieval town owes its checkerboardlike plan and solid Germanic look to the fact that in the thirteenth century, to protect its eastern outposts from Mongol invasion, the Hungarians invited Saxon traders to settle this area. Levoča

was one of the Saxons' creations. Gothic, Baroque, and early Renaissance houses in good repair abound. There are still fourteenth- and fifteenth-century fortifications, a handsome arcaded Gothic **Town Hall** (Radnice) with its original vaulting, and, in **St. James's Church** (Kostel sv. Jakuba), whose slender, graceful tower rises above the town, a masterpiece of European Gothic art, Master Pavel's carved and gilded Madonna. There are several small museums here of specialized interest.

Spišský Hrad

The largest castle in all Czechoslovakia, though now in ruins, is a most impressive site, perched as it is along a ridge above the town of Spišské Podhradie. The first thirteenth-century castle here turned back the Mongols. Down through the centuries it was built and rebuilt, for it was of considerable importance in the defense of the region. But in 1780 it was destroyed by fire, and no reconstruction followed.

Starý Smokovec

The earliest of the High Tatras resorts (now it and its neighbors, Nový, Horný, and Dolný Smokovec, are all one) was already attracting tourists in the eighteenth century and became a resort in the late nineteenth. Hotels, guest houses, and restaurants are set along well-laid-out paths. On a rise is the old-fashioned Grand Hotel. Below it there is a wide variety of hostelries. Starý Smokovec is a starting place for treks in the mountains, and there are skiing possibilities for all — from beginners to the highly experienced. Narrow-gauge railways from this starting point climb higher to **Hrebienok,** from which there are pleasant walks to be made, and to picturesque nineteenth-century **Tatranská Lomnica,** with its richly decorated wooden buildings. From it a cable car goes to 5,740-foot-high **Skalnaté Pleso,** where there is a lake and an astronomical observatory. Because of the popularity of the trip, it is wise to buy a ticket as soon as you arrive. The cable car does not operate on Tuesday. The other attraction here is the **Tatra National Park Museum** (Tatranské národná muzeum),

which recounts the history of the area and its resorts. It is open
Monday through Friday from 8:00 A.M. until 5:00 P.M. and on
weekends from 8:00 A.M. until noon.

ŽDIAR

In this five-mile-long village in the High Tatras, windows are
sometimes outlined in bright-red paint, domino spots decorate
the corner boards of others, and yellow fretwork embellishes still
others. There is a small museum of embroideries and costumes.
Unfortunately, only a handful of the cottages are still painted in
the old way.

GETTING THERE, SLEEPING,
EATING, AND ENTERTAINMENT

Czechoslovakia is approximately the size of Pennsylvania, but
highlands cross it and forested mountain ranges encircle it. The
visitor who would like to sample not only its impressive capital
of Prague, but its dozens of historic cities and towns virtually
untouched by war, its more than 3,000 castles, manor houses,
and stalwart fortresses, and its colorful villages would be well
advised to travel by car, for many of these sites are in out-of-the-
way places.

If renting a car, it is wise to make the reservation before leaving
the United States, for this guarantees the rental rate. Hertz, Avis,
Budget, and Auto-Europe at Box 1097 in Camden, Maine 04843
(Tel. 800-223-5555) have cars available in Czechoslovakia and
Čedok, the Czechoslovakian national travel agency, with offices
in New York at 10 East 40th Street, New York, New York
10016, will also make reservations. Alternatively, you can rent a

car in a neighboring Western country, but it may be difficult to obtain unleaded gas for a Western car in the East.

All rental car firms require partial prepayment on pickup in United States dollars or German marks or with a credit card. The final payment, as well, must be in hard currency. Maps of the country, indicating the location of gas stations, are available at car pickup points.

To purchase gas, coupons are required of foreigners and may be bought — only with hard currency — at banks, from Čedok, or at border crossings. In the event of a breakdown, Auto-tourist at Limužská, Prague 10, Malešice (Tel. 775521, or at the emergency number 154) can provide road help. Renting a car, however, should not be considered if you expect to be spending most of your time in Prague, for much of the heart of the city is closed to cars and there is virtually no parking.

Hiring a car, driver, and guide as an option will cost in excess of $130 a day; a car and a driver without guide about $70 a day.

Alternatively, Čedok at Na příkopě 18 offers tour packages of several days that include highlights of the country or day tours out of Prague, but if you plan to take one, leave plenty of time to make the arrangements. Efficiency is still not a strong suit anywhere in the East. Tourist information is also available at Pražská informační Siužba, Na příkopě 10 (Tel. 2754-44-44).

If you prefer public transportation, Czechoslovak Airlines (ČSA) serves major cities and Poprad in the Tatras as well, and there is inexpensive rail and bus service. The letters ČSD indicate Czechoslovakian State Railways and ČSAD the bus line, but few ticket sellers speak English. A tip for the independent traveler using public transportation: "Odjezdy" on posted schedules indicates departure times; "Příjezdy" arrival times. If you know in advance where you are going and when, ask Čedok for schedule information and buy your tickets from Čedok either in the United States or Prague. It is now possible, as well, to purchase an East Pass for rail travel in Austria, Czechoslovakia, Poland, and Hungary. Similar to Eurailpass, the East Pass allows five days of travel within a fifteen-day period for $160 or ten days of travel within a month for $250. East Passes must, however, be purchased in the United States. They are available from travel agents or Rail Europe (Tel. 800-345-1990).

Within Prague, buses and trams run from 4:30 A.M. to 11:30 P.M. and the tickets for them and for the Metro may be bought at newsstands. Put Metro tickets through a machine as you enter the station. If you are taking the bus or tram, follow the lead of other passengers in finding the ticket-punching machine on board.

Many airlines now fly from New York to Prague with ČSA offering nonstop service, and Air France, KLM, Lufthansa, and Sabena providing the best service but involving a change of aircraft. ČSA also offers service from Chicago via Montreal.

Prague is on the train route from Berlin to Vienna and Budapest. From Cracow and Moscow, there is service to Košice in Slovakia and from Warsaw or Budapest to Žilina in Slovakia. No visas are required for American tourists.

Further information on travel to and in Czechoslovakia is available from Čedok at 10 East 40th Street, New York, New York 10016 (Tel. 212-689-9720), or, in the Chicago area, from Cihak travel at 6302 Cermak Road, Berwyn, Illinois 60402 (Tel. 800-426-8826), a specialist in travel in Czechoslovakia.

It is important to bear in mind that hotel space is extremely limited in Prague and reservations must be made months in advance, although as accommodations begin to be available in private homes as well, information on private room rental may be obtained from Pragotour at U Obecního Domu 1, Prague 1, or by calling 422-231-7281 in Prague. But it is advisable, too, to reserve from Pragotour in advance. Prague Suites at $125 to $135 a night are also offered by Cihak Travel.

Meals in Czechoslovakia tend to be hearty — with pork (vepřová pečeně), slices of heavy bread or potato dumpling (knedlíky), and cabbage (zelí) or sauerkraut (kyselé zelí) omnipresent on menus in the Bohemian part of the country. Sometimes goose (husa) or duck (kachna) will be substituted for the pork. Thick gravy (the dumpling is used to sop it up) is also an essential part of these dishes.

The usual liquid accompaniment is beer (pivo), for which

Czechoslovakia is justly famous. Light, refreshing Pilsen Urquell brewed in Plzeň (Pilsen) has been a specialty of the country since the thirteenth century, but satisfying beers are brewed virtually everywhere. České Budějovice's Budvar (from which Budweiser gets its name) is also popular. In Czechoslovakia, beer is considered lacking if it hasn't a good head of foam. "Beer without foam," Czechs insist, "is like a woman without a smile."

But in southern Moravia and southern Slovakia, wine is a popular drink, too, and in many a village, visitors are welcome to try the local product (for a small fee) at a villager's house. Riesling and Traminer are frequently produced, but there are also good Moravian red wines (*červené víno*). In Bohemia, the wine region is around Mělník. The strong drink is plum brandy (*slivovice*).

Thinly sliced Prague ham (*pražská šunka*) is a popular appetizer as is smoked fish (*ryby*). Soup will often precede lunch or dinner. Potato soup with mushrooms (*bramborová polévka s houbami*) is eaten in mushroom season.

In Slovakia, the Hungarian influence remains in goulash (*guláš*).

Desserts, like the rest of a Czech meal, are on the heavy side. Apple strudel (*jablkový závin*) is among them. Particularly delicious — but not always easy to find — are juicy fresh plum dumplings (*švestkové knedlíky*).

With the exception of cabbage, green vegetables are virtually nonexistent. Among vegetables, mushrooms (*houby*) are popular and may well be the main feature of a spring menu.

Breakfasts (usually part of the hotel-room price) may be either bread and coffee or include meat and cheese.

Finding a table in a restaurant of your choice can be a problem anywhere in the country, but especially in Prague, and service, though it is improving in these new days of free enterprise, is still slow. An acceptable meal can be had for five to six dollars, but isn't hard for one person to spend thirty dollars for a good dinner with wine. It is common to ask to share a table.

There are several classifications of Czech eating establishments. In addition to restaurants (*restaurace*), there are wine restaurants (*vinárny*); pubs (*pivnice*), where there is some food but the emphasis is on the beer; cafés (*kavárny*); and self-service cafeterias (*jídelny*).

There follows, in alphabetical order by town, a list of better hotels and restaurants in major tourist sites.

BRATISLAVA

HOTELS

Forum Bratislava, Mierové náměstí 2 (Tel. 348-111). There is little charm to this high-rise modern hotel, but the food is fair in its restaurants and service is pleasant and welcoming.

Hotel Kyjev, Rajská ulice 2. This is not a distinguished hotel, but it is cozier than the Forum and the price, with breakfast and one main meal, is approximately $115 double, $70 single.

RESTAURANTS

Arkadia, Beblaveho 3 (Tel. 335-650). Goose liver is a good bet here.

Kavárna Bystrica is situated on the Bratislava Bridge (Tel. 513-45). Although the food isn't extraordinary, the view from above the Danube surely is.

Stará Stadovna, Cintorínská 32 (Tel. 511-51). This is a pub where the beer is what you *really* come for, but the simple fare is an inexpensive accompaniment.

Rybarsky Cech, Zízkova 1. Fish is the specialty in this pleasant restaurant.

Veľ'ki Františkáni, Dibrovovo náměstí 10 (Tel. 3330-73). In this Old Town (Staré Mesto) restaurant there is Gypsy music in the cellar, a courtyard for summer dining, and a proper indoor dining room.

TOURIST INFORMATION

Čedok, Stúrova 13 (Tel. 522-80).

ČESKÉ BUDĚJOVICE

HOTEL

Gomel, Miro 14 (Tel. 27941). This is a four-star hotel about a fifteen-minute walk from the center of town. It's nothing special, but it is the best that České Budějovice has to offer.

RESTAURANTS

Masné Krámy, Května třída 13 (Tel. 326-52). The fried fish is fine in this pub where the Budvar is less than a dollar for half a liter.

Zahradní in the Gomel offers good fare but little atmosphere.

KARLOVY VARY (CARLSBAD)

HOTEL

Grand Hotel Pupp, Mírové náměstí 6 (Tel. 221-21). Newly renovated after a drab period as the Grand Hotel Moskva, the Pupp is an elegant white-and-gold edifice splendidly set against a wooded hillside. The original hotel on the site was founded in 1701. It is notable for its early-eighteenth-century hall. A double room, including bed, breakfast, and lunch or dinner, is approximately $160, a single approximately $90. Just now, the hotel restaurant offers as good fare as you are likely to find in the town.

MARIÁNSKÉ LÁZNĚ

HOTELS

Golf Hotel, Zabud 55 (Tel. 27-12). This is a small, newly renovated deluxe hotel, set, as its name indicates, on a golf course a little out of town. Room, breakfast, and lunch or dinner is approximately $70 per person and the restaurant is good.

Palace Hotel Prana, Odborářů 67 (Tel. 222-23). A small turn-of-the-century hotel of faded elegance.

PRAGUE

HOTELS

Alcron, Štěpánská 40, Prague 1 (Tel. 235-92-96). This small (150 rooms), centrally located, older deluxe hotel off Wenceslas Square (Václavské náměstí) is undergoing restoration.

Esplanade, Washingtonova 19, Prague 1 (Tel. 22-25-52). This is a 65-room centrally located hotel near the National Museum and the main railway station, and is known for its Est-Bar Nightclub. The high-season rate is $135 single, $180 double.

Europa (Václavské náměstí 29, Prague 1 (Tel. 236-52-74). You couldn't find a more central location than the Europa's but for that very reason, it tends to be noisy. The price, however, is right at this three-star hotel where many rooms are without baths, about $100 for two in high season.

Forum, Kongresová ulice, Prague 4 (Tel. 41-01-11). This is an enormous (531 rooms), towering, modern hotel in a rather inconvenient location for the center of Prague, but near a subway station and the highway and equipped with all modern conveniences. A good bet for the business traveler. Two restaurants, a café, two bars and a nightclub, fitness facilities, and a pool and conference center. The lowest-price summer accommodations are $179 double and $159 single.

Inter-Continental, Náměstí Curieových 43–45, Prague 1 (Tel. 231-18-12). A splendidly located, elegant 400-room hotel on the river in the Old Town. A convenient walking distance to virtually all historic attractions. Sauna, health club, two restaurants, nightclub, business center. Doubles in summer are $195, singles $170.

Olympik II-Garni, Invalidovna, U Slumcové, Prague 8 (Tel. 83-02-74). This is distinctly a hotel for young people. The dining room is in the Olympik across the street. You need a tram to reach the city center, but the double room rate in summer is about $90. Rooms are often without bath.

Palace, Panská 12 (Tel. 23-71-51). This newly renovated, elegant Art Nouveau hotel (123 rooms) is little more than a block from Wenceslas Square. Its main dining room is renowned for its decor and its food.

Panorama, Milevská 7, Prague 4 (Tel. 41-61-11). This very modern 412-room, high-rise hotel with saunas, swimming pool, solarium, and gym is not centrally located but is on the Metro line.

Paříž, U Obecního domu, Prague 7 (Tel. 231-20-51). A small, fair hotel in the Old Town (Staré Město), newly renovated in Art Nouveau style.

Park Hotel, Veletržní 20, Prague 7 (Tel. 380-71-11). There is little charm to this modern hotel, nor is it centrally located, but when rooms are in short supply, it's always a possibility.

Three Ostriches (U Tří Pštrosů), Dražického náměstí 12, Prague 1 (Tel. 53-61-51-5). This is a charmingly situated seventeenth-century hotel in the Lesser Town (Malá Strana) just at the foot of the Charles Bridge. The rooms, however, tend to be small. Reservations should be made at least six months in advance.

RESTAURANTS

Espresso Kajetánka, Kajetánské zahrady. Enjoy a splendid view of the city from below the castle ramparts while you refresh yourself with coffee and snacks.

Hanavský Pavilón, Letenské sady 173, Prague 7 (Tel. 32-57-92). A turn-of-the-century restaurant with a terrace overlooking the Vltava. Splendid for summer dining.

Jewish Restaurant, Maiselova 18, Prague 1. Hardly fancy, but there's old-fashioned kosher home cooking at this little restaurant in the heart of the ghetto.

Klášterní Vinárna, Národní třída. This is a former Ursuline convent now notable for its flambéed *palačinky*. Its location near the National Theater makes it ideal for post-entertainment dining.

Opera Grill, Divadelní 24 (Tel. 26-55-08). Czech dishes are what the menu features in this elegant little restaurant. Wine, not beer, is the beverage offered. Reservations are essential.

Pelikán, Na příkopě 7, Prague 1 (Tel. 37-45-46). It's essential to reserve a table in this moderately priced restaurant with Czech and international fare.

Praha Expo 58, Letenské sady, Prague 7 (Tel. 37-73-39). There are French and Czech restaurants in this modern glass structure overlooking the river. It was this restaurant that offered Czech cuisine to the world at Brussels' Expo '58. The Czech food is hearty, in the national tradition. A dinner in the Czech restaurant costs between $25 and $30. Fancier (and more expensive — about $50 per person) is its French dining room.

Restaurace u Supa, Celetná 22, Prague 1 (Tel. 22-30-42). This beer hall in a restored Renaissance palace in the Old Town (Staré Město) is nothing special, but the beer and brew will fill you up and the price is right.

Rotisserie, Mikulanská 6. Fine food brings the crowds to this little restaurant.

Savarin, Na příkopě 10, Prague 1 (Tel. 22-47-78). There are a number of restaurants, cafés, and snack bars in this complex.

Staropražská Rychta, Václavské náměstí 7. The service is slow but the food well prepared and the ambience invitingly romantic in this elegant restaurant popular with tourists. Dinners are $10 to $12.

U Bonaparta, Nerudova 29, Prague 1. This is a popular beer bar in a pretty part of the Old Town (Staré Město), but it's a long climb to get to it.

U Fleků, Křemencova 11, Prague 1 (Tel. 29-24-36). This big, noisy, smoky beer hall consists of room after room and a big courtyard through which waitresses scurry with trays full of frothy dark beer brewed on the premises. The drinking is more to be recommended here than the eating. The latter is only fair, but the atmosphere makes it worth a visit.

U Golema, Maislova 8 (Tel. 26-18-98). This dark and quiet little restaurant in the ghetto where the Golem was said to roam in the Middle Ages takes its name from that man-made creature. The menu isn't extensive, but the food is good.

U Kalicha, Na bojišti 12, Prague 2 (Tel. 29-60-17). It was in this New Town (Nové Město) tavern that the adventures of Jaroslav Hašek's World War I soldier, the Good Soldier Schweik (Švejk), began, and drawings of characters from the book decorate its walls. The food is Czech and beer the drink to indulge in. There's always plenty of camaraderie — and noise — in this medium-priced colorful restaurant.

U Labutí, Hradčanské náměstí 2, Prague 1 (Tel. 53-94-76). Reservations are essential at this quiet first-class wine restaurant near Hradčany Castle. Closed on Sunday.

U Mecenáše, Malostranské náměstí 10, Prague 1 (Tel. 53-18-83). A small Lesser Town (Malá Strana) wine restaurant with a medieval setting.

U Palivce, Fugnerovo náměstí 1 (Tel. 29-03-70). Hearty, satisfying fare and fine beer at good prices. A lunch of soup, duck, cabbage, and dumpling, strudel and beer for under $7.

U Pinkasů, Jungmannovo náměstí 15, Prague 1 (Tel. 26-18-04). Beer's the thing at this popular beer bar.

U sv. Tomáše, Letenská 12, Prague 1 (Tel. 53-00-64). Dark ale and satisfying if undistinguished food at reasonable prices in a medieval setting make this Lesser Town (Malá Strana) restaurant, on the site of a fourteenth-century monk-run brewery, a good bet for the budget-conscious. The goulash is about $2; a mug of beer under one dollar.

U Zlaté hrušky, Nový svět 3, Prague 1 (Tel. 53-11-33). This first-class restaurant in restored eighteenth-century style is a good place for dinner after a castle visit. Wild game and Moravian wines are among the specialties. Reservations are essential.

U Zlaté konvice, Melantrichova 20. Only cold dishes are served at this moderately priced wine-cellar restaurant that is particularly popular with Prague's young.

U Zlatého hada, Karlova 18. In this eighteenth-century coffee house that students enjoy you can sit as long as you like over coffee and cake, a snack.

U Zlatého jepena, Celetná 11. There's plenty of color, but very casual service in this restaurant for the young set that is set in restored wine vaults.

U Zlatého tygra, Husova 17, Prague 1 (Tel. 26-52-19). This is an old-fashioned beer bar popular with older beer-guzzling sorts.

Valdštejnská hospoda, Valdštejnské náměstí 7, Prague 1 (Tel. 53-61-95). An attractive restaurant offering both Czech and international fare beside the Wallenstein Palace. Closed on Monday.

Vikařská, Vikařská 6, Prague 1 (Tel. 53-51-58). This is a good, moderately priced Czech-fare restaurant inside the Hradčany Castle complex. Because of its location, it is ever-popular with tourists at lunchtime, and reservations must be made.

Železné dveře, Michalská. A satisfying restaurant where Moravian wines are served and the prices are moderate.

ENTERTAINMENT

In Prague, there's always music in the air. It was at the **Tyl Theater** (Tylovo divadlo), after all, that Mozart's *Don Giovanni* received its world premiere. Bedřich Smetana was director of the National Theater from 1866 to 1874. Antonín Dvořák is remembered in a museum of his life here and Leoš Janáček's operas are performed not only here, but the world around. A major annual event is Prague's Spring Music Festival from mid-May to mid-June. Tickets to musical events may be bought in advance either through Čedok at Na příkopě 1-8 (Tel. 212-71-11), which is open Monday through Thursday from 8:15 A.M. to 4:15 P.M., Friday from 8:15 A.M. to 3:45 P.M., and Saturday from 8:15 A.M. until noon, except in summer, when it is open until 2:00 P.M. Information may also be obtained from Prăzska Informačni Sluzba, Na příkopé 20 (Tel. 254-44-44), and the American Hospitality Center at Malá náměstí 14 from 9:00 A.M. to 6:00 P.M. daily (Tel. 236-74-86) or Sluna at Václavské náměstí 18, Alta Passage, Prague 1 (Tel. 26-16-02), which is open Monday through Thursday from 9:00 A.M. to 6:00 P.M. and on Friday until 5:00 P.M.

Opera and ballet are generally performed at the handsomely restored nineteenth-century **National Theater** (Národní divadlo) at Národní třída 2, Prague 1; the equally handsome **Smetana Theater** (Smetanovo divadlo) is on Vítězného února 8, Prague 1. Tickets for performances at the National Theater and the **New Theater** are also available in advance in the Glass Palace of the New Stage, Národní třída 4, Monday through Friday from 10:00 A.M. to 6:00 P.M. and Saturday and Sunday from 10:00 A.M. to 2:00 P.M.

The city's major concert hall is the **Smetana Hall** (Obecní dům), náměstí Republiky 5, Prague 1. The publication *The Month in Prague,* which is in most hotels, will list musical and theatrical performances around the city. Many musical performances are in churches.

A theatrical performance that even non-Czech-speaking audiences can enjoy is the **Magic Lantern** (Laterna Magica), Národní třída 40, Prague 1 (Tel. 26-00-33), a multimedia presentation of film, live performances, and song. Tickets to it must be purchased at the theater's box office. Black theater performances, with stagehands dressed in black moving props "invisibly" against a black backdrop, are done, when the company is in town, at the **Theater on the Balustrade** (Divadlo na zabradl). Folkloric performances are given nightly in summer on **Slovanský Island** (Slovanský ostrov) near the National Theater.

Puppet shows are offered at the **Spejbl and Hurvínek Theater** (Divadlo Spejbla a Hurvínka), Římská 45.

For the best in nightclub entertainment the places to go are the **Est-Bar,** Washingtonova 19, Prague 1 (Tel. 22-25-52); **U Fleků,** Křemercova ulice 11; the **Alhambra Nightshow,** Václavské náměstí 5 (Tel. 22-04-67).

TOURIST INFORMATION
Čedok, Na příkopě 18 (Tel. 212-71-11).

SMOKOVEC (Starý, Nový, and Horný)
HOTELS
Bellevue, Horny Smokovec. This is a modern, satisfactory, clean resort hotel.

Grand Hotel, Starý Smokovec. There's an old-fashioned grandeur to this recently renovated 1905 hotel. The Starý Smokovec restaurant to try is the Tatranská kuria.

Park Hotel, Nový Smokovec. A clean and satisfactory but unexceptional small mountain hotel.

ŠTRBSKÉ PLESO
HOTEL
Hotel Patria (Tel. 925-91-5). This hotel is in very modern ski lodge style — plenty of bare wood and stone and a pleasant folk restaurant, the Slovenka, with reasonably good food.

TÁBOR
HOTEL
Palcát Interhotel (Tel. 2235/229-01). This 68-room hotel near the main square is clean, though unexceptional. The food in its dining room is, again, acceptable but nothing special.

TATRANSKÁ LOMNICA
HOTEL
Grand Hotel Praha (Tel. 963-01). This is a modernized, some-

what characterless but satisfactory hotel near the cable-car station.

RESTAURANT

Zbojnická koliba. Folk music accompanies the food (which is good) at this cozy (and smoky) restaurant.

Eastern Germany

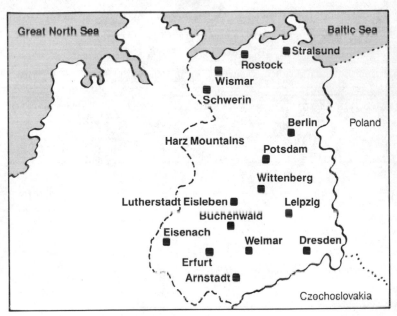

Great North Sea

Baltic Sea

Stralsund

Rostock

Wismar

Schwerin

Berlin

Poland

Harz Mountains

Potsdam

Wittenberg

Lutherstadt Eisleben

Leipzig

Buchenwald

Eisenach

Welmar

Dresden

Erfurt

Arnstadt

Czechoslovakia

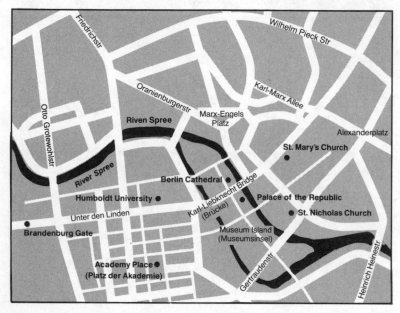

EASTERN BERLIN

$\mathcal{E}$xtending from the island of Rügen in the Baltic Sea to the mountains of Thuringia on the Czechoslovak border and to Poland on the east, eastern Germany — the former German Democratic Republic — makes up one fourth of today's Germany. It includes, in the historical scheme of things, Brandenburg, Mecklenburg, Saxony-Anhalt, Saxony, and Thuringia, once lands, like the rest of Germany, of electors, dukes, counts, margraves, prince-bishops, and kings. In this eastern area are the industrial city of Leipzig, the cultural cities of Weimar and Dresden, and, of course, much of Berlin. The Harz Mountains with their half-timbered houses, the sandstone cliffs of Saxon Switzerland, the birthplaces of Johann Sebastian Bach and Martin Luther are among the sites of the east that, for the four decades of Communist rule after World War II, have been accessible to Westerners only if they were willing to cope with endless bureaucracy.

In 1949, the German Democratic Republic was formed out of the Soviet-occupied zone. In 1961, with the erection of the Berlin Wall, the third of Berlin that had been the capital city's governmental and cultural heart was cut off from its grandest commercial area and prettiest park and some lovely residential streets. Before that, the history of the eastern part of the country was the same as the history of the west.

There was never a single German nation until 1871. Then Otto von Bismarck, prime minister of the kingdom of Prussia, managed to unite the thirty-five autonomous states and free cities that had been loosely joined into a German Confederation in 1815. For centuries, the German people — descendants of a number of tribes that occupied central Europe — had lived in hundreds of virtually independent states. Periodically, there had been rulers above them. In 800 Charlemagne was crowned emperor of the Romans by the pope — a title that also included his jurisdiction over the German lands he had conquered. A century later, Otto I bore the same title, and in the twelfth century, Frederick Barbarossa became head of something new — the Holy Roman Empire of the German Nation (das Heilige Römische Reich Deutscher Nation). In the thirteenth century, the princes of these states of the German nation elected Rudolf of Hapsburg as their emperor. But then, to assure that they would retain their own power, they devised a system of imperial elections in the next century that virtually guaranteed that their rulers would have no strength. And they didn't. Though the Austrian Hapsburgs occupied the throne of the Holy Roman Empire from the thirteenth to the nineteenth centuries, they never really succeeded in controlling the power of their princes.

When the Reformation came in the sixteenth century, it only reaffirmed the princes' jurisdiction, for the Catholic Church of Germany had become corrupt and Luther's revolt against it and the emperor who supported it pleased them.

In the Thirty Years' War (1618–1648), the Protestant princes fought the Catholic Hapsburg emperor. When it was over — after Catholic France and Protestant Sweden had been drawn into it and the Hapsburgs defeated — the country was in ruins, but the princes were strong. One of them, Frederick William I, the Great Elector, ruler of Brandenburg-Prussia, brought his state to prominence above the others. He established the first standing army in a German state and acquired territory on the Baltic Sea. He began an absolutist rule that was to continue in Prussia under strong militaristic and expansionist leaders like Frederick the Great, who, seeking to enlarge and enrich his state, entered the Seven Years' War (Third Silesian War) with Austria in 1756. Even though, as it turned out, he gained no land, he established Prussia as a power to be reckoned with.

After Frederick's death came Napoleon Bonaparte. Seeing fair game in the more than 300 largely militarily weak, separate German states, he conquered them, forcing the abdication of the Hapsburg emperor, the dissolution of the Holy Roman Empire, and the consolidation of Germany's 300 states into about 30. He did not, however, take control of Prussia, though he defeated and humiliated it. That humiliation helped lead to Napoleon's downfall, for it nurtured Prussian nationalistic fervor. By 1815, Prussia was strong enough to play a powerful role in the defeat of the Little General at Waterloo.

It was then that the confederation of autonomous states and free cities was substituted for the defunct Holy Roman Empire — but once again, state autonomy was paramount. More important, Prussia dissolved all internal tariffs in 1818 and established high tariffs on all goods that came from or passed through adjacent states. In a way nothing else could, this forced — for their economic well-being — the union of those other states with Prussia. Then in 1862, Bismarck became Prussia's prime minister and introduced his policy of blood and iron.

Determined that Prussia would become the ruler of all the German people, he went to war against Austria, whose leaders had for so many centuries been the Holy Roman Emperors. Prussia won the war. After that, Bismarck, with the help of a well-trained army, began to annex the German states in the north. Next he aggravated Napoleon III into starting the Franco-Prussian War and managed to lure southern German states into joining his side in that fight. The southern states thus fell under his control, too. Prussia was getting bigger and bigger.

But in 1888, after William II became the Prussian ruler and the German kaiser, Bismarck was dismissed. Internally, Germany prospered. Industry expanded. The population grew. But the kaiser lacked Bismarck's adroitness in dealing with other nations. When he sought more land for his increasing population, World War I resulted. When it was lost, Germany became a republic. But that Weimar Republic was short-lived. Germany was made to grovel under the Treaty of Versailles and heavy reparations. There was economic and spiritual depression across the land. Try as it might to bring law, order, and prosperity, the Weimar Republic couldn't. Right-wingers demanded more order; Communists demanded more social equality. Many small political parties were created.

In this unhappy climate, Adolf Hitler's charismatic message of the superiority of the German people was invigorating and appealing. In 1933, he was elected chancellor; in 1934, he took complete control. In 1936, he began annexing land. In 1939, with the invasion of Poland, World War II began. When it ended, Europe was in ruins and the German nation it had taken so many centuries to unite was split asunder.

But now that it is one country again, the eastern section, though left far behind for those four decades of communism, is modernizing and catching up with the west. Its adjustment will not be overnight, but even while it is going on, this new "Old World" Germany is a challenging, stimulating place for a visit.

BERLIN

Though a few curious tourists visited East Berlin on day bus tours after the 1961 erection of the Berlin Wall, and sometimes bold young travelers passed through Checkpoint Charlie independently, East Berlin was generally off Western tourists' itineraries for the twenty-eight years of the Berlin Wall. Those who did cross into the east returned depressed with the gloom in the air, the listlessness of the residents. But architecturally and artistically, the eastern part of Berlin had and has some of the finest attractions of the city.

Before its division, when Berlin was the capital of Prussia and of Germany, its eastern section was its intellectual and cultural heart. In the east, lined with government buildings, was Unter den Linden, Berlin's most beautiful thoroughfare; the Brandenburg Gate; the Pergamon Museum, one of the world's greatest museums; Humboldt University; the State Opera House; the Komische Opera, made famous by Walter Felsenstein; the Berliner Ensemble of Bertolt Brecht; the Schauspielhaus (Concert Hall); the Protestant Cathedral; and the city's loveliest churches. Many of the bombed buildings have been rebuilt, but often in massive, aesthetically unappealing Communist Modern style, and many back streets, where workers live, have never been reconstructed. Now that there is one Berlin again, the riches of this eastern sector have become easily accessible and western entrepreneurs are enlivening what was so grim. Static, unimaginative window displays have been replaced by enticing ones. Old state-owned restaurants offering humdrum food are becoming private restaurants with good food (albeit at high prices). New hotels are in prospect. The grimness is gone. Lights sparkle along the River Spree.

Brandenburg Gate (Brandenburger Tor), Unter den Linden: Erected at the end of the eighteenth century when neoclassical architecture was in vogue, this eighty-five-foot-high, 205-foot-wide gate, the symbol of Berlin, is the design of K.-F. Langhans. It was inspired by the entrance gate to the Acropolis in Athens. The quadriga, the bronze chariot that belongs on top but is now being restored, is pulled by four horses and driven by the goddess of Victory. It is the work of the early-nineteenth-century sculptor Johann Gottfried Schadow. In 1807, after his invasion of Prussia, a covetous Napoleon Bonaparte carried the ten-ton sculpture off to Paris and set it up on the place du Carrousel, where it remained till his defeat in 1814. When it was returned here and reinstalled, it was turned around to face east rather than the west, as it had before. Another change was made after World War II. When the statue, which was extensively damaged in a bombing raid, was recast, the Communist government of the east had the Iron Cross and the Eagle — symbols of the military and of Prussia — removed from the hand of Victory. All through the years of Communist East Berlin, the gate backed up to the Wall.

Unter den Linden: This spacious avenue gets its name from the trees that line it. The first of these were planted when the original street was laid out in 1647 on order of Frederick William, the founder of the Prussian monarchy. (Hitler had the trees cut down to widen the avenue for parades, but they were replanted.) This is the site of many handsome nineteenth-century buildings and monuments, now largely restored. Notable as you head east from the Brandenburg Gate is an equestrian statue of Frederick the Great, which was acclaimed when it was erected in 1851 as one of the grandest (forty-four feet high) monuments of its kind in Europe. For most of the time the Communists ruled here, it was banished to Potsdam, for it was under Frederick the Great that Prussia began the rise to power that ultimately led Germany into World Wars I and II. In 1980, however, the statue was returned to its original site.

Virtually opposite it, on the left-hand side of the avenue, is the **Old Palace** (Altes Palais), built in 1834–1836 by K.-F. Langhans and now the headquarters of Humboldt University, the three-story, neo-Baroque **German State Library** (Deutsche Staatsbibliothek), and more Humboldt University buildings. Originally the palace of Prince Henry, brother of Frederick the Great, the university that is now housed in the Old Palace was founded in 1809 by the statesman and philologist Wilhelm von Humboldt. His statue, along with that of his brother, the naturalist Alexander von Humboldt, stands outside. Karl Marx is among the university's noted graduates.

Across the way is the neoclassical **State Opera House** (Deutsche Staatsoper), designed in the eighteenth century by military-man-turned-architect Georg Wenzeslaus von Knobelsdorff. On the square between it and the Rococo **Old Royal Library** (with its curved front, sometimes said to resemble a chest of drawers) is **Bebelplatz,** where on May 10, 1933, the Nazis burned thousands of books. Into the flames went works by such frowned-upon German-born writers as Erich Maria Remarque and Thomas Mann. Poet Heinrich Heine had remarked prophetically in his time, "Where books are burned, people, too, are burned in the end."

Behind Bebelplatz is **St. Hedwig's Cathedral** (St. Hedwigs-Kathedrale), its exterior fashioned by Von Knobelsdorff after the Parthenon in Athens (with Frederick the Great, it is said, continuously looking over his shoulder). Totally destroyed in World War II, its exterior has been reconstructed exactly as it had been, but the interior is strikingly modern, with its ribbed dome, lights that dangle like Christmas-tree ornaments, and enormous pillars. On the lower level are handsome chapels whose oval stained-glass windows are in sea-glass colors. The church is open for viewing daily, except during services.

Beside the Opera House is the seventeenth-century **Palace Under the Lindens** (Palais Unter den Linden) with, behind it, in the recently restored red-brick **Friedrichswerder Church** (Friedrichswerderkische) on Werderscher Markt, a museum of the work of the nineteenth-century artist and architect Karl Friedrich Schinkel, who was largely responsible for the face of Berlin in its heyday.

Back on Unter den Linden opposite the Opera House is Schinkel's **New Guard House** (Neue Wache), designed with its Doric pillars rather like a fortified gate. It houses the eternal flame that marks the grave of an unknown soldier and unknown resistance fighter — "Victims of Fascism and Militarism."

Continuing east, the square, dark-red Baroque former **Prussian Arsenal** (Zeughaus) houses a fascinating **Museum of German History** (Museum für Deutsche Geschichte), where, though the explanations of the displays are in German, non-German speakers can recognize posters of a sultry Marlene Dietrich in her early acting days, Napoleon's hat recovered after the Battle of Waterloo, and photographs of the short-lived dirigible *Graf Zeppelin* of the 1930s. In the courtyard (Schlüterhof) outside (a little hard to find), the eighteenth-century sculptures of heads of dying warriors by Andreas Schlüter above the window arches should not be missed. The museum, however, is closed for restoration.

Marx-Engels Bridge (Marx-Engels Brücke): Designed by master architect-sculptor Schinkel from 1822 to 1824, this bridge across the Spree canal only returned to its former glory in 1981, when the statues of stages in the life of a warrior and of Victory teaching a child about heroes were returned from West Berlin. They had been hidden there for safekeeping during World War II. The marble statues, from designs by Schinkel but actually done by a variety of sculptors, were originally erected in the mid-nineteenth-century reign of Frederick William IV, the great builder of Berlin. Schinkel's own sculpture is represented here in the dolphin and sea horse on the balustrades. Across the bridge is Museumsinsel.

Museum Island (Museumsinsel): On this island to the left of Marx-Engels Platz, formed where the two branches of the River Spree meet, are the major museums of this eastern section of the city — the incomparable Pergamon, the Old and the New Museums, the National Gallery, and the Bode. The museums and their collections are described below.

Bode Museum (Bodemuseum): Though the interior of the former Kaiser Friedrich Museum is dark and gloomy and the displays old-fashioned, there is much of interest and value in this turn-of-the century neo-Baroque structure. Its Egyptian collection is one of the largest in the world, and its German medieval sculpture gallery contains works by Tilman Riemenschneider and Veit Stoss. In the Early Christian and Byzantine rooms are interesting Coptic art and a sixth-century mosaic from Ravenna. Particularly fascinating are items archeologist Heinrich Schliemann brought back from excavations at Troy in the nineteenth century. But much of the best that he unearthed was destroyed in the war, although it was stored in a supposedly indestructible tower. The Bode is open Wednesday through Sunday from 10:00 A.M. to 6:00 P.M.

National Gallery (Nationalgalerie): Though builder-king Frederick William IV did not succeed in having the cathedral that he longed for built in his lifetime, this national gallery, designed by Friedrich August Stüler and the king and built by H. Strack, was completed and is something of a memorial to Frederick William. Here is nineteenth-century sculpture by Johann Gottfried Schadow (sculptor of the quadriga on the Brandenburg Gate), Christian Rauch (at the Charlottenburg Palace in western Berlin he is represented by the equestrian statue of Frederick the Great and the reclining marble statue for the sarcophagus of Queen Louise of Prussia), Adolph Menzel, and the Italian Antonio Canova. There is some nineteenth-century French painting, but the museum is most noted for its German twentieth-century Impressionist and Bauhaus work. The gallery is open Wednesday through Sunday from 10:00 A.M. to 6:00 P.M.

New Museum (Neues Museum): This mid-nineteenth-century neoclassical building was still undergoing restoration at this writing. The Egyptian Museum and prehistoric art will eventually be in it.

Old Museum (Altes Museum): Designed in neoclassical style by Schinkel and erected between 1824 and 1828, this structure, with its Ionic portico of nineteen columns approached by a graceful flight of steps, is considered the architect's masterpiece. On top of the front are copies of the horse tamers from the Piazza del Quirinale in Rome.

The inside collection, as this book went to press, was disappointing — principally unimaginative work of the German Democratic Republic. But the print room (Kupferstichkabinett), if you know what you wish to see, is worth a visit. Not on display, but available in files, are Rembrandts, Dürers, and Cranachs; nineteenth-century German work by Käthe Kollwitz and Max Slevogt; and French prints by, among others, Rodin, Degas, and Toulouse-Lautrec. The museum's hours are Wednesday, Thursday, Saturday, and Sunday from 9:00 A.M. to noon and 2:00 to 6:00 P.M. and on Friday from 10:00 A.M. to noon and 2:00 to 6:00 P.M.

Pergamon Museum (Pergamon-Museum): Reconstructed here is the monumental Great Altar of Pergamon, believed to have been part of an enormous altar to Zeus erected in 180 B.C. in celebration of a Greek victory over the Gauls at Pergamon (Bergama in today's Turkey).

In 1870, German engineers were asked by the Turks to construct a railway in the Bergama area, and in a mountain where they were digging to lay the tracks, this altar was uncovered. Two thirds of what was found was reerected in this museum built expressly for it in 1930. The altar is built in terraces with friezes representing the victory of the gods, led by Zeus and Athena, over the Giants. Enormous figures of the wrestling gods and their opponents are executed with great drama.

Almost as impressive are the Ishtar Gate and the tiled Processional Way from Babylon lined with winged yellow lions and other mythological animals on a blue background and the throne room from Babylon in the sixth century B.C. days of Nebuchadnezzar II. (Not all that you see, however, is original. Some has been constructed to better display the original finds.)

A market gate from Miletus in Asia Minor and the facade of a Jordanian prince's palace of A.D. 743 are among the other extraordinary exhibits. The museum is open Wednesday through Sunday from 10:00 A.M. to 6:00 P.M.

Also on Museum Island, beside the Old Museum, rises the green copper dome of the former **Protestant Cathedral** (Berliner Dom). A neo-Renaissance structure erected at the turn of the century, only the exterior has been reconstructed as it was before World War II, when it was badly damaged. The interior now houses small art exhibits. The rectangular modern structure opposite it, with reflecting windows, served as the **Palace of the Republic** (Palast der Republik) in Communist days, and it was there that the Parliament met.

In planning to visit the museums of Museum Island, it is wise to double-check in advance at a tourist office to make sure what sections of each are open. In the past, whole collections have often been closed for months.

Soviet Memorial (Sowjetisches Ehrenmal), Treptower Park: Five thousand Soviet soldiers killed in the battle for Berlin in 1945 are remembered here by two walls of red granite symbolizing flags at half mast, a gray marble statue of Mother Russia, and a mausoleum topped by a bronze statue of a Soviet soldier with a rescued child in one arm and his sword resting on a shattered swastika in his other hand. The monument, though heavy and Socialist in style, is deeply moving and is the largest Soviet military monument outside the Soviet Union. The turn-of-the-century park in which it sits is a popular place for Sunday afternoon strolls.

Alexander Square (Alexanderplatz): This sprawling pedestrian square named for Russian Czar Alexander I, who visited Berlin in 1805, was the heart of the old East Berlin. (Before the war, it was the heart of the Old Town, of all Berlin. Virtually all of it, however, was destroyed by bombs and last-minute street fighting.) It can be reached from the Palace of the Republic by continuing up the wide avenue named for Karl Liebknecht until you reach the Lutheran **St. Mary's Church** (Marienkirche) on the right side of the avenue. Originally an early Gothic church of the thirteenth century, it was rebuilt in late Gothic style in the fifteenth century. A neo-Gothic spire was added in the eighteenth century. Damaged but not destroyed in the war, it has been rebuilt, and half-hour organ concerts are held here daily at 3:30 P.M. The interior is worth viewing for the sixteenth-century Dance of Death (Totentanz) fresco discovered during postwar reconstruction. Painted during a plague in Berlin, it shows a grinning Death dancing with victims. The church is open from 10:00 A.M. to noon and 1:00 P.M. to 5:00 P.M. weekdays and noon to 4:30 P.M. on Saturdays. On Sunday, services are at 10:30 A.M.

Behind the church in the **New Market** (Neumarkt) soars the **TV Tower** (Fernsehturm). A viewing platform is open from 8:00 A.M. to 11:00 P.M. from May through September and from 9:00 A.M. to 11:00 P.M. from October through April. The view may be hidden by smog in winter. In the base of the tower are exhibits and an espresso bar.

Another site here is the restored turn-of-the-century **Neptune Fountain** (Neptunbrunnen) and, across from that, the restored red-stone neo-Renaissance **Red Town Hall** (Rotes Rathaus) of the 1860s.

Alexander Place itself resembles an enormous, iceless, outdoor skating rink. Next to it rises the architecturally uninteresting Hotel Stadt Berlin; at right angles to that are the windows of the equally architecturally uninteresting Centrum Department Store. On the opposite side are the 1969 **World Time Clock** (Weltzeituhr), which reports the time in major cities around the world, and the Congress Hall. The centerpiece of Alexander Place is a large but characterless fountain.

St. Nicholas Quarter (Nikolaiviertel): This four-block area along the River Spree — except for the shell of the **St. Nicholas Church** (Nikolaikirche) — was nothing but rubble after the Second World War. In an effort to re-create some of the charm of Old Berlin, it was restored for the city's seven hundred and fiftieth anniversary in 1987.

Prefabricated pieces of concrete were plastered and stuccoed, painted pink and gold, and decorated with the Gothic arches and oriel windows of centuries past. Wrought-iron lamps and cobblestone streets completed the touristic creation, which attracts visitors galore to its sidewalk cafés in summer. Its rustic restaurants specialize in hearty fare like pea soup and sauerkraut in winter. Both food and clothing shops considerably more elegant than elsewhere in the eastern part of the city lure window-shoppers.

In the middle of it all was (and is) the red-stone St. Nicholas Church, part of which dates from the thirteenth century, making it the city's oldest church. It now houses part of the **Museum of Mark Brandenburg** (Märkisches Museum) — the section devoted to artifacts and pictures of medieval Berlin. (The main part of this museum of the history of the city and the Mark Brandenburg is at Amköllnischen Park 1020 and is open from 9:00 A.M. to 5:00 P.M. Wednesday through Friday; Saturday until 6:00 P.M. and Sunday from 10:00 A.M. to 6:00 P.M.) The church is open Tuesday through Friday from 9:00 A.M. to 5:00 P.M., Saturday until 6:00 P.M., and Sunday from 10:00 A.M. to 6:00 P.M.

Two other museums in the St. Nicholas Quarter are the **Museum of the Eighteenth-Century German Enlightenment** (Knoblauchhaus) and the **Ephraim Palace** (Ephraimpalais). Among Enlightenment figures whose memorabilia is displayed in the eighteenth-century Knoblauchhaus is that of dramatist and critic Gotthold Ephraim Lessing. The museum is open Tuesday through Saturday from 9:00 A.M. to 5:00 P.M. and Sunday from 10:00 A.M. to 5:00 P.M., but it is probably of minimal interest to any but those with a background in German literature. The building was one of the few survivors of the war in this part of the city.

In the reconstructed Rococo Ephraim Palace at the corner of Poetstrasse and Mühlendamm is a display of Berlin domestic history from the seventeenth through the twentieth centuries, with pictures of the capital in its thriving pre–World War II days. The house itself, a mansion erected in the mid-eighteenth century for Veitel Heine Ephraim, a Jewish banker and adviser to Frederick the Great, was destroyed by the Nazis in 1935. Parts of the exquisite mansion, however, were carried off to West Berlin. Making use of the returned pieces, the house has been rebuilt with the help of photographs and illustrations. Recently, it has been undergoing reconstruction, but its normal hours are 10:00 A.M. to 6:00 P.M. Tuesday through Friday and on Sunday, and on Saturday until 7:00 P.M.

Academy Square (Platz der Akademie): A right turn onto Wilhelm Kulz Strasse off Unter den Linden just after the statue of Frederick the Great leads to this former Gendarmenmarkt, where eighteenth-century gendarmes had a barracks. It is also the site of the restored Greco-Roman **Concert Hall** (Schauspielhaus), which was considered Schinkel's masterpiece; of the domed **French Church** (Franzosicher Dom) and its companion **German Church** (Deutscher Dom), and of many elegant dwellings. This square, in the eighteenth century, was considered one of Europe's most beautiful. Today there is much restoration work in the area, but the two churches and the Concert Hall have been largely reconstructed from the ruins. Visitors are welcome in the churches, but to see the interior of the Schauspielhaus, as of this writing, was still not possible, unless you were attending a performance.

The French Church, built in early Baroque style in the first years of the eighteenth century by two French architects, Louis Cayard and Abraham Quesnay, was constructed to serve the sizable Huguenot population invited here by Frederick William I when the Edict of Nantes, which had allowed freedom of worship to Protestants in France, was repealed. More than 200,000 French Huguenots fled to Brandenburg-Prussia, established themselves, and became an influential part of the eighteenth-century Berlin community. Their history in the city is recounted in displays in the church tower. The church is open Tuesday through Thursday and on Saturday from 10:00 A.M. to 5:00 P.M. and on Sunday from 11:30 A.M. to 6:00 P.M. It is still in use as a church.

The German Church, constructed at approximately the same time by Italian architect Giovanni Simonetti, is virtually the twin of the French Church. It serves a Lutheran congregation. At this writing its reconstruction was still in progress.

THE OUTSKIRTS OF BERLIN

KÖPENICK

Köpenick, a Berlin suburb, is noted for its palace and town hall.

Köpenick Palace: (Köpenick Schloss): Though it resembles a grand manor house more than a palace, this handsome structure built between 1678 and 1682 and now housing the **Museum of Applied Art** (Kunstgewerbemuseum) is the oldest palace still standing in Berlin. Historically, it is notable as the site where, in 1730, the eighteen-year-old prince who would become Frederick the Great was forced to witness the execution of the best friend with whom he had planned to escape the tyranny of his father, Frederick William I. Artistically, it is important today as a handsome restoration and for the porcelain, gold, and silver, including royal silver and golden jewelry of the eleventh-century empress Gisela. It is open Wednesday through Saturday from 9:00 A.M. to 6:00 P.M. and Sunday from 10 A.M. to 6 P.M. It can be reached by Number 27 bus from the S-Bahn station, Köpenick.

Köpenick Town Hall (Köpenicher Rathaus): This red-brick neo-Gothic town hall became part of German literary and folk history after the 1906 adventure here of shoemaker Wilhelm Voigt. A not-very-successful shoemaker, with a police record in addition, Voigt greatly improved his own self-esteem one day when he bought an old uniform of a captain of the guards in a pawnshop. Emerging onto the street, he saw a troop of soldiers and promptly took command of them, ordering them to join him in taking the Köpenick Town Hall and arresting the mayor. The soldiers dutifully did as they were told by the captain in the scruffy uniform, taking the contents of the municipal treasury while they were at it, for Voigt needed identity papers and hoped he would find them in it. When he finally opened the treasury box after having had his troops lock up the mayor and his staff in the Neue Wache, Voigt discovered it contained no identity papers, so he turned himself in to the authorities and ended up serving a brief prison term for theft. His exploit, however, captured public fancy and playwright Carl Zuckmayer based his *The Captain of Köpenick,* a Berlin hit of 1931, on it.

POTSDAM

Frederick the Great, with an artist's eye, selected Potsdam, a beautiful site on the River Havel, seventeen miles southwest of Berlin, as the site of his summer residence. Here there was not only the river, but woods and lakes. With an architect's eye, he chose his old friend Georg Wenzeslaus von Knobelsdorff, the Prussian army officer turned architect, to build it for him.

Both choices were exemplary, and though Frederick and Von Knobelsdorff parted company angrily in the end (Frederick really wanted to be his own architect and drew up the plans himself), before they did, a Rococo masterpiece had been created.

At the same time that Frederick asked Von Knobelsdorff to build a little residence for him, he entrusted him with rebuilding what had been Frederick's father's larger Town Palace (Stadt Schloss) in Potsdam. The latter, along with much of the town of Potsdam itself, was destroyed in World War II, but Frederick's summer palace of **Sans Souci** (Free from Care), in its extensive gardens, still stands.

One of Frederick's arguments with Von Knobelsdorff was about whether the palace, which sits on a hill, should be one story or two. Von Knobelsdorff wanted two and explained that palace rooms on a cellarless ground floor would be dank and cold. But Frederick, who loved gardens and the out-of-doors, liked the idea of stepping directly out into his garden. He won the argument, of course, and Sans Souci is a graceful single story structure with a rounded central dome. (He did not get the outdoor terraced vineyards he wanted because the Potsdam climate is too cold, so hothouses had to be built.)

Guests entering from the garden climbed a flight of steps and were met at the top by caryatids leaning forward between the windows. Today visitors enter from the other side. If you turn around before you enter, you will be looking through a semicircular colonnade of Corinthian pillars toward an artificial Roman ruin in the distance.

Inside the palace, stucco nymphs in relief dance above the doors. The long, narrow, white-and-gold **Little Gallery** is lined with paintings and statues. A bust of Frederick the Great, patterned from his death mask, is on a mantelpiece.

Off Frederick's study (reconstructed in the style of early neoclassicism in the late eighteenth century but with Rococo furnishings) is the evocative alcove — formerly a bedroom — where the king died in 1786 at the age of seventy-four in a chair that still stands there. The clock, which he always wound himself, stopped, it is said, at precisely the moment of his death, 2:20 A.M. on the seventeenth of August.

Among the prettiest of the rooms is the cheerful music room, with walls painted with birds, baskets of flowers, and dogs chasing rabbits. Mirrors are used to make it look wider and seem to bring the outdoors in. Murals of Ovid's *Metamorphoses* by Frederick's court painter, the Frenchman Antoine Pesne, adorn the walls.

Because he did not wish those waiting for him to be bored, the king (an admirer of all things French) hung French paintings in his reception room that he especially liked and hoped would also please his visitors.

The central hall of the palace is fashioned in miniature after the Pantheon in Rome. Off it are the guest rooms, one painted in Chinese style, two sedately redone in the 1970s with blue-and-white- and red-and-white-striped silk damask walls. The fourth, named for Voltaire, whom Frederick greatly admired (until the writer came for a visit), is decorated with parrots on its yellow walls and a bust of the French philosopher. Frederick had hoped he and Voltaire could have pleasant chats together about philosophy and literature, but they seem to have argued instead, and when Voltaire was gone, Frederick said he was "like a lemon . . . you can press out the juice and throw the rest away."

Reveling in the out-of-doors, Frederick made sure that his gardens were as lovely as his palace so that no visitor would miss strolling through them. They are filled with exuberance. Though Frederick had trouble getting the fountains to work in his lifetime, modern technology has them bubbling and spouting energetically.

At the foot of the graceful portal entrance to the palace grounds, Flora, the goddess of flowers, and Pomona, the goddess of fruit, stand on a wall between Corinthian columns. In a grotto, a statue of Neptune, god of the sea, brandishes his trident.

Frederick was a brilliant ruler, but a lonely, tortured man, always torn between wishing to be a great thinker (when he was young, he had written a criticism of Machiavelli's *The Prince* that he called the "Anti-Machiavelli"), an artist and patron of the arts, and a king. Unhappily married (rumors were that an illness in his youth made him impotent, and his wife did have a place of her own outside Berlin), he took great comfort in pets, and his two greyhounds are buried in the garden. "When I am there with them," he said, "then I, at last, will be *sans souçi —* without care." But Frederick did not get his wish. He was first buried in the Garrison Church in Potsdam. After the Second World War his remains were removed to the Hohenzollern family tombs in Hechingen in the west. Now they are expected to be returned here. Sans Souci is open from 9:00 A.M. to 5:00 P.M. April through September and from 9:00 A.M. to 4:00 P.M. in October, February, and March. In November, December, and January, it is closed from 12:30 to 1:30 P.M. and after 3:00 P.M. It is closed the first Monday in each month.

Love of art is obvious everywhere at Sans Souci, and Frederick is said to have established the first gallery solely for the display of pictures in the world. This **Picture Gallery** (Bildergalerie), its walls literally "plastered" with art, includes paintings by Breughel, Rubens, Titian, Watteau, Caravaggio, Van Dyck, and Rembrandt. There is also an **Orangery** in the garden with copies of forty-seven Raphael paintings and a charming little **Chinese Teahouse** with a tent-shaped golden roof and gilded sculptures of Chinese figures seated on it. The work of John Buring, this is considered one of the finest examples of the Chinoiserie style popular in eighteenth-century Europe.

The largest and most ostentatious building in the park is the late Baroque **New Palace** (Neuer Palais), which Frederick built to his people's dismay just after the nation had suffered through the Seven Years' War. Its resplendent interior includes a marble concert hall that seats 500 and a room inlaid with shells, its friezes studded with minerals and precious stones. Some of its rooms are decorated in silver, others in gold. It may be viewed the same hours as Sans Souci, but it is closed the second Monday in each month. The other buildings are open from 9:00 A.M. to 5:00 P.M. from May to October, but are closed for lunch.

Schloss Charlottenhof, which began as an unpretentious country house but was transformed into an Italian villa by Karl Friedrich Schinkel in the 1820s, is also open to the public, but the outside is the most interesting part. The Sicilian gardens around it are by nineteenth-century master landscape artist Peter Joseph Lenné.

Other buildings in the park include **Roman Baths** (Römische Bäder), a **Pheasantry** (Faisanerie), and the **Peace Church** (Friedenskirche). There is a **Military Museum** in the eighteenth-century **Marble Palace.** Edging Helliger Lake, the garden is a pretty, quiet place.

After Sans Souci, the principal attraction of Potsdam is **Schloss Cecilienhof.** Built as a 1912 copy of an English manor house, it was the site of the Potsdam Conference of 1945 that decided the fate of postwar Germany. The palace, which lies a little northeast of the town, was built from 1913 to 1917 for Kaiser Wilhelm II's son, Crown Prince Wilhelm, and named for his wife, Cecilia. Today it is part hotel and part museum. Cecilienhof is set in the **New Garden** (Neuer Garten) laid out by Frederick William II in the late eighteenth century and planted with more than 13,000 trees.

At the Potsdam Conference, a cryptic telegram that said "A baby is born," delivered to Harry S. Truman, brought the president the news that an atomic bomb had successfully been made. In the crown prince's Blue Study, Winston Churchill worked for a few days before the British government changed and Labour prime minister Clement Attlee took over.

Cecilienhof is open from 8:00 A.M. to 5:30 P.M. April to October and from 8:00 A.M. to 4:30 P.M. during the winter.

To the east of the palace grounds in the town of Potsdam itself, there are numerous sights: the **Church of St. Nicholas** (Nikolai-kirche) that Schinkel built, but that was destroyed in World War II, has been rebuilt; a pretty Baroque street, Wilhelm Staab Strasse, has also been restored. There is the reconstructed 1752 **Town Hall** (Rathaus), with Atlas bearing the globe on his shoulders atop the gable; a little colony of Dutch-style houses built in the eighteenth century; and the houses built for Russian singers invited to Frederick III's court in the nineteenth century.

SPREEWALD
The charming Spreewald of woods, canals, and marshes outside Berlin remains today, as it has been for centuries, a charming, quiet place for outings. It was here in the last century that German government officials elected to bring their mistresses for romantic rendezvous. All up and down its narrow canals sit little country houses in pretty gardens. The tourist on a boat excursion (boatmen pole longboats through reedy canals) feels almost like a voyeur passing by, for the gardens of flowers, gherkins (a product here), and houses are so near and the waterways so narrow. The three-hour spring-summer boat tours (it's amazing how quickly the three hours pass!) leave from the town of Lübbenau, making one stop for a visit to a museum of the Sorb people, a Slavonic race that once made up the larger part of the population here. Should you decide to visit the Spreewald, it is wise to bear in mind that virtually no English is spoken in such rural areas.

THURINGIA

Here in the green heart of Germany, where the hills are gently rounded and the valleys are fertile, is the Thuringian Forest and some of eastern Germany's most historic cities — Arnstadt, where

Johann Sebastian Bach took his finest job; Eisenach, where Bach was born and Martin Luther imprisoned; Erfurt, where Luther studied and was ordained; Weimar, home to poets Johann Wolfgang von Goethe and Friedrich Schiller and to painter Lucas Cranach the Elder, and where Franz Lizst taught music and the Bauhaus School of Art and Architecture was founded. Just outside of Weimar is the site of the Nazi concentration camp at Buchenwald.

ARNSTADT

Bach Church (Bachkirche): Johann Sebastian Bach was just eighteen when he was appointed organist and choirmaster here in 1703. With a light schedule, he was able to do considerable studying and composing; while he was here, he wrote his first compositions for the organ as well as toccatas and choral preludes. But he infuriated church authorities when he did not return as expected from a leave to study with master organist Dietrich Buxtehude. Bach is said to have walked the 290 miles to Lübeck, where he hoped to prove so exemplary a pupil that he would inherit the aging Buxtehude's job as organist at Lübeck's Marienkirche. But Buxtehude's daughter's hand in marriage, it turned out, was part of the arrangement. Bach declined it on the grounds that she was too old for him. He did not get the job but returned here to be reprimanded for both his tardiness and the new style of organ playing he had learned from the master. Happily, as criticism mounted, he was offered the organist's post in the parish church of St. Blaise in neighboring Mühlhausen.

Arnstadt Castle Museum (Schlossmuseum): Aficionados of miniatures will be in their element visiting Mon Plaisir, a collection of eighty Baroque and Rococo doll settings arranged in the early eighteenth century by the countess Augusta Dorothea von Schwarzburg-Arnstadt and local craftsmen. Four hundred costumed dolls are set in kitchens, at tea parties, in the market square, a cooper's shop, a wine cellar, and a barbershop, among other settings. The museum is open Tuesday through Sunday from 9:00 A.M. to noon and 1:00 to 4:30 P.M.

Arnstadt's other attractions include the thirteenth-century

Church of Our Lady (Liebfrauenkirche), with its two tall towers and impressive medieval interior; the sixteenth- and seventeenth-century burghers' houses and arcades around the market square; one turret of a sixteenth-century fortification; and the mauve **Town Hall** (Rathaus) with its gilded clock. A statue of Bach also decorates the square, and there is a **Bach Museum** of prints and programs.

EISENACH
This town of pink-and-gold half-timbered houses is called the finest town of the Thuringian Forest because of its picturesque site and for the great men — Bach and Luther — it has nurtured. In 1685 Johann Sebastian Bach was born in Eisenach; the young Martin Luther attended Latin School here, singing from door to door to help pay his room and board. Later, the adult Luther spent eight months in the Wartburg fortress that looms above the town. The minnesingers of the Middle Ages entertained at the landgraves' court and centuries later Richard Wagner, hearing of them on a visit, was inspired to write his opera *Tannhäuser.*

Bach House (Bachhaus), Frauenplan 21: Although this seventeenth-century mustard-yellow house with the statue of Bach in the pretty garden outside is not a structure in which the great composer ever lived, this is Eisenach's Bach museum, with memorabilia — letters and old engravings — and a music room.

In a room full of Baroque musical instruments — flutes, piccolos, lutes, cornets, a clavichord, a harpsichord, and a viola da gamba — either live or recorded Bach music is played for groups of visitors at the end of their house tour. The museum is open Monday from 1:30 to 4:30 P.M., Tuesday through Friday from 9:00 A.M. to 4:30 P.M., and Saturday and Sunday from 9:00 A.M. to noon and from 1:30 to 4:30 P.M.

Luther House (Lutherhaus), Lutherplatz 8: A teenaged Martin Luther was a boarder with family friends in this restored little late Gothic house in the years he attended Latin School here. Largely destroyed in World War II, the tipsy little house is now a museum of Bibles of Luther's day and items of the period of his school years. On the top floor are two small rooms, minimally furnished, where he is believed to have stayed. Now the property of the German Evangelical Church, the house is usually open from 9:00 A.M. to 1:00 P.M. and 2:00 to 5:00 P.M. weekdays and from 2:00 to 5:00 P.M. Sunday.

Reuter-Wagner Museum (Reuterhaus), Reuterweg 2: The Wagner memorabilia displayed in this villa — letters, photographs, and theater programs — is small, but it is said to be the next largest in size to that at Bayreuth. With no translations, however, it is of limited appeal to any but Wagner devotees. The museum also honors the nineteenth-century writer of humorous verse Fritz Reuter, whose home it was. It is open Monday through Friday from 9:00 A.M. tro 12:30 P.M. and from 2:00 to 5:00 P.M., and on Sunday from 9:00 A.M. to 4:00 P.M.

St. George's Church (Georgenkirche): In this little church on the marketplace, Johann Sebastian Bach, son of the trumpet player Johann Ambrosius Bach and his wife, Elisabeth, was christened in 1685. As a schoolboy, Martin Luther sang in the choir; later he preached from the pulpit. Both the composer and the reformer are remembered on the wrought-iron gate outside — Bach by his entwined initials, Luther with a cross and a heart. Though the church dates from the twelfth century, virtually nothing of that period remains. Seriously damaged in World War II, its interior is most notable for seventeenth-century paintings of Luther, his protector, Frederick the Wise, elector of Saxony, and the Holy Roman Emperor Charles V, and for its 4,835-pipe organ. Though churches with a Luther link are more likely to be open every day than other churches, it is wise to check in advance on their hours at the Eisenach Information Office near the railroad station, which is open weekdays until 5:00 P.M. and Saturday until 3:00 P.M.

St. Nicholas Church (Nikolaikirche): This Romanesque church with its octagonal tower was built at the end of the twelfth century and rebuilt at the end of the nineteenth. Beside it stands the late Romanesque St. Nicholas Gate (Nikolaitor), erected about 1200 as part of the town fortifications; it is the oldest city gate still standing in Thuringia.

Thuringian Museum (Thüringisches Museum), Markt 24: This elegant Baroque palace-museum has a fine collection of blue Thuringian porcelain. It is usually open Tuesday through Friday from 9:00 A.M. to 12:30 P.M. and from 2:00 to 5:00 P.M. On Saturday it is open from 9:00 A.M. to 4:00 P.M.

Wartburg: From the spring of 1521 till December of 1522, the reformer-monk Martin Luther was held in "protective custody" in this hilltop fortress built in the eleventh century for the landgraves of Thuringia. Outraged by the Catholic Church's practice of selling indulgences to mitigate the consequences of sin, Luther had criticized this and other church practices that he deemed dishonest. He posted his criticisms in 1517 on the Wittenberg Castle church door (*see* Wittenberg). Since the sale of indulgences was profitable to the Church, his criticism stung sharply and Charles V, Holy Roman Emperor, ordered him to come to the Council of Worms and recant. Luther attended as bid, but did not recant and was declared a "notorious heretic" by the council. Though he was given safe-conduct to return to his home in Wittenberg, his friend, the Saxon elector Frederick the Wise, questioned the validity of that safe conduct; for Luther's own protection he had him "abducted" and brought to this fortress above town, valley, and forest.

Here he substituted knight's garb for his monk's cassock, grew a beard, and adopted the identity of "Junker Jörg." It was hoped that during his absence from public life, furor over his "heresy" would subside. And while he was here — not very happily, for he felt guilty about not serving his people — he translated the New Testament from Greek into German to distract his thoughts. He accomplished this task in ten weeks and in so doing virtually created the modern German language.

The simple furnishings in the little room where he worked are the table on which he wrote, the whale's vertebra he used as a footstool, and a green-tile stove. (A spot on the wall, periodically renewed, is said to have been left when, in a fit of rage, he threw an inkpot at the devil.) On other walls hang copies of paintings his friend Lucas Cranach the Elder painted of him and the Greek scholar Philip Melanchthon of Wittenberg, to whom he smuggled copies of his work for corrections. There is also a copy of a

Cranach copper engraving of Luther as Junker Jörg and a copy of his German New Testament.

On German-language tours of the Wartburg, you also see the late Romanesque hall that has been restored with a cross-beamed ceiling as it was in the landgraves' day and on whose walls are late-nineteenth-century frescoes of life in the days of the landgraves by Moritz von Schwind. These include one of the Sängerkrieg — the medieval singing contest of German minstrels Wagner wrote of in *Tannhäuser*. There are also frescoes of the life of the thirteenth-century Hungarian St. Elizabeth, the generous and gentle wife of a Thuringian landgrave. Always concerned with the poor, Elizabeth, the story goes, was stopped by her husband one day as she took bread to them in her apron. When he demanded to know what she carried, she replied, "Roses," and when he made her open her apron to show him, the apron was, indeed, filled with roses.

Fifteenth- and sixteenth-century sculpture and carving may also be seen here. Concerts are held in the **Jubilee Hall** in summer. The Wartburg is open daily from 9:00 A.M. to 3:30 P.M.

ERFURT

Erfurt, one of the oldest cities of Germany, escaped major damage in World War II and can still show off its Gothic and Renaissance tradesmen's houses, twenty-two historic churches, and a monastery. Nevertheless, as this book went to press, refurbishing was under way and scaffolding impeded sightseeing in the heart of the **Old City** (Altstadt). Erfurt's principal sites follow.

Augustinian Monastery (Augustinerkloster): Young Martin Luther came to the University of Erfurt to study law, but his life's plan changed one summer afternoon in 1505 as he walked from the country to town. Caught without shelter in a terrifying thunderstorm, a lightning bolt struck him to the ground. Realizing how close he had been to death and grateful to God for having spared him, Luther, on the spot, dedicated his life to God's service. Two weeks after the incident, he changed his studies from law to theology and moved into this gray stone monastery, where he remained till 1511. Though considerably damaged during

World War II, most of the monastery has now been restored and you can see the reconstructed cell that Luther occupied, stroll in the Renaissance courtyard in which he strolled, and visit the **Church of St. Augustine** (Augustinerkirche), where the devout Luther, beset with inner conflicts, is said to have often lain prostrate in prayer on the cold stone floor. The monastery is open Tuesday through Saturday from 9:00 A.M. to 4:00 P.M. from April through October. From November through March, visitors may enter for guided tours only at 10:00 A.M., noon, and 2:00 P.M. Tuesday through Saturday.

Barefoot Church (Barfusserkirche), Barfusserstrasse: It was in this simple thirteenth-century Gothic church, restored in the nineteenth century and now undergoing restoration again, that Luther, in 1546, preached his last sermon.

Cathedral (Dom): Begun in the twelfth century and rebuilt in

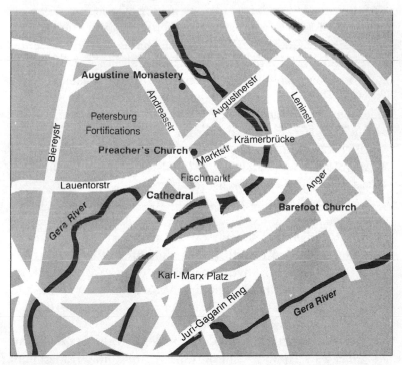

ERFURT

Gothic style in the fourteenth, this Catholic cathedral set on a hill in the center of the city is held up on arches — an unusual engineering feat in that day. Its interior is notable for a fifteenth-century stained-glass window of blue, gold, rose, and red, considered one of the loveliest in all Germany; a twelfth-century wall painting of St. Christopher; a bronze relief, *The Coronation of the Virgin*, by Peter Vischer the Younger; intricately carved fifteenth-century choir stalls; a twelfth-century carved Madonna; and a curious twelfth-century candelabra of a worshipper that is distinctly modern in its look. Except for Cologne Cathedral, Erfurt's Dom has the largest bell in the country, weighing more than thirteen tons. It peals forth annually on Christmas and Easter. In 1507, Martin Luther, after having completed his studies at Erfurt University, was ordained in this imposing cathedral. It is open from 10:00 to 11:30 A.M. and 12:30 to 4:00 P.M. Monday through Saturday, and from 2:00 to 4:00 P.M. Sunday.

Church of St. Severin (Severinkirche): This three-spired fourteenth-century Gothic Catholic church shares the hill above the old town square with the Catholic Cathedral. It is notable for its late Gothic baptismal font, a fifteenth-century alabaster relief of St. Michael, and the sarcophagus of St. Severin. It has been undergoing restoration.

Fish Market (Fischmarkt): From the fourteenth to the sixteenth centuries, Erfurt was a flourishing trading center and its successful merchants built many handsome houses around this square, where formerly the fish market was held. Among them are the sixteenth-century **House of the Red Oxen** (Haus zum Roten Ochsen) with an ox over the door and a devil (put there to frighten Satan himself away) on the pediment and the 1582 **House of the Broad Hearth** (Haus zum Breiten Herd) with its reliefs that illustrate the five senses by showing a woman looking in a mirror, playing music, smelling a rose, eating an apple, and touching a bird. Also in the Fish Market is the restored nineteenth-century **Town Hall** (Rathaus).

Other old structures worth looking for are the **Old Swan** (Alter Schwan), now a wine restaurant, near the Tradesmen's Bridge; the Gothic **House of the Tall Lily** (Haus zur Hohen Lilie) at the Domplatz (Cathedral Place); the **House of the Stockfish** (Haus zum Stockfisch) that is now a museum of the city on Leninstrasse; the **Bursa Pauperum**, near the river, a student hostel in the Middle Ages that is now undergoing reconstruction; the fifteenth-century **House of the Golden Star** (Haus zum Goldenen Stern); and the thirteenth-century **St. Michael's Church** (Michaelis Kirche) on Michaelistrasse, as well as a few ruins of the largely war-destroyed university.

Some of these houses have a round hole cut into the facade. In early times, on a day when beer had just been brewed, university professors' wives would place a wisp of straw in the hole to indicate that there was fresh brew to share inside.

Napoleon Bonaparte stayed in the eighteenth-century **Governor's Residence** (Statthalterei) in 1808 during the French occupation here. He invited Alexander I of Russia, whom he viewed as a potential ally, to be his guest; to entertain him appropriately, he imported the Comedie Française from Paris. Goethe was another of his guests here, and on the poet's visit, the Little Emperor tried unsuccessfully to woo him away from Weimar, where Goethe then lived, to Paris.

A fine museum here is the **Museum of Thuringian Folk Art** (Museum für Thüringer Volkskunde) at Juri-Gagarin Ring 140A. Carnival masks, toys, and Christmas decorations of the past are among its displays, some of which are captioned in English. The museum is open Wednesday to Sunday from 10:00 A.M. to 6:00 P.M.

A spring attraction of Erfurt is the annual International Landscaping and Horticultural Exhibition held on the outskirts of town.

Preacher's Church (Predigerkirche), Bahnhofstrasse: Constructed in 1228, this is one of the earliest pure Gothic churches in Germany, with a Gothic carved altar of note inside.

Tradesmen's Bridge (Krämerbrücke): By the ninth century, because of its situation on the route from Spain to Russia and on the East-West salt route, Erfurt was a prosperous tradesman's town. In the twelfth century, some enterprising tradesmen had a wooden bridge built across the River Gera on the Spanish-Russian trade route. Along the bridge, resembling the Ponte Vecchio in Florence, artisans opened shops and sometimes lived above them. Art and antique stores today have replaced the goldsmiths' and spice merchants' shops of the Middle Ages. From the park below, there is a fine view of this wooden span topped with its yellow-gold shops reflected in the river below.

Woad Warehouse Theater (Waidspeicher Theater): This reconstructed sprawling, half-timbered structure off Marktstrasse was used, in Renaissance days, as a storage place for woad, a locally produced blue vegetable dye. Until the advent of indigo from the East, woad was responsible for a considerable part of Erfurt's prosperity.

WEIMAR

From the 1700s until the 1930s it was music, art, culture, and philosophy for which this Thuringian city was renowned. At the

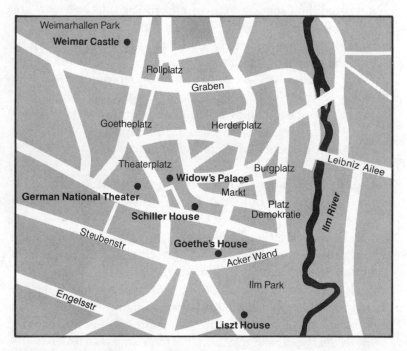

WEIMAR

end of the First World War, it briefly became a political place when the Weimar Republic, seeking to bring democracy to Germany, was proclaimed here. When that failed and Adolf Hitler rose to power, he chose Weimar as the site for the notorious concentration camp of Buchenwald. The glories of Weimar's happy early days still shine here, but the shadow of Buchenwald cannot be forgotten.

German National Theater (Deutsches National Theater), Theaterplatz: The constitution of the democratic Weimar Republic was signed in this little theater in 1919. In an earlier theater on the site, the works of Goethe and Schiller (whose statues stand in front) were performed in the nineteenth century, and Goethe, for a time, was the theater director.

Goethe House (Goethe Haus), Frauenplan: The Shakespeare of Germany — Johann Wolfgang von Goethe — spent nearly fifty years of his life in this restored Baroque-style patrician's house just above the town square. In 1832, at the age of eighty-three, he died in his little bedroom here.

In 1775, when he was twenty-six, Goethe first came to the then duchy of Weimar, invited by the eighteen-year-old duke, Karl August, who wished his little duchy of 6,000 to be a center of learning and culture. In those first years, Goethe spent much of his time entertaining the duke, directing the court theater, and directing road building, transportation, and mining in the duchy. Furious both at himself for the time he was wasting on paltry affairs and at the inefficient bureaucracy that was making him do so, Goethe disappeared in disguise one night in 1786, telling only his secretary that he was bound for Italy and a life of freedom. The letter he left for the duke requested a temporary leave of absence.

For two years, he played the vagabond, writing, painting, and absorbing the spirit of things Italian. In 1788, Goethe returned here — much to Karl August's delight. Karl August presented him with this house to do with as he would in 1794.

Goethe set to work on it with a vengeance, widening the entry stairs so they were in the Italian Renaissance tradition and filling rooms and corridors with plaster casts of ancient art he had

8. For most of his life, Goethe lived in this house in Weimar.

brought back from his travels. To display the majolica, rocks, and gems he had collected, he had special cabinets constructed, and in decorating this house that is now a museum he put to work theories of color he was then espousing.

Colors, Goethe was convinced, affected one's sensibilities, so he had his dining room painted a sunny yellow and his study a soothing green. Visitors to this fascinating house-museum will see all of this, plus facsimiles of Goethe manuscripts and drawings. The museum is open daily, except Monday, from 9:00 A.M. to 4:00 P.M.

Goethe's Garden House (Garten Haus), Park an der Ilm: It was in this little summer country house across the River Ilm from the heart of town that Goethe spent his first six Weimar years. Since the end of the nineteenth century it has been open to the public as a Goethe memorial, and most of the furniture in it dates from his stay here. You can see facsimiles of poems and drawings inspired in these surroundings. The garden outside is the writer's design. The Garden House is open daily, except Monday, from 9:00 A.M. to 12:00 P.M. and 1:00 P.M. to 4:00 P.M.

Liszt House (Liszt Haus), Marienstrasse: From 1869 until his death in 1886, the Hungarian-born pianist-composer Franz Liszt spent his summers here and gathered young students of music around him. Liszt, a devotee of Richard Wagner, brought many of that composer's operas to the Weimar stage. Memorabilia of Liszt on display in this handsome house on the edge of Ilm Park include the baton with which he conducted the first performance of *Lohengrin* here, the portable clavichord he took on his travels to keep his fingers limber, his piano, and his Hungarian passport. The museum is open from 9:00 A.M. to 12:00 P.M. and 2:00 P.M. to 4:00 P.M. daily, except Monday.

It was in today's high school opposite the Liszt House that from 1919 to 1925 the **Bauhaus School,** which emphasized the craftsman-designer concept, offered its precepts. On its faculty were Expressionists like the Swiss Paul Klee and the German-American Lyonel Feininger.

Marketplace (Marktplatz): Once reconstruction is completed, this marketplace should be picturesque. Behind it rises the seventeenth-century **Hotel Elephant,** from whose balcony in 1944 an ebullient Adolf Hitler announced that World War II was almost at its end, with Germany the victor. An earlier notable guest was Thomas Mann, who wrote of the hotel in *The Beloved Returns.* On one side of the square are the peaks and pinnacles of the Flamboyant Gothic nineteenth-century **Town Hall** (Rathaus) and across from that, decorated with colorful mermaids, is the house that Renaissance-Reformation painter Lucas Cranach the Elder occupied for a time.

Old Cemetery (Alter Friedhof), off Friedrich-Engels Ring: In a columned mausoleum here, in an oak sarcophagus, the poets Goethe and Schiller are buried. Also buried in the mausoleum, in a Russian Orthodox church addition of the 1860s, is the Russian-born Weimar grand duchess Maria Pavlovna, daughter-in-law of Karl August. The mausoleum is open daily, except Tuesday, from 9:00 A.M. to 1:00 P.M. and 2:00 to 5:00 P.M.

State Church (Stadtkirche), Herderplatz, Johann Gottfried von Herder, the philosopher-theologian by whose name this church is also sometimes called, came to this black-spired Flamboyant Gothic church as court preacher in 1776. One of Cranach the Elder's most notable paintings, an altarpiece of the Crucifixion, with Luther, John the Baptist, and the artist himself depicted, may be viewed here. It is open Monday through Friday from 2:00 P.M. to 5:00 P.M. and Saturday and Sunday from 2:00 to 3:00 P.M.

Schiller House (Schiller Haus), Schillerstrasse 12: This house-museum where the poet Friedrich Schiller, lured here by Goethe, spent the last three years of his life and wrote the drama *Wilhelm Tell* on which Rossini's opera is based was heavily damaged during World War II. The house is largely filled with playbills and posters announcing performances of his work, for virtually none of his possessions were intact after the war (except a clock on a wall that found its way to San Francisco but was sent back). You can visit the reconstructed attic room in which Schiller closeted himself for six weeks with a map of Switzerland on the wall and, his paper and pens before him, wrote *Wilhelm Tell*. Meanwhile, the rest of his family lived normal lives downstairs. The Schiller House may be visited daily, except Tuesday, from 9:00 A.M. to 4:00 P.M.

Weimar Castle (Residenzschloss), Burgplatz 4: A rich collection of paintings by sixteenth-century Lucas Cranach the Elder, friend and confidant of Martin Luther, and by Lucas Cranach the Younger are displayed in this onion-domed restored castle. It is open Tuesday through Sunday from 9:00 A.M. to 1:00 P.M. and 2:00 to 5:00 P.M.

Widow's Palace (Wittumspalais), Theaterplatz: When a fire damaged much of her palace in 1774, the then ruling duchess Anna Amalia, niece of Frederick the Great of Prussia, moved into this two-winged Baroque palace, where she continued to stay in the years after her son Karl August took over the governing of the duchy. Here, in the **Round Table Room,** she gathered about her a circle of artists, writers, and scientists to discuss the problems of the day; Goethe and his friend and mentor, Johann Gottfried von Herder, and the poet-novelist Christoph Martin Wieland, "the German Voltaire," were among them. Today the palace, which includes an extensive collection of paintings and costumes, is open to the public from 9:00 A.M. to 12:00 P.M. and 1:00 to 5:00 P.M. daily, except Monday and Tuesday.

If you have time, other sites worth seeing in Weimar include a pretty little Roman country house in **Ilm Park** that Goethe helped design for Duke Karl August; **Tiefurt Castle** (Schloss Tiefurt), set in a park about two miles east of Weimar and summer home to Duchess Anna Amalia (open daily except Monday and Tuesday, from 9:00 A.M. to 1:00 P.M. and 2:00 to 5:00 P.M.); **Castle Belvedere** (Schloss Belvedere), a Baroque hunting and entertainment castle with a Russian garden and orangery fashioned by Maria Pavlovna, under reconstruction; and **Castle Kochberg** (Schloss Kochberg), twenty-five miles outside of town, where the young Goethe paid frequent visits to Charlotte von Stein, a married Scotswoman who exerted a strong influence over him in his Weimar years. It is open daily, except Monday and Tuesday, from 9:00 A.M. to noon and 2:00 to 5:00 P.M.

A German-language museum devoted to the works of the philosopher Herder occupies the third floor of the Baroque **Kirma-Krackow House**, furnished in the style of a patrician residence of about 1800. The museum is under reconstruction but is expected to reopen in 1994.

BUCHENWALD

Down a wooded road on Etterberg Hill, barely seven miles northwest of Weimar, stand the ordinary-looking yellow barracks buildings with red-tile roofs that are what remain of this Nazi concentration camp. More than 65,000 men, women, and children from eighteen countries perished here from 1937 to 1945. Though technically a work rather than a death camp, many died of exhaustion from their slave-labor jobs, malnutrition, and inadequate living facilities. A stone bell tower and a modern monument mark the entry gate. The grounds and the museum that graphically recounts what took place here are open Tuesday through Sunday from 8:45 A.M. to 4:30 P.M.

THE HARZ MOUNTAINS

BAD FRANKENHAUSEN

Frankenhausen Monument (Gedenkstätte Frankenhausen): In this rotunda is the world's largest painting on canvas, 408 feet long by 46 feet wide, illustrating the 1525 Battle of Frankenhausen, a bloody battle of the Peasants' War. The work of Leipzig artist Werner Tübke, the painting's characters, which are twice life-size, include the 5,000 peasants who were slaughtered and the feudal lords and landholding princes who slaughtered them. The peasants had been urged to fight for their rights by Mülhausen clergyman Thomas Münzer. (The final straw, legend has it, occurred when a nobleman's wife insisted that the peasants find snail shells on which to wind her yarn.)

Depicted along with the battle participants are Luther, the humanist Erasmus, the reformer Ulrich Zwingli, the painters Lucas Cranach the Elder and Albrecht Dürer, the Greek scholar Philip Melanchthon, and Münzer, who was tortured and executed after the battle. This panoramic painting was completed in 1989.

LUTHERSTADT EISLEBEN

Martin Luther was born and died in this pretty little Harz Mountain town of 27,000; he is remembered in churches and museums.

Birth House (Geburtshaus): In this much-restored square Franconian house with a high-pitched roof, Martin Luther was born in November 1483 to copper miner Hans Luder and his hardworking wife, Margarethe. Less than a year later, the family moved to neighboring Mansfeld, but Eisleben claims Martin Luther all the same and has worked hard through the centuries to have his birthplace preserved as a memorial.

It hasn't always been easy. From 1806 to 1813 in Napoleonic days, the house was a school for poor children. Before that, it was gutted by fire. All the same, in 1917, on the four hundredth anniversary of Luther's birth, a bust of him by Johann Gottfried Schadow was unveiled in the yard and the birth house was formally opened as a museum. Though simply furnished in fifteenth- and sixteenth-century style, there are interesting period paintings of supporters of the Reformation on the top floor and a gleaming gold swan — the symbol Luther took — that alludes to Czech reformer Jan Hus's statement (as he was about to be burned at the stake), "You are roasting a goose, but after me there will come a swan you will not be able to roast." (*Husa* is the Czech word for "goose.")

Other contents of the house are old mining tools and pots, medals bearing Luther's portrait or symbol, and copies of Lucas Cranach the Elder's portraits of Hans and Margarethe Luder. The house is open from 10:00 A.M. to 1:00 P.M. and from 2:00 to 4:00 P.M. daily except Monday. An English-language tape is available as a guide.

Death House (Sterbehaus): This originally Gothic patrician town house was restored in late Gothic style in the nineteenth century and opened in 1894 as a memorial to Luther, who died here in February 1546. In the room in which he died are a curtained bed, a washstand, and a chest. Elsewhere in the house is the pall that covered his coffin at St. Andrew's Church in the town and a copy of one of the last letters he wrote to his wife. Luther, whose home was Wittenberg, died here of pneumonia contracted in a snowstorm on his way back from settling a land dispute in Mansfeld. The house is open daily, except Monday, from 8:30 A.M. to noon and 1:00 to 4:30 P.M. from May 1 to November 1 and from 9:30 A.M. to 3:30 P.M. the other months. There is frequently an English-speaking guide on duty.

Other Luther sites to visit here are **Sts. Peter and Paul Church** (Petri-Pauli Kirche), where he was baptized, and **St. Andrew's Church** (Andreaskirche), where his funeral took place.

Also of interest in the Harz Mountain region are medieval **Quedlinburg** and **Wernigerode,** rich in half-timbered dwellings, **Nordhausen,** where the old fortifications are now pleasant promenades, and **Naumberg,** with remarkable thirteenth-century statues in Peter-Pauls-Dom.

SAXONY

The former kingdom of Saxony has some of Germany's most picturesque mountains and two of its most important cities — Dresden, the cultural capital of the east, and Leipzig, renowned for its music and its trade fairs. Through Saxony flows the historic River Elbe, where Russian and American troops met in

World War II. In its city of Meissen, some of the world's finest porcelain is created. Richard Wagner was born in Saxony, and Johann Sebastian Bach spent his most productive years there. In Dresden — before it was completely demolished in World War II — Germany's grandest Baroque architecture stood and is now being re-created. Saxony offers historic cities, tranquil landscapes, and incomparable museums to the traveler. On no account should it be missed.

DRESDEN

Until February 13, 1945, this city straddling the River Elbe was unparalleled in Germany for the beauty of its architecture and its art. Known as the German Florence, it was largely the eighteenth-century creation of Augustus the Strong, elector of Saxony, king of Poland, and great-grandfather of France's Louis

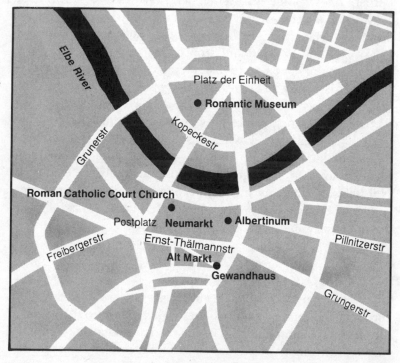

DRESDEN

XVI. It was one of the world's grandest Baroque cities, with cherubs perched on its fountains and rooftops. Its oval-domed Frauenkirche (Church of Our Lady) was the finest example of Protestant ecclesiastical architecture in the world. Its gold sandstone facades danced with alcoves, windows, and decoration.

But for two nights in February, a total of 1,300 British and American bombers pounded the city. The bombing caused an inferno that left 135,000 people dead, 75,000 houses and apartments demolished, and the Frauenkirche and the Semper Opera House, where Wagner's operas were first heralded, rubble.

Nearly half a century later, charred skeletons of buildings remain as a reminder of that ghastly time. But bit by bit, restoration *has* gotten under way. Painstakingly, the Opera House has been rebuilt, the Royal Palace is under reconstruction, and the Zwinger Palace, already once reconstructed, is being repaired again. And even though some 206 paintings were destroyed in the 1945 conflagration and hundreds are still unaccounted for, Dresden's painting collection is a treasure, its porcelain incomparable.

Dresden's major attractions follow.

Albertinum Museum: Originally a sixteenth-century arsenal, then a royal storehouse, it was not until the turn of the century that the Albertinum became a museum. Today it is one of Germany's finest. In its Gallery of the Old Masters (Gemäldegalerie Alter Meister) hang Raphael's *The Sistine Madonna,* Giorgione's *Sleeping Venus,* Rembrandt's *Portrait of a Bearded Old Man,* Jean Etienne Liotard's *The Chocolate Girl,* as well as Holbeins, Van Dycks, Veroneses, and the paintings of Old Dresden by the younger Canaletto (Bernardo Bellotto). Most of these were lovingly collected by Augustus the Strong's son and successor, Augustus III, who is said to have viewed *The Sistine Madonna* in a cloister in Italy when he was still a crown prince and determined to have it. Once he was on the throne he sent Count Heinrich von Brühl — himself an art connoisseur — to buy it for him. When it came, he moved his throne from the light of the window so *The Sistine Madonna* would have the better light. Technically, the Old Masters collection belongs in the Zwinger Palace, on which, it is hoped, repairs will be finished in 1992. But until then, these great works can be seen in the Albertinum. The Albertinum's own collection, in the **New Masters' Gallery** (Neue Meister Galerie), consists of eighteenth- and nineteenth-century paintings by, among others, Manet, Renoir, Van Gogh, Degas, and Gauguin, as well as German Impressionists. There is also an impressive armor display.

The most unusual collection in the Albertinum is the exhibit of bejeweled objects in the **Green Vault** (Grünes Gewölbe), so named for the green-painted burglar-proof and fireproof rooms with walls eighty inches thick in which it was kept in the Royal Palace. Five of these rooms survived the 1945 fire bombing — the only rooms in Old Dresden that did and still stand. When reconstruction of the palace is finally completed (it is just getting under way now), the late Renaissance and early rococo pendants of precious jewels, the ivory carvings by Bavarian Balthasar Permoser, the pearl- and emerald-encrusted gold crucifixes and swords, the sixteenth- and seventeenth-century goblets of gold and ivory and silver and coral will be moved there. The highlight of the Green Vault is the *Court of Delhi on the Birthday of One of Its Great Moguls* — 137 enameled, pure-gold figures of courtiers, animals, and birds in miniature, studded with diamonds and rubies by Johann Melchior Dinglinger, a Swabian who became the Benvenuto Cellini of Dresden. There is also an eclectic collection of fanciful objects of all kinds known as the **Chamber of Marvels**. The Albertinum is open from 9:00 A.M. to 5:00 P.M. on Tuesday and Thursday through Saturday, and until 6:00 P.M. on Wednesday. Closed Monday.

Beautiful Doorway (Schöne Pforte), Johanneum, Neumarkt: This richly decorated Renaissance doorway, now at the entrance to the **Transport Museum** with its exhibits of planes, ships, and trains, was once the door from the Royal Palace into the Royal Palace Chapel. The museum is open from 9:00 A.M. to 5:00 P.M. April to September, except Monday, and from 10:00 A.M. to 5:00 P.M. October to March, except Monday.

Brühl Terrace (Brühlsche Terrasse): Napoleon called this terrace above the Elbe "the balcony of Europe." Earlier, Augustus III's powerful chief minister, Count Heinrich von Brühl, for whom it is named, obviously felt the same way and had his palace built here. Though today the view across the Elbe offers boxy modern buildings rather than Baroque domes and the river traffic is largely limited to big, white, day-tripping boats, the terrace is still a pleasant place for a stroll. It is the site of the Albertinum Museum.

Church of Our Lady (Frauenkirche), Neumarkt: A figure of Martin Luther stands before the skeletal remains of what was once the largest and grandest Protestant church in Germany. It was erected in 1739 with money collected by Protestant burghers furious at the erection of the Roman Catholic Court Church. Its dome, "the Lantern," was a Dresden landmark. It seemed a miracle, when the 1945 fire storm had ended, that this church still stood, for no other complete structure in the Old Town had. But on the very next day, its sandstone cupola collapsed. As a monument to the anguish of war, the Frauenkirche has been left as it was then.

Church of the Holy Cross (Kreuzkirche), Altmarkt: This reconstructed Baroque church is known primarily for its boys' choir.

Golden Rider (Goldener Reiter), across Augustus Bridge in Neustadt: This larger-than-life gilded equestrian statue of Augustus the Strong, designed in 1736 by Wiedemann of Augsburg, marks the entryway to Neustadt, that part of Dresden on the right bank of the Elbe.

Mosaic Wall (Fürstenzug), Augustusstrasse: Because it was made of kiln-baked Meissen china, this elaborate mosaic wall of pictures of the rulers of Saxony from the twelfth through the twentieth centuries stood undisturbed through the flames that licked across this city in the 1945 fire storm.

New City (Neustadt): Nineteenth-century pink-and-gold burghers' houses have been reconstructed along the main pedestrian mall here on the Elbe's right bank. There is a **Romantic Museum** (a Romantic movement flourished here in the early nineteenth century), as well as ethnological and folk art museums and the elegant Hotel Bellevue. Still, there is little to see here in comparison to the attractions of the left bank.

Roman Catholic Court Church (Hofkirche), Terrassen Ufer, opposite the Augustus Bridge: Now a cathedral, this eighteenth-century Baroque church was designed by Italian architect Gaetano Chiaveri. Augustus the Strong had it built to please his Catholic subjects. Though its roof and interior were destroyed in 1945, its tower remained standing and most of its artworks had already been removed. It is notable for a 1722 pulpit, the work of Balthasar Permoser, and the last and largest (3,000 pipes) organ that eighteenth-century master organ builder Gottfried Silbermann ever made. Guided English-language tours of the cathedral are offered Monday through Thursday at 11:00 A.M. and 2:00 P.M., Friday and Saturday at 1:00 and 2:00 P.M., and Sunday at 1:00 P.M.

Royal Palace (Königlicher Palast): As this book went to press, a small museum of photographs of the palace as it was before the 1945 bombing and just afterward were on display along with fragments of friezes, pediments, and walls. The palace as such does not exist, only the fragments and a few rooms. Visiting hours are uncertain.

Royal Stables (Marstall), Schlossplatz: It only takes a minute to step off the street into this quiet reconstructed Baroque parade ground with gilded horses' heads and the coats of arms of Saxony decorating the arcades around it.

Semper Opera House (Semper Oper), Theaterplatz: This recreated opera house, opened with great fanfare in 1985, is a copy of the original theater built here between 1837 and 1841 by Gottfried Semper and rebuilt by his son, Manfred, after a fire in 1869. In the latest Opernhaus, all the colors and decorative effects of the second opera house (included marbleized stucco) have been returned.

In the square outside are statues of nineteenth-century King Johannes, ruler of Saxony and translator of Dante, astride his horse and of Carl Maria von Weber, who headed the Dresden Opera from 1816 to 1826. The opera house is open to the public on guided tours. Information on them is available at the Schinkelwache on Theaterplatz, the city's central ticket agency, which is open from 2:00 to 6:00 P.M. Monday; from 10:00 A.M. to noon and 1:00 to 5:00 P.M. Tuesday; from 1:00 to 5:00 P.M. on Thursday; and from 1:00 to 3:00 P.M. on Friday.

Zwinger Palace (Zwinger Palast): When fire destroyed this royal palace in 1701, Augustus the Strong began to realize a dream he had cherished for years — to build a palace comparable to Versailles, with gardens, fountains, and promenades for outdoor entertainments along the riverbank. As architect for this undertaking, he chose Matthäus Daniel Pöppelmann. Today's reconstructed Zwinger, which, sadly, is having to be restored again (apparently pollution has caused the sandstone of the postwar Zwinger to crack), was the outer court of the palace that Augustus the Strong had planned. Unfortunately, he did not live to see it completed. But he did see and enjoy the Meissen porcelain — the great wealth of eighteenth-century Dresden — that is displayed here.

Meissen came into being when a Thuringian alchemist, Johann Friedrich Böttger, took refuge in Dresden. He had fled Berlin after he was accused of being a magician for trying to turn base metals into gold. Even if Berlin authorities looked askance at such projects, pleasure-loving Augustus the Strong, who always needed gold to finance his many architectural projects, didn't. He eagerly welcomed Böttger and told him to show what he could do. Böttger never produced mineral gold, but continuing experiments already under way in Dresden to develop a porcelain to rival that of the Orient, he invented Europe's first porcelain.

Delicate but strong, it was an unqualified success. In Böttger's porcelain, Augustus had the riches he wanted. To make sure he did not lose his master porcelain maker, Augustus shut Böttger up to work, first in underground rooms along the river in Dresden, then in a castle down the Elbe in Meissen. Night and day, Böttger was expected to produce. He did, but he died a madman — some say from drink, others from the solitary nature of his work. In those Zwinger rooms that are still open, you can see

9. In Dresden this Meissen wall withstood the heat of the Allied fire storm in World War II.

some of his early red porcelain objects (red was the first color produced), as well as later porcelain pieces, including life-size animals and birds, tureens, and ginger jars. Meissen's most notable designers were Johann Gregorious Höroldt, Johann Joachim Kändler, and Johann Friedrich Eberlein. A scientific-instrument collection of early telescopes, globes, and weights and scales is also worth seeing here. The porcelain galleries are open Monday through Thursday from 9:30 A.M. to 4:00 P.M. and Saturday and Sunday from 9:30 A.M. to 4:00 P.M. The instrument collection is open from 9:00 A.M. to 4:00 P.M., except Thursday.

DRESDEN ENVIRONS

Both upriver and downriver from Dresden are inviting tourist destinations. In summer they can be easily visited on boat excursions of the White Fleet (Weisse Flotte). About seven miles upriver is the Baroque palace of **Pillnitz** on the right bank of the Elbe, colorfully designed by Zwinger architect Pöppelmann in an Oriental style with sloping roofs and sphinxes and a formal

French-style garden with an English-style addition. Augustus II called it his "pleasure seat." Its garden is open to the public.

Twenty miles north of Dresden is another mostly Pöppelmann creation, the large hunting castle of **Moritzburg** in a pretty island setting. It may be visited Tuesday through Sunday from 10:00 A.M. to 2:30 P.M.

Still farther upstream are the fortresses of **Königstein** and **Lilienstein** on opposite sides of the river. Beyond these rise the sandstone crags of Saxon Switzerland.

Downriver, about twenty miles above the city of Meissen, looms the late Gothic fortress castle of **Albrechtsburg**. Constructed in the fifteenth century, its history is recounted inside in nineteenth-century Romantic paintings. For a time in the eighteenth century, Meissen porcelain was manufactured inside. Rising beside the castle is a thirteenth-century High Gothic cathedral.

MEISSEN

Founded in 930, Meissen is one of Saxony's oldest towns, prettily set among hills and vineyards. At this writing, reconstruction in the half-timbered **Old Town** made it less attractive than it would otherwise have been, but work has been done on its fifteenth-century **Town Hall** (Rathaus) and the lovely sound of its porcelain carillon can be heard ringing from the **Church of Our Lady** (Frauenkirche). A somber curiosity here is the little memorial chapel to Meissen's soldiers killed in World War I.

At the porcelain factory on Leninstrasse, busloads of tourists are disgorged daily to see how Meissen is delicately hand-painted. To avoid the crowds, make your visit as early as possible. The demonstrations are given April through October from 8:00 A.M. to noon and 1:00 to 3:00 P.M. Tuesday through Sunday. If you want to buy Meissen, a small shop on the marketplace sells it.

HALLE

Halle, thirty-one miles northwest of Leipzig, has been a commercial and industrial city for years and, despite being frequently bombed in World War II, has much of interest to see.

Cathedral (Dom), Domplatz: It was in this thirteenth-century Gothic church that George Frideric Handel, born in Halle, was the organist for a time when he was seventeen.

Giebichenstein Castle (Burg Giebichenstein): Set above the River Saale a little outside of town on the Crollwitz tram line are the ruins of this imperial castle whose origins date from the tenth century. There is a pleasant walk along the river from this site.

Halle Museum (Halloren Museum), Manfelderstrasse 52: For centuries, Halle was known for the salt springs — *halis* — from which it gets its name. In this museum, in addition to exhibits detailing the extraction of the salt from the water, is the exquisite silver drinking cup collection of the old Salt Workers Guild. The museum, however, is open only one Sunday morning each month. Halle-Information at Kleinschmeiden 6 can provide information on which Sunday.

Handel House (Handel Haus), Grosse Nikolaistrasse 5: It was in this golden-yellow house below the marketplace that George Frideric Handel was born in 1685. Pictures and documents recount how his ability at the organ made itself evident when he was only ten. Though his father, a surgeon, wanted him to be a lawyer and he studied at Halle University, his love was clearly for music and drama, and he soon was en route to Hamburg, then a great opera center. He composed his first operas there and was nearly killed in a duel with a fellow musician — he was only saved because a button on his jacket deflected his opponent's sword. Exhibits tell of his later work in Italy and finally in England, where he spent a great part of his life as a court musician. There are period instruments and material on other Halle musicians in the house. Recordings of Handel music are played for visitors and, from time to time, Handel concerts are held here. In late May and June annually, Halle honors its favorite son with a Handel Festival. The museum-house is open Tuesday through Sunday from 9:30 A.M. to 5:30 P.M.

Market Church (Marktkirche), Marktplatz: In this four-towered sixteenth-century church where two of the towers are linked by a bridge, Johann Sebastian Bach's oldest son, Wilhelm Friedemann Bach, was the organist for eighteen years.

Moritzburg Castle Ruins (Moritzburg), Robert-Franz Ring: Erected in the sixteenth century by the bishop of Magdeburg, Moritzburg Castle was largely destroyed in the Thirty Years' War, but in the 1890s some reconstruction began. Today, this ruin, with its agreeable courtyard, is among the major sites for performances during the Handel Festival.

Museum Geisseltal, Domstrasse 5: Those with a geological bent should enjoy this rich and unusual collection of fossils of the Geisseltal region. Information on its hours is available from Halle Information on weekdays.

Rannischestrasse and Schmeerstrasse: Handsome town houses, often with richly decorated facades and upper stories, line these streets, but their old-fashioned charm is, to a considerable extent, undermined by tram wires and tracks and endless clatter.

Red Tower (Roter Turm), Marktplatz: This 276-foot-high Gothic clock tower contributes its splendid silhouette to the sunset skyscape of old Halle. By day, unfortunately, the skyscape is marred by the network of overhead electrical wires and, in recent years, by the smog from brown coal and the chemical industry.

LEIPZIG

The name "Leipzig" seems to have come from the Slavonic *lipa* for "linden tree." Commonly known as "the Fair City," since the twelfth century tradesmen have gathered here to display their wares. Situated on both the trade route between Poland and Thuringia and the route between northern Germany and Bohemia, it was the natural location, from earliest times, for trade fairs, which today are held twice yearly on twenty-four acres of exhibition land. Fair times, in September and March, are definitely *not* the time for tourist visits here. The shortage of hotel space means that some fair participants must be housed as far away as Dresden (ninety miles) and bused here. The tourist coming here should bear in mind, too, that a quarter of Leipzig was destroyed in World War II and its rebuilding was largely in Communist Modern style. It therefore lacks the picturesqueness of smaller historic towns of eastern Germany. Leipzig (population 549,230) is, however, a dynamic city. In 1989, Leipzig was the scene of the most active demonstrations against the Communist government of the German Democratic Republic. Leipzig's Gewandhaus Orchestra performs some of Germany's finest music. Its Opera House was the first in eastern Germany built after the Second World War.

After Berlin, Leipzig, in the days of the German Democratic Republic, was the most cosmopolitan and up-to-date of East German cities. In its new situation in the Federal Republic, it is determinedly retaining a position of importance.

Its major sites follow.

Auerbach's Cellar (Auerbachs Keller), Grimmaischestrasse 2 (Mädlerpassage): Since 1530 this restaurant has been a popular

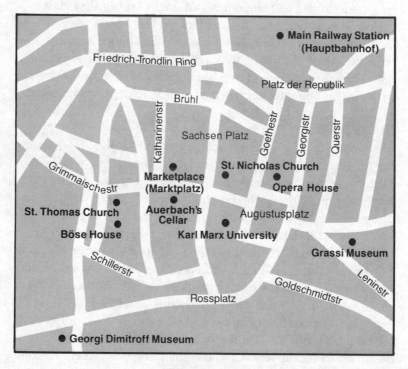

LEIPZIG

eating-and-drinking place with students — not the least of them Johann Wolfgang von Goethe, who studied law at Leipzig University. Later, when he wrote *Faust,* he had Faust and Mephistopheles ride off on a beer keg together from this wine cellar. The original Auerbachs Keller was torn down in 1912, but its reconstructed version remains as popular as its forebear. Statues of Mephistopheles, Faust, and fellow revelers stand at its door.

Böse House (Bösehaus), opposite St. Thomas Church: When Johann Sebastian Bach lived in Leipzig, this sixteenth-century house, now a Bach museum and the repository of Bach archives, was the property of merchant, art connoisseur, and Bach friend Heinrich Georg Böse. Bach lived just across the way in rooms provided by the St. Thomas Choir School, and he was a frequent visitor. Bösehaus now displays engravings of middle-class life in the Bach era, as well as books, music, musical instruments, and costumes of the early eighteenth century. A Bible with Bach's signature on it may be seen. The house is open Tuesday through Sunday from 9:00 A.M. to 4:30 P.M., and concerts are sometimes given in a charming concert hall.

Coffee Tree (Zum Kaffeebaum), Kleine Fleischergasse 4: In the dark interior of this restored seventeenth-century restaurant with a Turk under a coffee tree over the door, the nineteenth-century composer Robert Schumann edited his *New Journal for Music.* Schumann, like Goethe, had come to the university to study law, but he soon tired of it and spent his time at Gewandhaus concerts, giving concerts for his friends, practicing the piano, falling in love, smoking cigars, drinking, and reading poetry. Other frequenters of the Kaffeebaum were Liszt, Goethe, and Wagner.

Fine Arts Museum (Museum der bildenen Künste), Dimitroffstrasse: In the past, the upstairs of this former supreme court building of the Third Reich was devoted to the life of the Bulgarian Communist Georgi Dimitroff, who successfully defended himself against Hermann Göring, who had accused him of complicity in the 1933 fire that partly destroyed the Berlin Reichstag. Downstairs, in the art museum, is a collection of works by such old German masters as Martin Schongauer and Lucas Cranach the Elder. Works by Teniers, Van Eyck, and Metsu are also on display. The museum is open Tuesday through Friday from 8:00 A.M. to 5:00 P.M. and on weekends from 8:00 A.M. to 2:00 P.M. As this book went to press, it remained undecided whether the Dimitroff display would be kept.

Grassi Museum Complex (Grassi Museum), Johannisplatz: There is an outstanding display of musical instruments of the Bach period here. The museum hours are extremely variable, however.

Karl Marx University (Karl Marx Universität), Augustusplatz: Though there is little to interest the visitor here, the thirty-four-story jagged university tower, familiarly known as "The Jagged Tooth," has become a landmark of the city.

Katherinenstrasse: The handsome patrician houses (undergoing restoration as this book went to press) along this street attest to the importance of Leipzig as a commercial city after the Middle Ages. Fur was then, and continues to be, a major product here — furriers' shops line the side streets and the wide Brühl, the old center of the fur trade, and a fur fair is held annually. Of particular interest on this street is the eighteenth-century **Romanus House** (Romanushaus), with its statue of a flirtatious Hermes in front. Conrad Romanus, owner of the house, was responsible for the city's first street lights and for a sedan-chair service for theatergoers. Unfortunately, he overextended himself and is said to have stolen city funds and ended up in jail, so he actually spent little time in this much-decorated dream house.

Main Railway Station (Hauptbahnhof), Bahnhofplatz: Built in 1907–1915, this imposing structure, with its twenty-six tracks inside a shell of steel and glass, is one of Europe's largest railroad stations.

Marketplace (Marktplatz): Restored or reconstructed historic structures on this little marketplace include the **Old Town Hall** (Altes Rathaus), the **Old Weighing House** (Alte Waage), where foreign imports to the fairs were weighed in the old days, and the seventeenth-century **Kings' House** (Königshaus), where Saxon rulers stayed on state visits and entertained the royalty of other lands. Today the Kings' House houses a clothing shop.

Monument to the Battle of the Nations (Völkerschlachtdenkmal), three miles southeast of the Main Railway Station: This enormous structure commemorates the first major battle of modern times in which Russians, Prussians, Austrians, Bavarians, and Swedes successfully fought off the forces of Napoleon in 1813. Some 500,000 men were engaged in the battle, and 150,000 were killed or wounded. The monument is open (for climbs up the 500 steps to the top) daily from 9:00 A.M. to 4:00 P.M.

Neues Gewandhaus, Augustusplatz: This modernistic ten-year-old structure (there are no right angles in it) replaces the Gewandhaus that was destroyed in the Second World War. Established in 1743, the Gewandhaus Orchestra is the oldest professional orchestra in Germany. It gets its curious name, which means "Cloth Merchants' Trade Hall," from the fact that when it was first established, its headquarters were in a linen merchant's warehouse. Acoustics in the New Gewandhaus, whose conductor is Kurt Masur, recently named music director of the New York Philharmonic, are extraordinary. The concert hall may not be visited, except when there are performances.

Old Town Hall (Altes Rathaus), Marktplatz: This reconstructed sixteenth-century town hall, with its steep gables and arcades and Baroque clock tower, is one of the largest in Germany. Today it contains the **Museum of the City of Leipzig,** which includes a room of memorabilia of Felix Mendelssohn, who came here in 1835 as conductor of the Gewandhaus Orchestra. It is open Tuesday to Sunday from 10:00 A.M. to 6:00 P.M. (The Mendelssohn Room has been undergoing restoration.)

Opera House (Opernhaus), Augustusplatz: This modern structure was opened in 1960 with a performance of native son Richard Wagner's *Parsifal.* It is not open to the public except during performances.

Russian Memorial Church (Russische Gedächtniskirche), Philipp-Rosenthal Strasse and Semmelweissstrasse: This 1912–1913 golden-domed church honors the 22,000 Russians who died in the Battle of the Nations.

St. Nicholas Church (Nikolaikirche), Nikolaistrasse: Demonstrators for democracy gathered at this church in the autumn of 1989, and the candlelight protest marches organized here were of inestimable importance in toppling the Communist government of Erich Honecker and bringing East Germany into the free world.

In earlier times, J. S. Bach, though his primary affiliation was with St. Thomas Church, gave first performances of several of his major works at St. Nicholas. It is open Monday to Thursday, 10:00 A.M. to 6:00 P.M., Friday noon to 6:00 P.M., and Saturday 10:00 A.M. to 4:00 P.M.

St. Thomas Church (Thomaskirche), southwest of the Markt: A larger-than-life statue of J. S. Bach stands outside this thirteenth-century church where the composer came in 1723 at the age of thirty-eight to be cantor and director of the boys' choir and director of music at the university. He remained here until his death in 1750. During his years here, he wrote more than 300 cantatas, the Mass in B Minor, and the *Passion According to St. Matthew*. Today he lies buried near the altar. But it is not only Bach for whom this church is renowned. Martin Luther proclaimed the Reformation from the pulpit, and Richard Wagner was christened here in 1813.

Though originally Romanesque, St. Thomas's interior was transformed to Gothic in the late fifteenth century. The St. Thomas Boys' Choir sings here for the public each Friday at 6:00 P.M. and Saturday at 1:30 P.M., except in July and August. In addition, the church is open Monday through Saturday from 8:00 A.M. to 1:00 P.M. and 2:00 to 6:00 P.M.

Snack Market (Naschmarkt): It was not for the sale of snacks — candies and fruits — that this small marketplace received its name, but for the ceramic pots called *asche* (because they were baked in the ashes) that were sold here in early days. A statue of Goethe, who studied at Leipzig University, stands in this market, the site of an outdoor café now, and the richly decorated Baroque **Old Stock Exchange** (Alte Börse) is at the end of the market.

WITTENBERG
Had the reformer Martin Luther, a professor at the university of Wittenberg in the sixteenth century, not elected to post his

ninety-five theses that are the foundation of Protestantism on a church door here, the world would have been a vastly different place. In this little town with its long main street, its Renaissance Town Hall behind the marketplace, and its abundance of church towers, the memory of Martin Luther's most important hour has never dimmed.

Augustinian Monastery (Augusteum), Collegienstrasse 54: In 1508 the young monk Martin Luther took up residence in this Augustinian monastery that now contains a **Museum of the History of the Reformation** and a room in which Luther preached and lectured. He came to Wittenberg to teach at the university, where his dynamic preaching soon attracted attention. Both as a teacher-monk and later as a married man, he made his home in this now much restored sixteenth-century building. The museum and **Luther Room** (Lutherhalle), with a pulpit he used, are open from 9:00 A.M. to 4:00 P.M. daily, except Monday.

Castle Church (Schlosskirche), Schlossplatz: In 1517, an outraged Martin Luther affixed to the doors of this church his ninety-five theses attacking the Roman Catholic Church's policy of forgiving sins in exchange for monetary contributions. Written in Latin, the language of the educated, the theses might have gone relatively unnoticed had they not, unbeknownst to Luther, been translated into German and widely distributed in town. The monk-teacher was summoned to Worms to explain his theses to Holy Roman Emperor Charles V. It was on his return that he was "captured" by Saxon elector Frederick the Wise and hidden from papal authorities in Eisenach for the better part of a year (see Eisenach, in Thuringia).

The original wooden church doors have been replaced with impressive bronze ones that bear the Latin text of the theses. Inside the church, simple bronze plaques mark the burial places of Luther and his friend and adviser, the Greek scholar Philip Melanchthon. The church is open Tuesday through Sunday from 10:00 A.M. to noon and 2:00 to 4:00 P.M.

College Street (Collegienstrasse): At one end of this street is an oak tree marking the spot where Luther in 1517 burned the papal bull condemning him. Farther along, the Melanchthon

House is open as a museum, and, finally, the Augusteum is here.

Marketplace (Marktplatz): A statue of Luther by Johann Gottfried Schadow and one of Melanchthon by Friedrich Drake are centerpieces of this square, whose backdrop is the handsome High Renaissance **Town Hall** (Rathaus). Gabled Renaissance houses now containing shops edge part of the square, a popular sunning place for Wittenbergers in warm seasons.

Melanchthon House (Melanchthonhaus), Collegienstrasse 60: There is relatively little to see inside this Renaissance house-museum where Melanchthon lived in the sixteenth century, but here that Greek teacher and scholar is believed to have corrected Luther's translation of the New Testament into vernacular German from the Greek. During his "imprisonment" in Eisenach's Wartburg, Luther had sections of his manuscript, as he finished them, taken down to Melanchthon for his approval. There is a peaceful garden to visit behind the house where a little fountain has been bubbling from a spring on the edge of town ever since Melanchthon's day. The house is open Tuesday through Friday from 9:00 A.M. to 5:00 P.M. and on Saturday and Sunday from 10:00 A.M. to 12:00 P.M. and from 2:00 to 5:00 P.M.

Parish Church (Stadtkirche), off the Marktplatz: The towers of this fourteenth-century church in which Luther sometimes preached and where he married the former nun Catherine von Bora can be seen from the Marketplace. Inside is an altar triptych showing Luther in knight's disguise and Melanchthon. It is attributed to Lucas Cranach the Elder, who was mayor here. While Luther was incarcerated in the Wartburg (*see* Eisenach, in Thuringia), his followers in the Reformation altered the rules of their church so that priests might marry. The church is open daily, except Sunday, when services are held. Daily hours are from 10:00 A.M. to noon and 2:00 to 5:00 P.M.

Wittenberg also is the site, on Schlossstrasse, of a house where the painter Lucas Cranach lived and had his workshop. Cranach, who was mayor and councilor of Wittenberg several times, bought the house in 1520. On the front of it is a sandstone relief of the elector John Frederick, who once resided in Wittenberg.

THE BALTIC COAST

At present the Baltic Coast of eastern Germany is distinctly for the traveler who likes to go where the tourists aren't. Though there are miles of beaches here and the remains of once thriving medieval trading towns, wars and communism have taken their toll. There was much bombing of the cities, and the postwar priority was to build up-to-date, not necessarily aesthetically agreeable, housing rather than to restore the past. Here and there you will find soaring red-brick Baltic Gothic churches and step-gabled burgher houses, but often both will be in need of repair. Their medieval or Renaissance grandeur is likely to have beside it a purely functional contemporary structure. The same kinds of northern German architecture are better found in western Germany.

Along the beaches are workers' holiday complexes — strictly functional, with only occasional thatched-roofed cottages.

The curious traveler to eastern Germany with time to spare might, however, wish to explore the Baltic Coast a little. If so, the following sites are worth a stop.

ROSTOCK
Rostock is situated on the Warnow River about eight miles from the Baltic. In the fifteenth and sixteenth centuries, it was an important member of the Hanseatic League, a trade alliance, and its ships sailed to France and Spain, Norway and Russia. Its university, founded in 1419, was the first in northern Europe and numbered among its notable professors the seventeenth-century astronomer Johann Kepler. But in the seventeenth and eighteenth centuries, Rostock suffered from invasions and fires.

In the Seven Years' War of 1756 to 1763, it was occupied by the Swedes, the Prussians, and the Russians and in Napoleon's day by the French. Not until the mid-nineteenth century, when its sailing fleet was surpassed only by Hamburg's in Germany, did it begin to come out from under its centuries of hardship, and

10. A gate tower from the old town walls of Rostock.

after World War I, it developed an aircraft as well as a shipbuilding industry. These industries, of course, made it a prime bombing target in World War II. Until then, it had retained much of its old Hanseatic quality. Now most of its medieval structures are gone, but a few remain and there has been some rebuilding in the old style.

Most notable of the old structures still standing is the towering fifteenth-century Baltic Gothic **St. Mary's Church** (Marienkirche), with its seventeenth-century astronomical clock embellished with salamanders and cows. Unfortunately, the rest of its whitewashed interior needs painting.

Rostock's other tourist attractions include its turreted red-brick **Town Hall** (Rathaus) and the remains of its old town walls, in particular the fourteenth-century **Kröpelin Gate** (Kröpeliner Tor) on Kröpelinerstrasse, now the **Museum of Cultural History;** the restored Renaissance **Stone Gate** (Steintor) on Steinstrasse; the **Lagebush Tower** (Lagebuschturm); and the thirteenth-century Gothic **Cow Tower** (Kuhtor). There is also a zoo. There are restored step-gabled houses here and there, and an effort has been made to build modern dwellings with stepped gables to help them blend in with the buildings of the past.

SCHWERIN

Of principal interest in this city, now the capital of the Mecklenburg region, is the turreted castle, built on an island between two small lakes, where ducks and swans swim and weeping willows nod. Though as long ago as the twelfth century, the princes of Mecklenburg had their palace here, the present structure is nineteenth-century neo-Renaissance, inspired by the French Loire Château of Chambord. Parts have been restored and are now open, but as of this writing extensive repair work was being done on it.

Other sights of the city include the court theater next to the castle, the fifteenth-century red-brick Baltic-style cathedral, half-timbered houses, the Baroque Church of St. Nicholas (Schelfkirche), and the National Museum, which has some interesting seventeenth-century Dutch paintings.

STRALSUND

This former Hanseatic League city was severely damaged in World War II air raids. Reconstruction has been slow, but there are several outstanding structures — fifteenth-century **St. Mary's Church** (Marienkirche) on the **Neuer Markt,** an enormous red-brick Baltic Gothic structure, with an octagonal tower and steeple. The tower affords a fine view of the city. The lacelike, late-fourteenth-century **Town Hall** (Rathaus) in the **Alter Markt** — elegant and graceful but in need of much repair — is said to have been built with ransom money paid for imprisoned fourteenth-century noblemen. Opposite the Town Hall at Alter Markt 5 is the house of former burgomaster Bertram Wulflam; it has a splendid red-brick, pilastered, fourteenth-century gable topped with copper turrets. To the left of this, the pretty gable-fronted house of the fifteenth century has been remodeled in Baroque style. The height of these patrician houses allowed several stories of storage space for merchandise inside. If you stroll around the town, look for other Gothic, Renaissance, and Baroque houses.

Stralsund also offers the fourteenth-century **St. Nicholas Church** (Nikolaikirche) in the **Alter Markt,** which is rather like the Marienkirche but undergoing repair, and the fourteenth-century **St. James Church** (Jakobkirche) on Böttcherstrasse, which is also being rebuilt. There is an interesting **Oceanographic Museum** (Meereskundliches Museum) open Wednesday through Sunday from 10:00 A.M. to 5:00 P.M. in the former **St. Katherine's Monastery** (Katherinenkloster) on Mönchsstrasse. Housed here, too, is the **Museum of Cultural History** (Kulturhistorisches Museum), with exhibits of the old-time fisherman's life of this Mecklenburg area.

From Stralsund, there is regular ferry service to the little island of Rügen with its rich bird life and impressive white chalk cliffs overlooking the sea. Ships of the White Fleet (Weisse Flotte) go from both Rügen and Stralsund to picturesque Hiddensee, a narrow strip of meadow and heath and dunes where, in the village of Kloster, playwright Gerhart Hauptmann lived and died and where Thomas Mann frequently visited.

WISMAR

Like Rostock, Wismar was an important member of the Hanseatic League, and, like Rostock, it suffered invasions from Sweden. It was also heavily bombed by English and American planes just as World War II neared its end, and only one of its three redbrick Baltic Gothic churches, the **St. Nicholas Church** (Nikolaikirche), survived without damage. All that remains of thirteenthcentury **St. Mary's** (Marienkirche) is its tower, while **St. George's** (Georgenkirche) is, for the moment at least, only a shell. Still, Wismar is a pleasant town to explore. There are step-gabled houses around the **Market Square** (Marktplatz), which is among the largest in northern Germany. Most impressive among these houses is Number 20, the red-brick **Old Swede** (Alter Schwede), named because of its seventeenth-century occupation by Swedish forces. Built in 1380, it is notable for its triple-pilastered gable and its tiles and for being the oldest Gothic brick house in Wismar. The gabled brick houses were those of the well-to-do patricians in these and other Hanseatic towns, while the small, timber-framed houses belonged to craftsmen and the middle class.

Number 15, a double-gabled house, was the headquarters of the Swedish commandant. In one restored corner of the square is the sixteenth-century copper-roofed water tower that supplied water to Wismar through wooden pipes till the turn of the century.

Other attractions of Wismar include the sixteenth-century **Princely Court** (Fürstenhof), once a seat of the dukes of the region and now housing the city archives. Wismar's three-story **New Court** (Neuer Hof) is a particularly outstanding example of Baltic Renaissance architecture.

GETTING THERE, SLEEPING, EATING, AND ENTERTAINMENT

Now that there is one single Germany, traveling to and within the former German Democratic Republic — an area about the size of Tennessee — is easily done once again. As this eastern part of the country is rich in cultural, historic, religious, and scenic sites, exploring it is well worth doing. There are still inconveniences, of course — first-class hotel space is lacking, and restaurants that have been in government ownership are just becoming private. The bureaucrats who, in the forty-one years of communism, controlled most of the country's museums and tourist offices are still not all gone, and the days and the hours that tourist facilities and museums are open may, as a result, be uncertain and depend on local whim. Hotel and shop clerks, similarly, may not yet have adjusted to the more efficient ways of the West — particularly in smaller communities — but visiting eastern Germany, all the same, will be less arduous than visiting other countries of the East. Though English is not widely spoken, people are increasingly learning it.

Pan Am offers nonstop service from New York to Berlin, Lufthansa from Newark to Berlin, and there is change-of-plane service from Atlanta, Boston, Chicago, Dallas/Fort Worth, Los Angeles, Miami, Philadelphia, Washington, San Francisco, and St. Louis on many airlines. Dresden and Leipzig may also be reached with one-stop change-of-plane Lufthansa service from the East Coast of the United States.

Though it will be some time before all railway tracks in eastern Germany are ready to receive the high-speed trains that have been traveling in the west, a rapid InterCity Express now links Frankfurt with Berlin with continuing InterCity service to Dresden and Leipzig. GermanRail Flexipass and GermanRail Junior Flexipass (for those between eleven and twenty-six) may now be used for travel throughout the country and are available in the United States, at a saving, for five, ten, or fifteen days of travel within a month. Both first- and second-class passes are sold and may be used on InterCity Expresses as well as on ordinary trains. Eurailpasses, which also must be bought in the United States before departure and offer savings, are now good in eastern Germany. Further information is available from travel agents, from German Rail, 747 Third Avenue, New York, New York 10017 (Tel. 212-308-3100), or RailEurope, 226 Westchester Avenue, White Plains, New York 10604 (Tel. 800-345-1990).

Those who would like to drive through eastern Germany will find roads good on the whole. Hertz and Avis rental cars are available in major cities and Auto-Europe at Box 1097 in Camden, Maine 04843 (Tel. 800-223-5555) makes advance reservations for cars in Berlin. It is generally cheaper to reserve a car before departing for Europe. Road assistance is provided in emergencies by Allgemeiner Deutscher Automobil Club (ADAC).

More detailed information is available from the German National Tourist Office, 747 Third Avenue, New York, New York 10017 (Tel. 212-308-3300).

Because in Communist years, it was the showcase city of Berlin that was kept best supplied with foodstuffs, the number of restaurants offering fine fare elsewhere (except in Leipzig) was limited then and continues to be. But everywhere there are regional specialties that have not been forgotten. In Berlin, a meaty pig's knuckle (*Eisbein mit Sauerkraut und Erbsen*), cooked with dried peas and sauerkraut, is a satisfying midwinter dish. Cold giant meatballs (*Bouletten*) are often found in Berlin bars. *Berliner Pfannkuchen* — jelly doughnuts — are a favorite sweet. Pea soup with salt pork and croutons (*Löffelerbsen mit Speck*) and a mixed grill (*Schlachteplatte*) are other Berlin specialties. In the Spreewald, eel in a green-herb sauce (*Aal grün*) and freshwater fish may be on menus.

Thuringia is renowned for its sausage and its sauerbraten with dumplings (*Thüringer Sauerbraten mit Klossen*). Along the Baltic Coast, fish restaurants (*Gastmahl des Meeres*) are the places to dine. A thick soup like green pea soup (*Erbsensuppe*) often opens a meal. Good salads will be beet (*rote Rüben*), cabbage (*Kraut*), or cucumber (*Gurken*). Potatoes (*Kartoffeln*) or dumplings (*Knödel*) are part of virtually every dinner.

The specialty of Leipzig is *Leipsziger Allerlei* — a succotash-like combination of peas, carrots, asparagus, and mushrooms that sometimes is given an additional fillip by little balls of minced crab and veal.

As this book went to press, the cakes and ice-cream confections of eastern Germany were invariably too sweet and the flavor of artificial ingredients overwhelming. For the visitor's waistline, this is just as well, for the breads of Germany — mainly dark — are varied and tempting. Breakfasts (generally included in the hotel-room price) are a fine time to try them, for rolls, dark and salt breads, along with eggs, ham, wurst, and cheese are usually offered. Neither beer nor wine is exceptional in eastern Germany, though grapes are grown in the hillsides near Meissen and in the Saale and Unstrut valleys, where a dry white wine is produced. As for beer, virtually every town has its own brewery. (A

Berlin beer specialty is *Berliner Weisse mit Schuss* — a light beer with fruit juice in it.)

There follow, in alphabetical order by town, a selection of hotels, restaurants, and entertainments in the principal tourist centers.

BERLIN
HOTELS

Berolina, Karl-Marx Allee 31 (Tel. 210-9541). Accommodations are satisfactory but not charming in this 350-room hotel near Alexanderplatz. The two restaurants include one specializing in Berlin cuisine.

Domhotel, Platz der Akademie (Tel. 220-4509). Opened in 1990, this 450-room deluxe hotel is in the heart of eastern Berlin's historic district in close proximity to the Schauspielhaus that is now the home of the Berlin Symphony Orchestra. Its amenities include three restaurants and a business center offering translating and interpreting services.

Grand Hotel, Friedrichstrasse 158-164 (Tel. 209-20). The height of elegance, this 370-room hotel that opened in 1987 surely lives up to its name. It was the first hotel in Eastern Europe to be included in *Great Hotels of the World*. Service is impeccable, rooms luxurious. It has four restaurants offering special fare. In **Le Grand Silhouette,** the menu is French; in **Zur Goldenen Gans,** Thuringian; in **Forellen Quintet,** dishes — mainly fish — of the Spreewald are served; in the **Peking,** the cuisine is Chinese. The **Café Bauer** offers fine cakes and pastries. The double room rate in low season, including breakfast, was $355 as this book went to press, the single room rate $280.

Metropol, Friedrichstrasse 150-153 (Tel. 220-40). This 320-room hotel refurbished in 1989 caters, in particular, to businessmen and is lacking in the luxuriousness and the posh quality of the Grand and the Dom. Its convenient location is within a block of the Friedrichstrasse S-Bahn station, however. The double room rate is about $210, the single rate $170. There is a fitness room, a nightclub, and a pool.

Palasthotel, Karl-Liebknecht Strasse 5 (Tel. 24-10). In the past, tour groups have frequented this enormous (600 rooms), sprawling hotel where there are twelve restaurants to choose from for those who prefer hotel dining to coping with eating outside a hotel. Rooms — many of them overlooking the River Spree — are adequate but lacking in charm. High-season room rates are about $200 double, $115 single. The Palast has a nightclub, a fitness room, and a pool.

Stadt Berlin, Alexanderplatz (Tel. 2190). Large Russian and Eastern European tour groups were the principal clientele in Communist days of this very standard hotel on Alexanderplatz. Its best features are its *Bierstube,* the **Zille-Stube,** serving typical Berlin fare, and its thirty-eighth-floor restaurant, which has a fine view out over the city.

Unter den Linden, Unter den Linden 14 (Tel. 22-003-11). The location of this 310-room hotel is first rate, near theaters, museums, and historic sites, but it is satisfactory rather than inviting.

RESTAURANTS

Bear in mind that restaurants, like hotel rooms, are still in short supply, so it is essential to make reservations.

Alte Munze, Karl-Liebknecht Strasse and Karl-Marx Allee. Old Berlin dishes like *Schweinhaxe* (pigs' feet), *Hackepeter* (steak tartare, pork, and onions), *Eisbein Schmalz* (lard spread made with fried onions and bacon), and *Schusterjunge* (dark rolls) are served with beer here.

Am Marstall, Marx-Engels Forum 1020 (Tel. 212-4569). This is an elegant and expensive restaurant, but it is usually worth the price. A dinner for two might be $50. Reservations are essential.

Bierschanke in der Gerichtklause, Poststrasse 28. Typical Berlin pork dishes are offered in a picturesque setting.

Ephraim Palais, Poststrasse 16 (Tel. 2171-3164). This dressy restaurant on the Spree has a good menu and high prices.

Ermeler Haus, Am Märkisches Ufer 10 (Tel. 275-5113). Fine German fare is served in the little Spreeside restaurant in the basement here.

Keller Restaurant Brecht Haus, Chauseestrasse 125 (Tel. 282-3848). Upstairs is a **Bertolt Brecht Museum** with tours of the rooms where dramatist Brecht and his wife, Helene Weigel, spent their last days. (It is open Monday through Thursday from 9:00 A.M. to 6:00 P.M. and Saturday and Sunday from 10:00 A.M. to 6:00 P.M. In the cellar, decorated with Brecht memorabilia, is this restaurant. It is not open on weekends.

Moscau, Karl-Marx Allee 34 (Tel. 279-4062). If a Russian meal appeals rather than a German one, you might try this spacious restaurant where there is good live music in the evening.

Neubrandenburger Hof, Wilhelm-Pieck Strasse and Borsigstrasse. This is a popular restaurant (Mecklenburg cuisine is the specialty) with dishes at popular prices.

Offenbach-Stube, Stubenkammerstrasse 8. There's good German cuisine here, but unless you take a taxi, it will be hard to find.

Restaurant Wolga, Haus der Sowjetischen Wissenschaft und Kultur, Friedrichstrasse and Otto-Nuschke Strasse. Russian dishes are the specialty in the restaurant started by a former cosmonaut, but they seem to be rarely available.

Turnstuben, Französischer Dom, Platz der Akademie (Tel. 229-3463). A small, intimate, and agreeable restaurant with food that is good but not outstanding.

Weinrestaurant Ganymed, Schiffbauerdamm 5 (Tel. 282-9540). Almost next door to the Berliner Ensemble, this is a favorite with theatergoers and intellectuals. It has a wide choice of items at high prices.

Zur Letzen Instanz, Wasenstrasse 14-16. Situated next to the old Appeals Court, this is a colorful, old-fashioned restaurant with simple German fare.

Zur Rippe, Poststrasse 17 (Tel. 2121-4932). A cozy little restaurant where spareribs in wine sauce are the specialty and prices are reasonable.

For coffee and cake after an afternoon of sightseeing, in addition to Café Bauer are **Café Spreeblick,** Spreeufer 1020, in the St. Nicholas Quarter; **Café Fredericke** at Friedrichstrasse and Claire-Waldorf Strasse; **Café im Palais,** Poststrasse 16 (for the older set); and **Chez Felix** on Schiffbauerdamm near Bahnhof Friedrichstrasse.

ENTERTAINMENT

Music and theater have been a vital part of the city's culture for a long time. Even in Communist days, the theater of the eastern part of Berlin, following in the tradition of Expressionist directors like Erwin Piscator and Max Reinhardt and playwrights like Brecht, has been innovative and imaginative. Though Berlin music has never been so renowned as that of Leipzig, an opera, a concert, or a stage production is well worth attending on a visit here. Tickets are most easily purchased in advance at the Reiseburo on Alexanderplatz.

Berlin Sinfonia Orchester, Oberwallstrasse 6-7. When it is not on the road, the Berlin Symphony Orchestra plays in the stunningly restored Schauspielhaus.

Berliner Ensemble, Bertolt-Brecht Platz 1 (Tel. 28-880). Such classic Brecht dramas as *Mother Courage* and *The Caucasian Chalk Circle,* Shakespeare and Molière plays, and Carl Zuckmayer's *The Captain of Köpenick* are the sorts of productions done in this world-famous Expressionist theater that Brecht founded. Even non-German-speakers, if they are acquainted with the works being presented, should enjoy an evening of theater here. The present director was a pupil of Brecht. The box office is open Monday from 11:00 A.M. to 5:00 P.M., Tuesday through Friday from 11:00 A.M. to 1:30 P.M. and 2:00 to 6:00 P.M., and Saturday from 5:00 to 6:00 P.M.

Deutsche Staatsoper, Unter den Linden 7 (Tel. 372-205-4556). In this rebuilt eighteenth-century opera house with a Corinthian facade, Richard Strauss was the conductor for twenty years. The box office is open Tuesday through Saturday from noon to 6:00 P.M. and one hour before performances.

Deutsches Theater, Schumannstrasse 13-14 (Tel. 287-1225). Enjoyment of performances at this theater will depend largely on knowledge of German.

Die Diestel, Friedrichstrasse 101 (Tel. 207-1291). This principal cabaret in the eastern part of Berlin will be amusing largely to those with a good understanding of German. The box office is open Tuesday through Friday from 3:00 to 7:00 P.M. and Saturday and Sunday from 5:00 to 7:00 P.M.

Friedrichstadtpalast Revue Theater, Friedrichstrasse 107. In this enormous theater, musical revues are performed, or what has been a stage can become a skating rink or pool for aquatics. The quality of presentations is "iffy," however.

Komische Oper, Behrenstrasse 55-57 (Tel. 229-2555). This opera company headquartered just beside the Grand Hotel is known for its development of new ideas. The box office is open Tuesday through Saturday from 2:00 to 6:00 P.M. and for an hour preceding performances.

TOURIST INFORMATION
Martin-Luther Strasse 105 (Tel. 21-23-27-87) or Alexanderplatz.

DRESDEN

HOTELS

Hotel Bellevue, Koepckestrasse (Tel. 566-20). This handsome hotel overlooking a park on the banks of the River Elbe is an expansion of a seventeenth-century restored burgher's house. Baroque elegance is evident everywhere — including in the room furnishings. Among its four restaurants, one specializes in French cuisine and another in Polynesian. The **Pöppelmann Café** looks out on the garden. A pool, sauna, and translation and dispatch services for businessmen are among the amenities. The room rate for two, off-season, is between $225 and $300, but there is no prettier place to stay in Dresden.

Dresdener Hof, Am Neumarkt (Tel. 48-410). This brand-new 335-room deluxe hotel is situated in the heart of what remains of historic Dresden, within a ten-minute walk of the Opera House and the Zwinger and the Albertinum museums. The interior decoration is influenced by the Bauhaus School. The hotel's ten restaurants include one — **The Gourmet** — offering fine French fare and another serving Italian food. A swimming pool, sauna, health club facilities, and a businessmen's center are among the amenities. Rates are comparable to those at the Bellevue.

Hotel Astoria, Ernst-Thälmann Platz (Tel. 47-51-71). The Astoria's location, near the zoo, is not especially convenient, but accommodations, though simple, are clean, and its two restaurants provide good fare.

Hotel Königstein, Prägerstrasse (Tel. 48-560). Though labeled a three-star hotel, this is an extremely basic, satisfactory hotel without charm, but with a location near the main railway station and within reasonable walking distance of the cultural attractions of the city. A single room is approximately $100, including breakfast.

Hotel Lilienstein, Prägerstrasse (Tel. 48-560). This is virtually a twin to the Königstein — another high-rise Soviet-style structure with boxlike rooms with sagging beds and an enormous, uninviting lobby. It is, however, clean and adequate; the prices are about $100 for a single, including breakfast.

Hotel Newa, Leningraderstrasse 34 (Tel. 496-7112). The principal advantage of this architecturally uninteresting first-class hotel (as opposed to the deluxe quality of the Bellevue and the Dresdener Hof) is its proximity to the main railway station. There is also good food in its Russian restaurant. It does not, however, meet the standards of a first-class United States hotel. The off-season double room rate is between $125 and $150.

RESTAURANTS

Äberlausitzer Töppl, Strasse der Befreiung 14. Fish and good dark beer are the specialties here.

Kügeln Haus, Strasse der Befreiung 14 (Tel. 5-27-91). Located in a restored nineteenth-century burgher house on the north side of the Elbe, this is a restaurant with old-fashioned charm and style. Service is thoughtful, and the decoration — engravings and woodcuts of notable singers and actors of Dresden's past — is attractive. Reservations are required.

Luisenhof, Bergbahnstrasse 8 (Tel. 3-68-42). Accessible by cable car, and a little on the outskirts of the city, Luisenhof — rebuilt after the war in neo-Baroque style — has a romantic setting above the Elbe. Dancing is offered some evenings. Reservations are required.

Meissner Weinkeller, Strasse der Befreiung 14 (Tel. 5-27-91), is in the cellar of the town hall of Augustus the Strong's time and has an air of the past and good local specialties and wines.

Pirnaisches Tor, Pirnaischer Platz near the Zwinger. Fish is among the better offerings in this modern self-service restaurant.

Wroclaw, Prägerstrasse 15 in the International Restaurant (Tel. 4-95-51-34). This restaurant offering Polish fare is situated close to the main tourist hotels and provides an acceptable meal at a reasonable price.

ENTERTAINMENT

Culture Palace (Kulturpalast), Thälmannstrasse. The Dresden Philharmonic Orchestra concerts are given here.

Church of the Holy Cross (Kreuzkirche), Altmarkt. Ever since the Middle Ages, the boys' choir concerts performed here have been memorable. The practice has been to offer them Saturday at 6:00 P.M.

Semper Opera (Semper Oper), Theaterplatz. This splendidly reconstructed opera house is *the* place to go for the evening if you are in Dresden in opera season. (The house is dark from early July to mid-August.) Tickets, however, are generally in short supply, so it is wise to get them as far in advance as possible either at the box office or through a hotel concierge. It was at the Semper Opera House that Richard Wagner's first successful opera, *Rienzi,* was premiered in 1842 and Carl Maria von Weber from 1816 to 1826 was among its most notable directors.

TOURIST INFORMATION

Prägerstrasse 10/11 (Tel. 4-95-50-25).

EISENACH

HOTELS

Wartburghotel (Tel. 51-11). This small hotel is splendidly situated above the red roofs of town. Its dining room serves game and Thuringian specialties in a hunting-lodge atmosphere.

Parkhotel, Wartburgallee 2 (Tel. 52-91). This is a friendly and clean hotel, but the comfort is strictly basic. Many rooms are without baths, and the plumbing down the hall may or may not work. The dining room is, like the hotel, adequate but unexciting.

RESTAURANTS

Zwinger, Bahnhofstrasse/Nikolaitor (Tel. 52-91). This is an inexpensive restaurant not far from the Nikolaitor that tends to be crowded at lunchtime. Wild game is often on the menu.

ENTERTAINMENT

Stadtcafé, Karlstrasse 35-35 (Tel. 30-54). Dining and dancing and a weekend revue are the principal attractions.

TOURIST INFORMATION

Bahnhofstrasse 3-5 (Tel. 48-95 or 61-61).

ERFURT

HOTELS

Erfurter Hof, Am Bahnhofsvorplatz 1-2 (Tel. 51-151). This turn-of-the-century hotel opposite the main railway station has recently been renovated. Thuringian fare is served in the dining room.

Kosmos, Juri-Gagarin-Ring 126-127 (Tel. 55-10). High-rise and modern, but that is about all there is to recommend this 332-room hostelry.

RESTAURANTS

Alter Schwan, Gothardtstrasse 27, Altstadt (Tel. 29-116). A small and cosy Old Town restaurant, much frequented by locals. Reservations are required.

Café zur Krämerbrücke, Krämerbrücke. This charming little café with better-than-average sweets sits right at the foot of the Krämerbrücke. A window seat affords a good look at passersby.

Zur Hohen Lilie, Domplatz (Tel. 2-25-78). Sweden's seventeenth-century king Gustavus II lived for a year in this step-gabled, centrally located house that is now a pleasant small restaurant and nightclub. Reservations are essential.

TOURIST INFORMATION

Trommsdorffstrasse (Tel. 2-62-67), or Bahnhofstrasse 37.

LEIPZIG

The Leipzig-bound visitor should bear in mind that during fair times in spring and fall it will not be possible to find accommodation for miles around.

HOTELS

Hotel Am Ring, Augustusplatz 5-6. This is an adequate, but not inviting first-class hotel near the Gewandhaus.

Hotel Astoria, Platz der Republik (Tel. 72-220). This centrally located 305-room hotel across from the main railway station is modern and supremely conveniently situated. Among its four restaurants there is one, **Pelz-Klause,** specializing in Saxon fare.

Hotel International, Trondinring (Tel. 71-880). Small (85 rooms) and restored, there's a pleasant old-fashioned quality to the International, but its location is noisy.

Hotel Merkur, Gerberstrasse (Tel. 79-90). This luxurious 27-story Japanese-built hotel provides by far the most luxurious accommodations and best service in Leipzig. It is equipped with a swimming pool, sauna, and health club facilities as well as a business center. Its Japanese restaurant, **Sakura,** is a favorite among Leipzigers. A single room is about $102, a double $145.

Hotel Stadt Leipzig, Richard-Wagner Strasse (Tel. 26-88-14). This 34-room hotel opposite the main railway station has, in recent years, been a center for tour groups. It is distinctly lacking in charm and its rooms tend to be small, but it is clean and satisfactory. Its specialty restaurant, **Vignette,** serves international cuisine.

Hotel Zum Löwen, Rudolf-Breitscheid Strasse (Tel. 72-220). Ordinary and modern but acceptable, the Zum Löwen has the disadvantage of being on a noisy streetcar track.

RESTAURANTS

Because of the large number of fairgoers coming here each year, a restaurant directory has been published and is available from some newsstands and the Leipzig Information Office on Sachsenplatz near the Brühl. It is always wise to make restaurant reservations in Leipzig.

Auerbachs Keller, Grimmaischestrasse 2 (Mädlerpassage) (Tel. 20-79-90). Surely the most renowned restaurant in Leipzig, it was in the original restaurant that Goethe set the *Faust* scene in which the doctor rides away on a beer keg with Mephistopheles. Though the original restaurant (where Goethe spent many an hour in his Leipzig student days) was torn down in 1912, the re-creation is similar. Statues of Faust, Mephistopheles, and fellow revelers stand outside the door.

Burgkeller, Naschmarkt 1-3 (Tel. 29-56-39). Average food is offered here at reasonable prices in a good central location.

Café Cather, Katherinenstrasse 15. Lace curtains, whispering ladies, and delicious marzipan cakes help make the little Café Cather a popular spot for afternoon coffee.

Gasthaus Bartelshof, off the Markt (Tel. 20-09-75). Set in a courtyard off the Markt, this old restaurant has recently been undergoing restoration.

Gastmahl des Meeres, Dr. Kurt-Fischer Strasse (Tel. 29 11 60). Once a swamp (*Brühl*) occupied much of the land where this city now rises. In those days, fish was plentiful. Although that's no longer the case, this fish restaurant is ever-popular.

Paulaner, Klostergasse 3 (Tel. 20-99-41). Spread over three floors in two buildings near the Markt, this is a pleasant, if unexciting, place for dining.

Restaurant Stadt Dresden, Wintergartenstrasse 7010 (Tel. 20-92-37). Reservations are absolutely essential at this popular modern restaurant serving both national and international dishes. Be sure to look for the wall painting of Dresden's history.

Thüringer Hof, Burgstrasse 19-23 (Tel. 20-98-84). There's beer-cellar character to this restaurant that is popular with students and is particularly known for Thuringian specialties like game and delicately spiced bratwurst.

Weinrestaurant Falstaff, Georgiring 9 (Tel. 28-64-03). Situated near the Opera and the Gewandhaus, this elegant restaurant is popular with music lovers and is, accordingly, pricey.

Zills Bier Tunnel Plovdiv, Barfussgaschen 9 (Tel. 20-04-46). Bulgarian fare, with an emphasis on charcoal broiling, is the specialty in this reasonable, pretty restaurant. Reservations are essential. Closed on Sunday.

Zum Kaffeebaum, Kleine Fleischergasse 4 (Tel. 20-04-52). Filled with literary and musical associations, this is where Goethe and Schiller liked to dine and where Robert Schumann edited his *New Journal of Music.* Pictures of artists and singers decorate the walls, and today's artists and musicians are among its frequenters. Though Zum Kaffeebaum in its early eighteenth-century days was simply a coffeehouse, as the Baroque carving of a Turk under a coffee tree above the outside door suggests, today meals are served. Reservations are required.

ENTERTAINMENT

Neues Gewandhaus, Augustusplatz (Tel. 713-20). Germany's oldest professional orchestra, established in 1743, performs regularly, except July and August, in this splendid modern concert hall that has been acclaimed as an acoustical gem. Because of the orchestra's stature, performances are often sold out, but hotel concierges can sometimes arrange for them. The Leipzig Information Office (Zentraler-Informations-Service) at Sachsenplatz 1 (Tel. 7-95-90) and the box office also sell tickets — if there are any left. It is wise, however, to write in advance for a ticket. The Gewandhaus is open only during performances, but organ concerts are given Saturday at 5:00 P.M.

Opernhaus, Augustusplatz. This monumental opera house, whose original was destroyed in World War II, opened in 1960, the first major postwar theater erected in the eastern part of Germany. Obtaining a ticket to it is not quite so difficult as obtaining a ticket to a Gewandhaus performance, but almost. Hotel concierges and the Leipzig Information Office may be helpful.

Thomaskirche (southwest of the Markt). Here, where Johann Sebastian Bach was cantor and the teacher of the boys' choir,

today's remarkable boys' choir performs Friday at 6:00 P.M.
and Saturday at 1:30 P.M., except in July and August.
TOURIST INFORMATION
Sachsenplatz 1 (Tel. 7-95-90).

POTSDAM
HOTELS
Hotel Cecilienhof, Neuer Garten (Tel. 23-141). Forty-two of
the rooms in historic Schloss Cecilienhof, where the Potsdam
Agreement was signed in 1945, have been turned into agreea
ble hotel rooms, many of them overlooking a garden. There is
good dining in the restaurants. Though Potsdam is hardly a
central location for the visitor to Berlin, this is a very pleasant,
luxurious place to stay at a more reasonable cost than in the
city.
Hotel Potsdam, Lange Brücke (Tel. 4631). For those who prefer
a country to a city setting, this hotel is an alternative, but it is
a seventeen-story, block-style hostelry lacking the charm of
Cecilienhof.
RESTAURANT
Restaurant Bolgar, Klement-Gottwald Strasse 35 (Tel. 2-25-05).
This is a restaurant with a Bulgarian ambience.
TOURIST INFORMATION
Friedrich-Ebert Strasse 5 (Tel. 2 30 12).

ROSTOCK
HOTELS
Neptun, Promenade, Rostock-Warnemünde (Tel. 53-71 or 53-
81). Situated on the beach of Rostock's outer harbor of War-
nemünde, this 350-room hotel has fine views, a swimming
pool, fitness rooms, and restaurants. It is, however, a twenty-
five-minute S-Bahn ride from the Rostock rail station.
Warnow, Hermann-Drucker Platz (Tel. 37-381). This centrally
located, refurbished modern hotel isn't anything fancy, but it's

acceptable. Among its three restaurants one, the **Riga**, offers Russian cuisine.

RESTAURANTS

Gastmahl des Meeres, August-Bebel Strasse 112-113 (Tel. 22-301). Fish, of course, is what should be sampled in this Baltic city. This fish restaurant prepares it simply, but well.

Ostseegastatte, Lange Strasse 9. There is nothing special about this seafood restaurant except that some English is spoken and an English-language menu is available.

Jägerhütte, Barstofer Wald (Tel. 23-457). Wild game is the specialty of this restaurant near the zoo.

TOURIST INFORMATION

Schnickmannstrasse 13-14 (Tel. 2-26-19).

SCHWERIN

HOTEL

Hotel Stadt Schwerin, Grünthalplatz (Tel. 52-61). This is a centrally located, very average modern hotel with two restaurants.

RESTAURANT

Alt Schweriner Schantstuben, Schlachtermarkt, is a simple, satisfactory restaurant in the Old Town.

TOURIST INFORMATION

Markt 11 (Tel. 86-45-09).

WEIMAR

HOTELS

Belvedere, Belvederer Allee (Tel. 24-29). Just completed opposite the park on the River Ilm, the Belvedere has all the amenities — a swimming pool, solarium, sauna, business center, and three restaurants, including **Notre Jardin**, which features vegetarian cuisine. Its location, however, is about a mile from the city center.

Elefant, Marktplatz (Tel. 641-71). For 200 years, this hotel on the marketplace has been welcoming guests — Johann Sebastian Bach, Franz Liszt, Richard Wagner, Thomas Mann, and Adolf Hitler among them. Much renovated, it has lost some of its charm in the reception area, but not its sweeping grand staircase or spacious, airy rooms. The food in its restaurants, the **Stadt Weimar** and the **Elefantenkeller,** is nothing outstanding, but it is considered about the best in town. Its **Nachtklub Bajadere** is one of Weimar's few night spots.

RESTAURANTS

Gastatate Alt-Weimar, Prellerstrasse 2 (Tel. 20-56). Musicians and artists have long frequented this simple but good restaurant. It is ever-popular with National Theater actors and attendees.

Gastmahl des Meeres, Herderplatz 16 (Tel. 45-21 or 47-21). This is a simple fish restaurant where prices are reasonable, but it is open weekdays only.

Goethe Café, Wielandstrasse 1 (Tel. 34-32). Coffee and cake are offered here in an attractive, old-fashioned ambience.

Konzert-Kaffee or Café-Esplanade, Schillerstrasse 18 (Tel. 29-10). Upstairs is the place to go for coffee and cake or a drink after the theater.

Zum Weissen Schwan, Frauentorstrasse 23. Once an eighteenth-century inn, Zum Weissen Schwan has now been restored and is a restaurant operated by the Hotel Belvedere.

ENTERTAINMENT

German National Theater (Deutsches National Theater), Theaterplatz (Tel. 75-50 or 75-53-53). Ballet and opera, as well as drama, are offered in this historic theater site. Hotel concierges, as well as the box office, are good sources of tickets. In July and August, the theater is dark.

TOURIST INFORMATION

Markstrasse 4 (Tel. 21-73).

Hungary

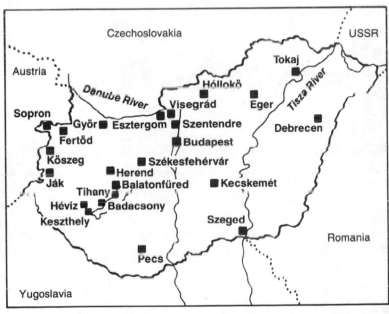

Czechoslovakia

USSR

Austria

Tokaj

Hóllokö

Danube River

Visegrád

Eger

Tisza River

Sopron

Győr

Esztergom

Szentendre

Debrecen

Fertöd

Budapest

Köszeg

Székesfehérvár

Herend

Ják

Tihany

Balatonfüred

Kecskemét

Héviz

Badacsony

Keszthely

Szeged

Romania

Pecs

Yugoslavia

When the Magyars from the Ural Mountains of Russia galloped down into the gentle Carpathian Basin below the Carpathian Mountains and the Alps at the end of the ninth century, they were hardly the first settlers here. Before them, there had been Stone Age peoples, Scythians of the Iron Age, blond Celts, Avars, and Slavs. In the first century A.D., the Roman emperor Augustus had created the Roman province of Pannonia in today's western Hungary. The Romans had thrived, building camps, towns, bridges, and baths till the marauding tribes — Vandals and Huns among them   drove them out.

When the forebears of the Hungarians (no connection with the Huns) left their home on the steppes, some headed for what is now Finland, which explains why Hungarians and Finns share something of the same language. The Magyars who came to the Carpathian Basin were a people renowned for horsemanship, with warriors so skilled that they could befuddle their enemy by shooting arrows behind them as they rode forward. These vigorous travelers from the north elected Árpád to be their ruler and drank their fealty to him from goblets filled with their own blood.

Though they had found a pleasant grassy place to live, it still took seventy years for these hard-riding, hard-fighting men of the steppes to settle down. Before they were finally stopped near Augsburg in today's Germany by the Holy Roman Emperor Otto I, they had raided as far west as the Pyrenees, south into Italy, east to Constantinople, and north to modern-day Belgium. Not until their resounding defeat at Augsburg did they give up their wild marauding ways. Árpád's great-grandson, Prince Géza, decided it would be wise to convert to the Christian faith of those who had defeated him, while his son Stephen (canonized for his efforts) embarked on an all-out battle against paganism, burying alive not only his pagan enemies but their horses, their wives, and their children.

Stephen invited missionaries from abroad to come to convert his people. In gratitude, Pope Sylvester II of Rome had him crowned Christian king on Christmas Day in the year 1000.

Under Stephen, the nation began to be organized and received its first laws. After him, however, unrest ensued, culminating in 1241 with a Mongolian invasion that left half the population dead, the country in tatters, and King Béla IV in refuge in Dalmatia. Though some criticized him for fleeing the invasion, once the Mongols had left, Béla returned to try to rebuild his nation, constructing fortresses and moving the capital from low-lying, devastated Pest to the hill of Buda and surrounding it with high walls.

With the end of the Árpád dynasty in 1301, Charles Robert of Anjou in France was invited to become king. He proved an admirable choice, as did his son, Louis, who has gone down in Hungarian history as Louis (Lajos) the Great. In Louis's rule, the University of Pécs was built. Mining thrived, with gold in such high production that, in the fourteenth century, Hungary was Europe's greatest gold producer. Hungary's borders expanded to include Galicia, Dalmatia, and Poland.

But after Louis, who left no sons, once again there was murder and mayhem. When it ended, another foreigner, Sigismund of Luxembourg, sat on the Hungarian throne. His reign saw the Turks advance into Western Europe, and though he tried to stop them, he was not successful. Eminently successful, however, was his successor, János Hunyadi of Transylvania, a deft and gallant military man who stopped the Turks with spectacular fighting at Nándorfehérvár (now Belgrade). But that was his last battle; the next day he succumbed to the plague.

Happily, he left behind him a son with all of his abilities — and more. Matthias Corvinus (a raven — *corvinus* in Latin — is said to have carried messages to him) became Hungary's great Renaissance king.

Under Matthias, Hungary became the greatest country of Central Europe. All Europe's leading scholars came to his court;

trade prospered; the first Hungarian book was printed. Matthias developed a strong central government that limited the power of the barons. His wife, Beatrix of Naples, brought with her from Italy artists and artisans to decorate the royal castle at Buda with fireplaces of red marble and majolica tile floors and stoves. Papal delegates applauded it as finer than any palace in Rome. The king, meanwhile, was collecting one of the largest libraries in the Renaissance world.

On Matthias's death, however, the government fell apart. With Hungary weakened, the Turks readied to invade again. At the Battle of Mohács, which a bitter Hungary has never forgotten, the young Hungarian king Louis II died and his 20,000 men were defeated. The Turks marched on to capture Pécs and Buda. For the time being, they stopped there. But the nervous Hungarians, hoping for help against the Turks — in a move they would long regret — selected an Austrian Hapsburg to be their king.

So it was that by the mid-sixteenth century, northern and western Hungary were in Hapsburg hands. Transylvania, though an "independent principality," was paying tribute to the Turks to keep them away, and central Hungary was directly under Turkish rule.

Not until 1683 were the Turks forced beyond the Danube, and not until 1849 were the Hungarians able — briefly — to oust the Hapsburgs and declare their country a republic. But their happiness was short-lived. Austria's eighteen-year-old ruler, Franz Joseph, called on the tsar of Russia to help put down the rebellious Hungarians. In the fighting that ensued, Hungary lost two of its greatest freedom fighters — the poet Sándor Petöfi was killed and the fiery orator Lajos Kossuth was forced to flee to America. The Hapsburgs instituted stern absolutist rule.

This lasted until 1867. By that time, there was unrest again in the Hungarian population and the Hapsburgs gave in to the demands for more Hungarian autonomy by establishing the dual Austro-Hungarian Empire.

It was in this partnership role with Austria that Hungary was forced into World War I on the German side, and it suffered considerably. When the war ended, there was, briefly, a Hungarian

Republic, then a Hungarian Soviet Republic, then a right-wing government. As punishment for its involvement in the war, Hungary was forced to cede to neighboring countries two thirds of its land and three fifths of its people. By the terms of the 1920 Treaty of Trianon, all of Transylvania, with its nearly 2 million Magyars, went to Romania.

All the same, when Germany tried, at the onset of World War II, to lure Hungary into its camp, most Hungarians weren't interested. They even allowed Polish soldiers, after the invasion of Poland, to take refuge here. When the Nazis promised them the return of Transylvania, however, the Hungarians were won over and in March 1944 the Germans occupied Hungary. By October, the Russians had arrived, and the battering of Budapest, where the Germans had their headquarters in Buda Castle, began. By the time they were finally routed in February 1945, a large percentage of the capital's buildings had been destroyed.

After the war, a People's Republic was proclaimed. For a while, following Stalin's death in 1953, promising economic and social reforms got under way. But in 1956, when even more freedom and an end to communism were demanded, Russian troops came to quell the revolution. By the time the revolution ended, more than 3,000 were dead; the country's leader, Imre Nagy, had been executed; thousands had been imprisoned; and some 200,000 had fled to other lands. In Nagy's place, János Kádár was installed.

At first intensely disliked, Kádár came to be rather admired as he avowed that "he who is not against us is with us" and introduced some private initiative in both business and farming. Goulash communism thrived and other Eastern countries were jealous of Hungary's comparative prosperity.

Finally, in the fall of 1989, Hungary opened the Iron Curtain that had separated East from West when it allowed East German refugees to cross its border into Austria. Hungary — and all of central Europe — has been a changed place ever since.

In Hungarian, last names appear before first names, so in this guide, András Hess Square in Hungarian is Hess András tér.

BUDAPEST

The Danube River flows *by* Vienna, but the Danube River *is* Budapest. It is its centerpiece, its heart, its pulse. Its relationship with the city is even more intimate than that of the Seine with Paris or the Arno with Florence. The vista on a sunny summer's day from the castle heights to the graceful sweep of the brown-gold Danube, or, on a clear night, across the river's velvet blackness, over the diamond brooch of the Chain Bridge, to the castle high on the Buda side of the river, is unforgettable.

On the right side of the river are the green Buda Hills, the old town where restored pink-and-gold Baroque houses with elaborate facades stand beside Renaissance and medieval ones. Rising above them is the Gothic lace of Matthias Church.

On the left bank — Pest — the neo-Gothic spires of the Parliament building spear skyward. There are bulbous nineteenth-century turrets and cupolas, colorful Art Nouveau tiles over shop fronts, bustling pedestrian malls and inviting coffeehouses.

In the first century A.D., the Romans established a camp here on the site of a Celtic settlement and called it Aquincum, probably naming it after its thermal waters. In the second and third centuries, it became the capital of the Roman province of Lower Pannonia, with both a fortified camp guarding the border of the Roman Empire and a trading city. Then, in the fifth century, Attila's Huns drove out the Romans — Roman fortifications notwithstanding. Buda is said to have been the name of one of Attila's brothers.

When the Magyars came in the ninth century, they built on the right side of the river on the low land that is now fashionable Óbuda. Meanwhile, a community grew up on the Danube's Pest side.

After a Mongolian invasion in 1241, during which the invaders first devastated low-lying Pest, then crossed the Danube on ice to destroy Buda, King Béla IV ordered Buda Castle constructed and the Budapest of today began to take shape.

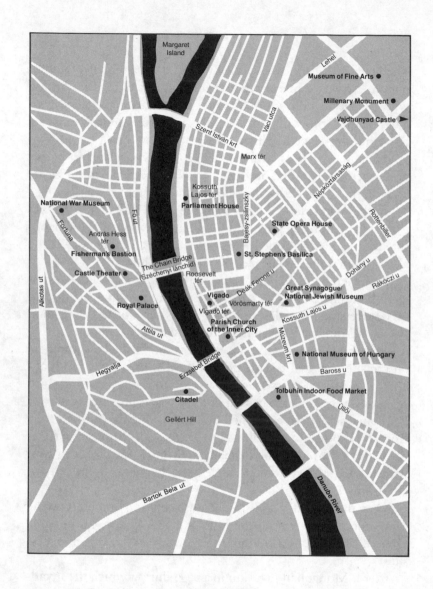

BUDAPEST

BUDA

CASTLE HILL AREA

The principal sites of the castle area of the Buda side of the capital follow.

András Hess Square (Hess András tér): The first book printed in Hungary, *The Buda Chronicle,* was produced in a workshop in Number 4 in 1473 by printer András Hess. The shop is now a restaurant. Although the square is named for András Hess, the statue in its center is of Pope Innocent XI, who was a powerful force in convincing the Christians to drive out the Turks in 1686.

At Number 3, the red hedgehog bas-relief was the sign of the **Red Hedgehog Inn** (Vörös Sün) that occupied the premises in 1760. It is one of the city's oldest structures, now a private house.

Castle Theater (Várszinház), Szent Gyorgy tér: In this restored golden-yellow Baroque building, the first play ever performed in Hungarian was produced in 1780. Once a Carmelite monastery and in the Turkish days a pasha's palace, this structure has also been a casino. But in 1787, it was redesigned as a theater by the Hungarian architect Farkas Kempelen (especially renowned for the chess "machine" he invented that once checkmated Napoleon). Here, he employed his genius in the acoustical field, and Hungarians like to tell proudly how Beethoven played here. Today, however, the good acoustics are sometimes too good, and one hears sounds from the street outside.

Fishermen's Bastion (Hálaszbástya), Hess András tér: Frigyes Schulek, the architect responsible for the nineteenth-century renovation of Matthias Church, was a man abounding in ideas. When he was through with the church, he thought up these picturesque ramparts and turrets above the Danube to go with it. It is uncertain whether in the days of actual fortification the fishermen's guild really manned the bastion that was here, but the modern one has been given their name.

Fortune Street (Fortuna utca): In the Middle Ages, French craftsmen lived and worked here, and the street was named Francia utca for them; in the eighteenth century, it took the name of the Fortuna Inn (now the not particularly interesting **Hungarian**

Museum of Commerce and Catering — Magyar Kereskedelmi és Vendéglátóipari Múzeums). Elsewhere along the street, at Number 14, there are Gothic design elements to be seen; at Number 6, where the facade is nineteenth-century, the building itself eighteenth, and the foundations medieval, a relief of Cupid is over the door.

Hilton Hotel, Hess András tér: The construction here in 1976 of a modern hotel that incorporates the ruins of a Dominican church and monastery of the Middle Ages and an eighteenth-century Jesuit college was the subject of much discussion, but now its shimmering sides, which reflect the towers of Matthias Church, have been generally accepted.

Lord's Street (Uri utca): On both sides of this longest street in the castle district are houses of many periods. Below the street at Number 9, in caves that served as a hospital in World War II, there is now a grisly **Waxworks Museum** that is open from 10:00 A.M. to 6:00 P.M., except Tuesday. On the fifteenth-century house at Number 15, a carved lion holds a coat of arms. At Number 31, there is a Gothic facade. Number 53, once a Franciscan monastery, became the headquarters of the Jacobins in the eighteenth century, when the French ideals of liberty, equality, and fraternity made their way here briefly. The Jacobin leaders were caught and imprisoned here before their execution on Blood Meadow below Castle Hill. There are Baroque-style statues at Number 54-56.

Magdalene Tower (Magdolna Kapisztrán), Kapisztrán trán tér: This restored tower, now an art gallery, is all that remained at the end of World War II of the thirteenth-century Church of St. Mary Magdalene. For a while, during the 150 years of Turkish occupation, its use as a Christian church continued to be allowed and Protestants and Catholics shared it, but it was eventually turned into a mosque.

Matthias Church (Mátyás-templom), Szentháromsúg tér: Handfuls of golden coins and bouquets of snowy flowers seem to have been tossed on the roof of this church that crowns Castle Hill — and to have stuck. That is the way Matthias's tiles have been fashioned to look. If you are not bedazzled by the colorful roof, surely you will be by the delicate tracery of the High Gothic south facade and the soaring splendor of the neo-Gothic steeple.

Béla IV started construction of this Coronation Church in the thirteenth century, and every king thereafter, into the fifteenth century, added architectural touches. In the nineteenth century, after it had been turned into a Turkish mosque for a time, struck by lightning, and damaged by fires, it was decided to unify all of its earlier styles in the rebuilding. The present, largely neo-Gothic structure is the result.

Inside, the columns, window frames, and vaulting are bright with geometric and floral designs in paisley-like designs and colors. Here, King Matthias Corvinus (whose coat of arms — the raven — can be seen on the left if you enter the church through the Mary Portal on the side) married both his wives, Catherine Poděbrad and Beatrix of Naples.

As often called the Coronation Church as the Matthias Church, Charles Robert of Anjou was the first king crowned here, in 1310 — after seven years of controversy over whether he was a legitimate king. The people of Buda had chosen Wenceslas of Bohemia to be their ruler but the nobles and the pope preferred the Frenchman. In the controversy that resulted, the pope excommunicated the people of Buda; the people of Buda retaliated by excommunicating the pope. When tempers died down, Charles Robert was finally crowned.

The next important coronation here was not until many centuries later (Székesfehérvár, about fifty miles from Budapest, became the usual coronation place). But in 1867, Franz Joseph of Austria, to assure that he would be considered the legitimate ruler of the Austro-Hungarian Empire, was crowned here. Franz Liszt composed his *Hungarian Coronation Mass* for the occasion, and the flags that to this day fly above the nave are those of all Hungary's counties at that time. The next king to be crowned here was Charles VI in 1916. Both coronation thrones may be seen in the oratory; in the crypt are ecclesiastical vestments and church silver and gold. To the left of the side door, in the Loreto Chapel beside the South Tower, is a red-marble Virgin said to have miraculous powers. The chapel tends to be dark, however, and the statue hard to see. The Virgin was a thanks offering to the church by Louis II in the sixteenth century after he had escaped an assassination attempt. In 1686, when the church had been in Turkish hands for more than a century and in use as a mosque, the red-marble Virgin, long-disappeared, is said to have appeared in a crack in the church wall — a warning that the church's days as a mosque were numbered. And they were.

In the square to the side of the church stands an equestrian statue of St. Stephen. In the square in front is the eighteenth-century **Trinity Column,** erected with public donations by those who had survived the plague, in gratitude for their survival and in hopes of continued protection. ("The bigger, the better" seems to have been the thought, for this column replaced an earlier, smaller one.)

Concerts, organ recitals, and choral singing can be heard here.

National War Museum (Hadtörténeti Muzeum), Toth Árpád sétány: This is of limited interest, but the resplendent uniforms of the past, the elegant crossbows, the pikes, and the cannonballs with ornaments on them will appeal to some. It is open Tuesday through Sunday 9:00 A.M. to 5:00 P.M.

Outside the museum's left wing is a memorial stone commemorating the death in battle in 1686, at the age of seventy, of the last Turkish vizier here, Abdurrahman Abdi Arnaut Pasha, and recalling him as "a valiant foe."

Parliament Street (Országház utca): In the Middle Ages, this was the main street of the area. Number 17 is a Baroque house constructed from two medieval houses; Number 18 is a rebuilt fifteenth-century house; Number 20, fourteenth-century. At Number 22 you can look for Renaissance sgraffito and eighteenth-century Baroque embellishment. Part of Number 28 was once used as the Parliament.

Royal Palace (Budavári Palota), Szent György tér): The impressive structure that stands here today was virtually completely rebuilt after World War II, as was all of Castle Hill. Using the palace as their headquarters, the Germans dug themselves in on the hill in the face of the arrival of Russian forces. All winter long, in 1944–1945, the Russian bombardment of the hill continued, and by the middle of February, when the Russians finally took control, only one in every four buildings was undamaged.

But long before that, the palace that Béla IV had constructed had disappeared. Today, bits and pieces of that thirteenth-to-fifteenth-century palace have been restored, but most of what you see is a re-creation of the nineteenth-century neo-Baroque palace that stood here when the war began. You can see remains from the earlier periods in the palace cellar.

Of particular interest outside the palace is the romantic 1904 **Matthias Fountain**, which shows the great Renaissance king on a hunt. It recounts the legend of the disguised king's encounter with a fellow huntsman's daughter and of the love that stirred in them both. But she died of a broken heart when she discovered Matthias was the king and feared he had forgotten her. Later (if one accepts that legend as true) he married Beatrix of Naples. Beatrix brought with her to the Hungarian court fine Italian artists who added Renaissance elements to the palace that helped to make it one of the loveliest in Europe. Indeed, it is said that the Turkish sultan Suleiman was so impressed with what he saw that he wished to take it all back with him to Turkey.

Inside the **Historical Museum of Budapest** that is housed here are handsome medieval statues. In the **Hungarian National Gallery** are some of the finest fifteenth- and sixteenth-century altarpieces in Central Europe. The **Széchenyi Library**, one of Europe's largest in Matthias's day, has magnificent illuminated manuscripts among its 2,500 volumes.

The palace, museums, and library are open Tuesday through Sunday from 9:00 A.M. to 5:00 P.M.

Ruszwurm, Szentháromság tér 3: As long ago as 1500, this pastry shop was a bakery. Later it was a confectioner's, a pastry cook's, and a cake baker's. But always the fragrance of baked goods has been wafting from this little building. Unfortunately, it is too small for today's hungry clientele, and finding a table for coffee and cake in its Biedermeier-style dining room may require quite a wait.

Statue of Prince Eugene of Savoy (Savoyai Jenó), Szent György tér: At the Danube entrance of the palace this bronze 1900 statue of the Austrian prince Eugene of Savoy by József Róna marks one of the best viewing places to look down the Danube and across it to Pest. It was Eugene who led the victorious Christian forces that drove the Turks from Buda in 1686.

Mihály Táncsics Street (Táncsics Mihály utca): This was largely a Jewish area in the Middle Ages, and in the **Jewish Oratory** at Number 16 (open from April to October, Tuesday through Friday from 10:00 A.M. to 2:00 P.M., except the second weekend of the month, when it is open until 6:00 P.M.) are gravestones and other memorabilia of that era.

In the **Erdödy Palace,** at Number 7, Beethoven stayed when he was playing in Budapest, and Béla Bartók had his studio here.

Tárnok Street (Tárnok utca): Sixteenth-century frescoes adorn the front of the restaurants at Numbers 14 and 18. The **Golden Eagle** (Arany sas), at Number 18, is an eighteenth-century pharmacy turned museum. It is open from 10:30 A.M. to 5:30 P.M., except Monday.

Vienna Gate (Bécsi Kapu), Becsi Kapu tér: Through this 1936 reproduction of one of the old gates of the city, you get a good view of the green Buda Hills. To the right of the gate is the Európa-liget, a small grove of trees brought to the Hungarian capital by the mayors of major cities across Europe in 1972.

R I V E R B A N K

Below the hill, along the riverbank — the Viziváros — there are also sights to be seen.

Buda Castle Funicular: Linking the square at the Buda end of the Chain Bridge with the Royal Palace is a funicular that was the second steam-powered funicular in the world when it was opened in 1870. It was destroyed by bombs in World War II, but has been reconstructed with copies of the old carriages, though the power is now electric.

Castle-Garden Kiosk (Várkert Kiosk), Castle Hill: The stroller along the Buda riverfront cannot miss this domed structure with statues in front; it was created in the 1870s and is now part of a

Youth Park. Below it are a neo-Renaissance arcade and stairs. Both were the work of Miklós Ybl.

Chain Bridge (Lánchid): When this best-beloved of the eight bridges that cross the Danube in Budapest was finished in 1849, it was the first permanent bridge to span the river here. Its designer was an Englishman, William Tierney Clark; its engineer a Scot, Adam Clark. The money for its construction came from taxes on the nobility ingeniously "arranged" by Count Istvan Széchenyi. As a young man, he had come home from army service for the funeral of his father, but had missed the funeral because he had to wait a week to cross the river. The pontoon bridge in use then could be crossed in warm seasons, but when there was floating ice in winter — as was the case when Count Széchenyi was hurrying home — it was of no use. The count determined that one day a permanent bridge (considered impossible because of the width of the Danube in Budapest) would be constructed.

On a visit to England, he found the two Clarks and brought them here to build what became one of the longest suspension

11. Young lovers on the Buda side of the Danube River.

bridges in the world. In the War of Independence from the Austrians, the bridge escaped destruction. A century later the Germans did blow it up, so the present bridge is a reconstruction. Stone lions guard the bridge at both ends, and an old myth here is that their sculptor, scolded for having carved lions without tongues, was so ashamed that he drowned himself in the river.

Rudas Baths (Gyógyfürdő, near the Elizabeth Bridge): Green pillars support the octagonal roof of this impressive, for-men-only bath built in 1556 by a Turkish pasha. It is open daily and charges about $2 to get in.

St. Anne's Church (Szent Anna-templom), Báthyányi tér: Pretty little St. Anne's Church, built between 1730 and 1760 by an unknown architect, is a charming, graceful Baroque edifice with twin towers that is considered one of Hungary's best Baroque structures.

Semmelweis Museum of the History of Medicine (Semmelweis Orvostörténeti Muzeum), Árpád utca 1-3: Medical and surgical instruments from many lands in many centuries are on exhibit here (and explained by multilingual guides) in this house where Ignáz Semmelweis, who discovered how to prevent childbed fever, was born and is buried. It is open Tuesday through Sunday from 10:00 A.M. to 5:00 P.M.

Tomb of Gul Baba (Gul Baba Siremléke), Mecset utca 14: Buried in this tomb of carved-stone blocks is a sixteenth-century Turkish dervish and poet whose name (if it is romantically translated) means "Father of Roses." During the years of Turkish occupation, this was a popular Moslem pilgrimage place.

Turkish Baths (Király Gyógyfürdő), Fő utca 82-86: Two sixteenth-century Turkish pashas are responsible for the originals of these baths. In the nineteenth century, after the Turkish departure, they were redone in Baroque style and named for their renovators, the König (Király in Hungarian) family. Now as then, they are extremely popular. Patrons lock their clothes inside latticework cubicles, don apronlike garments, and head down the labyrinthine tile corridors to the steaming baths beneath an octagonal roof. After steaming and resting, they return to their cubicles to dress. If they are *very* hungry or *very* thirsty, there is a buffet serving sandwiches and cake. Minimal English is spoken. Monday, Wednesday, and Friday are for men; Tuesday, Thursday, and Saturday for women.

GELLÉRT HILL (GELLÉRTHEGY)
For the finest possible panorama of this Hungarian capital you should go to the top of this 770-foot-high hill named for the Venetian bishop St. Gerard (in Hungarian, Gellért). Bishop Gellért had joined Stephen I in his enthusiastic and determined conversion of the Magyars to Christianity. But some of those who did not wish to be Christianized captured him, tied him to a barrel studded with nails, and rolled him off this hill into the Danube. (A statue of him converting a pagan faces Elizabeth Bridge [Erzsébet hid].)

From here on a clear day, you can see the rooftops of low-lying Pest on the opposite bank and the wooded slopes of the Buda bank, Margaret Island (Margit sziget), and the industrial Csepel Island (Csepel sziget), splitting the brown-gold river, and even a part of Szentendre Island (Szentendre sziget) in the distance.

Citadel (Citadella): This fortress perched on top of the hill was erected by the Austrians after the Hungarian War of Independence in 1848–1849. It now houses a restaurant, a small hotel, viewing platforms, a disco, and shops. It is worth a visit because of the splendid views it offers.

Gellért Baths (Gellért Szálló és Gyógyfürdő), Szent Gellért tér in the Gellért Hotel: In this grand old Art Nouveau hotel on the riverfront, renovated after extensive World War II damage, you can bathe beneath domes of colored glass, where lions spew forth mineral water, or you can swim in an outdoor pool with waves. There is also an invigorating bubble pool whose water sparkles from carbon dioxide.

It is said that a hermit in ancient days established a reputation for his cures with the waters from the spring here, and the thirteenth-century St. Elizabeth, daughter of Andrew II, established a bath on this spot for the sick. The mud from the spring is also reputed to have therapeutic qualities. Indoor as well as outdoor baths are open to the public.

BUDA HILLS

Liberty Hill (Szabadság-hegy): This scenic hill may be reached by the **Pioneer Railway** (Úttörővasút). The seven-and-one-half-mile-long narrow-gauge railway climbs through woods in the Buda Hills with youngsters serving as conductors, stationmasters, and ticket sellers. Only the engineers are adults. To reach it, you must take the cogwheel railway that leaves from near the Hotel Budapest. It operates in summer.

MARGARET ISLAND (MARGIT SZIGET)

This prettily treed, mile-and-a-half-long island, Margit sziget in Hungarian, once the summer residence of the Roman garrison commander, later a royal game preserve and a medieval convent site, is today a public park. On it are open air baths and a swimming pool, gardens, an open air theater, spa hotels, a little zoo, a reconstructed twelfth-century chapel, and the picturesque ruins of the Dominican convent built there by Béla IV in the thirteenth century. Here he sent his nine-year-old daughter, Margaret, for whom the island is named, after he had promised her to God if the Mongols would quit his city. Margaret remained in the convent until her death nineteen years later, performing miracles and good works that led to her eventual canonization.

ÓBUDA

Here, on the Buda side of today's Árpád Bridge, the Romans settled in the first century A.D., naming their kingdom Aquincum for its mineral waters. Earlier, there had been a Celtic settlement on the site. Near the camp, archeological remains show the Romans established a town with an enormous amphitheater — larger, indeed, than Rome's Colosseum — and villas, baths, and a forum.

Aficionados of Roman ruins will find plenty of them here — the amphitheater; first-century public baths; the second-to-third-century **Hercules Villa,** with a splendid floor mosaic depicting the hero after whom the villa is named; and the **Aquincum Museum and Archeological Site,** an open air museum whose ruins give some idea of what the layout of the second-to-third-century Roman town must have been like. Brochures in several languages serve as a guide. The ruins here are open May to October from 10:00 A.M. to 6:00 P.M., except Monday.

The town apparently thrived till the fifth-century arrival of the invading Huns. Attila, pleased with it, seems to have settled here for a time (honoring his brother Buda by renaming it for him).

In the twelfth century, palaces were constructed of the stones from the Roman town, but after the Mongols stormed through in the thirteenth century, it was deemed wiser to have the fortified castle and city center on the higher ground of today's Castle Hill, and Óbuda declined in importance. In 1873, Óbuda, Buda, and Pest gave up individual autonomy to become Budapest. Today there is a cobblestoned square here with life-size statues of strollers in the rain by contemporary sculptor Imre Varga. Art galleries, restaurants, and wine bars in Baroque houses surround the square.

In the restored eighteenth-century **Zichy Mansion** at Number 1 Fő tér, works of Op artist Victor Vasarely and writer-poet-painter Lajos Kasak are displayed. At Laktanya utca 7, more sculptures by Varga fill the little museum that bears his name. The museums are open Tuesday through Sunday from 10:00 A.M. until 6:00 P.M.

PEST

Low-lying Pest is the economic heart of this capital city. In Roman days, like its neighbor across the river, it had its Roman camps, but they were less important than Aquincum. In the Middle Ages, craftsmen lived here, and that bustling, trading tradition continues today. There is surely much for visitors to see and enjoy in Pest, but where Buda is for strollers, Pest — except for its coffeehouses and riverfront promenade — is for the energetic, as the sights here are far apart.

Pest's principal sites follow.

Great Synagogue (Zsinagóga), Dohány utca 2-8: When this double-onion-domed, Moorish-influenced synagogue was built from 1854 to 1859, the Jewish community it served was 30,000. By World War II, there were 250,000 Jews in Budapest, and though today that number has been reduced to 80,000, this continues to be the largest synagogue in Europe. Unfortunately, repair work has kept it closed for some time.

Hungaria Café, Erzsébet körút 9-11: Giants in stone hold up the columns of the New York Palace, an office building on whose ground floor is this historic literary café. When it was opened at the turn of the century, it is said, Budapest's literary lights threw the key into the Danube — to assure that the café would stay open around the clock. Actors, writers, and journalists frequented it in its heyday from the teens of this century to the early thirties, and many a writer did his writing here. World War II, of course, changed all that, and there was bombing damage. Now the Hungaria has been reopened and its renovated Art Nouveau interior is an eyeful. These days the people it attracts are principally tourists.

Millenary Monument (Millenniumi emlékmü), Hősök tere: This monument, whose centerpiece is the archangel Gabriel atop a 118-foot-high column, was erected in 1896 in honor of the one thousandth anniversary of Árpád's conquest of the Hungarian lands. Gabriel is shown bearing the Hungarian crown because he supposedly advised Pope Sylvester II to accept Stephen as a Christian king. On the colonnade on both sides of the pillar are statues of Hungarian kings and freedom fighters. After World War II, the freedom fighters replaced the Hapsburg emperors who had previously been part of the monument. The enormous empty square on which the monument is set has become a favorite spot for skate-boarders.

Museum of Fine Arts (Szépművészeti Múzeum), Hősök tere: The Old Masters — particularly the Spanish Old Masters, Velázquez, Murillo, and El Greco — are especially well represented here. Indeed, the collection is said to be second only to that in Madrid's Prado. But there are also fine Flemish and French Impressionist paintings, including works of Rembrandt, Frans Hals, Van Dyck,

Rubens, Van Eyck, and Pieter Breughel the Elder; Monet, Gauguin, Cézanne, and Renoir. The museum's rich Italian collection suffered a temporary blow a few years ago when intruders climbed up some scaffolding and stole two Titians and a Raphael. Police quickly recovered the paintings in a satchel buried in a forest before any serious damage had been done.

National Jewish Museum (Zsidó Múzeum), Dohány utca 2-8: On the site of this museum, adjoining the Great Synagogue, Theodor Herzl, the founder of the Zionist movement, was born in 1860. Though anti-Semitism in Central Europe in his day led him to the concept of a Jewish state, the 250,000 Jews of pre–World War I Budapest were extremely important in the city's development. They were active in the press, the law, banking, in dustry, medicine, the arts and literature, and construction. Hungarian Jews have made worldwide contributions, too. Writers Arthur Koestler, Ferenc Molnár, and Felix Salten; journalist Joseph Pulitzer; entertainers Paul Lukas and Peter Lorre; the Gabor sisters; Theodore Bikel; and magician Harry Houdini were all born in Budapest. This museum of medieval Torahs and seventeenth-century ceremonial objects remembers their contributions with Seder plates from the Jewish-founded Herend porcelain factory. But in a dimly lit room are articles of clothing from concentration camps, drumheads made from Torahs, and other remembrances of the Holocaust. Several Holocaust graves are in the courtyard. You learn here, too, of efforts by such heroes as Swedish Raoul Wallenberg to rescue Hungary's Jewish population. It is open Monday and Thursday from 2:00 P.M. to 6:00 P.M., Tuesday, Wednesday, Friday, and Sunday from 10:00 A.M. to 1:00 P.M.

National Museum of Hungary (Magyar Nemzeti Múzeum), Múzeum körút 14-16: Hungarians troop to this nineteenth-century neoclassical museum to see the Royal Crown and Regalia. Twice the crown has been hidden away from hostile governments. During the days of the Austro-Hungarian Empire, the patriot Lajos Kossuth buried it in Transylvania. In World War II it was smuggled to Germany by Fascists fearful of what would become of it if it fell into Russian hands. Later, it came to the

United States, and in 1978 President Jimmy Carter returned it to Hungary with great ceremony.

Gleaming on velvet in a darkened room the double crown's upper part is said to be the very one Pope Sylvester II presented to Stephen I in 1000, making it one of the world's oldest royal crowns. Its lower part was given to King Géza I in 1074 by the Byzantine emperor.

As the story goes, the pope was undecided about whether to give this diadem of gold bands, pearls, precious gems, and cloisonné with its cross with two bars to the king of Portugal or to Stephen — until the archangel Gabriel told him Stephen should be his choice. Over the years the crown has been stolen, as well as hidden, and in a fall on one of those occasions, its cross was bent.

Also in the darkened display room are the orb and royal sword and a scepter with a tenth-century rock crystal head, believed to have been made in England. The museum is open Tuesday through Sunday from 10:00 A.M. to 6:00 P.M.

Paris Arcade (Párisi Udvar), Felszabadulás tér: Built in 1911, this handsome shopping arcade is notable for its domed glass ceiling and castlelike winding stairs, its wrought-iron work, and the stained glass over its doors.

Parish Church of the Inner City (Belvárosi-templom): At the foot of the Elizabeth Bridge rise the two Baroque towers of this church, whose construction began in the twelfth century with stones taken from Roman walls, but which has virtually every architectural style in its interior, including a Muslim prayer niche — a mihrab — from Turkish days, when it was converted to a mosque. Franz Liszt, who lived nearby from 1867 to 1875, often played on its organ. In a sunken area beside the church are the restored remains of a third-century Roman camp.

Parliament House (Országház), Kossuth tér: This enormous domed neo-Renaissance building along the riverbank, with its pinnacles and columns, Gothic windows and arcades, is best seen from the Buda side of the river. Among its adornments are 233 statues: Hungarian kings, Transylvanian princes, and military leaders. The interior of the building is open to the public only with a guide. Tours are offered at 11:00 A.M. and 2:00 P.M. weekdays when Parliament is not in session.

Construction of this wedding cake–like structure, which has 691 rooms and is 870 feet long, began in 1885 and ended seventeen years later. By the time the building was opened, its designer, Imre Steindl, was dead. In the square in front of the building are statues of Ferenc Rákóczi, a leader in the eighteenth-century battle against the Austrians, and Lajos Kossuth, briefly the governor of an independent Hungary after the Hapsburgs were driven out in 1849. When they returned to power, he emigrated to the United States. **Lajos Kossuth Square** (Kossuth Lajos tér), where the statues stand, in recent years has been the site of political gatherings. Also on the square is the **Ethnographic Museum** (Néprajzi Múzeum) — not very Hungarian in its contents, but a good museum of African, Eskimo, and Pacific artifacts. It is open Tuesday through Sunday from 10:00 A.M. to 6:00 P.M.

Rózsavölgyi House, Martinelli tér 5: It requires good eyesight to see the ceramic tile design on the upper stories of this innovative 1912 building that today houses quite ordinary streetfront shops. In the eighteenth century, there was a market here. Nearby, on crowded little Martinelli tér, is an enormous modern parking garage.

But if you cross the street from Number 5 and look up, the romantic ceramic tiles of Number 5 and the colored glass Art Nouveau mosaics on Number 3, two doors away, can be captured by a camera — or simply admired by the eye.

St. Stephen's Basilica (Bazilika), Szent István tér: The largest Roman Catholic church in Budapest, constructed with fifty different kinds of marbling, can hold 8,500 people in its rather dark and gloomy interior. Work on this structure began in 1851 and did not end until 1905, by which time both the designer who began it and the designer who had replaced him had died. In addition, the dome had collapsed. Cracks were discovered in it by Miklós Ybl, the architect who replaced the first architect, József

Hild. Barely a week after his discovery, the cracks cracked more, and with a shudder, the dome tilted and fell. The problem was that the pillars holding up the dome had sunk unevenly into the soft earth.

Although the structure of the dome may have been questionable, that of the cellars was not, and in World War II, the National Gallery's art treasures were kept safe deep below the earth. The church, known technically as a basilica minor, was begun in neoclassical style but continued by its second architect in neo-Renaissance style. The third architect, József Kauser, added neo-Baroque touches to the interior. Inside, St. Stephen is honored with a bust, a Carrara-marble statue, scenes from his life in bronze relief, and a painting of him on his deathbed, entrusting Hungary to the Virgin Mary, since he had no offspring.

State Opera House (Magyar Állami Operaház), Andrássy út or Népköztársaság: This impressive neo-Renaissance building was designed, as was St. Stephen's Basilica, by Miklós Ybl and built between 1875 and 1884. The first conductor (1837) of the state opera, Ferenc Erkel, is remembered, along with Franz Liszt, by statues in the places of prominence on the facade. The Muses are also part of the statuary and on high — if you can see them — are, among others, statues of Mozart, Scarlatti, Gluck, Beethoven, Wagner, Bizet, Verdi, and Smetana. In the richly decorated interior of the hall are three-ton bronze chandeliers and much period painting. Gustav Mahler and Otto Klemperer are among those who have been permanent conductors here.

Tolbuhin Indoor Food Market (Vásárcsarnok), Tolbuhin körút 1-3: It's hard not to grow hungry among the mounds of golden and red peppers, the fragrant salamis and spices, the fat sausages and smoked fish that are displayed in this enormous turn-of-the-century glass and iron-ribbed food hall, where you can eat standing up at the counters. Upstairs, vendors sell embroidered skirts and blouses and table linens of varying quality and at varying prices, but it is more fun shopping in the market than in the more formal handicraft stores. Occasionally, though less and less frequently, you see peasant women in country dress selling their produce here.

Váci Street (Váci utca): This main shopping street of the city is lined with attractive boutiques, bookstores, cosmetic stores, furriers, handicraft shops, florist shops, a modern shopping mall, and some restaurants and smaller hotels. Similarly, in the pedestrian alleyways off it, attractive goods are displayed. Sometimes, what is in the window is more inviting than what you find inside, but among Central European shopping streets, Váci utca is far and away the best. Actually, it has been a main strolling street of Pest since the seventeenth century. Then the fashionable would promenade on it to show off their finery. Catering to them, the shops grew more and more exclusive. Its buildings today are largely eighteenth- and nineteenth-century. Note the Art Nouveau shop window at Number 9.

Vajdahunyad Castle (Vajdahunyad vára), Városliget: Reconstructed Hungarian architectural styles from Romanesque through Baroque days make up this fairy-tale-like castle which was created as part of the 1,000-year celebration in 1896 and proved so popular that it was never taken down. The complex includes copies of the entrance to the Romanesque church in the village of Ják in western Hungary, a Gothic cloister, the fifteenth-century feudal Transylvanian castle of János Hunyadi (the original is now in Hunedoara, Romania), and the Baroque castle at Gödöllő in Eastern Hungary. The castle, whose Baroque section houses a **Museum of Agriculture,** rises picturesquely on an island in the middle of the park's Lake Városliget. In front of it stands a statue of its creator, Ignác Alpár.

Of interest in the castle courtyard is the hooded statue of the unknown priest who is believed to have been a scribe to thirteenth-century King Béla IV and who wrote down the early history of Hungary.

In the park, there is a statue of George Washington, erected in 1906 with contributions from the half-million Hungarian emigrants to the United States at the end of the nineteenth and the beginning of the twentieth centuries. The park is home to a zoo of about 4,000 animals.

Vigadó, Vigadó tér: The name of this nineteenth-century concert hall with its ornate facade covered with sculptures means "merrymaking"; inside there is not only a concert hall seating 640, but a restaurant, an art gallery, a ballroom, a small theater, and a handsome grand staircase. The present building is a 1980 reconstruction of the earlier one where Johannes Brahms, Franz Liszt, Béla Bartók, and Gustav Mahler played. Today's acoustics, however, are considerably better than the acoustics of their day. Unfortunately for those who wish simply to *see* the interior rather than attend a concert, only the foyer is open to nonconcertgoers and that only after 1:00 P.M.

Vörösmarty Square (Vörösmarty tér): The pedestrian section of Váci Street begins at this inviting square, where artists paint portraits of visitors and musicians perform in the warm months by the statue that honors the nineteenth-century Romantic poet Mihály Vörösmarty.

They like to tell the story here of the beggar who contributed a prized coin toward the statue's erection, and they point out the coin embedded in the statue, blackened over the years. Carved at the base of the statue is a line from a Vörösmarty poem calling for loyalty to Hungary.

Vörösmarty's Café, Vörösmarty tér: Many people still call this café on Vörösmarty Square after the Swiss confectioner Emile Gerbeaud, who bought it in 1864 and brought it renown. By either name, it's an intriguing place to have strong black coffee and cake piled high with cream — one of its specialties is *konyakos meggy*, a dark chocolate cake with sour cherries in it. Inside, the decorated ceilings are high, the tables small and cozy. Indoors or out, there's plenty of time to people-watch while awaiting coffee and cake or a glass of sweet Tokaji and a *dobostorta*, a many-layered cake with chocolate cream filling and a glaze of caramelized sugar, for service is notoriously slow.

Western Railway Station (Nyugati pályaudvar), Marx tér: Built by the same company that built the Eiffel Tower in Paris, this great cast-iron structure of 1874–1879 really is not for travelers going west, but north and east. But regardless of nomenclature, it is one of Europe's handsomest train stations. To be sure that no trains would be delayed during construction, this station was built around the already existing one, which was only torn down when the work had been completed.

THE DANUBE BEND

About twenty-five miles upstream from Budapest, the eastward-flowing Danube River makes a sudden bend to the south and slips between the craggy Visegrád Mountains on one side and the Börzsönyi Mountains on the other. Forests where kings once hunted swoop down to the riverbank. Medieval ruins perch above it. Small pastel towns sit tranquilly along the shore. In 1989, it looked as if all this was in danger. To meet Hungary's and Czechoslovakia's combined needs for energy, their Communist governments agreed to build a hydroelectric dam here. But at the final hour, Hungarian environmentalists' warnings of potential flood danger and destruction of the natural environment were heeded. Though some construction had begun on the riverbank, it has been stopped and dam plans quashed. The Danube Bend — site of some of Hungary's most historic moments — appears to be out of danger, and Hungarian vacationers, for whom this stretch of river has long been a prime attraction, are smiling again.

The principal attractions of the Danube Bend follow.

ESZTERGOM

This medieval capital of Hungary lies across the Danube from Czechoslovakia. In Roman days, this site was called Strigonium, and it was here that the emperor Marcus Aurelius wrote much of his philosophical *Meditations*. Here, too, the Árpád Dynasty's Duke Géza, father of Stephen I, built a palace in 972 in which that sainted king was born and crowned. Next, Catholic Stephen built a cathedral.

Until the end of the twelfth century, this continued to be an important political as well as religious center, and many a European knight bound for the Crusades was welcomed here. Even after the thirteenth-century Mongolian invasion, when Béla IV moved the political capital of the country to Buda, Esztergom continued as Hungary's religious capital, which it is to this day. Its domed basilica, begun in 1822 but not completed until 1856, is the nation's largest church. Franz Liszt composed his *Esztergom Mass (Missa Solemnas zur ein Weihung der Basilika in Gran)* for its consecration.

In the basilica, all that remains of the medieval cathedral that once stood here is the dark little red-marble **Bakócz Chapel** (Bakócz-kápolna), built for the ambitious Archbishop Tamás Bakócz, who had dreams of being a pope. His dreams died when, despite having made a costly trip with an enormous entourage to Rome, a Florentine Medici won the position. Although his luck in Rome was bad, Bakócz continued to be a great admirer of the Italian Renaissance. He had his chapel here fashioned with walls of carved red marble in Tuscan style; its white-marble altar was carved in Florence. Altogether, this is one of the finest pieces of Renaissance architecture in Hungary. Unfortunately, its handsome detail is hard to see because it is far away and the cathedral is dark.

In the church treasury (kincstár) is outstanding religious art, including the thirteenth-century golden cross on which Hungarian kings took their oath of office, chalices, and stunning Calvary crosses — one of which, adorned with the raven coat of arms of King Matthias and studded with pearls and precious gems, is considered a masterpiece of European goldsmithery. The basilica is open daily, except Monday. From April 1 to October 31, its hours are 9:00 A.M. to 5:00 P.M., and from November 1 to March 31, 9:00 A.M. to 3:00 P.M.

The palace built by King Stephen's father was hidden from view for centuries. During the Turkish invasion, much of it was knocked down and Hungarian soldiers built fortifications inside. Sand eventually covered all that remained of the structure. Not until the 1930s, when a rock from the Citadel ramparts fell into a garden, did anyone know that the palace where King Matthias's widow, Beatrix, and many archbishops had lived still existed. Today you can see the Italian frescoes in the **Royal Chapel** and allegorical murals in the **Hall of Virtues.** On the arches supporting the **Renaissance Hall** are the signs of the zodiac.

Built by Béla III, the twelfth-century king whose two wives had been French, the French Gothic influence can be seen in the columns of the Royal Chapel that resemble those of St. Trophimus at Arles. What are believed to be carved heads of the French architect who designed it and his Hungarian aide are on the chapel wall. The castle is open from 9:30 A.M. to 4:30 P.M. daily, except Monday.

Christian Museum (Keresztény Múzeum), near the river: The nation's best provincial art collection is housed in the Primate's Palace here. Along with outstanding examples of fifteenth-century and sixteenth-century Hungarian painting and carving are works by Sassetta, Lorenzo di Credi, Fra Filippo Lippi, and Lucas Cranach, among others. The museum is open daily, except Monday, from 10:00 A.M. to 6:00 P.M. but only until 5:00 P.M. in winter.

SZENTENDRE

This twelfth-century golden-yellow Baroque town, with its narrow cobblestoned streets and squares, its red-tile roofs and Serbian and Greek Orthodox churches, and its views out above the river, became a center for artists in the early years of this century. Today most of the artists are gone, but art galleries, restaurants, ice-cream parlors, and tourist boutiques abound. If you can avoid the tour-bus crowds and remain above the commercialism, Szentendre can be architecturally rewarding. It owes some of its attractiveness to the fact that in 1690, when the Turks invaded Belgrade, many of Belgrade's Serbian residents fled and a goodly number settled here. Though their wooden Byzantine churches have been replaced by Baroque ones, some retain this Eastern heritage. The main sites follow.

Belgrade Church, or Greek Orthodox Cathedral (Sabornatemplom), Alkotmany tér: Several things are worth viewing in this simple towered Orthodox Cathedral set in a garden — an iconostasis, a red-marble altar, and impressive wrought-iron gates. You need to be let in by the sexton.

Ferenczy Museum, Fő tér 6: Károly Ferenczy (1862–1917), painting here in his youth, lured other painters to Szentendre. His work and that of his children — one a tapestry weaver, one a sculptor, and the third a painter like his father — is displayed in this museum that bears their name. It is open more or less from 10:00 A.M. to 5:00 P.M. daily.

Greek Orthodox Memorial Cross (Görögkeleti Emlékkereszt), Marx tér: This wrought-iron Rococo cross was erected by Serbian merchants in 1763 in gratitude for having escaped the plague.

Margit Kovács Museum, Vastagh György utca: In what was once a Serbian merchant's residence are the often biblical, sometimes grotesque but never uninteresting somber ceramics that Margit Kovács, who died in 1977, gave to the town. It is open from 9:00 A.M. to 5:00 P.M. daily.

Serbian Ecclesiastical Art Museum (Szerb Egyháztörténeti gyüjtemény), Engels utca 5: This contains the nation's outstanding collection of Eastern Slavic art, but one must be let in by the sexton.

Serbian Orthodox Church of the Annunciation (Blagovestenska-templom), Fő tér: On the outside of this 1752 Baroque church is a fresco in fair repair of St. Constantine and St. Helena. Inside is an early-nineteenth-century gilded iconostasis carved of limewood by a Serbian carver. There is an admission charge.

Szentendre Village Museum (Szabadtéri Néprajzi Múzeum), two miles outside of town: This continually growing collection of parts of villages from various regions of the country is being charmingly put together. In summer you can watch regional craftsmen at work. Tours in English are possible if advance arrangements are made by calling first. It is open from the beginning of April to the end of October.

VISEGRÁD

In the fifteenth century, the 350-room marble palace overlooking the Danube here at its horseshoe turn was described to Pope Sixtus IV as a "paradise on earth." It was occupied first by the Angevin ruler of Hungary, Charles Robert, in the fourteenth century. In the fifteenth century, when King Matthias Corvinus and his bride, Beatrix of Naples, moved in, they transformed it into a magnificent structure with fountains that alternately poured forth red and white wine and with gardens, balconies, and bastions overlooking the slow-flowing Danube. The porticoes were white, and the courtyard was filled with statues. In these idyllic surroundings, the Wallachian prince Vlad the Impaler, prototype of Dracula and brother-in-law of Matthias Corvinus, was kept under house arrest for twelve years. After the Turkish invasion of 1543 and a subsequent settlement here by Germans, who expropriated the castle's building blocks to construct their own homes, little remained of the sumptuous quarters.

Between invaders, looters, and weather, gradually the palace totally disappeared. Only old letters and stories told of it. Twentieth-century archeologist János Schulek, son of the restorer of Budapest's Matthias Church, was convinced, however, that it had not *really* disappeared and that, sooner or later, if he kept at it diligently enough, it would be found. Just before World War II, he was rewarded when a vine grower digging in his backyard struck an underground wall. After the delays of the war, excavation of this site and reconstruction of the palace got under way.

Today you can see a Gothic arcaded passageway, a Renaissance loggia, and part of a Renaissance fountain; the thirteenth-century fortified Solomon's Tower; such artifacts as a red-marble Madonna and Hercules riding a seven-headed hydra; and the Citadel where the Hungarian crown jewels were kept for a time until a maid stole them. (They were recovered, and, thereafter, more carefully guarded). From the Citadel you have a fine view of the river.

In summer, tour boats from Budapest make Visegrád a regular stop. The ruins are open from 9:00 A.M. to 5:00 P.M. daily, except Monday, from May through October and from 8:00 A.M. to 4:00 P.M. from November through April.

WESTERN HUNGARY

South and west of the Danube, Transdanubia — western Hungary — stretches to the Austrian border, its centerpiece the green-blue, two-to-nine-mile-wide, forty-eight-mile-long Lake Balaton, the largest lake in Central Europe. (In this chapter the lake's attractions will be considered in another section.) Transdanubia is farm and vineyard country. Its northern part has more valleys and hills than most of this generally flat plains nation. Like the Austrian neighbor of which it was once a part, it is filled with golden villages and onion domes.

Castles are nestled in the wooded hills on the Austrian border. Although not very high, these hills are called the Hungarian Alps. Boar, deer, and water birds proliferate in the woods and marshes along the Danube in the **Gemenc National Park and Game Preserve.**

The Romans called Transdanubia "Pannonia," and most of Hungary's Roman remains are here. This is also Hungary's most industrial area. The highlights of western Hungary follow.

FERTŐD

Prince Nicholas Esterházy, Nicholas the Magnificent, paid a visit to Louis XIV's Versailles on a diplomatic mission for the empress Maria Teresa in the early years of the eighteenth century. He was among the Hungarian noblemen who had supported her when others of his countrymen would not because she was a woman. He valiantly fought for her against the armies of Prussia's Frederick the Great, and the rewards she heaped on him were abundant. Among other positions, she made him the Austro-Hungarian Empire's ambassador to London's Court of St. James's.

Prince Nicholas enjoyed the life that he led, thanks to her munificence, though he had not been poor before — the Esterházy family owned ninety palaces across the Austro-Hungarian Empire. But when the prince saw Versailles, he knew he must have one more palace. There must be a Versailles in his country, too. This elegant structure formerly called Esterházy Palace, on the shore of Lake Fertőd, is what he built.

From all over Europe, stonemasons, cabinetmakers, and architects came to construct it. From Versailles itself came the gardener. For its opening in the fall of 1770 there were Chinese lanterns and fireworks, balls and feasts. And for twenty years Esterházy — as it was then called — thrived as a center of entertainment and culture. Franz Joseph Haydn came to conduct a choir and an orchestra for the prince and stayed for the most creative part of his life.

But after the death of Prince Nicholas in 1790, his son used the palace rarely, preferring one he had at Eisenstadt, closer to Vienna. By the nineteenth century, Esterházy had been virtually abandoned, and when the Russians reached Hungary in 1945 it was fair game for looting.

Twenty-five years ago, Hungary began to restore the palace, which is now an impressive and flourishing tourist attraction. You can only visit on guided tours, which are not always in English, but a translation sheet will be provided on request at the admissions office. Inside, you can see the room Maria Teresa occupied on state visits, "just close enough to the prince's chamber to be convenient for him," guides say with a giggle; a Carrara marble reception room; a chinoiserie room; and a glittering gold-and-white music room, where Cupids with trumpet flowers spring from the walls. In the high-ceilinged concert hall, performances are offered on Saturday nights from May to September.

After taking the tour, find time simply to lounge on the grounds outside for a while, to explore the gardens, and to go out beyond the elaborate, forged front gates and admire the splendor of the good years of the Austro-Hungarian Empire. The palace is open, except Monday, from 8:00 A.M. until noon and 1:00 to 5:00 P.M., or 4:00 P.M. between October 15 and April 15.

GYŐR

Though this is an industrial town with a truck factory, the old center is an unexpected pleasure. Above the narrow, cobblestoned winding streets and alleys near the cathedral are Baroque houses, and here and there the second stories of Gothic houses protrude out over the streets.

Győr (whose German name is Raab) sometimes is called the Town of Four Rivers, because it lies on the Rába, the Rábca, and two branches of the Danube. In the nineteenth century, it was Hungary's most important grain center after Budapest. It is also known as the only town in the nation where Napoleon, coming north from Italy in 1809 and defeating Hapsburg force after Hapsburg force en route, ever spent a night. The Hungarian nobility made a fruitless attempt to stop him here. The house where he stayed, now a picture gallery, is at Alkotmány utca 4.

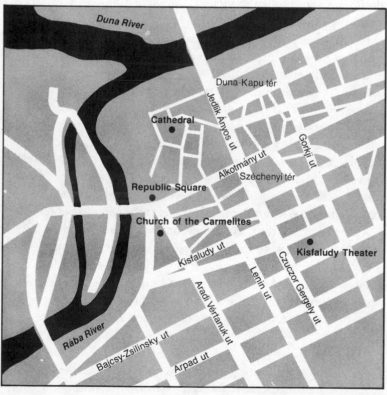

GYŐR

Győr's sparkling rivers arched with bridges and the boats that ply the waterways give it a special ambience and contribute to its vigorous bustling quality. Down on the riverfront, fishwives hawk silvery catches, and on the river's edge, anglers patiently await nibbles.

A morning or afternoon passed simply strolling Győr's narrow, winding streets, looking in shop windows and discovering unexpected squares, is time well spent. During Saturday morning market time, Győr is full to overflowing, and the very vigorousness of the commerce is exciting. The city has many attractions.

Ark of the Covenant, Gutenberg tér: This 1731 statue was erected, it is said, by Charles III after his soldiers had knocked the monstrance displaying the host from a priest's hands during a scuffle.

Church of the Carmelites (Karmelita-templom), Köztársaság tér: This eighteenth-century Baroque church is known for its graceful exterior proportions and its rich interior. Among the statues is one of Mary of the Foam, who is believed to be able to guard against the Rába River's overflowing.

Cathedral (Dóm), Káptalan dóm: Begun in Gothic style in the eleventh century, when King Stephen established an episcopal see here, virtually every century has added something of its own style. There are Baroque and neoclassical additions, and inside the well-preserved walls and altar are aswirl with Rococo frescoes by a Viennese master of the Rococo, Franz Anton Maulbertschi. One of Hungary's most stunning pieces of religious art, the silver-gilt reliquary bust of St. Ladislas, of about 1400, may be seen in the chapel that bears his name. Nearby, through a little garden, is the sprawling golden **Bishop's Residence,** built around a watch tower.

Kisfaludy Theater, Schweidel utca: With its exterior ceramic design by Op artist Victor Vasarely, this marble-and-glass structure is one of Hungary's finest modern theaters.

Margit Kovács Museum, Jedlik Annyós utca: The ceramics of this twentieth-century artist, who was born in Győr, can be seen by the public from 10:00 A.M. to 6:00 P.M. daily, except Monday, from October to March.

Miklós Borsos Museum, Martinovics tér: This museum of twentieth-century art is open from 10:00 A.M. to 6:00 P.M. in summer. From October to March, hours are 9:30 A.M. to 4:30 P.M. It is closed on Mondays.

Republic Square (Köztársaság tér): The column in the center of the square commemorates the retaking of Buda Castle from the Turks in 1686. The Baroque houses are also worth seeing.

Széchenyi Pharmacy (Széchenyi Patika): Aficionados of old pharmacies may enjoy the handsome woodwork and painted ceiling of this one. Open afternoons only from 2:00 to 5:00 P.M. and closed Monday and Tuesday.

Town Hall (Tanácsház), opposite the railroad station: This enormous neo-Baroque structure with a musical clock was built at the turn of the century.

Much of Győr's charm lies in the fact that it is still relatively undiscovered by any but Austrian tourists, but this also means that virtually no English is spoken — even in the local tourist and Ibusz offices.

JÁK

Because the Mongols never reached this part of Hungary, Ják's thirteenth-century **Benedictine Abbey Church** still stands and is Hungary's finest example of Romanesque art. Many statue heads were lopped off by the Turks, however, so that only the figure of Christ above the portal and the two apostles immediately beside him are the originals. But it is as much for its perfect proportions as for its sculpture that Ják is of tourist interest. At the turn of the century considerable restoration work on the church was done under Frigyes Schulek, who was also in charge of restoring the Matthias Church in Budapest.

KŐSZEG

In 1531, 1,000 Hungarians succeeded here in stopping 60,000 Turks en route to Vienna. Neither their valiant leader, Miklós Jurisics, nor the ordinary townsmen who fought beside him have ever been forgotten. For nearly a month the Turkish tents had been erected outside the city. The women and children of the village had fled. Some men favored flight, too, but Jurisics insisted that he — and they — could stop the Ottomans. Kőszeg had been built, after all, with an eye to stopping invaders. The houses in the center of town near the castle had been set one slightly behind the other in a sawtooth way so that the enemy was easily felled as it marched toward the ramparts. The houses are in the same position today.

For the traveler grown tired of touring, Kőszeg is delectably small. The population is only 12,000, and you can easily visit the center of the old town in an hour or two.

Above the door of the restored yellow- and red-striped **Town Hall** (Tanácsház) on the square (Jurisics tér) is the coat of arms of Jurisics, its savior. Some of the houses along the square (Numbers 7 and 14) are Renaissance structures. Others are seventeenth-century Baroque and eighteenth-century. The fifteenth-century **Church of St.** James (Szent Jákob-templom) is one of Hungary's finest structures with fifteenth-century frescoes on the right front wall. The **General's House** (Tábornokház) is a seventeenth-century linking of two medieval houses. The seventeenth-century **Church of St. Emmerich** (Szent Emmerich-templom) is part Baroque, part Gothic, part Renaissance.

In the reconstructed fourteenth-century **Castle** is a good museum of old weapons and displays recounting the history of the remarkable defense of the town. The castle is open daily, except Monday, from 10:00 A.M. to 6:00 P.M.

PÉCS

They call this lovely gold-and-pale-green community in the Mecsek Hills "Museum City" after its dozen cozy small museums, each guarded in a friendly fashion by middle-aged ladies in smocks. Several of the museums are along the same street, but in Pécs, that doesn't really matter. Although the population is 150,000, the Old Town is compact and easy to visit.

When Roman Pannonia flourished, this was its capital. In the fourth century it became Christian and remained so so steadfastly that in the eleventh century Stephen I made it a bishopric. Hungary's first university was founded here in the fourteenth century. In the fifteenth it was the home of one of Hungary's most-renowned poets, Jánus Pannonius, who was its bishop.

But in 1543, the Turks moved in, and Turkish mosques and minarets — though today they mark churches or museums — still rise above the city. Its principal attractions follow.

Amerigo Tot Museum, Káptalan utca 2: Here, the works of the twentieth-century Hungarian-born sculptor who did the bulk of his work in Italy is displayed on the level below the Zsolnay Collection (*see below*). The hours are from 10:00 A.M. to 4:00 P.M., except Monday.

Barbican: Excavation and restoration of these thirteenth-century walls that once encircled the city did not get under way until the 1960s and still continues.

Cathedral (Dóm), Dóm tér: This enormous, four-towered, many-times-reconstructed cathedral in its present form has a nineteenth-century neo-Romanesque look, but it is believed to have had its beginnings before the ninth century. It burned down innumerable times and each time was rebuilt with a difference. For a while, during the Turkish era, one of its towers was transformed into a minaret and the building was used as a mosque. Inside it is flat-ceilinged, with gleaming blue-and-gold decorations and largely nineteenth-century religious paintings. There is a striking red-marble Renaissance altar in its **Corpus Christi Chapel.** The exterior is notable for its imposing situation at the top of a sloping walkway and for the statues of the twelve apostles by Mihály Bartalits on its colonnaded entrance. Most of its genuine Romanesque artifacts are now in the nearby **Jánus Pannonius Lapidarium.**

The cathedral is flanked, as you face it, by the neo-Renaissance **Bishop's Palace** on the left and the eighteenth-century neoclassical **Chapter Archives** and **Parish Rectory** on the right. Check at the tourist office for visiting hours.

Csontváry Museum, Janus Pannonius utca 11: This museum is devoted solely to the colorful works of self-taught, post-Impressionist Tivadar Csontváry Kosztka (1853–1919), an assistant druggist, only recognized as a painter after his death. Much of his work, including what is generally considered his masterpiece,

Baalbek, is of biblical subjects. Museum days and hours are from 10:00 A.M. to 6:00 P.M., except Monday.

Elephant Block (Elefánt Épület), Jókai tér: Over the door of the former Elephant Block Drugstore, a handsome elephant head lures the hungry to the Elefánt Söröző, where there is a bar downstairs and a formal dining room upstairs. The various historic buildings that compose this block are in different architectural styles — one eclectic, one Baroque, one neoclassical, one Romantic.

Jakovali Hassan Mosque, Rákóczi út 2: This sixteenth-century mosque with its minaret beside it is one of the best-preserved Turkish period buildings in Hungary. Unfortunately, it is squashed between unappealing structures in an unappealing street and can really only be seen in its entirety from the Pannonius Hotel opposite. Its interior, however, has been well restored.

Flowers and excerpts from the Koran decorate the inside of the octagonal dome. There is a carved pulpit, and prayer rugs

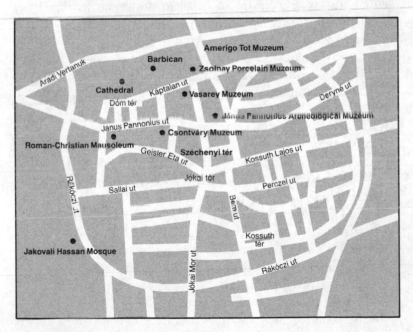

PÉCS

and carpets cover the floor; you expect somehow, in the subdued light, to hear the muezzin calling worshippers to prayer. In the small museum behind the mosque are Turkish armor and ceramics. The mosque and museum are open daily, except Wednesday, from 10:00 A.M. to 6:00 P.M.

Janus Pannonius Archeological Museum, Széchenyi tér 12: A collection of archeological artifacts of the area from prehistoric to Árpád dynasty times is housed in a Baroque building. Though displays are captioned in English as well as Hungarian, they are of limited interest. The museum is open from 10:00 A.M. to 4:00 P.M. daily, except Monday.

Main Square (Széchenyi tér): Rising at the top of this tilted city square is the domed stone-and-brick **Parish Church** (Belvárosi plebánia-templom). In the sixteenth century, this was the mosque of Gazi Kassim Pasha. The largest Turkish building still standing in Hungary, the mosque was constructed of stones from a Gothic church that had occupied the site. Inside, next to the main entrance, is a mihrab, a Moslem prayer niche, that faces Mecca. There are red-and-white half moons and Arab calligraphy on the walls, striped arches, windows with grilles, and above it all the great blue-and-gold dome. Of course, today a figure of Christ on the cross hangs in the prayer niche and the music is Catholic church music, and the effect is curiously moving. Atop the dome outside, the cross rests on the Muslim crescent moon. The church is open from noon to 5:00 P.M. daily.

Halfway down the square, on the left from the church, the big orange **Nádor Hotel** (Nádor Szálló) of the early years of this century is undergoing renovations. Its café has long been a popular gathering spot for local residents. The mustard-yellow clock-towered **Council Hall** with wrought-iron and white frostinglike decoration is a 1907 eclectic structure. The **Baranya County Courthouse** is another notable building in eclectic style on the square, and an amusing detail of this Art Nouveau former Pécs Savings Bank is the ceramic band of bees storing honey (as you should store money in a savings bank).

In the center of the square is a statue of the Trinity. In the square, too, is an equestrian **Statue of János Hunyadi,** hero in the war against the Turks and father of King Matthias Corvinus. Just across from the statue, ox-headed Art Nouveau gargoyles coated with green enamel spout water at the **Vilmos Zsolnay Memorial Fountain.** Behind it rises the former **Church of the Good Samaritan** (Irgalmasrend-templom), now the property of Pécs Medical University.

As you circle the square, look at Number 6, the restored house with a wrought-iron balcony and a dragon over the gate. Though it hardly appears so in its present eclectic form, it had its origin in the Middle Ages. The Ibusz Travel Company is in the Baroque building at Number 8.

Though sightseers pause to look up at the square's statues, and strollers cut across it admiring its red tulips in spring, today's square is a far cry from the bustling one that was here in Turkish days when turbaned vendors sold at bazaars and purchasers haggled with them and the muezzin was called from the minaret that is now gone. But the variety of colors and architectural styles of the buildings that surround it still make it one of the most attractive squares in Hungary.

Roman-Christian Mausoleum (Ōskeresztény mauzóleum), Dóm tér: Accidentally uncovered as recently as 1975, this fourth-century Christian tomb with frescoes of Daniel in the lions' den and Adam and Eve on the walls is a rare find, indeed, in Central Europe. It is open daily, except Monday, from May 1 to October 31 from 10:00 A.M. to 1:00 P.M. and from 3:00 to 6:00 P.M.

Vasarely Museum, Káptalan utca 3: This golden-yellow house on a pretty cobblestoned courtyard where flowers tumble from the walls is where Op artist Victor Vasarely was born in 1908. His work, done long before Op Art was the fashion of the sixties, is the attraction here. The museum is open daily, except Monday, from 10:00 A.M. to 4:00 P.M.

Zsolnay Porcelain Museum, Káptalan utca 2: Even if you are not a devotee of Art Nouveau, the Renaissance and Baroque structure in which this collection is housed is of interest. Its earliest section dating from 1324 was Pécs's first house. Upstairs, aficionados of Art Nouveau will have a heyday among glistening ceramics — pineapples and snakes and mushrooms on vases, a birdcage fashioned of leaves and flowers with an owl on top. There is a wonderful, awful madness of color and design in this work of Vilmos Zsolnay, who founded a small firm to make ceramics and later developed his own famous glossy glazed terra cotta here in 1865. His firm grew to be enormously successful, and examples of the factory's production throughout its history are in the rooms full of showcases. It is open from 10:00 A.M. to 4:00 P.M. daily, except Monday.

SOPRON

Although Sopron has a population of more than 50,000, the tourist wandering the cobblestoned streets of the horseshoe-shaped Old Town would certainly never know it once inside. To get to the Old Town from the more modern town, just look up for the green top of the 200-foot-high Watch Tower.

Situated just at the Austrian border, Sopron was actually given to Austria after World War I and the breakup of the Austro-Hungarian Empire. But its largely Hungarian population was more than a little unhappy at the decision. A plebiscite was called, and

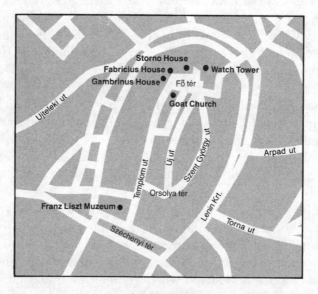

SOPRON

overwhelmingly Sopron voted to be Hungarian. Even during the long years of Communist rule, with prices low in the East and Western currency much in demand, Austrians freely came over to Sopron for a day's shopping or a visit to the hairdresser's. This hasn't always pleased the Hungarians, who grumbled about the Austrians as prices rose in their little town and astute shopkeepers sought to cater to Western-currency customers. Now, however, all seems forgotten and forgiven in this largely bilingual community where the ambience and the cuisine are quite as much Austrian as Hungarian.

Sopron had its beginnings as a Celtic settlement; when the Romans came, they named it Scarbantia. In view of its good location on the north-south trade route and the east-west route of the Byzantine merchants, they made it an inviting stopping place. It remains attractive: 115 of its buildings are labeled historical monuments and 240 are dubbed as of historical interest. With that much to preserve and restore, however, it is more than likely that if you come here in the next few years you will find scaffolding interfering with picture taking and venerable structures closed for repairs. Before putting Sopron on an itinerary, it would be wise to check with Ibusz in Budapest about the status of restoration work at the time you are planning a visit.

Sopron has retained much that is old because neither Mongols nor Turks found their way here. Roman ruins are regularly unearthed and there are more medieval Gothic elements here than in any other Hungarian town (though often they became part of structures of a later period). In World War II, it did suffer bombing raids, but that destruction uncovered new Roman ruins. To enjoy Sopron, tarry, looking up at the giants' heads above doors, the stucco floral garlands, the Madonnas in niches, the angels, lions, and coats of arms on facades, and drink in the colors — pink, gold, blue — albeit still being repainted. The principal sites follow.

Church Street (Templom utca): At Number 1 is the **Chapter House,** a small museum of medieval capitals said to represent the deadly sins. Its curator is enthusiastic, but you must stand a long time listening to religious history and jokes, all in Hungarian.

The house is open from 10:00 A.M. to noon and 2:00 to 4:00 P.M., except Monday. At number 2 the Baroque Esterházy Palace is now a **Mining Museum** of extremely limited interest to foreigners. Its hours are from 10:00 A.M. to 6:00 P.M., except Wednesday, in summer and from November to March from 10:00 A.M. to 4:00 P.M.

Fabricius House, Fő tér 6: Don't miss the handsome courtyard of this seventeenth- to eighteenth-century house. Its contents are those of an eighteenth-century aristocrat's home. It is open 10:00 A.M. to 6:00 P.M., except Monday.

Franz Liszt Museum, Május tér 1: In Raiding, a short distance from Sopron, Franz Liszt was born in 1811, son of a steward for the Esterházy family who was himself a minor musician. Recognizing his son's talent, the father quickly got him started in a musical life. Liszt gave his first concert in Sopron when he was nine. In this museum outside the town center, there is Liszt memorabilia, as well as historical material about Sopron. It is open from 10:00 A.M. to 6:00 P.M. in summer, except Monday, and from November to March from 10:00 A.M. to 5:00 P.M. The museum is of interest primarily to Liszt fans.

Gambrinus House, Fő tér 3: In the Middle Ages, this then Gothic building, now with a Baroque cast-iron balcony, was Sopron's Town Hall.

Gate of Loyalty (Hüségkapu), at the base of the Watch Tower: Though it looks much older, this archway that separates the Old from the New Town was erected in 1921 in honor of the residents' decision, by an overwhelming 72 percent, to be part of Hungary. The words "*Civitas Fidelissima*" carved on it mean "Most Faithful Town," and a grateful Hungarian is shown surrounded by loyal citizens.

Goat Church (Kecske-templom), Fő tér: Legend has it that the construction of this Gothic church was begun in the thirteenth century thanks to a grazing goat that unearthed a pot of gold coins. The alert goatherd snatched them away before they could be consumed and, grateful for his find, gave most of the money for the construction of the church. A less colorful story says the church got its name from the coat of arms of the donor who paid for the construction. It has long been a popular church in the nation, and three queens have been crowned here and five Diets held.

Lenin Street (Lenin körút): A number of old structures still stand on this main street of the New Town, including the **White Horse Inn** (Fehér 16) at Number 55, where composer Franz Joseph Haydn sometimes stayed when he was not at Esterházy Palace and where Johann Strauss reportedly wrote *A Night in Venice*.

New Street (Új utca): At Number 11 are the remains of a fourteenth-century synagogue; at Number 22, a medieval house now serves as a museum of Jewish artifacts. Both have recently been undergoing repairs, so if you wish to go inside, see in advance if the repairs are complete. There are handsome lancet windows at Number 16. When strolling this street be sure to look up at the facades.

Orsolya Square (Orsolya tér): Golden-yellow medieval arcades are an attraction here.

Outer Gate (Előkapu): The entryway into the Old Town has several medieval houses on it.

Pharmacy Museum (Patika Múzeum), Fő tér 2: This little museum is of interest only to the specialist. The museum is open from 10:00 A.M. to 6:00 P.M., except Monday.

St. George Street (György utca): At Number 12, note the loggias and courtyard of the **Eggenberger House**. The **Erdödy Palace** at Number 16, with its shell-and-floral decorations, is considered Sopron's finest example of Rococo architecture. Neither is open to the public.

Storno House, Fő tér 8: This late Renaissance palace with Baroque touches is now an interesting museum of household effects of Sopron's past. Ferenc Storno, who lived here beginning in 1821, was a restorer and painter of taste, and the family collection of furniture, clocks, and other household effects is well arranged. The house is open from 9:00 A.M. to 6:00 P.M. daily, except Monday, in summer and until 5:00 P.M. in winter. Unfortunately, an entrepreneurial Sopronian has turned its ground floor into a pizza parlor.

Trinity Column (Szentháromság-szobor), Fő tér: This elaborate Baroque pillar covered with cherubim has recently been undergoing restoration. It is regarded as one of the finest Baroque pillars in Hungary.

Watch Tower (Tűztorony): This symbol of the city, as you learn on a guided tour, has a foundation that was part of the original Roman city gate. On top of it is a Romanesque structure, then a sixteenth-century Renaissance middle, and, finally, the seventeenth-century Baroque bulbous tower and clock. All of these styles are masterfully blended. For centuries a watchman looked out from the arcaded balcony to the Lővér Hills that are Sopron's backdrop to make sure no hostile forces were approaching and to raise a warning if they were by blowing his bugle. And he would scan the city for possible fires — bugling again if he saw flames — for Sopron has suffered several blazes. In time, this bugling function took over and the watchmen became better known as musicians who entertained townspeople with their melodies than protectors of the community. The tower (124 steps affording a splendid view of the red roofs of old Sopron) may only be seen on non-English-speaking tours, but a translation card is available. It is open Tuesday through Saturday from 9:00 A.M. to 6:00 P.M. as is the adjoining small museum of Roman artifacts.

THE LAKE BALATON REGION

Silvery Lake Balaton, with an area of 266 square miles, Central Europe's largest lake, is the favorite national playground for Hungarians. With an average depth of ten feet and never more than forty, it is ready to receive swimmers, windsurfers, and yachtsmen early in the spring, and they can continue to enjoy it until late in the fall. It is rich in fish — forty-two different kinds — with fogas, a pike-perch, the most popular of all. And also because it is so shallow, ice fishing and skating can begin early in the winter season. On the slopes of the Badacsony Hills to the north, fine white wines are produced. Hungarian connoisseurs say Badacsonyi Szürkebarát (Pinot Noir) is this country's finest wine. Fourteen-acre Lake Héviz, about four miles from the western end of Lake Balaton, is one of the largest thermal lakes in the world.

But the Balaton area's attractiveness and its proximity to Budapest — about eighty miles southeast of the capital — have also led to development. Along its shores, vacation villages with thatched roofs and espresso bars have sprouted, and though efforts are being made to control pollution, the lake's western end has a pollution problem. For these two reasons Balaton is less likely to be so appealing to the foreign traveler as other parts of the country and, on a short itinerary, should probably be bypassed. Its principal attractions follow.

BADACSONY

This flat-topped hill on the northern shore of Lake Balaton is among Hungary's most interesting natural attractions. Basalt columns 180 to 200 feet tall are ranged behind each other like organ pipes on Badacsony and Szentgyorgyi Hills, which are splendid vine-growing regions. From the top of the Badacsony, there is a fine view of the columns, the vineyards, and the lake below.

As long ago as Avar and Roman days, vines were lovingly nurtured on these slopes. Roman altars to the gods of wine have been found and the Avars are said to have buried their dead with grape seeds to assure that there would be wine aplenty for them to enjoy in the afterlife. Vine growers here attribute the success of their vineyards not only to the sun that streams down from above and the way the hills and forests to the north protect the vines on the hillsides from cold winds, but to the way the vines "see" their own reflection — get light — on the undersides of their leaves from the sun striking the lake waters. They talk, too, of how strength comes to the vine roots from the fires of the volcanoes that once erupted here.

Badacsony's most famous wines, which you should surely taste on a visit, are Kéknyelű (Blue Stalk), Riesling, and Szürkebarát (like the Pinot Gris of Alsace). At the top of the mountain, there is a good viewing point, a museum, and a restaurant. The Baroque restaurant was formerly the home of Balaton-inspired poet Sándor Kisfaludy. Badacsony is full of tourists.

BALATONFÜRED

For nearly 250 years, the mineral springs here have been attracting health seekers. In the eighteenth century, the mineral waters, said to be efficacious in the treatment of lung and stomach problems, were mixed with the whey from goat's milk to make them better still. Though taking the waters is unlikely to be of interest, the park along the lake is a lovely one. Plane and poplar trees shade it, and statues decorate it. One of them is of the Indian poet Rabindranath Tagore, who came here ill in 1926 and was so delighted with the state of his health when he left that in gratitude he planted a linden tree along the bank. Since then, other satisfied visitors have planted trees, and the result is a charming, shady lake-front park. Vineyards and orchards are on the hills above the town. From here there are ferries across the lake to Tihany.

HEREND

In 1826 Vince Stingl from Sopron began making earthenware here. A talented and adventurous craftsman, he soon had expanded his interest to porcelain, but he was an artist, not a businessman. It was not until Mor Fischer, in 1839, took over management of the little factory here that Herend china began to be known.

In the beginning, Fischer established the porcelain's reputation by making replacements for discontinued lines that had originally been made by major concerns like Germany's Meissen and France's Sevres. Then, boldly, Fischer took an original design that he called the Chinese butterfly pattern to show at the Great Exhibition in London in 1851. It was a smash success — with, among others, Queen Victoria attending. After that Herend porcelain was famous.

Now, as then, it is still hand-painted — every orange dot on a roly-poly pig's side, the stamen of every flower. And visitors may watch on guided tours of a showroom, then explore the **Museum of Herend History,** with its 1850s Far Eastern patterns, its Romantic figurines of the 1860s, its historical and folkloric figurines of the 1920s. There is also a shop. The showroom and museum are open daily, but not Sundays or holidays, from 8:00 A.M. to 4:30 P.M. from April 1 to October 31 and from 8:00 A.M. to 4:00 P.M. from November 1 to March 31. To be assured of an English-speaking guide, you should make arrangements in advance through Ibusz in Budapest.

HÉVIZ
Thousands come annually to Europe's largest thermal spring to take the baths, said to be helpful to those with rheumatism, arthritis, and neuralgia. Its turreted turn-of-the-century buildings, its rare pink water lilies, and the fact that you can still swim outdoors here in October and not feel cold at all are among its attractions. It is not, however, a destination to go far out of your way to see. Lake Héviz, just a few miles from his palace, was a favorite with Count György Festetics, who helped develop Héviz as a spa in the eighteenth-century heyday of spas.

KESZTHELY
The highlight of this second-largest town (after Balatonfüred) on Lake Balaton is the palace just above the lake that Count György Festetics built here in 1745. In addition, however, Keszthely is a less frenetic place for a Balaton holiday than most of the lakeside communities.

If you are not expecting to go as far west in Hungary as the Esterházy Palace at Fertőd, the palace provides a taste of the elegance and grandeur of Hungary in its Austro-Hungarian Empire days.

The count who had this beige-and-white palace constructed was something of a Renaissance man. He established Europe's first agricultural institute in 1797, and the bright leather and gilt of his 52,000 volumes on science and literature gleam from the shelves of his paneled library. He invited the leading literary lights of the nation to his palace each spring to share ideas. The count had this palace built in Baroque style, but a restoration in 1883 made it neo-Baroque. It may only be visited on Hungarian-language guided tours, but a translation card is available.

Along with the library of handsome carved oak (now part of the National Széchenyi Library), there are paintings of cattle, counts, and hunting scenes; fine china and family hunting trophies; and Turkish and African weapons to be seen. The palace's contents have been so remarkably preserved thanks to the Russian general whose forces took the area in World War II.

A university history teacher in the Soviet Union, the general recognized the value of what he saw at the palace. (The last family member, a young widow with a child, had fled abroad as the Russians approached, leaving everything behind.) When it was determined that the palace was to be a Russian military hospital, the general had all its fine furniture taken to one wing, the door locked, and a sign "Serious Epidemic. Do Not Enter" affixed to the door. In 1949, what he had saved became the nucleus of today's palace-museum. It is open from 9:00 A.M. to 5:00 P.M. daily, except Monday, from October to April. The visitor here should not fail to stroll the French gardens to admire the statuary and the wrought-iron gate and the stucco horses on the palace facade.

SZÉKESFEHÉRVÁR

This first Hungarian capital, where Prince Árpád is believed to have pitched camp about A.D. 800, has suffered enormously over the centuries. During the Turkish occupation the church where Árpád kings were crowned was blown up and much of the rest of the medieval town destroyed. Though it was rebuilt in the eighteenth century, in World War II, 6,000 of its 7,000 houses were either destroyed or severely damaged. Today, many parts of the Old Town, where painstaking reconstruction is being done, are covered with scaffolding. This limits its interest to tourists, of course, but since it is just off the main route between Balaton and Budapest, it is worth a brief stop to see the old buildings around István tér and Szabadság tér. There is the richly decorated pale-green nineteenth-century **City Hall;** the fourteenth-century Gothic

St. Anne's Chapel, the only medieval building that still stands here; the ornate golden-yellow **Bishop's Palace** built with stones from the Coronation Church the Turks blew up. Behind it, in the **Garden of Ruins,** for aficionados of archeological sites, are medieval foundations and tombstones. But it is pleasant to stroll the narrow cobblestoned pedestrian streets lined with carefully restored gray-and-pink and green-and-gold Baroque structures, with intricate wrought-iron railings on their balconies. Hungary's oldest pharmacy, the **Black Eagle** (Fekete Sas), built in the eighteenth century, is here.

TIHANY

A few thatched roofs, but more of red tile, top the old stone fishermen's cottages on this windswept peninsula, much of which, today, is bird sanctuary and national park. The eleventh-century crypt of the Baroque **Abbey Church** is Hungary's oldest medieval structure and the burial place of King Andrew I, who founded a Benedictine monastery here and brought Russian Orthodox monks to the area. The present ornate church where putti with golden wings play on the organ is rich in similar carvings, most done by wood-carver-lay-brother Sebestyén Stuthoff, who turned to the Church after the death of his fiancée. (She is said to be the angel kneeling on the Altar of the Virgin Mary on the left side of the church.) Outside the church are two distinctly modern statues — Amerigo Tot's *His Majesty the Kilowatt* and Imre Varga's *The Founder,* King Andrew in basalt and aluminum.

Next door is a museum of the history of the Balaton area, of minimal interest but for the stunning view it affords of the lake below. It is open from 10:00 A.M. to 6:00 P.M. daily, except Monday.

Tihany also has an open air museum with a fisherman's guild-house in it that is open except Tuesdays, pleasant walks through the sweet-smelling lavender fields and the apple orchards in spring, an exceptionally rich fishing lake, and a second lake that serves as a bird sanctuary. On Csokonai utca and Petőfi utca are a few of the original gray-stone cottages of the village, their windows and doors outlined in white. Once a feverish volcanic area, there are yellowish-white volcanic "cones" — rocks — still to be seen. If you visit Tihany, come early in the day before the bus-loads and boatloads of tourists arrive, for it is a tourist heaven.

VESZPRÉM

In this unofficial capital of the Badacsony Hills, it is **Castle Hill** (Várhegy) that is most notable. The castle area is reached through the **Gate of Heroes** (Hősök kapuja), built in 1936 from stones of the fifteenth-century castle gate. Nearby, from the top of the part medieval and part Baroque **Fire Tower** (Tűzt orony), there is a fine view of the town and the surrounding countryside.

Tolbuhin út leads to the square that is the site of both the neo-Romanesque **Cathedral of the Church of St. Michael** and the Baroque **Bishop's Palace** (Püspöki palota). The palace was constructed by Jákáb Fellner from stones of the old medieval palace that had occupied the hill from the eleventh century. At that time, Veszprém became a bishopric, and Stephen I's wife, Gisela, had a cathedral constructed here. The thirteenth-century **Gisela Chapel** (Gizella kapolna), with its Byzantine frescos, stands beside the Bishop's Palace. It may be visited from May 1 to October 31 from 9:00 A.M. to 5:00 P.M. The cathedral that now stands here dates largely from the early twentieth century, though its original was a Romanesque church.

THE GREAT PLAIN

More than half of Hungary is flat — given over to the endless Great Plain. In the old days, the only punctuation in this endless landscape was an occasional low-slung, whitewashed farmhouse, a row of birches along the road, pheasants and geese, and hay mounds like sleeping elephants. Nowadays, there are occasional pink-and-white villages, apple and apricot orchards, and wheat and rice fields. In summer, the sun of this endless, unbroken landscape can produce mirages.

In medieval days, this 12,355,000-acre Great Plain, which goes south from Budapest to Yugoslavia and east to the Soviet

Union and Romania, was forested, and villages abounded. The annual flooding of the River Tisza, pesky though it was, enriched the soil for farming. But the Mongolian invasion in 1241 and the Turkish occupation wiped out most of the villages, with their nervous inhabitants moving into the towns where there was more protection. After that, the great, flat, green land became a pasture for animals — till nineteenth-century technology took control of the river and there was no more flooding. But neither was there the rich alluvial soil that had nourished the grasses on which the cattle, sheep, and pigs fed, but a great deal of alkaline wasteland instead. Happily, in the last few decades, the installation of canals has nourished the Great Plain with water again and arable farming has returned. But two areas of the old Great Plain — the Hortobágy Puszta and the Bugac Puszta — have been left as old animal grazing lands and turned into national parks. From Budapest, Ibusz organizes day trips, in season, to the Bugac Puszta, part of **Kiskunság National Park.** There, the horse herders of the plain — in broad-brimmed black hats, baggy

12. One of the famous horsemen of the Hortobágy Great Plain wearing a costume that has remained unchanged for centuries.

pants, and pale-blue shirts — put on horse shows for visitors, and there is a museum of pastoral life and an inn.

In the larger **Hortobágy National Park** (630 square miles) and considerably farther east, the grassy *puszta* — plains-land — stretches as far as the eye can see. Here, too, are museums and riding demonstrations by horsemen. There is nothing sophisticated about the tourism here. Visitors clamber into open, horse-drawn wagons and are jounced across rutty roads to see a herd of long-horned gray Hungarian cattle and flocks of twisted-horn racka sheep near at hand, to visit barns with roofs of thatch that sweep almost to the ground, to look out for storks, cranes, and curlews in the distance, and to watch cowboys standing balanced on the backs of their horses.

If it rains, the visitor will get wet watching the show. If it is sunny, he will get burned. But there is something attractive in the very rusticity of this adventure, as long as you are patient and not expecting Disney World organization.

Unless you come to the Hortobágy as part of an organized tour, you may or may not be fitted aboard a wagon, and the chances are, in any case, that the long, bumpy ride out onto the plain will not depart when it was scheduled to. Try to find out in advance from Ibusz in Budapest when shows are expected to take place. If the tour is late, you will have time to go to the **Shepherds' Museum** and look in the dusty showcases at the shaggy sheepskin coats the men of the plains wear in winter; learn of the black Hungarian sheepdog, the *puli*; see powder horns carved by the cowboys and the shepherds in long winters of the past; and admire the musical instruments they have played.

The **National Park Museum** has statistics on the number of animals still raised on the Great Plain, some captions in English, and a museum of the art of the Great Plain. There is a restaurant-bar where the tours begin, and even if there is little to eat, there is always plenty of apricot or bitter herb brandy *(unicum)* to drink. In the village of Hortobágy is a nine-arched stone bridge — the longest stone bridge in Hungary. Skeptics said it couldn't be built, but it was and is now known familiarly as "the bridge on nine holes."

And it is not out of the question, while you wait for a tour to originate, that you might, on a hot midsummer day, see a church steeple or a village mysteriously appear, then disappear, on the vast sizzling plain.

The principal cities in the neighborhood of the Great Plain and their main attractions follow.

DEBRECEN

Debrecen is renowned for its position as an entry point into the Hortobágy Great Plain and as a center of Protestantism, "the Calvinist Rome."

In 1552, it was decreed that only Protestants could settle here. As it turned out, the ruling made little difference, for three years later the Turks moved in, making Debrecen a property of the sultan, and the sultan interfered little with the activities of the Calvinists. Once the Turks were gone, the Catholic Hapsburgs tried converting the Calvinists, but they stood firmly by their faith. (One of the less attractive elements of Calvinism was the mass persecutions of witches, both here and in Szeged until 1768, when the Austro-Hungarian government stopped them.)

Debrecen's proximity to the Hortobágy increased its prosperity considerably. The Hortobágy cowhands, raising their long-horned gray cattle on the plain, started their cattle drives to Vienna and Prague from Debrecen.

The city's principal sites follow.

Calvinist College (Református Kollégium), Kálvin tér: In 1538 this theological school was first established by Hungary's Calvinists, who were strongly influenced by the egalitarian ideas of the English Revolution. Many of the preachers came from Debrecen and fomented their liberal ideas among its peasants and fiercely denounced the landlords from the pulpits. As well as being a great center for religious thought and social reform, the college gained renown in the field of language and for its splendid library. Though a fire in 1802 destroyed much of the building, courageous students saved the books, which today number more than 500,000 and make it the second largest (after Budapest's) library in the nation. In 1849 the Hungarian Chamber of Deputies led by Lajos Kossuth met in the **Oratory.** Both the library and the wood-paneled oratory are open to the public. Hours are Tuesday through Saturday from 9:00 A.M. to 5:00 P.M. and Sunday from 9:00 A.M. to 1:00 P.M., but it is wise to check in advance with the local tourist office (Hajdutourist) to the right of the Great Church to be sure that a custodian is on duty.

Csokonai Theatre, Kossuth Lajos utca 10: This extravagantly Romantic nineteenth-century structure, part Moorish, part Byzantine, was built in the 1860s; allegorical figures and poets adorn its facade.

Déri Museum, Múzeum utca: The major attractions inside this neo-Empire-style museum of the 1920s are the fine collection of embroidered felt cloaks worn on the Hortobágy and the nineteenth-century Hungarian art. (A charming tale of these cloaks is that in the old days a potential suitor would leave his cloak behind on the porch of his beloved, after having paid a call. If she was willing to accept his attentions, she would take the cloak inside; if not, she left it on the porch.) Most notable of all the art is *Ecce Homo* by Mihály Munkácsy, a work that was widely exhibited around the world, and much lauded, at the end of the last century.

Golden Bull Hotel (Hotel Arany Bika), Kossuth Lajos tér: This white-pillared 1882 structure, replacing a seventeenth-century inn, is somewhat down-at-the-heels these days, but the main dining room still has its stained-glass ceiling of yesteryear and dazzling chandeliers.

Great Church (Nagy-templom), Vörös Hadsereg: This Maria Teresa yellow, nineteenth-century neoclassical church with its colonnaded front, the largest Protestant church in Hungary, has a simple, undecorated grandeur inside. Because of its size (it can accommodate 5,000) it was here in 1849 that patriot Lajos Kossuth called for the independence of Hungary from Austria.

On top of the church, in the left-hand tower, is a five-ton bell, made from cannons captured in the Thirty Years' War by György Rákóczi I, ruler of Transylvania.

Little Calvinist Church (Kis-templom), Széchenyi utca: This little Baroque church, constructed between 1720 and 1726, was remodeled and given its present curious bastion when its onion dome was destroyed in a storm.

Memorial Gardens (Emlék Kert): The pillar in this garden behind the Great Church memorialized forty Debrecen Calvinist ministers and teachers who were sold as galley slaves in the seventeenth century, but miraculously freed by a Dutch vessel to make their way back home again.

Old County Hall (Régi megyeháza), Vörös Hadsereg útja 54: Devotees of Art Nouveau will be entranced by the Zsolnay ceramic ornamentation and stained glass of this 1912 structure where the city council meets.

Unfortunately, many squat, ugly, modern buildings have been constructed in recent years in the heart of old Debrecen, so it lacks the historic and architectural unity and charm that it must once have had. However, you can still find some pretty old houses and churches along Széchenyi utca and around Kálvin tér and Béke útja.

KECSKEMÉT

While much of Hungary was suffering under its 150 years of Turkish domination, this "town of the goat," as its name translates (each convert to Christianity was said to have been given a goat in the Middle Ages), was one of those that was a protectorate of the sultan, and as such it thrived. Situated in fertile, fruit-growing land, Kecskemét established a firm reputation for itself in the nineteenth century with its sweet apricots, most of which were transformed into potent but smooth *barackpálinka* — apricot brandy — and for its largely white wines. This reputation continues. It is also a bright, open town with squares gay with flowers and made architecturally lively by Hungarian Art Nouveau (or Secessionist) buildings.

Great Catholic Church (Nagy-templom), Kossuth Lajos tér: This vibrant late-eighteenth-century Baroque yellow-and-white "pigtail style" church is so called because of the sculpted braids at the tips of its columns. Inside, every surface is covered with painting. Its designer was a priest, Oswald Gáspár. On its facade are memorials to those who died in the War of Independence against the Austrians. It is said that to lure youngsters into that conflict, soldiers came to the square in the evening to dance and sing, promising the younger boys comradeship, popping soldiers' hats on their heads, and leading them away.

József Katona Theater, Lestár tér: This neo-Baroque theater, with its draped figures supporting the facade and its black wrought-iron canopy, has recently been restored.

For visitors with more special interests, there is a small **Toy Museum** (Játékmúzeum) and a small **Museum of Primitive Hungarian Art** (Magyar Maiv Festok Múzeum), virtually side by side. The **József Katona Museum** is largely concerned with archeological finds, and the **Zoltán Kodály Institute of Musical Education** (Kodály Zoltán Zenepedagógiai Intézet) is here. The nineteenth-century composer Zoltán Kodály was born in Kecskemét, and on the first floor of his institute there is a small museum about him and his work. It is open Monday through Friday from noon to 1:00 P.M. and 4:00 to 6:00 P.M. and Saturday and Sunday from 10:00 A.M. to 6:00 P.M.

The visitor to Kecskemét, as to most small Hungarian cities, may have difficulty finding English-speakers in the streets and in the local tourist offices. Similarly, few brochures will be in English, but provincial folk tend to go out of their way for strangers who look lost, to jump off their bicycles to assist as best they can in finding sites the visitor seeks.

Szabadság tér: Two of Kecskemét's most famous buildings are on this square — the Art Nouveau **Ornamental (Cifra) Palace** and the Romantic Moorish-style white structure with a black dome that is the former synagogue. The Ornamental Palace (you need binoculars to see its merry pansy decorations in the tile below the roof) is one of Hungary's finest examples of its special Art Nouveau style. The interior of the synagogue, built between 1862 and 1871, was destroyed by the Nazis and the building is now being used as a **House of Technology**. It is rarely open to the public.

Town Hall (Városháza), Kossuth Lajos tér: This salmon-pink turn-of-the-century structure with its cupolas, turrets, and tile decorations, its wrought iron over the glass front door, and its stucco grapes dangling, is a Gusztáv Pártos and Ödön Lechner design (Lechner is known in Budapest for his Postal Savings Bank and Geological Institute designs). Floral, but no human forms abound on its facade. Inside, colorful nineteenth-century historical paintings by Bertalan Székely, including Árpád, Hungary's founding father, and other leaders signing an agreement in blood making Árpád chief, decorate the walls.

On a rock split asunder in front of the Town Hall it is written, "Kecskemét's Greatest Son Broke His Heart Here," a reference to the playwright József Katona, who dropped dead of a heart attack outside in 1830.

SZEGED

This is the city of sunshine, paprikas, salami, and the Great Flood. It is in the heart of paprika country, and those crimson peppers are nurtured by the many days of sunshine here. It is the city of salami, and pork from pigs raised only here give the meat a special flavor. It is the city of the Great Flood because in 1879, when the Tisza River on which it sits rose over its banks, 5,500 of its 5,800 houses were destroyed and Szeged had to be virtually entirely rebuilt.

In the reconstruction, embankments were erected along the river and the entire city raised. The new city was built in something of a ring plan with the streets that make up its outer ring gratefully named for those world cities that gave money to help in its reconstruction — and many cities did. (Moscow was not among them, but in Hungary's Communist years, the Russian capital's name was substituted for Berlin's, though Berlin had been a donor. Now, however, Moscow is gone and Berlin is back.)

In Szeged's early days, it is said, Attila, king of the Huns, had his City of Tents here, and from it in the fifth century A.D., he set off on conquering forays to other lands. And it was here that he died, after a night of great merriment and feasting. He was thrown into the yellow Tisza in a coffin of gold, silver, and bronze, it is said, for which archeologists still are looking. It was near Szeged, too, that Árpád, founder of Hungary's first dynasty, was selected ruler of the Magyars and fealty to him was drunk in human blood. Szeged's principal attractions follow.

Cathedral Square (Dóm tér): The two-towered dark-red-brick neo-Romanesque **Votive Church** (Fogadalmi-templom) was built here between 1912 and 1929 with contributions from the city's aldermen in gratitude for having survived — as little of the city did — the 1879 flood. It is one of Hungary's largest churches, and its 10,180-pipe organ is Hungary's largest.

In front of it rises the squat twelfth-century **Tower of St. Demetrius** (Szent Dömötor-torony). When plans got under way for the construction of the Votive Church, a Church of St. Demetrius already occupied the selected site. When it was blown up to make way for the new construction, this squat Romanesque tower was uncovered and it has been allowed to remain. The rest of Cathedral Square has pretty arcades with busts of famous figures in Hungarian history and the arts under the arches. The Votive Church is attractive architecturally but permanent wooden bleachers erected outside the church for summer festive events destroy what would otherwise be a pleasing square. In addition to the church, the university and the Bishop's Palace border the square.

New Synagogue, Gutenberg utca 20: If there is one building worth seeing in this fifth-largest Hungarian city it is the stunning New (1903) Synagogue. Unfortunately, it is still undergoing extensive postwar restoration. Its mosaic dome of white, blue, and gold represents the world. The stained-glass windows are scenes from Jewish life. Much of the interior is Carrara marble, and the outside is faced with yellow brick. Set in a little garden, it was designed by Lipot Baumhorn and his son, Rabbi Immanuel Low. Many consider it the world's most beautiful synagogue, but it is not easy to get inside, so it is wise to go first to Szeged Tourist on Victor Hugo utca 1 to see if arrangements can be made with the caretaker. Little English is spoken in Szeged.

Széchenyi tér: The golden-yellow **Town Hall** here, like that in Kecskemét, was designed by Ödön Lechner and Gusztáv Pártos. Originally in Baroque style, after the flood it was redone in an eclectic design. Statues, an allegorical fountain representing the

Tisza, and many pretty plantings are also part of the spacious square's design.

NORTHERN HUNGARY

Northern Hungary bordering Czechoslovakia is a wooded upland of deciduous trees like oak, beech, and ash that in the spring are the freshest and most delicate of greens. Because, by Hungarian standards, this is high land, it can be misty and mysterious when fog is caught in pockets in the mountains. Wild boar and deer dwell in the forests. Apple trees bloom in the spring in the front yards of white houses with red-tiled roofs. Ducks waddle and geese strut in farmyards. Sometimes there are vineyards on the hills, for this is the land of Tokaji — Hungary's most famous wine — "a golden flame locked up within a bottle," the nineteenth-century poet Sándor Petőfi called it.

Northern Hungary's principal attractions follow.

EGER
Baroque Eger is renowned for its heroic and successful defense of its fortress with 2,000 men against more than 100,000 Turks, for the strong red Bull's Blood (Egri Bikavér) wine that gave them courage, for its medieval library, and for the northernmost minaret in Europe. Though reconstruction work in recent years has interfered somewhat with sightseers' vistas, there are still many accessible sites and much charm to the narrow streets, arcaded buildings, wrought-iron gates, and Baroque towers and domes of the **Old Town.**

Situated in a valley between the lavender peaks of Hungary's highest mountains, the Mátras, and the wooded Bük Hills, the natural backdrop for this city's historic monuments (third in number of historic monuments after Budapest and Sopron) is superb.

Eger was among the first Magyar settlements in the Carpathian Basin and was made a bishopric by King Stephen in the eleventh century. In the thirteenth century, the Mongols came, devastating countryside, cathedral, and the old mud castle that stood on the hill. It was afterward that Béla IV ordered construction of a stone fortress on the hilltop. This made the town seem secure enough so that immigrants from many parts of western Europe came to settle here. It is always wise to check Ibusz in Eger at Bajcsy-Zs. tömbbelsö to find out visiting hours for all sites in town. Eger's principal sites follow.

Cathedral (Dóm), Szabadság tér: This second-largest cathedral in Hungary (after Estergom), with its six Corinthian columns and long flight of steps, was built in neoclassical style in the early nineteenth century. The monumental statues on the steps, designed by a Venetian sculptor, Marco Casagrande, are of the Hungarian king-saints, Stephen and Ladislas, and the apostles Peter and Paul. The cathedral was the brainchild of controversial bishop János László Pyrker, who, out of sorts with the Baroque specialist architect he had originally hired, got involved in a lawsuit with him when he hired József Hild, another Baroque architect, to do the work instead. Though the cathedral was completed in a very short time — only five years — money was beginning to run out before it was finished, so its interior is not so perfectly done as it might have been.

County Council Hall (Megyél Tanács Iroda), Kossuth Lajos utca 9: Step into the courtyard here to see the intertwined tendrils of the wrought-iron gate fashioned by the eighteenth-century smith Henrik Faziola, who came to Eger from Würzburg. He not only designed and constructed the most beautiful wrought-iron gates and window bars of the city, but also analyzed ore found in the Bük Mountains and started an ironworks.

István Dobó Square (Dobó István tér): A large statue that recounts the events of the battle of 1552, whose leader was Captain István Dobó, is the centerpiece of this square, which is also the site of the two-spired Baroque gold-and-cream **Minorite Church** (Minorite-templom) of 1771. Although the exterior of this church, designed by a Prague architect, has been restored, the interior remains in need of restoration. When the structure was built, the chief of the Minorites, the name given to the Franciscans by St. Francis, was roundly criticized because of the elab-

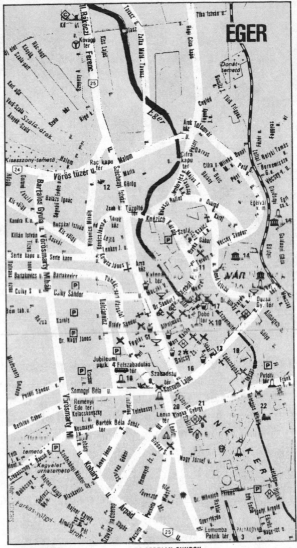

EGER

1 COUNTY HALL
2 EGERTOURIST OFFICE
3 STATION (RAILWAY)
4 BUS-STATION
5 HOTEL EGER
6 HOTEL PARK
7 MOTEL TOURIST AND TOURIST HOUSE
8 CAMPING-SITE
9 CATHEDRAL
10 CHURCH OF THE MINORITES
11 MINARET
12 SERBIAN CHURCH
13 FAZOLA-GATES
14 DOBÓ I. FORTRESS MUSEUM AND PICTURE GALLERY
15 GÁRDONYI MEMORIAL HOUSE
16 LICEUM LIBRARY, OBSERVATORY
17 DOBÓ STATUE
18 LIBERATION MONUMENT
19 COUNTY LIBRARY
20 GÁRDONYI GÉZA THEATRE
21 THE HOUSE OF TECHNICS
22 OPEN-AIR BATH

13. Musicians preparing for an outdoor concert in the main square at Eger.

orateness of his structure, for Minorites were supposed to be austere. The twentieth-century eclectic **Town Council Building** and arcaded shops also edge the square, as, unfortunately, does a modern department store that is distinctly out of place.

Fortress (Vár Kapu): In the fifteenth century, this was a leading Renaissance town, and it seemed fair game to the Turks who came here in 1552. Happily for the Hungarians, spies let them know in advance that a Turkish attack was in prospect, and István Dobó, who would be remembered ever afterward for his heroic defense of this fortress, filled its underground labyrinth of caves with ammunition and enough food for half a year and awaited the expected attack. On the eleventh of September, the Turks arrived "to kick down the sheepfold," their leader said.

For thirty-eight days, more than 100,000 Ottoman soldiers battered at Eger's fortress. The 1,935 Hungarian men, women, and children inside fought back, pouring pitch and boiling oil on their attackers and hurling stones down on their heads. One device the Hungarians had for ascertaining when and where the Turks were planning to use mines to blow up the fortress was a pea on a drum. If the pea began to move, the Hungarians knew a cut was being made for a mine (thus shaking the pea), and they would cut countermines. Finally, it is said, a Turkish soldier called up from below on the thirty-eighth day, "You in the castle are valiant; now you have no more to fear; there will be no more siege, since the pashas, to their great sorrow, are leaving for home."

You can tour the dark, grim underground casemates of the fortress with a guide or explore its stony hill from 9:00 A.M. to 5:00 P.M. daily, except Monday. There is a **Castle Museum** (Dobó István Vármúzeum) filled with Turkish and Hungarian weapons and armor and coins of the period, and a fine view of the green copper church towers, the slender minaret, and the red roofs of the city from the fortress ruins.

Unfortunately, the valiant fight of István Dobó in 1552 was not the last battle fought here. Thirty-four years after the first siege there was a second, and this time it was mercenaries who were in the fortress and chose to capitulate. For the next century, this city was not only under Turkish rule, but was a Turkish provincial capital.

The reasonably good state of preservation of the fortress can be attributed to the Hapsburgs, who, in the aftermath of the War of Independence, ordered all fortresses destroyed. Their method of "destroying" this one was to bury it in sand, which, it turned out, helped in its preservation.

Kethuda Minaret, Károly Knézits utca: From 1596 till 1687 the Turks ruled Eger, building mosques, minarets, and baths, but all that remains today is this single fourteen-sided minaret, 131 feet high, built of carved stones. The mosque of which it was a part was torn down in 1841. This is the northernmost minaret still standing in Europe.

Lyceum (Ho Si Minh Tanárlképzö Föiskola), Sabadság tér: This beautifully proportioned Baroque structure with its "pigtail" decorations was designed by Jákab Fellner (one of his other great works is the Bishop's Palace at Veszprém) and József Gerl. Its superb library includes more than 1,000 volumes in a room with elaborate furniture in Louis XVI style and a fine ceiling fresco of the Council of Trent. Its graceful staircase and its observatory are other outstanding features. Originally, this was to have been a university, and plans for it were laid by Bishop Ferenc Barkóczy, who, in 1761, selected Gerl as the architect of his school. But before work on the project got under way, Barkóczy quit his archbishopric in something of a huff and Bishop Károly Esterházy took over and hired Jákab Fellner, the Esterházy family's architect. The library is open from 9:30 A.M. to 12:30 P.M. daily, except Monday. The observatory is open from 9:00 A.M. to 1:00 P.M. from May 20 to July 10 and is closed during the Christmas and New Year seasons.

Palace of the Vice Provost (Kispréposti lak), Kossuth Lajos utca 4: This lovely Rococo house has a balcony with wrought-iron sides that is the handiwork of master smith Henrik Faziola.

Széchenyi utca: All along this street are outstanding Baroque buildings. Extravagant Rococo ornamentation above the doorway and around the windows of the early-eighteenth-century, Jesuit-built **Cistercian Church** make it worth looking at. The Rococo decoration was added in the second half of the eighteenth century at the time that the Cistercians took it over. The **Archbishop's Palace** at the corner of this street and Szabadság tér was built in the early eighteenth century with later neoclassical additions. Outstanding are the wrought-iron gates to the garden.

The house at Number 13 was built by Giovanni Battista Carlone, an Italian architect who settled in Eger.

Wine Taverns, Szabadság tér and Dobó István tér: For sampling the wines of this region, wine taverns abound. In addition to the deep-red, potent Egri Bikavér, which some say is not being produced with the care it once was, local wines to try are Medoc Noir, a dark dessert wine; Egri Leányka, fragrant and herb-flavored; and Muskotály (muscatel). You can also taste them in the wine cellars of the Szépasszony Volgy (Beautiful Woman) Valley, about a twenty-minute walk from the cathedral.

HOLLÓKŐ

A handful of mainly elderly people live in this little village of fifty-four preserved houses, one chapel, and one church that UNESCO has deemed a World Heritage worth saving. They are the Palóc people, an ethnic minority that has managed better than most, because of their out-of-the-way location, to preserve old costumes, architecture, and traditions.

Hollókő women are inclined to wear their costume of the past — long, lacy black-pleated skirts, black shawls, and black stockings. (Because the village is often used as a film setting, however, it's a little hard to tell whether costumes are being worn for filmmakers and tourists or because residents like them.) But the village itself is certainly picturesque. Its streets are cobbled and its little white houses noted for the round tiles like giant coins that protect the interiors. Picket fences enclose the small gardens. You can see what remains of a thirteenth-century castle the Hapsburgs blew up on a hill above the village, and if the weather is good, it is a short, easy climb to it. You can visit the **Weaving Museum,** open in summer from 10:00 A.M. until 4:00 P.M. Off-season, you may be able to find someone to let you in anyway. (The village's total population is only about twenty families, so someone is sure to know someone who has the key.) Language, again, can be a problem, though sign language will get you far.

There is also a simple little church and a teahouse, the latter open Tuesday through Friday in season from 9:00 A.M. to 4:00 P.M. and from 9:00 A.M. to 6:00 P.M. on Saturday and Sunday. The church's hours are variable. Hollókő folk — most of whom make their living nowadays from tourists (a few still farm) — are pleased to show off their village and will even offer primitive overnight accommodations.

TOKAJ

Had it not been for the prospect of a fall raid by the Turks, this little village whose name is of world renown might never have been known at all. Though grapes had long been grown on the surrounding hills and wine produced, until the middle of the seventeenth century the wine was neither better nor worse than most Hungarian white wines. But Mate Sepsi-Laczkó, a Calvinist clergyman who was also a vine grower, having heard one October that the Turks were en route, postponed till November his harvest of grapes. That, magically, did it. The grapes began to rot slightly in the hot sun; a fungus shrank them and shriveled and thinned their skins, but increased their sweetness, and Aszu, the golden Tokaji sweet dessert wine of Hungary, was born. Louis XV of France, toasting his paramour Madame de Pompadour with Tokaji, supposedly pronounced, "It is the wine of kings and the king of wines." And Pope Benedict XIV, the recipient of a gift of Tokaji Aszu from the empress Maria Teresa, reportedly heralded it with the words "Blessed be the land that has produced you; blessed be the woman that has sent you; blessed am I who drink you."

There is relatively little to see in Tokaj but plenty to drink. The most famous of the wine cellars is the **Rákóczi Cellar** at Kossuth tér 13. There are twenty-four passageways filled with wine and a cellar for tasting and buying as well. The cellar is open from 8:00 A.M. until noon and from 12:30 to 7:00 P.M. Elsewhere in town, there are other wine cellars.

Tokaj also has a **Wine Museum** of limited interest (open 9:00 A.M. to 5:00 P.M., except Monday), an eighteenth-century **Town Hall,** a few castle remains, a pleasant view of the town from the bridge over the Tisza River, cobblestoned streets, and stork nests in the chimneys of old houses.

Getting There, Sleeping, Eating, and Entertainment

Of all the countries of Eastern Europe it is Hungary that is best prepared to receive visitors from the West. Its capital city of Budapest, divided in two by a ribbon of the River Danube, is both elegant and vivacious; its residents yearn to please. Famous as Hungary is for composers Franz Liszt and Béla Bartók, as well as for Gypsy violinists, music continues to play an important role in the life of the city. Fine cuisine plays an even more important role. There are shopping streets to stroll in, their windows bright with hand embroidery from the countryside; Danube cruises to take; cobblestoned streets lined with reconstructed Renaissance and Baroque houses to explore.

Budapest is easily reached nonstop from New York on Malev Hungarian Airlines and Pan Am. The two airlines share a flight several days a week. (There is also joint Malev Pan Am service from Los Angeles and Chicago.) With a change of planes in their capitals, most European carriers flying from the United States offer service daily to Budapest.

A little bigger than Austria, to which it was once linked as part of the Austro-Hungarian Empire, Hungary is largely a fertile plain — but for heights along the Danube, some forested northern highlands, and the hills of Transdanubia. Though it is landlocked, its 266-square-mile Lake Balaton is Central Europe's largest freshwater lake.

On its sweeping plain, rare gray cattle roam in national parks and skilled horsemen (*csikós*) herd sleek Arab and Lipizzaner horses that tourists ride in summer and fall. Wild birds abound on the plain; mirages add mystery to it. All across Hungary are golden-yellow towns to see where history was made — where Turks and Austrians were fought by Magyars yearning for independence.

Because the terrain is mostly flat, traveling by road — even when distances are considerable — is speedy. Major routes are good and reasonably well marked. But there is a sameness to the landscape. Budget, Avis, and Hertz all have car rental service in Budapest, or you can make arrangements with Auto-Europe at Box 1097 in Camden, Maine 04843 (800-223-5555). Gas may be bought at any service station, and the Hungarian Automobile Club, MAK (Tel. 1-666-404), provides road service and also rents cars. Alternatively, there is reasonably good rail service. Both Eurail Flexipasses that are sold by the French National Railroad's and the German Federal Railway's New York offices and East Passes, which must be bought in the United States (available from Rail Europe at 800-345-1990 and from travel agents), reduce the cost of rail travel to and in Hungary. The Flexipass is for travelers arriving from the West, East Pass for those coming from Austria, Czechoslovakia, and Poland. Timetables with an English translation are available in Budapest's international stations.

Budapest is on international train lines from many European cities, including Paris, Munich, Vienna, Zagreb, Rome, Cracow, Warsaw, Prague, and Berlin. Depending on their place of origin, trains arrive at one of three stations — Keteti, Nyugati, or Deli. It is also possible to reach the Hungarian capital by hydrofoil from Vienna. Arrangements should be made in advance through Ibusz at Felszabadulás tér 5 or at the departure point on the Belgrad Rakpart in Pest, where Mahart, the boat line, has an office.

Like train travel within the country, bus travel is reasonably good. Bus departure times are clearly marked at stations and, at Budapest's main bus station at Engels tér, there is usually someone who can speak a little English. It is wise, whenever possible, to purchase your ticket well in advance of travel for — even in Budapest — there are bound to be glitches.

Within Budapest, the Metro is a quick and easy way to travel, but remember it stops running at 11:00 P.M. Tickets may be purchased at tobacco shops and newsstands. They may also be used on trams and the suburban railroad. Day passes as well as passes for individual journeys may be purchased.

Though both accommodations and restaurants in Budapest are plentiful, that is not the case in the countryside. There, except for the resort communities around Lake Balaton, good accommodations can be hard to find. Restaurants may be in short supply, too. Hungarians, however, enjoy good food and see to it that it is provided in even the smallest restaurant. Among the specialties you should not miss are *gulyás leves* (goulash), which is more of a soup than a stew in Hungary. Its ingredients include green pepper and red paprika to add bite, tomatoes, onions, beef or pork, and dumplings. In Szeged, it is fish soup (*Szegedi halászlé*) with carp, pike-perch, and plenty of paprika that is the popular dish. *Paprikás ponty* (carp in paprika sauce) is another fish specialty. So is *rácponty* (carp with peppers, tomatoes, onions, and sour cream).

Pörkölt is pork stew that is more like the American idea of goulash. Sour cream and dumplings are its usual accompaniment, along with a cooling cucumber salad. Then there are stuffed peppers (*töltött paprika*).

Quite as good as the meat and fish dishes of Hungary are the poultry entrees. Fried goose liver (*liba máj*) is considered one of the finest (and is surely among the costliest) of entrees. Preparing chicken with paprika (*paprikás csirke*) gives it untold pizzazz. Flaky pastry (*rétes*) filled with ground nuts or poppyseeds never fails to be a tempting dessert. Then there are Gundel pancakes and *dobostorta*, a rich, thin-layered cake.

Hungarian wines are not to be missed. Sweet Tokaji is best known abroad, but hearty red Egri Bikaver (Bull's Blood of Eger) also has gained renown, and there are good white wines from the shores of Lake Balaton. On the Great Plain, *barackpálincka* (apricot brandy) is a favorite drink.

There follows, in alphabetical order by town, a list of better hotels and restaurants in major tourist sites.

BALATONFÜRED

HOTELS

Annabella, Beloiannisz utca 25 (Tel. 86-42-222). This is a 348-room modern hotel on the lakeside that opens in mid-April and closes in mid-October. It offers sports facilities and a private beach.

Marina, Széchenyi utca 26 (Tel. 86-43-644). This 358-room, three-star hotel has its own beach for guests.

BUDAPEST

HOTELS

Astoria, Kossuth Lajos utca 29 (Tel. 11-73-411). This small, refurbished, turn-of-the-century hotel in downtown Pest is moderately priced and its restaurant's cooking is good.

Atrium Hyatt, 2 Roosevelt tér (Tel. 13-83-000). This glitzy high-rise, a stone's throw from the Danube (and with a fine view of it) on the Pest side of Budapest looks — atrium lobby and all — as if it had been transported from the United States. The hotel includes every comfort, several restaurants, a pool, sauna, business center, English-speaking help. The high-season single room rate is approximately $161, double $205, including breakfast.

Béke Radisson, Teréz körút 97 (Tel. 13-23-300). As the Britannia, this 238-room grand hotel was popular with important Fascists in World War II days. Now refurbished, it attracts Hungarian visitors to the capital. It is not far from the Western Railway Station.

Buda-Penta, Krisztina körút 41-43 (Tel. 15-66-333). This new 400-room hotel in a pretty Buda setting has a fine view of Castle Hill, several restaurants, a pool, and sauna, but you need to take the Metro to reach the heart of the city.

Budapest Hilton, Hess András tér 1-3 (Tel. 17-51-800). The special attraction of this hotel on Castle Hill on the Buda side of the Danube is the thirteenth-century church that is part of it. Though it has 323 rooms, there is a much more intimate quality to it than to the grand hotels on the Pest side. It is distinctly in the heart of the city's tourist district and includes a casino.

The high-season single room rate, without breakfast, is $210, double $265.

Duna Inter-Continental, Apáczai Csere János utca 4 (Tel. 11-75-122). Right on the riverfront on the Pest side, this 340-room high-rise affords superb views of the Danube. Its restaurants include a terrace café with a water view. There are also a swimming pool, squash court, and facilities for business guests. The rooms, however, are smaller than in some of the other new modern hotels. The high-season single room rate, including breakfast, is $191, double $222.

Erzsébet, Károly Mihály utca 11 (Tel. 13-82-111). This is an old-fashioned three-star hotel, refurbished and well located in downtown Pest.

Flamenco, Tas Vezér utca 7 (Tel. 12 61 250). This is a handsome new Spanish-run hotel in a lovely green Buda setting. It has a swimming pool, sauna, and gym, as well as a man-made lake on its spacious grounds. Among its several dining rooms is one offering Spanish specialties.

Forum, Apáczai Csere János utca 12-14 (Tel. 11-78-088). This well-managed hotel has a spectacular location on the Danube's Pest bank. There are 408 rooms, a pool, sauna, gym, and businessmen's facilities. Among its restaurants is the Silhouette, one of Budapest's finest.

Gellért, Szent Gellért tér 1 (Tel. 18 52 200). If you want to feel that you are *really* in Budapest, the Art Nouveau Gellért on the Pest bank of the Danube, renowned for its baths and its elegant old-fashioned decor, is the place to stay. A double room with breakfast is about $150.

Grand Hotel Hungaria, Rákóczi út 90 (Tel. 12 29-050). This refurbished old hotel near the Eastern Railway Station is Budapest's largest. Its prices are slightly lower than at more centrally located hotels, though it is in the Hungarian four-star category.

Metropol, Rákóczi út 58 (Tel. 14-21-175). An old-fashioned two-star hotel with prices that are reasonable. The location and the service here are right.

Nemzeti, József körút 4 (Tel. 13-39-160). Situated on a main

Pest boulevard, the four-star Nemzeti has restored turn-of-the-century elegance and a good restaurant.

Novotel, Alkotás utca 63-67 (Tel. 18-69-588). This new hotel on the outskirts of the city has the advantage of fine views from every room. There is a swimming pool, a sauna, and a variety of restaurants. A single room including breakfast is about $115, a double about $150.

Palace, Rákóczi út 43 (Tel. 11-36-000). Situated on Pest's walking street, this three-star hotel may not be the quietest in Budapest, but it is certainly in the heart of the city. Not all rooms have baths.

Ramada Grand Hotel, Margaret Island (Tel. 11-11-000). Recently acquired by the Ramada Inn chain, this 1873 hotel at the north end of Margaret Island has a tunnel connection to the Thermal Hotel for those who would like to use its spa facilities. Good Hungarian food is served in its **Széchenyi Restaurant.**

Taverna, Váci utca 20 (Tel. 13-84-999). This is a centrally located (on Pest's pedestrian mall), modern, three-star hotel where prices are reasonable.

Thermal, Margitsziget (Tel. 13-21-100). This 206-room Margaret Island hotel is notable for its thermal baths and for the fine cuisine in its dining room. It also includes a swimming pool and nightclub. There is bus service to Pest.

Thermal Aquincum, Árpád Fejedelem utca (Tel. 13-21-100). This is a brand-new (1990) luxurious modern hotel set in the quiet of sylvan Margaret Island and offering a wide variety of health spa treatments.

RESTAURANTS

Alabárdos, Orszagház utca 2 (Tel. 15-60-851). The goose liver is a special treat in this fine small restaurant on Buda Hill.

Apostolok, Kigyó utca (Tel. 11-83-704). Gypsy music accompanies the first-class fare at this Art Nouveau restaurant–beer hall in the pedestrian area of Pest. Goulash, sausage, and cold goose liver, winter salami and red caviar go well with the good beer.

Barokk. Elegant food is offered at this new little restaurant near the State Opera House. Reservations are essential.

Bécsi Kávéház, Forum Hotel, Apáczai Csere János utca 12-14. The cream cakes are one of the best confections to sample at this hotel-café.

Bohémtanya, Paulay Ede utca 6 (Tel. 12-21-453). Prices are fine, the food good, and the ambience young at this little restaurant near Deák tér.

Café Hungaria or **New York Café,** Erzsébet körút 9 (Tel. 12-23-849). As this book went to press, it was rumored that this historic and imposing café restaurant that is worth a visit to see, but not necessarily to dine in, was for sale. Its cuisine could definitely do with a make-over. The building itself, destroyed in World War II, has been rebuilt in all its Rococo grandeur.

Fortuna, Fortuna utca 4 (Tel. 17-56-857). This is an elegant first-class tavern in the Castle Hill section of Buda.

Gundel, Állatkerti körút 2 (Tel. 12-21-002). This restaurant near the city park and the zoo is old and established. Károly Gundel, its founder in 1910, is remembered for a famous Hungarian cookbook, but both the food and the ambience have changed (the restaurant was remodeled in the 1970s), and neither lives up to Gundel's past reputation. There is, however, a famous Gundel dessert — a pancake filled with nuts and topped with chocolate sauce — that is still memorable.

Kacsa, Fő utca 75 (Tel. 13-53-357). Elegant dishes are prepared at this small Buda restaurant near the Danube.

Kisbuda, Frankel utca 34 (Tel. 11-52-244). Good food in good portions is served here in an attractive Buda garden setting in summer near the Margaret Island Bridge.

Kiskakukk, Pozsonyi utca 12 (Tel. 13-21-732). Wild game is the specialty at this moderately priced restaurant on the Pest side near the Margaret Island Bridge.

Kispipa, Akácfa utca 38 (Tel. 14-22-587). This is a popular, moderately priced Pest restaurant. Good value for the money.

Korona, Dísz tér. This coffeehouse near the castle is a good place for a stop after an afternoon of castle touring.

Légrádi Testvérek, Magyar utca 23 (Tel. 11-86-804). A very elegant restaurant where diners sit in armchairs and are served by waiters in cutaways. Goose livers anywhere are delicious; here they are especially so. Légrádi, obviously, is an expensive Pest restaurant. Reservations are essential.

Lukács, Andrássy út 70. Vanilla, chocolate, and chocolate cream layers topped with hazelnut cream in a *Lukács torta* are what make up the specialty confection of this marble-and-gold-decorated café that has been renowned for its confections since the nineteenth century.

Margitkert, Margit utca 15 (Tel. 13-54-791). Old Hungarian dishes and charcoal-broiled meats are the specialty of the refurbished nineteenth-century Buda restaurant near the Margaret Island Bridge. Gypsy music is the accompaniment. Reservations are essential.

Ménes Csárda, Apáczai Csere János utca 15 (Tel. 11-70-803). Foreign visitors are the clientele for this restaurant behind the Forum Hotel with costumed waiters. Pork and duck are specialties, and there is Gypsy music and a folklore show.

Nancsi néni, Ördögárok utca 80 (Tel. 11-67-830). A small, unpretentious restaurant with fine food, but bear in mind that it may be crowded.

Ruszwurm, Szentháromság tér 3. This is said to be the oldest coffee and pastry shop in Budapest, in existence since 1827. Unfortunately, it is very small, and as it is situated near the castle it is very crowded at almost all times of day.

Silhouette, Forum Hotel, Apáczai Csere János utca 12-14 (Tel. 11-78-088). Some of the best food in Budapest is served in this hotel restaurant.

Sipos, Fő tér 6 (Tel. 18-88-745). The surrounding neighborhood is nothing to get excited about, but the fish is at this Óbuda restaurant.

Százeves, Pesti Barnabás utca 2 (Tel. 11-83-608). There's considerable charm to the oldest restaurant in Budapest, which is set in a small Baroque palace. In keeping with the surroundings, the price for *süllő*, a white-fleshed fish found only in Lake Balaton, is high. Gypsy musicians play during the dinner hour.

Szindbad, Markó utca 33 (Tel. 13-21-087). Reservations are essential at this small first-class restaurant near the Western Railway Station.

Vadrózsa, Pentelei Molnár utca 15 (Tel. 13-51-118). Be sure your wallet is fat before a visit to this Buda garden restaurant that has come to specialize in serving well-to-do foreigners with éclat.

Vigadó, Vigadó tér 1 (Tel. 11-81-598). The food is surprisingly good in this beer hall inside the Vigadó Concert Hall in Pest.

CAFÉS

Angelika, Batthyány tér 7. This is something of a hangout for the literary set who feed their creative impulses with its coffee and cake.

Gerbeaud, Vörösmarty tér. The pastries are delectable, the coffee what coffee should be, and the Tokaji wine smooth in this old-fashioned coffeehouse outside of which, in summer, you can watch all the activities of bustling Vörösmarty Square. The extremely slow service will give you plenty of time to ogle or rest tired feet. Emile Gerbeaud, whose name it bears, was a Swiss invited from Geneva in the 1880s to establish a Budapest coffeehouse that would be the rival of Vienna's coffeehouses. He succeeded, and his café became a favorite stopping place for composer Franz Liszt and writer Ferenc Molnár, among others. Among its specialties are an apple strudel called *almás rétes* and chocolate and hazelnut tortes.

Wiener Kaffeehaus, Forum Hotel, Apáczai Csere János utca 12-14. Sweet specialties here include *meggy torta,* a sour cherry torte, and *Rigóbomba torta,* a rum-soaked cake with raisins and chocolate icing.

Zsolnay Kávéház, Hotel Béke Radisson, Teréz körút 97. Try the chestnut cake (*gesztenye torta*) topped with cream and crushed pistachios, or strawberry layer cake, and enjoy a blissful, fattening afternoon listening to the piano player at this grand old café.

ENTERTAINMENT

The **National Philharmonic Central Ticket Office** (Országos Filharmónia Központi Jegy-irodája), Vörösmarty tér 1 (Tel. 11-

76-222), is open Monday through Friday from 11:00 A.M. to 6:00 P.M. for the purchase of classical and pop-concert tickets. The Theater Central Ticket Office (Szinházak Központi Jegyi-rodája), Andrássy út 18 (Tel. 11-20-000), is open Monday through Friday from 10:00 A.M. to 7:00 P.M. for the purchase of tickets to theater, opera, musicals, and ballet.

Academy of Music (Zeneakadémia), Liszt Ferenc tér 8 (Tel. 22-14-406). The acoustics in this 1,200-seat auditorium, where orchestral and chamber music is performed, are considered among the finest in Europe.

Budai Vigadó, Corvin tér 8 (Tel. 11-59-657). Folk ballet and dance performances are presented.

Erkel Opera (Erkelszínház), Köztársaság tér 30 (Tel. 13-30-540). Modern dance and opera are performed.

Matthias Church (Mátyás-templom), Szentháromság tér. Con-certs and organ recitals as well as fine choir singing at Sunday services are musical highlights.

MOM Cultural Center (MOM Kulturális Központ), Csörsz utca 18 (Tel. 15-68-451). Folkloric programs are offered in summer.

Municipal Operetta Theater (Fővárosi Operett Szinház), Nagy-mező utca 17 (Tel. 13-20-535). Musical comedy, generally of the American variety, is offered.

Opera House (Állami Operaház), Andrássy Nepkoztarsasag út 22. Hungarians are devotees of opera and have been since the seventeenth century. Tickets may be purchased at the box of-fice at Dalszinház utca Tuesday through Saturday from 10:00 A.M. to 2:00 P.M. and 2:30 to 7:00 P.M. and Sunday from 10:00 A.M. to 1:00 P.M. and 4:00 to 7:00 P.M.

Vigadó, Vigadó tér. In this concert hall, which has virtually per-fect acoustics and was reconstructed in 1980 after World War II shelling (but kept behind its nineteenth-century Hungarian facade), chamber music concerts are performed.

TOURIST INFORMATION

Ibusz, Felszabadulás tér 5 (Tel. 11-86-866). Telephone informa-tion in English is available from Tourinform (Tel. 11-79-800) from 8:00 A.M. to 8:00 P.M. Railway schedules, daily events, and currency rates are given.

DEBRECEN
HOTEL
Arany Bika, Vörös Hadsereg utca 11-15 (Tel. 52-16-777). This 285-room, three-star historic hotel is the principal one in town. Its restaurant is well known.
RESTAURANTS
Gambrinus, center city. This is a popular, centrally located restaurant.

Régiposta Étterem, Széchenyi utca 6. This restaurant, serving reasonably good meals, is in the oldest house in town.

Szabadság Restaurant, Vörös Hadsereg utca 29, is a reasonable restaurant in the center of town.

EGER
HOTELS
Eger Hotel, Szálloda utca 1-3 (Tel. 36-13-233). This modern three-star hotel lacks charm, but many of its rooms have a pleasant view of the park.

Hotel Minaret, Harangöntő utca (Tel. 36-20-473). This cozy little hotel has only seventeen rooms, but they are attractive indeed.

Park Hotel, Klapka György utca 8 (Tel. 36-13-233). Although this hotel is a little dated in its look, it is a clean and reasonable spot for an overnight stay.

Senator-ház, Dobó tér 11 (Tel. 36-20-466). This is a cozy little eleven-room hotel in a Baroque building.
RESTAURANT
Fehér Szarvas, Klapka utca 8 (Tel. 1322-33). Wild game is why diners come here from all over the country.
TOURIST INFORMATION
Ibusz, Bajcsy-Zs. tömbbelsö (Tel. 36-12-526).

ESZTERGOM
HOTELS
Esztergom, Prímás-sziget (Tel. 81-68). This is a small (34-room) modern hotel.
RESTAURANT
Úszó Halászcsárda, Esztergom Island (Tel. 230). This "fisherman's inn" offers not only fish cooked in Hungarian style but a wide variety of other Hungarian dishes.

FERTŐD
RESTAURANT
Haydn. This is a pleasant small restaurant just outside the palace.

HÉVIZ
HOTELS
Thermal Hotel Aqua, Kossuth Lajos utca 13-15 (Tel. 11-090). Many amenities and a wide variety of treatments are offered at this modern spa hotel on the shores of Lake Héviz.
Thermal Hotel Héviz, Kossuth Lajos utca 9-11 (Tel. 11-190). Guests at this four-star spa hotel have the advantage of a casino along with their spa treatments.

KECSKEMÉT
HOTELS
Aranyhomok, Széchenyi tér 3 (Tel. 76-20-011). This modern hotel is equipped with a swimming pool and is centrally located in the heart of town.
Három Gúnár, Batthyány utca 7 (Tel. 76-27-077), is a small restored historic hotel.
RESTAURANT
Három Gúnár. The hotel dining room offers the best food in town. Its specialty is goose — *gúnár*, the hotel's name.

PÉCS
HOTELS
Palatinus, Kossuth Lajos utca 5 (Tel. 72-33-022). This small hotel is in a renovated historic building.

Pannonia, Rákóczi utca 3 (Tel. 72-13-332). Being modern and centrally located are the principal attractions of this somewhat characterless hotel.
RESTAURANT
Elefánt Söröző, Jókai tér 6 (Tel. 134-49), is a charming old-fashioned restaurant offering many Hungarian specialties.
TOURIST INFORMATION
Ibusz, Széchenyi tér 8 (Tel. 72-12-148).

SOPRON
HOTELS
Lővér, Városi utca 4 (Tel. 99-11-061). This resort hotel is set in an attractive location in the woods, but on the outskirts of town.
Palatinus (Tel. 99-11-395). This is a small, centrally located hotel.
Sopron, Förvényverem utca (Tel. 99-14-254). Modern and attractive, the Sopron is set in a pleasant spot just above town and caters well to foreign guests.
RESTAURANTS
Cesar Pince, Hátsókapu 2. Although a wine cellar, food is also served here.
Corvinus, Fő tér.
Vörös Étterem, Lenin körút 25.

SZEGED
HOTELS
Hungária, Komocsin Zoltán utca 4 (Tel. 62-21-211). This modern hotel is attractively set on the riverbank.
Royal, Kölcsey utca 1 (Tel. 62-12-911). This is a two-star, older, centrally located hotel.
RESTAURANTS
Alabárdos, Oskola utca 13. A pleasant restaurant in a cellar setting.
Halászcsárda, Roosevelt tér 12. This is a fish restaurant on the riverbank.
TOURIST INFORMATION
Ibusz, Klavzál tér 2.

SZENTENDRE
RESTAURANT
Aranysárkány, Vöröshadsereg utca 2 (Tel. 116-70). Though this restaurant in the center of town is always too crowded, the food (with French touches) is well prepared. Reservations are essential.

TIHANY
HOTEL
Club Tihany, Rév utca 3 (Tel. 86-48-088). Bungalows as well as a 330-room hotel are part of this shore-front complex with many sports facilities.

Poland

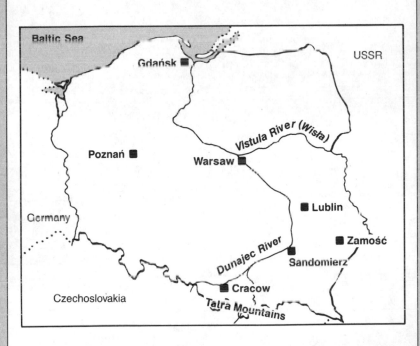

Baltic Sea

Gdańsk ■

USSR

Poznań ■

Warsaw ■

Vistula River (Wisła)

Germany

Lublin ■

Czechoslovakia

Dunajec River

Zamość ■

Sandomierz

Cracow

Tatra Mountains

*H*ad it not been for the indomitable spirit of its population, Poland would have permanently disappeared from the face of Europe long ago. With aggressive Prussia on the west, Russia on the east, the Austro-Hungarian Empire on the south, and Sweden just across the Baltic Sea, Poland has been eminently attractive to all. Though there are hills and mountains in the south, most of the land is low, with rivers the only natural barriers. As it is, Poland was overrun by Tartar hordes; taken over by Teutonic Knights; raided by the Swedes; three times partitioned by Austria, Prussia, and Russia; and virtually wiped out by the Germans in World War II. But, always, somehow — whether in exile in a foreign land, on a battlefield, or in the underground — the patriots of Poland have seen to it that their nation rose again.

Today's Poles are said to be the descendants of a Slavic people called the Lechici. Their original settlement was on the Danube, but the Romans drove them north to the Oder and Vistula rivers. Herdsmen, hunters, and farmers, they lived the independent, separate lives of such people until dangers forced them to come together in the tenth century A.D. under their first historic prince, Mieszko.

It was he, facing invasions by Christians to the east, who deemed it wise politically to become a Christian himself and make his people Christian. His son, Boleslaus I, further strengthened the tie with the Church of Rome by becoming friends with the Holy Roman Emperor. Ever since Boleslaus's day, Roman Catholicism has been a major political as well as religious force in Poland. Polish joy was unbounded when Cardinal Karol Wojtyla of Cracow became Pope John Paul II.

As well as being a good and clever Catholic, Boleslaus was an able soldier who greatly expanded Poland's territory. Unfortunately, in the twelfth century, the last of that line, Boleslaus, the Wry-mouthed, helped to diminish those conquests by dividing the land, on his death, among his four sons. This so weakened the country (turned into dukedoms and principalities) that it fell easy prey to outsiders. The Holy Roman Emperor Frederick Barbarossa annexed some of it. A century later, the Tartars thundered in. The Prussians and the pagan Lithuanians came next. A desperate Duke Conrad of Mazovia, in 1226, unable himself to keep these intruders out, invited the Teutonic Knights, a semi-religious military order organized in northern Germany to assist in the Crusades, to help him out. They accepted with enthusiasm, and having ousted Conrad's enemies, proceeded to annex Polish land themselves and found their own state. Poland seemed to be falling apart.

But in 1333 Casimir the Great came to the throne. He skillfully managed to revive and rebuild the kingdom, make peace with the Teutonic Knights, and control the nobles. To improve the economy, he brought in Jewish craftsmen and tradesmen ousted from Russia. Altogether, he gave Poland thirty-eight years of a Golden Age. When he died without a male heir, he left Poland to his nephew, Louis of Hungary. Louis's skillful contribution was to arrange the marriage of his twelve-year-old daughter, Jadwiga, to a thirty-eight-year-old pagan Lithuanian duke, Ladislaus Jagiello, by convincing her that it was her Christian duty to help in the duke's conversion. This union ended Lithuanian attacks, and again, as in Casimir's day, in this late fifteenth- and early sixteenth-century period — known as the Jagiellonian dynasty — peace and prosperity reigned in Poland. Foreign artists and architects (Italians in particular) brought their designs and ideas to the Polish kingdom.

In 1572, when there was no heir to the throne after King Sigismund II Augustus died, it was decided that thereafter Poland's kings would be elected by the nobles. Sometimes these kings were Polish; sometimes they were foreign; among them was a Frenchman, Henri of Valois, and Stephen Batory, prince of Transylvania. Almost always they had trouble controlling the nobles who had elected them.

Again, invaders — this time Turks and Russians — threatened the country. Although King John III Sobieski fought valiantly and defeated the Turks at Vienna in 1683, thereby preserving Christianity in the West, by the second half of the eighteenth century, Poland was weak again (the nobles were usurping power) and Russia, Prussia, and Austria were able to take more than a quarter of its territory and a third of its people in what has come to be called the First Polish Partition (1772).

In 1793, there was a Second Polish Partition, and more of Poland's extensive territory was divided among the three powers. In 1795 with the Third Partition, Poland disappeared from the map. That was when patriotic Polish legions decided to throw their strength on the side of Napoleon against the Russians, Prussians, and Austrians in hopes of help from him in return.

For a brief time, his successes got them what they wanted. After conquering Prussia, he created the duchy of Warsaw and the free city of Gdańsk (Danzig) out of the land the Prussians had held. Though they were under French rule, France was a friend, and it seemed, at least, a start again for Poland.

But when Napoleon fell in 1815, so, too, did the duchy of Warsaw — this time into the hands of the tsar of Russia — while Gdańsk went back to the Prussians. More unhappy times were in store for Poland for nearly 100 years.

An independence movement formed in 1848 was cruelly crushed. Poles were exiled to Siberia in the 1860s, and many fled to other parts of Europe and the United States. In World War I, when the Russians were on the Allied side and the Austrians and Prussians on the side of the Central Powers, the Poles — depending on where they lived — were drafted into one army or the other and often Poles fought against Poles. It was not until 1918, when Prussia and Austria lost the war and Russia was in the throes of its own revolution, that Poland became its own master again.

But its joy was not to last long. On September 1, 1939, Hitler entered Poland from the west, set on its complete destruction. Six million lives were lost, more than half of its major cities and one third of its farmlands laid waste. Yet Poland survived and — even in the face of communism — was reborn.

The Polish spirit never really accepted communism. Entrepreneurial Poles always managed to have second jobs and to remain somewhat aloof from their government. In the 1970s, the independent trade union Solidarity was formed. It had its martyrs, but martyrdom brings out the best in Poles.

And now, at last, Poland is independent again. It is eager to show off its accomplishments and natural attractions — the old cities magnificently re-created from the rubble of war; its indomitable spirit; its mountain landscape and remote wooden villages; its painted glass and paper cutouts, wood carvings, and embroidery; the tranquil Mazurian lakes (there are more than 3,000 in its northeast); untamed forests; and the golden dunes along its Baltic beaches.

WARSAW

A mermaid princess swimming in the River Vistula here — so the story goes — saw on the riverbank a handsome prince who had lost his way on a hunt. Wishing to be of help, she sang him melodious songs so he would follow her to the home of the fisherman, Wars. Both Wars and his wife, Sawa, welcomed the prince, fed him, and gave him the directions he sought. Pleased with the results of her good deed, the mermaid urged the prince to build a city where Wars and Sawa dwelt and to name it for them. It would be a happy and glorious city, she said, a city of world renown.

The enamored prince did as bid. The mermaid proved right in promising that Warsaw would be a city of renown, less right about its being a happy place.

Situated almost exactly in the center of continental Europe, Warsaw was a busy trading center and the seat of government of a twelfth-century dukedom called Mazovia. In the sixteenth century, it became part of the kingdom of Poland and eventually the Polish capital. As such, with its fine central location, it was fair game for conquerers — the Swedes in the seventeenth century; the Prussians in the eighteenth; Napoleon, the Austrians, and the Russians in the nineteenth; the Germans and the Soviet Union in the twentieth.

As the world knows, some 800,000 Varsovians were exterminated during the five years of German occupation in World War II, and 85 percent of the city was destroyed. Of the city's 957 buildings of historical value, about 800 were only rubble when the Soviets "liberated" this city in January 1945.

Within two weeks, Poland decided that its capital would be not only rebuilt but that its most important historic sites would be reconstructed to look as they had before. This was possible thanks both to prewar architectural students' studies of old Warsaw and to the paintings of Bernardo Bellotto (the younger Canaletto), who had painted many detailed cityscapes during his years as court painter in the eighteenth century.

Poles who had fled the city began to return, willing to live in the rubble while they helped to rebuild their capital. They salvaged old stone to provide the right "old" look for the new structures. All tram tracks, trams, and buses had been blown up by

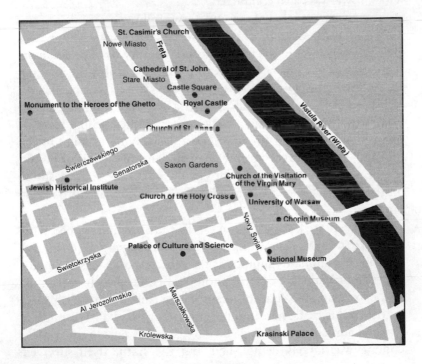

WARSAW

the Germans, so pedal taxis were the sole means of transportation. There was virtually no place to live except in dank cellars. But somehow, the Varsovians managed to clear away the debris, bury their dead, and start reconstruction. Some are critical of the "artificial" look of today's **Old Town** (Stare Miasto), where horse-drawn carriages wait to take visitors on tours of the narrow cobblestoned streets, outdoor artists paint portraits, and café tables have replaced market stands. While it is certainly true that behind the reconstructed pink-and-gold and pale-green Renaissance, Baroque, and Gothic houses there are modern restaurants, museums, and souvenir shops, the effect is nonetheless impressive, especially so when you think of how it all came about. Within twenty-five years of its destruction, historic old Warsaw — all but its castle — had been completely rebuilt. And today it is lived in and shopped in by ordinary folk as well as by tourists. In the 1970s, the red Royal Castle with its tall central clock tower was also completed.

The principal sights of the Old Town follow.

Barbican (Barbakan): This dark-red turreted brick wall, whose original was built in the mid-sixteenth century by a Venetian architect to protect the northern part of the city, is now the dividing line between the Old Town and the **New Town** (Nowe Miasto). The street through the wall is also a popular sunning spot in warm weather for young artists and craftsmen selling jewelry, paintings, and amber (the Baltic Sea, less than 200 miles to the north, is renowned for its amber). You can walk inside or on top of the wall for a fine view of the Vistula and of the popular statue of the rather warlike mermaid Syrena, who bears a sword in one hand.

Castle Square (Plac Zamkowy): The tall column topped with a bronze statue of King Sigismund III Vasa carrying the cross and a sword (Kolumna Zygmunta) is the centerpiece of Castle Square and one of Warsaw's favorite monuments. Originally erected in 1644 to honor the sixteenth-century Swedish-born Polish king who built his castle here and made Warsaw the Polish capital, it was dynamited with a vengeance by the Germans in 1944. The column was largely demolished, but the statue itself survived and in 1949 was one of the earliest public monuments to be re-erected.

Cathedral of St. John (Katedra Św. Jana), ulica Świętojańska: Because this red-brick, fourteenth-century church was the center of much of the fighting in the 1944 Underground uprising, the Nazis took their revenge, dynamiting and burning what was left after the fighting. Now rebuilt in its original Gothic style, it is among the most popular places of worship in Warsaw. Unless you go when there is a service, nowadays it is hard to do more than get into the entryway of Warsaw churches. But if you arrive at a service, you can explore the cathedral afterward; in the crypt are the tombs of Henryk Sienkiewicz — who received the Nobel Prize in Literature in 1905 and is noted for his novel *Quo Vadis?* — and Cardinal Stefan Wyszyński, primate of Poland, who spent three years in prison for his faith in the 1950s.

Church of the Visitation of the Virgin Mary (Kościół Nawied-zenia N.P. Marii), ulica Koscielna: This fifteenth-century Gothic church above the Vistula, whose original was the oldest church in New Warsaw, a district that began in the fifteenth century, is particularly notable for its adjoining sixteenth-century red brick bell tower, a landmark of the city.

Freta Street (ulica Freta): The Gothic and Baroque **Church of St. Hyacinth** (Kościół Św. Jacek), at Numbers 8-10, whose original was built in 1638 and its companion Dominican monastery created a little later, was entirely rebuilt after its total destruction in World War II with contributions from Polish-Americans.

In the original house at Number 16, Maria Skłodowska, who became Madame Curie and, with her husband, Pierre, discovered radium, was born in 1867. On a tour of the house, if you can find an English-speaker to accompany you, you will learn how the energetic young woman, unable to attend the University of Warsaw because of her sex, went to work in an agricultural laboratory to earn enough to pay for an education in Paris. At the Sorbonne, she met Pierre Curie. Though the house has been faithfully reconstructed to be as it was when her mother took in students as roomers to supplement the income of Marie's teacher-father, only a desk, a bookcase, and a clock remain of the original furnishings. The museum is largely filled with family photographs, busts, and her awards (she won a Nobel Prize in 1911). At the age of sixty-seven, Marie Curie died of leukemia, and some of the papers from her laboratory are still believed to be radioactive. The house is open from Tuesday to Saturday from 10:00 A.M. to 4:30 P.M. and Sunday from 10:00 A.M. to 2:00 P.M.

Jewish Cemetery (Cmentarz Zydowski), ulica Okopowa 49-51: Broken cemetery stones make up the wall at the largest Jewish cemetery in Europe. You can spend half a day strolling among the stones of the centuries and, with the help of a translator, read the angry outcry on memorial tablets of children and grandchildren remembering the murder of their forebears at Nazi hands.

Jewish Historical Institute (Zydowski Institut Historyczny), ulica Aleje Swierczewskiego 79: Faded photographs and memorabilia of the days of the Ghetto and the Ghetto uprising are displayed here. Museum hours are 10:00 A.M. to 3:00 P.M. weekdays, Saturday 9:00 A.M. until noon.

Krasiński Palace (Pałac Krasińskich), Plac Kracińskich: The original of this northern Italian Baroque palace was built in the seventeenth century by Tylman of Gameren from Utrecht for a provincial governor. At the time of its construction, it was lauded as grander even than the Royal Castle, and it was particularly renowned for its rich exterior sculpture. Though it was destroyed in a fire in 1783, it was restored (and restored again after World War II) and is considered by architectural historians to be one of Europe's finest Baroque palaces. It now contains special collections of the National Library.

Monument to the Heroes of the Ghetto (Pomnik Bohaterów Getta), ulica Ludwika Zamenhofa and ulica Mordechai Anielewicza: At the end of the eleventh century the first Jews came to Poland — victims of the pogroms in Western Europe. More came in the thirteenth century and finally, in the fourteenth, Casimir the Great extended an invitation to still more. By the early fifteenth century, some were listed on the city tax rolls. Down through Warsaw history, there continued to be a sizable Jewish population, working-class Jews living in their own area and intellectuals, in limited numbers, living among Gentiles. Relations were not always amicable, but neither were they always bad.

In August 1939, when World War II began, the Jewish population was 380,567, a third of Warsaw's population. It was the largest Jewish population in any city in the world, except New York. At the war's end, only about 300 Warsaw Jews were still alive. Those who died are memorialized here with this stark, striking monument in a small green park surrounded by modern apartment buildings. Here, before the war, Dr. Ludwik Zamenhof, the inventor of Esperanto, lived, and it is for him that the street where this monument rises got its name.

The monument, designed by Nathan Rappaport, depicts, in bronze, Jews fighting the oppressor and Jews leaving the Ghetto. Ironically, the Swedish granite on which it is mounted was ordered by Hitler for a victory monument for Berlin. But when the war ended, the granite was still in Sweden, and the Swedes thought it appropriate to offer it to the Jews of Warsaw.

Although since 1940 this area has been called a ghetto, before that it was simply the city's Jewish quarter, where working-class Jews lived. The professionals — doctors, bankers, businessmen willing to be assimilated, to speak French, German, or Polish and to send their children to Polish schools and dress them in Polish clothes — were allowed to live throughout the city, provided there were no more than two Jewish families to each block.

But in 1940, this Muranów area was marked off to be the sole place of residence for Jews, and any who lived outside were forced to move inside. With insufficient space for them all, they lived twelve to fifteen to a room. Food was scarce, sanitation abominable. Illness soon killed thousands. Then in 1941, to make matters worse, a high wall was erected around the Ghetto with 400,000 people confined in a 988-acre area inside.

In the summer of 1942, the Nazis began to order groups of Jews to appear at Umschlagplatz for journeys "elsewhere." Not until near the end of 1942, when only 50,000 remained in the Ghetto, did word filter back that "elsewhere" for those who left was either the concentration camp at Auschwitz (Oświęcim) or the one at Treblinka. Most of those who remained in the Ghetto were young people working at forced labor in factories. For a while they thought that because they were able-bodied, they were needed by the Germans and would remain untouched. But in 1943, Heinrich Himmler decreed that the "Jewish problem in Warsaw was to be resolved completely." Orders went out to the young Ghetto residents that they were to go to the loading platform at Umschlagplatz. Now knowing the fate that faced them, they refused. On Easter Monday in 1943, the Germans decided to move them by force. As it turned out, that proved impossible. Led by thirty-four-year-old Mordechai Anielewicz, with little ammunition but great valor, about 300 ghetto residents fought the tanks and the flamethrowers of the Germans from April 19 till May 16. The uprising, of course, was doomed to failure; its leaders committed suicide, but it remains one of history's most valiant battles against an oppressor.

Old Town Market Square (Rynek Starego Miasta): With one exception, only the ground floor facades of the medieval, Renaissance, and Baroque houses that stood here before World War II remained by the war's end. But beginning with those bits and pieces, the Varsovians miraculously reconstructed the damaged buildings. In the Middle Ages, the number of windows you were allowed depended on your position in life. The more windows across the front of a house, the larger the house. Two-windowed facades signified that the buildings were originally artisans' quarters, bourgeois homes had three windows, and noblemen's houses had four.

Among facades of particular note on the northwest side of the square is the **Warsaw History Museum,** where an absorbing fifteen-minute film on the city's destruction is shown. In the reconstructed burgher houses, now a museum, the history of Warsaw from its earliest days is also shown in models and pictorial displays, and there are telling identity cards, posters, and photographs from the World War II period. At Number 28, look up to see the Baroque statues at the top. Number 32 is a seventeenth-century patrician mansion. The museum hours are Tuesday and

Thursday from noon to 7:00 P.M., Friday and Saturday 10:00 A.M. to 3:00 P.M., and Sunday 10:30 A.M. to 4:30 P.M.

Number 36, the **House of the Moor** (Pod Murzynkiem), was a spice trader's house — the head of a Moor over the Renaissance door signifies this. It is the only building on the Old Town Square that stood firm during Nazi bombardments.

At Number 27 on the west side of the square is the **Fukier Winery** (Winiarnia Fukiera). This tavern, with Renaissance medallions and swans and sgraffiti, was originally built in 1566 and occupied by the Polish branch of the German Fugger banking family. Except for the war years, it has been a place of merry-making for centuries. Its courtyard is particularly attractive (you enter it not from the square but at ulica Piwna 44), and you can get a good drink of wine here. On the first floor there is a wine museum of limited interest.

Number 32, whose original building dated from the fourteenth century, is notable for its sixteenth-century sculpture of St. Anne.

Number 19, the **Crocodile House** (Pod Krokodylem), now has

14. The Old Town Market Square in Warsaw.

a restaurant in the cellar, where it is extremely difficult to get a table, and a popular coffeeshop on the first floor. Its original was built in 1608 by the mayor of Warsaw.

A good tale is told about Number 29, the **Giza House.** When sixteenth-century King Sigismund II Augustus's wife died, he was so distraught that his councilors went to a well-known sorcerer, Pan Twardowski, to see if he could conjure up her ghost and thereby restore the king to sanity. He didn't quite. Instead, once he had promised the king that his wife's ghost would appear, the sorcerer substituted pretty Basia Gizenka. As the sorcerer surmised, the king became as smitten with her as he had been with his wife.

On the south are Number 7, the Giza family's **Golden House** (Złoty Dom), which gets its name from its late Renaissance facade decoration, and the Lion House (Pod Lwem) at Number 13, which has a mid-fifteenth-century bas-relief of a lion and a sundial as part of its decoration.

The highlight of the east side is the **Orlemus House,** Numbers 18-20, the **Adam Mickiewicz Museum of Literature,** devoted to the unhappy life of the nineteenth-century Lithuanian-born poet of that name. Although he was viewed as the greatest Slavic poet after Pushkin, he was forced to spend much of his writing life in exile in Paris, frequently jobless. He died of cholera in Istanbul. It is open Monday, Tuesday, and Friday from 10:00 A.M. to 3:00 P.M., Wednesday and Thursday 11:00 A.M. to 6:00 P.M., and Sunday noon to 5:00 P.M.

The Old Town Market Square is thronged with tourists in summer, for it is a remarkable evocation of a proud past. In those ghastly immediate postwar years, when demolished Warsaw needed schools, hospitals, and housing, it first chose to restore its history in a way no other European city or nation did. Today many entrepreneurial young Poles, recognizing the touristic as well as the historic value of the Old Town Square, have become postcard sellers, ice cream vendors, and musicians there, but what is important is that the square is there at all.

Palace of Culture and Science (Pałac Kultury i Nauki), Plac Defilad: From the thirteenth floor of this enormous Stalinesque "wedding cake," there is a fine view out over the city, the Vistula, and the surrounding countryside.

Pawiak Prison (Więzienia Pawiak), ulica Dzielna 24-26: This notorious Gestapo prison is now open as a museum. Outside, on a tree stump, are tacked the names of those who died here. It is open Wednesday from 9:00 A.M. to 5:00 P.M., Thursday and Saturday 9:00 A.M. to 4:00 P.M., Friday 10:00 A.M. to 5:00 P.M., and Sunday 10:00 A.M. to 3:00 P.M.

Royal Castle (Zamek Królewski): For twenty-two years after the end of World War II, there was discussion about whether this seventeenth-century royal castle should be reconstructed, with some contending that the rebirth from the ashes of the Old Town had been extraordinary enough. In 1971 it was decreed that the castle should be rebuilt. By 1974, with the help of many private donations, it was. Incorporated into it were hundreds of pieces of the original stone fireplaces and doorways that patriotic Poles had sneaked out of the rubble left when the Germans blew up the castle in fury. Their anger followed the valiant nine-week 1944 uprising of the Polish Underground when the Russians were reported to be coming close.

Even before that, in the first days of Nazi occupation in 1939, museum staff members had smuggled to safekeeping small pieces of furniture, tapestries, paintings, and plaster. Today's visitors can see those original pieces of stone and sculpture back in the original places, surrounded by the reconstructed whole for which they were the models. Guided one-hour tours (the only way you can see the castle) must be booked at least a day in advance, and an English-language tour must be requested. As of this writing, no English-language guidebook was available.

Because from 1572 on, Polish nobility elected their kings, the Royal Castle has served both as the royal home and as the meeting place for the Parliament. On the ground floor, overlooking the River Vistula, are the **Parliamentary Rooms** (Sejm), decorated with twelfth-century Flemish tapestries and portraits of the dukes of Mazovia, who built the very first fortification here in the thirteenth century.

In the seventeenth-century **Jagiellonian Rooms** that also overlook the Vistula is a considerable collection of original sixteenth-century furniture, porcelain, and art that survived the war, including the telling Flemish tapestry, *The Tragedy of the Jews*.

But surely the most interesting room of all is the **Canaletto Room** in the **Royal Apartments,** for its walls are virtually covered with the paintings of Warsaw that Bernardo Bellotto (who called himself Canaletto after his noted painter-uncle) made from 1767 to 1780, when he was court painter. It was these paintings, so architecturally specific, that were so important in the postwar re-creation of this capital city.

Enshrined in the little **Royal Chapel** off the Canaletto Room is the heart of Tadeusz Kościuszko, hero of the American Revolution and leader of the fight against a Russian invasion of Poland in 1794.

As you tour these royal chambers, guides tell of famous paintings removed from their frames, rolled up, and carried off in rucksacks to protect them from the Germans, and of other works of art lost to Poland by looters over the centuries but sheepishly returned from many lands when it was learned that the indomitable Poles were restoring this castle.

In the original magnificent mirror-lined ballroom, Napoleon Bonaparte, meeting the wives of Warsaw dignitaries at an official gathering, was reportedly stunned — and said so — at the number of lovely Varsovian women he saw. (One of them, the countess Maria Walewska, surrendered herself to his advances in the hope, so the story goes, that her tenderness would make him kind to Poland.)

Portraits and busts of Polish royalty are everywhere among the multicolored marble columns of the Royal Apartments, and in what were the royal children's rooms the paintings of nineteenth-century historical romanticist Jan Matejko are displayed — monumental, inspiring paintings of the Parliament and of battles. In the **Knights' Hall** are more paintings of grand historic scenes by the Italian painter Baciarelli. The castle is open from Tuesday to Saturday 10:00 A.M. to 2:30 P.M. and Sunday 9:00 A.M. to 2:30 P.M.

St. Casimir's Church (Kościół Sw. Kazimierza), Rynek Nowega Miasta: This domed, octagonal Baroque church was originally built in 1683 as a thanks offering of French-born Queen Maria Casimir, grateful for the resounding victory of her husband, King John III Sobieski, against the Turks near Vienna. It was a victory that stopped the Ottoman Empire's westward expansion. Architect for the structure was the Dutchman Tylman of Gameren.

Warsaw Uprising Plaque (Tablica Ku czci Powstania Warszawskiego), ulica Długa and ulica Miodowa: This is a memorial to the more than 5,000 who sought to escape from the Old Town through its sewers in the sixty-three-day Second Warsaw Uprising of 1944. Many were drowned; many more were killed by German hand grenades pitched into the sewers. Some died of starvation. A few survived.

Royal Way (Trakt Królewski): Warsaw's Royal Way, beginning at Castle Square, continues to Wilanów Palace, about six miles from the center of the city. All along, as it changes its name from Krakowskie Przedmieście to Nowy Świat to aleje Ujazdowskie, are reconstructed palaces that are now government office buildings, pastel Baroque houses, restaurants, shops, churches, university buildings, and embassies. In geographical order, as you leave the Royal Castle, they follow.

Church of St. Anne (Kościół Św. Anny): For years, Polish princes swore allegiance to their kings in front of this imposing fifteenth-century church with its eighteenth-century neoclassical facade. Happily, most of the church, with a rich Baroque interior, survived the devastation of World War II.

Church and Monastery of the Barefoot Carmelites (Kościół Karmelitow Bosych): This late-seventeenth-century neoclassical church is easily recognized by the sphere on top with a serpent biting an apple on it. Inside are resplendent Baroque altars. As with all Polish churches today, entering it at any but service times may be a problem.

Radziwiłł Palace (Pałac Radziwiłkow): A striking equestrian statue of Prince Jósef Poniatowski, nephew of Poland's last king, Stanislaus II Augustus, and commander of the Polish forces under Napoleon, stands in the courtyard of this imposing neoclassical palace that now is the meeting place of the Council of Ministers. The original statue of the prince, dressed like a Roman emperor on his horse, was designed by Danish sculptor Bertel Thorvaldscn. Aftcr it was destroyed by the Germans in World War II, Copenhagen provided this substitute.

Church of the Nuns of the Visitation (Kościół Wizytek): Frédéric Chopin played the organ in this late Baroque church with its saints on high. The church suffered almost no war damage. Inside, its boat-shaped, eighteenth-century pulpit is of particular interest.

University of Warsaw (Uniwersytet Warszawski): A neo-Baroque gateway topped with the Polish eagle marks the entrance, on the same side of the street as the Radziwill Palace, to the complex of seventeenth- and eighteenth-century restored palaces that today are the buildings of the university.

Church of the Holy Cross (Kościół Św. Krzyza): Across Krakowskie Przedmieście from the university stands this two-turreted Baroque church with Christ carrying the cross outside. Inside, the heart of nineteenth-century Polish composer Frédéric Chopin is in a pillar with clusters of banners and flowers around it. If you pass half an hour or so in this richly gilded church you are certain to see some music lover, homemade bouquet in hand, come to honor Poland's greatest composer. In the same pillar is the heart of Nobel Prize–winning novelist Władysłav Reymont.

Academy of Fine Arts (Akademia Sztuk Pieknych), Krakowskie Przedmieście 5: Aficionados of composer Chopin might wish to try to find their way to the second-floor room arranged in Empire style where Chopin lived briefly before going abroad. There is one grand piano and two uprights in the room, but none were his.

Copernicus Statue: The sixteenth-century Polish astronomer Mikołaj Kopernik (Copernicus is the Latin form of his name) is honored here by another Thorvaldsen statue. During the World War II occupation the Germans attached a plaque suggesting that the astronomer was German, not Polish. A Polish Underground organization removed it. In retaliation, the Germans took down another popular Polish monument, a memorial to eighteenth-century shoemaker Jan Kilínski, who led a revolt against the Russians. Even in the face of the horrors of war, the Poles' reply was a new plaque on Copernicus, this one informing the Germans: "In retaliation for the destruction of the monument to Kilínski, I prolong the winter for another six weeks. Nicolaus Copernicus Astronomer."

Chopin Museum (Muzeum Chopin, Gninski Residence), ulica Tamka 41: In this re-created seventeenth-century Ostrogski palace, photographic and manuscript displays recount (unfortunately not in English) Frédéric Chopin's life abroad. Chopin left Warsaw at the age of twenty, encouraged by Italian composer Niccolò Paganini, who, on a visit, was astounded by the young man's talent. (When he was only eight, Chopin had had a Polonaise published.) Exhibits recount how the youthful composer longed to return home after an initial trip to Paris, but the 1830s were revolutionary times in Poland — with much antagonism to Russian influence over the government. Chopin wrote his E Minor Etude in honor of his friends in the revolutionary movement. Critics acclaimed it as sounding like "guns hidden in flowers . . . you can feel 'La Marseillaise' in it." So the composer was warned that it would be inadvisable for him to return home.

Chopin's affair with French writer George Sand is recorded. There are facsimiles of letters and compositions and the piano on which he did his last composing before his death at the age of thirty-nine in Paris.

(An incidental legend connected with this palace-museum tells of a lake in its cellars filled with gold and guarded by a golden duck. When a soldier visiting the palace happened upon the lake, the duck generously presented him with a bag of lake gold, but warned him that he must spend it wisely. Of course, the soldier didn't, and when he returned hoping for more gold, the palace cellar was just like any other cellar — quite empty of both lake and gold.) The museum is open from 10:00 A.M. to 2:00 P.M., except Sunday.

Blikle's (Bliklego Ciastkarnia), Nowy Świat: If you continue along Krakowskie Przedmieście Street after it becomes Nowy Świat (New World Street), the delectable fragrances and the crowds are likely to lure you into this 100-year-old confectioner's. During World War I, when Charles de Gaulle was a young French army officer giving advice to the Polish army on how to fight the Soviets, he was a frequent visitor here. After he became president of France, Blikle's continued to supply him with its light, sweet doughnuts. If you are tempted to buy one (and you should), don't expect prompt, efficient service. You will get your doughnut in due time — the better for the wait — and then you can munch it as you continue your sightseeing.

National Museum (Muzeum Narodowy), aleje Jerozolimskie 3: This enormous and architecturally very ugly museum (Poland's largest) has seven halls filled with ancient, medieval, Polish, and foreign art. Of principal interest are the early frescoes brought back from a cathedral at Faras in Nubia (now the Sudan) by a Polish archeological expedition in the 1960s. Dramatic historical paintings by the nineteenth-century's Jan Matejko include *The Battle of Grünwald,* at which King Ladislaus Jagiello and Russian, Lithuanian, and Czech armies defeated the Teutonic Knights. In the thirteenth century, the knights, invited to Poland to help rid it of invaders, had taken over many Polish lands. In World War II, the canvas was spirited away and buried. Because the Teutonic Knights were Germans, the Nazis offered a 10 million mark reward for the painting's recovery. But it was not until after the war that it was unearthed from its secret hiding place. There are also Bellotto views of Warsaw here.

The museum is open Sunday and Tuesday from 10:00 A.M. to 5:00 P.M., Wednesday, Friday, and Saturday until 4:00 P.M., and Thursday from noon to 6:00 P.M. It is closed on Monday, public holidays, and the day after any public holiday.

Łazienki Park (Łazienki): Few countries have such gracious parks of canals, ponds, lakes, and flowers and statues, palaces, and theaters. Laid out between 1764 and 1795 under the direction of King Stanislaus Augustus, Łazienki Park is popular with young and old, Varsovians and visitors, who stroll along its myriad paths, watching ducks feed, enjoying the flowers, visiting the palaces, and, in season, attending the concerts.

In 1775 King Stanislaus Augustus built himself a **Summer Pal-**

ace (Pałac na Wodzie) on the willow-lined lake here. It is a graceful building designed by his royal architect, Domenico Merlini, in Polish neoclassical style with a colonnaded portico. This style of architecture, of which there are other examples in the park, is sometimes called Stanislaus Augustus style. The park takes its name from a bathhouse that once occupied the site.

Stanislaus Augustus was originally a Polish prince who got his start in politics as ambassador to the Russian court at St. Petersburg. While there, he and a lively young German princess had an affair for a time, but the princess was the intended of Russia's Peter III. When Peter died, under somewhat mysterious circumstances, his German-born widow became Catherine the Great. After Stanislaus Augustus became Poland's titular king, he and the empress continued their on again, off-again relationship. At the end, they were distinctly off, when the Polish king grew tired of being a Russian pawn and sought independence. Catherine forced him to abdicate and put him under house arrest in Russia.

But for many years before that, this father of the Polish Renaissance had enjoyed the loveliness of his park and his more than twenty palaces. The king invited artists, poets, and writers to weekly dinners at this palace each Thursday. From this stems the tradition that on Thursdays all museums in Poland are free of charge.

In 1944, the Germans elected to blow up the palace after removing its art. As it turned out, they never had the time to do it. After sousing it with gasoline and drilling 400 holes for their explosive charges, the imminent arrival of the Russians forced them to flee. The damaged, but not destroyed, little palace on the island — a perfect neoclassical structure — is now completely restored. Some of the interior is country-style with pebble-studded walls, some Baroque, and some controlled, superb neoclassical. In the king's picture collection (from which much was taken) there are still many Dutch masterpieces. It is open to the public daily, except Monday, from 10:00 A.M. to 3:00 P.M.

Also on the lake is an open air **Amphitheater** (Teatr na Wyspie) that is a copy of the theater at Herculaneum. The stage is separated from the audience by water. There is an **Orangery** in the park that has a little court theater inside with marbleized walls that are actually wood and decorations that include a frieze of countries of the day. At the southern end of the park is a later orangery.

The park's other attractions are the **White House** (Biały Domek), where France's Louis XVIII, brother of ill-fated Louis XVI, lived for a while in exile in the early nineteenth century and where Stanislaus Augustus is said to have kept his mistresses; the rather stiff late-eighteenth-century **Belvedere Palace** that is now the home of the president; a cottage Stanislaus Augustus gave to the soothsayer who predicted his election to the kingship; and the controversial **Chopin Monument.** The monument was not universally popular before the war, but after it was broken up by the Germans for scrap, it was recast and joyously reerected. (The Art Nouveau–like statue has Chopin seated beneath an enormous weeping willow tree which becomes the pianist's hand as you look at the back of it). Wacław Szymanowski was its sculptor. On summer Sundays, concerts are given here at noon and 4:00 P.M.

Church of St. Anthony and St. Boniface (Kościół Św. Antoniego i Binifacego), ulica Czerniakowska: Some call this seventeenth-century domed Greek-cross church, designed by Tylman of Gameren, Warsaw's most beautiful church. Its interior is richly decorated with baroque frescoes and stucco angels, leaves, and tendrils, and it escaped the war unscathed.

Praga: Until the 1970s, this area across the River Vistula was the site of a popular and colorful flea market. The market has moved now to the Remberow district and with it a good deal of the color of Praga has gone, but it continues to have certain attractions. These include **Praga Park** (Park Praski) and the **Zoo** (Ogród Zoologiczny), the turn-of-the-century neo-Gothic **Church of the Archangel Michael and St. Floria** (Kosciot Archaniół Michała i Sw. Floriana), and the Byzantine-style onion-domed **St. Mary Magdalene's Orthodox Cathedral** (Katedra Prawosławny Św. Marii Magdaleny) on ulica Świerczewskiego.

Wilanów Palace and Gardens (Wilanów): This graceful pale-yellow Baroque palace was started by King John III Sobieski, victor over the Turks at the siege of Vienna, in 1677 and not completed until 1729, long after the king's death. John III, who preferred country to city, purchased the land where the palace now sits, along with two neighboring hamlets, to assure that he would have woods and waters around him, though he was still not that far from the capital.

Plans for a palace here had already been laid out by the property's previous owner, but little work had gotten under way, so the king and his beloved French wife, Maria, erected a palace of his own choice, embellishing it over the years as the nation's treasury allowed it. The palace today is filled with portraits of Polish royalty and nobility. (Particularly interesting are the seventeenth- and eighteenth century hexagonal portraits on tin of the deceased that were attached to coffins but removed before burial, and the iron jewelry women wore in mourning.) In the king's bedchamber, the canopy over his bed is said to have been made from the tent of the Turkish leader at the siege of Vienna who, in the Turkish way, throttled himself after his defeat with a silken cord sent for that purpose by the sultan. There are richly painted beamed ceilings, stucco Baroque decorations that look like marble, gilded armchairs, and chandeliers. Not all of this is of King John's day. After his death, the palace passed through many hands and underwent many changes.

During World War II, when the palace was used as a sanitarium for wounded Luftwaffe officers, much of the furniture was removed and some structural damage done. It has been elegantly restored and some of the original furnishings reacquired. Designed and decorated, as was Louis XIV's Versailles, by a whole school of craftsmen, the overall effect of the Baroque palace and its accompanying French-style gardens is stunning. Directing the work on it and master architect for it all was a Polish-Italian, Agostino Locci.

Also on the palace grounds, in the former Riding School, is the **Poster Museum** (Muzeum Plakatow), of some interest to those who like graphic art, which is quite noted in Poland. The palace

is open daily, except Tuesday, and holidays from 9:30 A.M. to
2:45 P.M., but not the day after public holidays or the first Sunday in the month. Because it is now such a popular site, it is wise
to arrange in advance with Orbis for a guided English-speaking
tour.

THE OUTSKIRTS OF WARSAW

BROCHOW

Towering over the flat Mazovian landscape here is the restored
red-brick Renaissance **Church of St. Rochus** (Kościoł Św. Roch),
where Frédéric Chopin's parents, Nicolas Chopin and Justyna
Krzyzanowska, were married in 1806 and where the newborn
Frédéric was christened in 1810. Three round towers and a defense wall protect the church, one of the few fortified churches
remaining in Poland. Unfortunately, except at the time of services, access to the inside is unlikely.

KAZIMIERZ DOLNY

It was Casimir (Kazimierz) the Great, whose name it bears, who
founded this town on the River Vistula in the fourteenth century.
Legend has it that he installed his Jewish mistress, Esterka,
nearby, linking his castle to hers by an underground tunnel. Be
that as it may, by the sixteenth century, this was a thriving port,
with grain from neighboring nobles' lands shipped down the
river to Gdańsk and salt herring brought back in exchange.
There were forty-five granaries here at the end of that century
and many fine houses. Later, Kazimierz Dolny fell on hard times,
but in the last century, artists suddenly discovered its **Old Town
Square,** faced with some of Poland's handsomest Renaissance
houses.

The most impressive of these are the two houses of Nicholas
and Christopher Przybyla, well-to-do merchant brothers. On
Nicholas's house, there is an enormous figure of his patron saint.

On Christopher's, his saint is carrying the Christ Child on his shoulders and using a tree as a stave. Both houses have arcades, ornate attic stories, and much-decorated windows. Elsewhere around the square, facades are decorated with saints on the moldings.

Below the square on ulica Senatorska, overlooking the Grodarz stream, monsters and griffins adorn the equally lovely seventeenth-century Mannerist **Cele's House,** again a rich merchant's house that is now the local history museum. It includes a history of the Jews of the area, but all is in Polish. (On the outskirts of town is an impressive memorial to the Jews of Kazimierz Dolny — a split tablet on a hillside made from cemetery gravestones.) In town, near the museum, a popular bakery offers bread in the shapes of roosters and crayfish.

At the top of the square is the parish church begun in Gothic style, burned in 1561 and rebuilt in the seventeenth century. Inside are a 1620 organ and Renaissance and Rococo features, but entry into the church can be a problem.

Above the church are the few remains of Casimir the Great's **Castle** and **Three Crosses Hill** (Góra Trzech Krzyży), memorializing townspeople who died of the plague in the early eighteenth century.

For the time being, at least, Kazimierz Dolny remains largely a quiet, unspoiled place (though souvenir shops occupy some of the Old Town Square).

ŁOWICZ

In the **Regional Museum** here, open daily, except Monday, from 10:00 A.M. to 4:00 P.M., is a fine collection of folk arts and crafts of the region — colorful paper cutouts that were a popular folk decoration in the last century and the beginning of this one, painted Easter eggs, costumes, weaving, and gaily painted furniture. Behind the museum are several local peasant cottages that have been moved to the site.

In the surrounding countryside, particularly in the village of Zlaków Koscielny, the thatched-roofed, blue-washed cottages

are a living part of the village-scape. In the village of Zlaków
Borowy, other "working" farm cottages may be seen; some are
open to the public.

ŻELAZOWA WOLA

Frédéric Chopin was born in 1810 in a pretty little restored cottage here, thirty-five miles outside Warsaw. This is a countryside
of onion fields and haystacks swirled around tall poles; ducks,
chickens, and horse-drawn wagons; and long straight roads.
Here Frédéric's French-born father was tutor in the wealthy
Skarbek family, to which his mother was distantly related. Set
among willows, maples, birches, with a stream (though it is
called the River Utrata) flowing by, it is easy to see why inspira-
tion might come in such tranquillity. Chopin lived here only for
the first year of his life (legend has it that the village band was
playing mazurkas as he was being born, which influenced him
ever afterward). The family, however, returned summers
throughout his childhood, and this is said to have been his favorite place. The cottage, which the state acquired in 1929, had only
recently been opened as a museum when World War II began.
Much of the Chopin memorabilia that had been lovingly collected was carried off by the Germans and an army unit was
quartered here. Fortunately, the six-room cottage has been restored, and though it is not rich in Chopin memorabilia, there
are enough furnishings to give it a homey sense.

On a bright summer day, it is a sun-filled house, and on Sundays from May till the end of October, pianists of note play Chopin works in the music room and the melodies can be heard
everywhere in the garden. On display indoors are facsimiles of
some of his earliest compositions and letters to his parents, a
copy of his birth certificate, and family portraits, including a
copy of the Delacroix painting of Chopin that hangs in the
Louvre. In the surrounding park are thousands of plants and
trees donated by Chopin admirers from around the world. The
house is open Tuesday to Sunday 10:00 A.M. to 5:00 P.M. and
day trips are offered from Warsaw by Orbis.

CRACOW AND ITS ENVIRONS

As long ago as the Middle Ages, Cracow (Kraków) was acclaimed as the most beautiful of all the cities of Poland. With its hilltop Renaissance castle, its spacious marketplace, red-brick church towers, the golden dome of its cathedral, and narrow streets edged with elaborate Gothic facades, it remains, six centuries later, Poland's loveliest city.

As such, of course, it attracts tourists by the thousands and at the height of the summer season the crowds milling in the castle

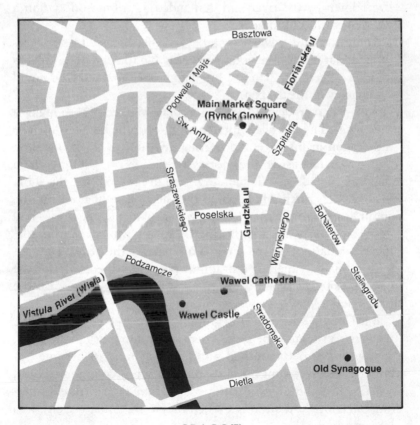

CRACOW

courtyard and snapping pictures of the flower sellers' stalls at the Main Market Square are hardly an enhancement to its pictur-esqueness. Accommodations may be hard to find and restaurant reservations difficult to get. Plans for a visit should be made well in advance of a journey — and a Polish-speaking guide is almost essential to finding your way into the castle and the cathedral. But it is all worth the hassle.

Cracow began, legend has it, when a prince named Krak built a fortified castle on Wawel Hill above the River Vistula, where today's Wawel Castle stands. He called his settlement Kraków, for himself. It was not an altogether happy place, as a dragon lived down by the river and demanded as tribute one virgin a week to garnish his dinner.

The distraught townspeople begged their prince to do some-thing about it, and the good Krak, unable to solve the problem himself, offered the hand of his daughter to anyone who could rid Cracow of the dragon.

A shoemaker devised the plan that worked. He bought a sheep, killed it, and filled it with sulfur. Then he boldly took it to the dragon in his cave and encouraged him to try it, insisting that it was far tastier and more tender than the young women the dragon had been demanding. The dragon fell for the shoe-maker's sales pitch. He gobbled the sheep, caught fire from the sulfur, leapt into the river to gulp water to quench the fire — and drank so much water that he burst. Cracow was saved from fur-ther depredation and the shoemaker married the prince's daugh-ter. To this day, there is a dragon cave below the castle for the benefit of tourists and a dragon statue spitting flames on the banks of the Vistula.

But Cracow's historical beginning was in the eighth century, when the Vistulan tribe settled here and trading began. In 1000, a bishopric was established and Cracow in 1038 became Po-land's capital. It continued to be a thriving community until 1241, when the Tartars galloped in from the north, murder-ing, pillaging, and burning. When they were gone, the city was largely rebuilt.

In the next three centuries, some of the city's finest structures were built: a university was established by Casimir the Great, which during the days of Casimir's great-niece, Queen Jadwiga, and her husband, King Ladislaus Jagiello, was much expanded. (On her death, she left her jewels to the university.) Today it is known as the Jagiellonian University.

In the early sixteenth century, when King Sigismund I — Sigismund the Old — married an Italian princess, Bona Sforza, she brought with her Italian Renaissance ideas and Cracow became Poland's center of art and culture. But a fire in the castle in 1595 gave the king at that time, Sigismund III (Sigismund Vasa), king of Sweden as well as of Poland, an excuse to transfer his residence to Warsaw so it would be nearer to his other kingdom.

In the centuries that followed, Cracow declined, as it was attacked and invaded by Swedes and Austrians. In the nineteenth and twentieth centuries, Cracow enjoyed something of a comeback until World War II, when the Germans made Wawel Castle the seat of their government in Poland. They sent its Jewish population and its university professors to concentration camps as they sought to destroy its intelligentsia. They would have destroyed Cracow's historic structures, too, had Soviet Marshal Ivan Koniev not reached it before they could.

The principal sites of Cracow follow.

Barbican (Barbakan): Even though relatively little remains of Cracow's medieval fifteenth-century red-brick defensive walls, with observation turrets fashioned after those at Carcassonne in the south of France and Arab military fortifications, this round red-brick tower built for defense — the Cracow "stew pot" as it is called — is one of the largest structures of its kind in Europe.

Floriańska Street (ulica Floriańska): Restoration work along this street has revealed many Gothic facades that had been covered in later years by later styles. Worth a stop are the **Jan Matejko House and Museum** at Number 41, rich in memorabilia of the painter (if you are a fan of his monumental historical canvases), and the **Jama Michalika Café** (Michalik's Den), with its Art Nouveau room. On the glass partitions and glass ceiling are fanciful flowers and a spider with a dragonfly caught in her web. The woodwork is dark, the atmosphere welcoming and cozy.

Here, with extremely slow service, you can have light meals, good ice cream, and coffee. As is the case in many restaurants and cafés in Poland, tables are shared, increasing the comradeship (if the strangers brought together can speak each other's language, and even if they cannot). The café, formerly a literary cabaret, has, over the years, been especially noted for its political puppet shows.

At Number 14 is the **Hotel pod Róża** (Under the Rose), Cracow's oldest hotel, and, though recently renovated, in need of further renovation. But its management proudly makes it known that Franz Liszt and the Russian tsar Alexander I have been among its guests. Above its Renaissance door, in Latin, it is written, "May this house stand until an ant drinks the water of the seas and a tortoise goes around the world."

Grodzka Street (ulica Grodzka): All along Grodzka Street, today one of Cracow's main shopping streets, are handsome Gothic and Renaissance houses, and if you venture into the little alleys between shops and houses, you will find many charming courtyards, often with more shops and workshops. On the street, as well, are interesting churches — **St. Andrew's** (Św. Andrzeja), an eleventh-century stone church that was not destroyed in the thirteenth-century Tartar invasion; the Jesuit **Church of Sts. Peter and Paul,** Cracow's first Baroque church, with its line of larger-than-life-size statues of apostles in swirling robes. A little bit off Grodzka Street at the Place of the Spring of Nations (Plac Wiesny Ludow) is the **Franciscan Church,** which is known for its Art Nouveau stained-glass windows by painter-poet-dramatist Stanisław Wyspiański. Across the street is the Baroque **Bishop's Palace,** where Pope John Paul II lived during the dozen years he was archbishop in Cracow.

Kazimierz: When World War II began, a quarter of Cracow's population was Jewish, almost all of it settled in this district of winding narrow streets. By the war's end, it was virtually deserted. Its **Old Synagogue** at Szeroka Street 24, started in the fifteenth century, had been damaged and looted, but, in fact, none of the six synagogues in this district had actually been destroyed. Today, the Old Synagogue has become a Museum of the History and Culture of Cracow's Jews, but the **Remu'h Synagogue,** more than 400 years old, is functioning again. All around it are some 700 Renaissance and Baroque tombstones unearthed during excavations after World War II and a Wailing Wall made from tombstones that the Nazis shattered. The museum is open Wednesday, Thursday, and weekends from 9:00 A.M. to 3:00 P.M. and on Friday from 11:00 A.M. to 6:00 P.M.

Other highlights of Kazimierz include the rich **Ethnographic Museum,** housed in the Old Town Hall at Wolnica Square and filled with wood carvings, paintings on glass, country cottage rooms, paper cutouts, and pottery. Nearby, in the Christian section of Kazimierz, are two enormous Gothic basilicas, the **Church of St. Catherine** (Kościół sw. Katarzyny) and the **Pauline Church** (Paulinow) on the cliff. The museum is open Wednesday to Saturday from 9:00 A.M. to 4:00 P.M. and Monday from 10:00 A.M. to 6:00 P.M.

Kanoniczna Street (ulica Kanoniczna): The Renaissance town houses along this street were undergoing restoration as this book went to press. Many of them were once the homes of church canons, identified as such by the hats carved over the doors.

Main Market Square (Rynek Główny): Often called the Drawing Room of Cracow, this is one of Europe's largest market squares. In warm seasons, it is bright with the stalls of flower sellers and their gay umbrellas. Pigeons — bewitched princes, it is said — feed happily in its great open spaces. In any season, it is an architectural delight. Centerpiece of it all is the arcaded 328-foot-long **Cloth Hall** (Sukiennice) with its flowing Renaissance "Polish attic" — a false front that hides a steep sloped roof essential in the snows of Cracow. Grotesque Renaissance masks add vitality to its facade. Inside on the lower floor today are souvenir and handicraft shops; the second floor, the **Gallery of Polish Painting** of the National Museum, is largely filled with works of the eighteenth and nineteenth centuries. It is open from 10:00 A.M. to 4:00 P.M. Friday through Monday, from noon to 6:00 P.M. Thursday, and closed Tuesday and Wednesday.

Behind the Cloth Hall is the Gothic **Town Hall Tower** of brick and stone (the rest of the town hall has been torn down). Today the tower houses a museum of the city and in its cellar a popular café and theater.

Rising above the marketplace are the two unequal towers of the red-brick **Church of the Virgin Mary** (Kościół Mariacki). Every hour on the hour, a bugler trumpets four times from its heights. He interrupts his bugling each time, so it will sound as the first bugler's did in the thirteenth century when an arrow pierced his heart as he was trumpeting a warning that the Tartars were coming. The two towers differ in height, it is said, because two brothers were assigned the task of constructing them in the fifteenth century. One worked much faster than the other, and the slower brother, in a fit of jealousy at the other's speed, murdered him with a sword that now hangs in the Cloth Hall. Then the murderer, aghast at what he had done, jumped from his tower to his death, thereby leaving his work forever of unequal height.

The inside of the church is notable for a Jan Matejko painting of angels playing musical instruments and the rich blues and reds of its fourteenth-century stained-glass windows, but, above all, for its wooden altar triptych by master German wood carver Veit Stoss — in Polish, Wit Stwosz. It is believed to be the largest wooden Gothic altar triptych in Europe. Though the altar is supposed to be opened and illuminated at noon daily, it may or may not be. It would be wise to check opening and illumination times at the Orbis information office and to arrive at least fifteen minutes in advance of opening time to be ahead of the crowd.

The opened altarpiece depicts the death and Assumption of the Virgin. Her gentle expression and the apostles' realistic looks and stances (they are believed to be modeled after Cracow burghers) are memorable. Art historians call it one of the greatest examples of medieval wood carving still in existence.

When it is closed, the altar shows scenes from the life of Christ and the Virgin. (But when it is closed and there are no lights illuminating it, it is virtually impossible to view the work.)

Also attributed by some to Stoss, a Nuremberg-born carver who came to Cracow in 1477 and did most of his work here, are the stone crucifix in the church's righthand aisle and the cross in the chancel.

During World War II, the Germans, claiming Stoss as one of their own, removed the altarpiece to Germany, but in 1946, it was brought back here, restored and returned to its original place.

The oldest building in the Old Town Square is little stone **St. Adalbert's Church,** largely Romanesque and built at the end of the eleventh century. Visitors of Polish heritage will be interested in the plaque in the square marking the spot, in 1794, where patriot Tadeusz Kościuszko urged rebellion against the Russians who had partitioned the country.

Around the square are handsome Gothic and Renaissance houses.

St. Florian's Gate (Brama Floriańska): This 115-foot-high brick gate with its rectangular tower managed to survive the general nineteenth-century demolition of this city's old defense system, thanks to the efforts of a historically minded professor, who campaigned energetically for their preservation. Taking the place of those walls and towers destroyed is a stretch of green called the **Planty,** where students sun and study in season, mothers push strollers, and children bounce balls.

St. John Street (ulica Św. Jana): The **Czartoryski Museum,** at Number 19, is a branch of the National Museum. Among other valuable paintings, it houses Leonardo da Vinci's *Lady with an Ermine* and Rembrandt's *Landscape with the Good Samaritan,* a Bellini *Madonna and Child,* and a Giordano *Flight into Egypt.* The armory in an adjoining building has striking Oriental military souvenirs of Polish fighting against the Turks. The museum is open from 10:00 A.M. to 3:00 P.M. Saturday through Tuesday and on Friday from noon to 5:30 P.M.

The **Collegium Maius** here, built in 1400, is the oldest university building in all Poland. With its red-brick walls and Gothic gables, its arcades, and its graceful flights of stairs leading to second stories, it is a lovely sight to behold. Entry into the courtyard is easy. Unfortunately, getting beyond it into the **Museum of the History of the University** seemed almost impossible as this book went to press. It is open only from noon to 2:00 P.M. and not on Sunday and holidays.

Though Dr. Faustus is said to have studied here and dabbled in the alchemy that would bring him to ruin in Goethe's play, and the Cracow magician Pan Twardowski (he who "conjured up" his dead queen for bereaved King Sigismund II Augustus) is said to have worked here, too, the Alchemy Room where they experimented is closed now to the public. So is the Common Room with its antique astronomical implements (Nicolaus Copernicus was a student here), wood carvings, tapestries, and carpets; and the Jagiellonian Room with its coffered ceiling decorated with rosettes.

Wawel Castle: This red-brick complex of copper domes, towers, and walls rising on Wawel Hill over the Vistula does not, as you climb toward it, give much indication of the glories awaiting inside. But its graceful arcaded Renaissance courtyard is considered by many the finest of its kind in Europe, and the treasures of art in its seventy-one rooms are incomparable. In its **Armory** gleam Turkish shields and tournament armor, chain mail and javelins, and armor with feathered "wings" to prevent its wearer from being lassoed.

In its **Treasury** is Szczerbiec — the Jagged Sword — the iron-and-gold coronation sword of Poland's kings. (It got its name, it is said, when a Polish king, invading the Ukraine, knocked three times with it on the gate of Kiev, thereby damaging its blade. Taken away by the Prussians during the Third Polish Partition in 1795, because it was not all gold it happily escaped the fate of the crown jewels, which were sold and their gold melted down to make coins. Returned to Poland just before World War II, the sword was smuggled to London and then Canada before the Germans occupied the castle.)

The castle's 136 sixteenth-century tapestries ordered from Brussels by King Sigismund II Augustus are its most valuable collection, brilliant in color and thrilling in design, and they decorate the walls of virtually every room. Many are said to have been designed by Peter Paul Rubens and their patterns destroyed on order of the king to assure they would be one of a kind. Along with the coronation sword, the tapestries spent the war years in Canada.

Wawel Castle also houses one of the world's largest collections of Turkish and Persian tents — with dazzling red-and-gold interiors of damask, leather, and canvas — but this collection may only be seen by previous arrangement with the Educational Division of the castle.

As for the rooms themselves, one of the most interesting is the **Chamber of Deputies** with its ceiling of carved wooden heads — some allegorical and some of historical personages of the sixteenth century. Legend has it that once when King Sigismund Augustus was about to deliver a judgment here, he was warned by a voice from one head, "King Augustus, be just."

The structure itself had its beginning in the eleventh century. In the fourteenth century it became a Gothic castle, but it was in the sixteenth century that the present Italian Renaissance touches were so splendidly blended into the existing Polish Gothic fortress. The royal rooms are open Tuesday, Thursday, Saturday, and Sunday from 10:00 A.M. to 3:15 P.M. and Wednesday and Friday from noon to 6:00 P.M. They are closed on Monday. The Treasury and Armory are open daily except Monday from 10:00 A.M. to 3:00 P.M.

Wawel Cathedral: Since the eleventh century, three cathedrals have occupied this riverfront site. The main part of what stands here today — where kings have been crowned and buried for centuries — is flamboyant Gothic, but it is surrounded by Renaissance and Baroque chapels. Not to be missed among them is the Renaissance **Sigismund Chapel**, often acclaimed as the finest Renaissance chapel north of the Alps. Set in niches in its white marble walls, carved in red marble, are the sarcophagi of Sigismund I, his son Sigismund II Augustus, and Queen Anna, daughter of Sigismund I.

Also of interest is the red marble tomb of Casimir the Great, with the marble king sleeping peacefully on it, and the Holy Cross Chapel (Kaplica Św. Krzyża), where the carving of the dead king, Casimir IV, is the work of Veit Stoss.

In the cathedral transept on a pink marble base is the elaborate silver casket of St. Stanislaus, done in Baroque style by a Gdańsk silversmith of the seventeenth century. Stanislaus, an eleventh-century bishop, was at odds with his king, Boleslaus II (Boleslaus the Brave), and was murdered either by the king or by royal order.

Another highlight of the cathedral is the Romanesque **St. Leonard's Crypt,** where Polish patriot Tadeusz Kósciuszko (who fought in the American Revolution) is buried among fourteen Polish kings, their wives, and their children. Then there is the view from the cathedral tower where Poland's largest bell hangs, the twenty-six-foot-circumference Sigismund, cast from enemy cannon captured in 1520.

AUSCHWITZ (OŚWIĘCIM)

Forty miles southwest of Cracow is this harrowing reminder of the Nazi extermination policy of World War II. What remains today are echoing brick buildings, barbed-wire fences, silent streets, watch towers, photographs, torture chambers, and rooms filled with mountains of pots and pans and other familiar household goods that innocent victims brought here thinking they were simply being moved to some new place. There are toys, false teeth, and false limbs taken from the men, women, and children — 2 million from twenty-eight countries — who died of overwork or malnutrition or were killed here. A moving film in the **State Oświęcim-Brzezinka Museum** shows the Soviet liberation of this concentration camp on January 27, 1945. Still standing above the entry gate is the black iron sign that welcomed new arrivals to the camp: *"Arbeit Macht Frei"* — "Work Makes Freedom."

A short twenty-minute walk away are the barracks and ruins of the gas chambers and crematoria of Birkenau (Brzezinka), which the Germans blew up as the Russians approached. From the monument there the rail lines that brought the thousands of victims to the camp can still be seen. Left much as it was in the days when its barracks were occupied, Birkenau — from which there was no reprieve — is, if anything, an even more sinister sight than Auschwitz. Both camps are open from 8:00 A.M. to

7:00 P.M. from June through August, until 6:00 P.M. in May and September, until 5:00 P.M. in April and October, and until 3:00 P.M. in the winter months. Both films shown and guidebooks sold are multilingual.

Częstochowa

Annually, a million and a half Catholics come to the **Jasna Góra Monastery** in this industrial city for a glimpse of the Black Madonna, an icon of the Virgin Mary said by some to have been painted by St. Luke himself and to be endowed with miraculous powers. In the seventeenth century, when Swedish armies invaded Poland and almost the whole country capitulated, this fourteenth-century Paulist monastery — with its Black Madonna — stopped them. In 1430, when a Tartar soldier, tantalized by the silver on it, sought to steal it, he found it growing heavier and heavier and was so infuriated, so the story goes, that he slashed the Virgin's face with his sword. Her face bled, and the scar remains to this day.

In any case, the elaborate Baroque Monastery of Jasna Góra with its needlelike tower and its bedazzling white-and-gold interior is the most sacred place in this 90 percent Catholic country. In August, pilgrims walk close to 200 miles from Warsaw to Częstochowa, and in any season, schoolchildren, teenagers with backpacks, toddlers on their fathers' shoulders, the weary elderly carrying shopping bags, bright-faced nuns and priests, and brawny workmen can be found on their knees here or crushed together waiting for the 6:00 A.M. and the 3:30 P.M. unveiling of the Black Madonna to the roll of drums and trumpet fanfare. (At noon and at 6:00 P.M. the Madonna is veiled again.)

There is also a church **Treasury**, filled with ecclesiastical robes, church silver, and gifts that worshippers have left behind at the shrine. It is open daily from 9:00 to 11:00 A.M. and 3:30 to 5:30 P.M. Outside the church are nineteenth-century Stations of the Cross.

Visitors must bear in mind that the great number of the devout and of tourists who come to this site are inviting to pickpockets, and it is wise to be alert to their possible presence.

WIELICZKA

If the tours of the **Salt Mines** here were not so long (more than two hours) and you could be assured of an English-speaking guide, a visit here, just seven miles from Cracow, would be a pleasant break from historic sightseeing. Unfortunately, as this book went to press, the tours still needed streamlining. But here, 442 feet down, visitors go on a mile-and-a-half walk through tunnels into a seventeenth-century chapel carved from salt by pious miners and lit by rock-salt chandeliers, past playful gnomes and pretty princesses carved of salt, up stairways carved of salt, into ballrooms cut out of salt, and an "assembly plant" where German occupiers planned the manufacture of airplane engines. There is also an underground sports complex for today's miners with volleyball and tennis courts carved from the salt and a sanitarium for respiratory diseases. For 1,000 years the Wieliczka Salt Mines have been a major source of salt, and to this day 200,000 tons of salt a year continue to be mined here.

It all began, it is said, when Kinga, daughter of the king of Hungary and affianced to a Polish prince, learned there was little salt in the land to which she was going. Her father, as dowry, therefore gave her a Hungarian salt mine. Into it, she accidentally dropped her engagement ring. Sorrowfully, she proceeded on her way to Cracow, but was moved to stop suddenly, and she ordered her servants to dig. Digging, they found not only her ring but this rich bed of salt that had followed her. The mine is open from 8:30 A.M. to 6:00 P.M. daily.

ROUND ABOUT ZAKOPANE

It is only ninety miles if you travel by road from Cracow to Poland's most popular winter resort of Zakopane, and the only sensible way to make the trip is by bus or car (cars may be rented or arrangements made for cars and drivers in Cracow). Though road signs are generally spread far apart on most Polish roads, they are better spaced on this much-touristed route.

Not far outside Cracow you begin to be in the country, climbing undulating green hills brightened by red-brick farmhouses. Brown cows are tethered by the roadside. Haystacks sprout in fields. The road winds past fields into woods. It edges the turbulent Raba River. In villages are dark-brown wooden churches with sharply pitched roofs and covered sleeping porches outside for weary travelers. Some of these porches — constructed with wooden pegs — have been here since the seventeenth century. If the weather is good, an elderly babushkaed lady or two may have come to pray and leave flowers — though not necessarily inside (for like the city churches of Poland, country churches, too, are now often closed when there are no services).

In time, the white peaks of the Tatra Mountains that separate Poland from Czechoslovakia come into view. The road dips into **Nowy Targ,** an unexceptional town but for its marketplace, where, on Thursdays, country women may be out selling wool or wool sweaters and hats and mittens. In the neighboring village of **Poronin** the Russian revolutionary Lenin lived for two years. When World War I started, the patriotic highlanders (goral) of this Podhale region told police about the curious Russian in hiding in their village, and he was arrested.

Though the embroidered white felt legginglike pants and the round flat hats of the highlanders are seen less and less nowadays, on Sunday old-timers tend to put on their finery.

Zakopane — and those alluring Tatras — is about fifteen miles from Nowy Targ.

Z A K O P A N E

For the foreign traveler this most popular of Polish winter resorts may not be the place for a visit in winter because of the overcrowding by Poles and limited hotel space. But in spring, summer, and fall, the countryside is a delight for lovers of the out-of-doors. Zakopane itself at first glance seems little more than a wide main street edged with sales stands, where hand-carved wooden objects (frequently tacky), bulky handmade woolens (at extraordinarily low prices), and gay flowered babushkas (if you are tempted to buy one, make sure it is not from Hong Kong or Brooklyn) are sold. And while you shop, you can nibble on ewe's milk smoked cheese molded in an egg shape and sold at street-side stands.

But below the main street, beyond the Tatras Museum and the big gray stone church on the hillside, along Kościeliska, Krupówki, and Zamoyskiego streets, are chaletlike wooden highlanders' houses — steep-roofed structures with white-framed windows and cutouts of moons and suns over the doors. They sit behind long wooden fences with peaked "hats" on the fence posts.

With a car, there are any number of excursions you can make from Zakopane — to the village of **Chocholow,** where the eighteenth- and nineteenth-century blond wood houses, fitted together like Lincoln Logs, are scrubbed clean outside with soap and water once every year. There are funicular trips up **Gubałówka Hill,** caleche or walking trips into a valley — **Dolina Kościeliska** — where streams race, woods close in, and mountains loom. Morskie Oko (Eye of the Sea) is the largest lake in the Tatras. Fifteen peaks soar above it, and their reflection shimmers on its still silvery surface. Buses, if you choose not to drive, will take you to most of these.

Twenty-three miles from Zakopane is the fifteenth-century **Dębno Podhalańskie Church** with its high-pitched roof that almost descends to the ground. If you can arrange it, the time for a visit is just before 11:00 A.M. on Sunday, when the women in flowered skirts, their heads covered with long, fringed white scarves, and a handful of old men in highlander costume will be gathering outside to attend Mass. Inside, the simple church is decorated with stenciled animals and flowers applied five centuries ago.

THE DUNAJEC

En route to this river from Zakopane, the road edges the sheer cliffs of the granite part of the High Tatras (closer to Zakopane they are of limestone). Tall, fanciful gingerbreadlike houses with many-angled tin roofs sit at the backs of fields. Giant woodpiles in yards suggest long, hard winters. At **Czorszczyn,** eager highlander boatmen in embroidered felt vests and hats decorated with shells (an ancient sign of wealth) wait by the river from May to September to take passengers on their rafts of hollow tree trunks tied together. Their spectacular hour-and-a-half boat trip dashes around rapids, passes Czech and Polish villages and fields, and where the river narrows passes between towering rock walls. Though there always seem to be boatmen awaiting passengers, it may be wise to book in advance at Orbis in Zakopane. A historic curiosity at Czorszczyn is **Niedzica Castle** above the river. Legend has it that the last Peruvian Inca princess managed somehow to get here, where she died at the end of the eighteenth century, leaving behind information about Inca treasure at the bottom of Peru's Lake Titicaca.

THE BALTIC COAST

GDAŃSK

On September 1, 1939, World War II began at this Baltic seaport when a German battleship, ostensibly on a "courtesy" call, opened fire on the little Polish garrison at Westerplatte, a peninsula just five miles north of the city. On March 30, 1945, when the war was over for Gdańsk, 90 percent of the city had been destroyed.

But, like Warsaw, there was no thought of not reconstructing this historic port that had risen to economic prominence in the fourteenth century when it was part of the Hanseatic League of merchants of northern Europe that included Lübeck, Hamburg, and Bremen.

One of the oldest cities in Poland, Gdańsk (Danzig in German) is mentioned as existing as a community of more than 1,000 in A.D. 997. But in 1308, the Teutonic Knights — that curious body of semireligious militarists of the Middle Ages — who, in 1226, had accepted a request to help settle a local power dispute here, took over this city, killing thousands of its inhabitants, tearing down its fortifications, and burning its houses. Then, the knights imported Germans to replace the population they had killed. The knights held the city until the mid-fifteenth century, when its

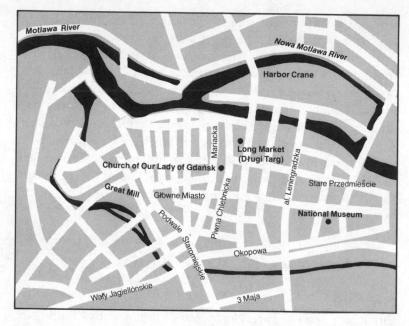

GDAŃSK

population overthrew them, declaring Gdańsk a free city but putting it under Polish protection. For the next 150 years, with its Hanseatic connection, Danzig was one of the richest ports on the Baltic. It owes much of its fine architecture to this period, about 1600, when architects and builders from the Low Countries found their way here and began building in their traditional style with tall, stepped facades.

But in the seventeenth century, the city was attacked by the Swedes and in the eighteenth century by the Russians and the Prussians. From 1807 to 1813, when Napoleon gained it during his continental campaigns, Danzig was briefly declared a free city, but after his defeat, the European powers meeting at the Congress of Vienna returned it to Prussia. It remained Prussian until the Treaty of Versailles (1919). Then the Allies, to provide Poland with access to the sea, gave it free-city status again, linking it to Poland by a "corridor" twenty to thirty miles wide that separated East Prussia from the rest of Germany. With Germans in the majority in the population, it was bound to be a bone of contention between the two nations. When the Poles refused Hitler's demand that it be returned to Germany, the bombardment of Westerplatte, followed by full-scale war, was ensured.

In its postwar years, not only was the **Old Town** thoughtfully and authentically rebuilt, but the port and the shipyards that were its lifeblood stirred again — stirred so vigorously, indeed, that it was at the Lenin Shipyard here that, in December 1970, food riots so shook the government that twenty-seven protesting workers were shot by the police and the Solidarity Trade Union, led by charismatic Lech Wałesa, was born a decade later.

The principal points of interest of the city follow.

Chlebnicka and Piwna streets (ulica Chlebnicka and ulica Piwna): Along these streets are some of the most delightful of Gdańsk's burghers' dwellings. Capping the balustrades of the enormous stoops are glowering dragons' and lions' heads and huge stone globes the size of a giant's bowling ball. For the most part, these structures house shops today.

Church of Our Lady of Gdańsk (Kościół Mariacki), ulica Piwna: This towering red-brick church, the largest Gothic church in Poland, supposedly holds 25,000 people. Built from the fourteenth to the sixteenth centuries, the Church of Our Lady was seriously damaged in World War II. It has been entirely rebuilt, and its 245-foot tower is a city landmark. Among interior high points are the harrowingly realistic Gothic crucifix and the charming fifteenth-century Madonna of Gdańsk, said to have been carved in one night by a young man scheduled to be executed for murder the next day. Civic authorities were so dumbfounded by the beauty of his creation that they declared him innocent and set him free on his supposed execution day.

Great Mill (Weilki Młyn), ulica Wielki Młpyny: This seven-story mill, originally built by the Teutonic Knights in the fourteenth century, was the largest mill of its kind on the Baltic at that time and could produce twenty-two tons of flour a day. Largely destroyed in 1945, it was rebuilt in 1962, but now it is an amusement arcade.

15. Gdańsk waterfront. At the right is the fourteenth-century crane tower used to unload ships.

Harbor Crane (Żuraw Gdański), Motława Quay: This medieval crane has come to symbolize Gdańsk and its waterfront prosperity. It was built in 1333 not only to hoist cargo into vessels and fit ships' masts, but also to serve as a gateway that was part of the harbor fortifications. It was only partially damaged in 1945 and now houses the **Maritime Museum,** which is open Tuesday, Wednesday, Friday, Saturday, and Sunday from 10:00 A.M. to 4:00 P.M. and on Thursday from noon to 6:00 P.M. Nearby, on the picturesque quay, tourist boats leave in summer for Westerplatte and the beaches of the Hel Peninsula. It is easy to while away an afternoon here watching the ferries, yachts, merchant vessels, and other boats come and go.

Large Armory (Wielká Zbrojownia), ulica Piwna: With its elaborately decorated Flemish-style facade, this sixteenth-century brick and sandstone structure, built in 1609, is a masterpiece of Gdańsk Renaissance architecture.

Long Street (ulica Długa): It was along this route that Poland's kings and queens came in ancient days on their way to gatherings at the soaring red-brick Town Hall. The route begins at the sixteenth-century Flemish-built **High Gate** (Brama Wyżynna). Once a gate through the city ramparts, it was left standing alone when the ramparts were removed in the nineteenth century. Inside the High Gate is the hip-roofed **Prison Gate** (Brama Wyżynna) with its torture room and prison tower. Beyond that is the Italian Renaissance-style **Golden Gate** (Złota Brama), topped with allegorical figures. Next, as this royal road actually begins, rises the **House of the Fraternity of St. George** (Dwór Bractwa Św. Jerzego), a late Gothic brick structure with a statue of a dragon at the top. All along the royal way the narrow, gable-fronted houses are embellished with medallions, garlands, and frescoed mythological scenes and with statues adorning the parapets.

The royal road ends and the **Long Market** (Długi Targ) begins at the dark-red-brick Flemish Renaissance **Town Hall** (Ratusz) with its slender 269-foot-high tower on which a gilded sixteenth-century statue of King Sigismund II Augustus stands. Both its exterior and its interior are dazzling. Much of the interior decoration — paneling and elaborate wrought-iron grilles, stucco unicorns, and flowers and cherubim, and its intricately carved spiral staircase and doors were removed in 1943 after American bombing of neighboring Gdynia had begun. Fearing that Gdańsk would be next, the precious interiors of Gdańsk's Town Hall were hidden in villages. As it turned out, there was no American bombing of Gdańsk, but both Germans and Russians occupied the city and much that has been saved would have been lost to them had it not been removed. An hour among the sixteenth-century allegorical paintings and carvings (virtually all the sixteenth- and seventeenth-century work here is Netherlands Mannerist) in the **Red Room** and the **Fireplace Room** (the fireplace held up by carved turbaned Turks) is time well spent. The Town Hall is open Tuesday and Wednesday, from 10:00 A.M. to 4:00 P.M., Thursday and Friday from 11:00 A.M. to 4:00 P.M., and Saturday and Sunday noon to 6:00 P.M. It is closed on Monday.

Beside the Town Hall is the seventeenth-century **Neptune Fountain** (Studnia Neptuna) with Neptune's trident spurting

16. A burgher's house with its typical ornate stoop on Mariacka Street in Gdańsk.

water and a wrought-iron railing decorated with the Polish eagle all around it. Behind the fountain rises the white stone **Artus Mansion** (Dwór Artusa), which has a seventeenth-century Flemish Baroque facade and medallions of kings on its decorative portal. The building was originally constructed as a meeting place for the wealthy burghers of Gdańsk and later became the Wheat Exchange. It is now an exhibition hall.

Other fine houses are Flamboyant Gothic Number 43, with a Renaissance portal, and Number 42, the seventeenth-century Golden House (Złota Kamienica), with its tendrils of grapes, its heads of royalty, and high-relief mythological battle scenes between the windows. But anywhere you look there are mythological figures on balustrades, beautifully shaped gables and attics, tall windows, and frescoes.

The Long Market pedestrian mall ends at the Renaissance Green Gate (Żielona Brama).

Mariacka Street (ulica Mariacka): Along this cobblestoned little street are colorful reconstructed Baroque and Renaissance houses, notable for their ornate stoops and for the gargoyles and dragons that spew forth rainwater from the drainpipes.

National Museum (Muzeum Narodowe), ulica Toruńska 1: Though there are interesting examples of Dutch and Gdańsk furniture, textiles and china, portraits and Dutch and Flemish art, it is Flemish artist Hans Memling's fifteenth-century *Last Judgment* that is the museum's principal attraction. Actually, it doesn't belong in Gdańsk at all.

Commissioned for a church in Florence, it was on its way to Italy aboard an English ship in 1473 when the English vessel got into combat with a vessel from Gdańsk and was captured. The Gdańsk captain took what he wanted — including the Memling tryptich — and it ended up in the Church of Our Lady of Gdańsk. It has, however, hardly stayed there since — but it has never gotten to its intended Italian destination either.

In 1807, Napoleon took it. When he fell, the Prussians got it and returned it here. In World War II, the Germans took it away again. The Russians found it in Germany, took it to Leningrad, and in 1956 returned it to Gdańsk. The museum is open daily, except Monday. On Tuesday and Thursday its hours are from noon to 6:00 P.M., Wednesday and Friday from 10:00 A.M. to 3:00 P.M., Saturday from 11:00 A.M. to 4:00 P.M., and Sunday from 10:00 A.M. to 4:00 P.M.

Three Crosses Monument (Pomnik Trzech Krzyżów), Lenin Shipyard: This stainless steel memorial to the workers killed here in 1970 was erected when Solidarity was established as a trade union in 1980 and the Communist government of Poland began to be challenged by the people.

MALBORK

Thirty-six miles from Gdańsk is this brooding dark-red-brick stronghold, built in the thirteenth, fourteenth, and fifteenth centuries as the headquarters of the Teutonic Knights. The largest feudal complex in Europe, it is the perfect castle of dungeons and cobblestoned courtyards, a moat, arcades, and vaulted ceilings. It is filled with shields, swords, armor, and helmets for jousting and for war, with crossbows and ivory-inlaid pistols. There is a museum of amber pieces — pendants, beads, altars, and lumps with plants and animals inside — for it is along the shore in the neighborhood of Gdańsk that this golden solidified resin is washed ashore.

Sometimes there are guided tours in English, but often you must roam the castle on your own, helped by a guidebook with a little English in it — if there are any in stock.

After its centuries as the residence of the grand master of the Teutonic Knights, Malbork became a Polish royal residence when the knights fell from power. In the eighteenth century, Frederick the Great of Prussia turned it into a military barracks. It suffered considerably in World War II but has been restored. It is open May 1 to September 30 from 9:00 A.M. to 4:00 P.M., the rest of the year till 3:00 P.M., except Monday, when it is always closed.

OTHER POINTS
OF INTEREST

Among the Eastern European countries, Poland, with 120,700 square miles, is the largest. Approximately the size of New Mexico, it is the eighth largest nation in Europe. If you are visiting Poland on limited time you must, therefore, choose your destinations wisely. Up until now, only the "musts" of a Polish holiday have been included, but if you have the time, the following places might be added to your itinerary.

BISKUPIN

This 100-acre, 2,500-year-old fortified swamp settlement was discovered by archeologists at the bottom of a lake and reconstructed. As you stroll its wooden streets and pass its little wooden dwellings, it transports you back to the days of the Iron Age. It can be visited from May 15 to October 15 during daylight hours.

FROMBORK
From 1497 to 1512, the astronomer Nicolaus Copernicus was canon of the great red-brick Gothic cathedral here and did some of his finest work. Though the town itself, which was founded by merchants from Lübeck in 1310, was severely damaged during World War II and the destroyed buildings have been replaced, for the most part, with modern structures, the cathedral suffered relatively little damage. Its repaired organ is considered one of the finest in the country. It is notable, as well, as the burial place of the astronomer and for a museum of his life and works that is open Tuesday through Sunday from 8:00 A.M. to 3:30 P.M. in winter and from 10:00 A.M. to 4:30 P.M. June through September.

KĘTRZYN
It was in a tearoom outside the **Wolf's Lair** (Wilczy Szaniec) here in the days when this was East Prussia that, on July 20, 1944, Claus Schenk, the count von Stauffenberg, a cavalry officer fearful for the future of Germany under Hitler, attempted, with several other army officers, to assassinate him. In those days, the acres of bunkers that today are dilapidated, cracked, and overgrown were Hitler's impregnable headquarters for conducting his campaign against the Soviet Union. On that hot July day, the count carried a briefcase with two bombs in it to a meeting with Hitler. As it happened, because of the heat the meeting was held in the cool of a teahouse outside.

Setting the bombs to go off in ten minutes, von Stauffenberg left his briefcase on the floor near Hitler and excused himself five minutes before the bomb was to go off. He left the room, ostensibly to answer a telephone call.

In those five minutes that von Stauffenberg was out of the room, the briefcase was moved — not because it was suspect — simply because it was in the way. The bomb exploded as anticipated; four men died and three were injured, but Hitler suffered only minor burns and scratches and punctured eardrums. (Had the meeting been in the concrete bunker whose walls would have contained the explosion, Hitler, it is speculated, would have been killed. Instead, the feeble wooden structure of the teahouse simply blew away.)

By nightfall, the count and three fellow-officers implicated were dead — shot after a brief court-martial. In the ensuing weeks, 2,000 others were executed for allegedly having had a part in the conspiracy.

In 1945, as the Russians drew close, the Germans tried to blow up the bunkers, but the buildings were too sturdy to destroy and they remain here, hidden in underbrush, for World War II buffs to see. The nearest major town is the lake resort of Giżycko.

ŁAŃCUT

Łańcut, ten miles from Rzeszów, is one of Poland's loveliest palaces. This ivy-covered seventeenth-century pink-and-cream country house, once a castle with star-shaped fortifications that repulsed all invaders except Charles XII of Sweden, has been altered and renovated many times. In the late nineteenth century, the Potocki family rebuilt it in French Baroque style and filled it with art treasures from all over the world; to be sure that they had a complementary backdrop, the Potockis hired decorators from everywhere to adorn the palace interior. When word came of the imminent arrival of the Russians in 1944, Count Alfred Potocki packed as many family treasures as he could into eleven wagons and hastened away to Switzerland with them. Now enough pieces have been returned to make the sumptuous palace worth a visit. Perhaps its highlights are its white-and-gold eighteenth-century **Theater** and a pretty **Orangery**. In the **Coach House** is one of Europe's richest collections of carriages. The palace is open Tuesday through Friday 9:00 A.M. to 3:00 P.M., Saturday to 4:00 P.M., and Sunday till 6:00 P.M.

LUBLIN

This prettily situated city escaped the war virtually untouched. For that reason, it has a veracity of atmosphere that is missing in the perfectly constructed and painted restored cities. But it has a weary look from wear and tear and is undergoing restoration. Until 1939 it had one of Poland's largest Jewish communities. Sites particularly worth seeing are the **Old Market Square** (Rynek Starego Miasta) with its Renaissance houses, the **Lublin Museum** that is housed in the castle whose grim history includes five years as a Nazi prison, the **Church of the Holy Trinity** (Kościół Św. Trójcy), and the **Church of the Dominicans** (Kościoł Dominikanów). About two and a half miles outside the city are the barbed wire, watch towers, and barracks of the **Majdanek Concentration Camp,** where more than 360,000 people from twenty-eight countries were killed by the Germans. It is open daily, except Monday, from 8:00 A.M. to 3:00 P.M.

Poznań

One of Europe's leading international trade fair cities, Poznan isn't a place for a visit in June or September, its two fair times, but when the crowds aren't here there are many handsome architectural structures to see in this former Polish capital. This is a famous musical center as well. The Poznań Boys' Choir (Słowiki) is of international renown, and the **Museum of Musical Instruments** (Muzeum Instrumentów Muzycznych) at Old Market Square 45 (Rynek Starego Miasta) is one of Europe's best. Several of Chopin's pianos are here.

Other attractions of the city (55 percent of which was destroyed in World War II) include the reconstructed, richly decorated **Old Town Hall** (Ratusz), considered by many Poland's finest Renaissance structure. Originally Gothic, it was completely redesigned in the sixteenth century by Giovanni Batista Quadro from Lugano. A special attraction is its clock from which, at noon each day, two goats appear and bob their heads twelve times. A copy of the old town pillory (paid for from prostitutes' fines), a handsome Rococo fountain, and arcaded medieval shops are also part of the Old Market Square.

Also of interest is the red-brick Gothic **Cathedral of St. Peter and St. Paul** (Katedra Św. Piotra i Św. Pawła) on **Cathedral Island** (Ostrów Tumski).

SANDOMIERZ

Thanks to a skillful maneuver by a Russian colonel who managed to move the battle for the river crossing away from here in World War II, this splendid medieval city above the Vistula still stands. Twice destroyed by the Tartars, it was fortified and prospered in the days of Casimir the Great, but suffered again both from the Swedes in the seventeenth century and from the Germans in this century. Highlights include the **Market Square** (Rynek) with its Gothic **Town Hall** (Ratusz), the Gothic **Cathedral** with its Byzantine-Ruthenian murals, and the **Opatów Gate** (Brama Opatówska), built in the fourteenth century, part Gothic and part Renaissance.

TARNÓW

Although today this is largely an industrial town, there are interesting early houses around the cathedral square, handsome Renaissance tombs inside the **Cathedral**, and, in the **Mikolajowski House** opposite it, built into the city walls, a **Diocesan Museum** of Gothic country church carvings and paintings as well as paintings of biblical scenes on glass from all over Central Europe.

TORÚN

In the fourteenth century, this town on the River Vistula halfway between Warsaw and Gdańsk was a proud and a prosperous member of the Hanseatic League. The rich red-brick warehouses that still stand along the riverbank, the imposing churches, and the square-towered Flemish Gothic Town Hall all bear witness to this heyday. So, too, do the richly ornamented, tall-gabled houses still to be found here and there on side streets and around the marketplace. It was in one of these high-gabled houses, at ulica Kopernika 17, that the astronomer Nicolaus Copernicus (Mikołaj Kopernik) was born in 1473. Now a **Museum,** it contains both memorabilia of this scientist who pronounced that it was the sun that was the center of the universe and the furnishings, china, and decorations characteristic of a Torún burgher's home in the fifteenth century. It is open Tuesday, Wednesday, and Thursday from 10:00 A.M. to 4:00 P.M., Friday from 11:00 A.M.

to 5:00 P.M., Saturday from 10:00 A.M. to 3:00 P.M., and Sunday from 9:00 A.M. to 3:00 P.M.

Other sites worth seeing are the **Town Hall** (Ratusz) with its museum of medieval church art, including a particularly impressive collection of fourteenth-century stained-glass windows; the red-brick Gothic **Church of St. Mary** (Kościół N.P. Marii) near the marketplace; and the oldest church in Toruń, the overpowering twelfth-century **Church of St. John** (Kościół Św. Jana) on ulica Żeglarska. It is known for its thirteenth- and fourteenth-century Gothic frescoes, its stained glass, a vibrant Baroque interior, and its enormous bell. (Like all churches in Poland nowadays, however, these two may be difficult to get inside.) Town Hall museum hours are Tuesday, Wednesday, and Friday from 10:00 A.M. to 4:00 P.M., Thursday from 11:00 A.M. to 5:00 P.M., Saturday from 10:00 A.M. to 3:00 P.M., and Sunday from 9:00 A.M. to 3:00 P.M.

Along the riverbank are many of the gates and towers of the fourteenth-century fortifications, including a leaning tower it is impossible to stand erect against, and the ruins of the castle of the Teutonic Knights who originally built the town, but were driven out when their castle was largely destroyed by the people of Toruń in 1454.

Unfortunately, Toruń has suffered from industrial pollution and from the construction of modern facades on old buildings in the town's center. If you look up on the Market Square, however, there is still some Hanseatic design to be seen. The **Star House** (Dom pod Gwiazda) is particularly notable.

WROCŁAW

After Warsaw, Wrocław was the most destroyed of Polish cities in the Second World War. It has been largely rebuilt, though not always with an eye to reconstructing an entire area to look as it did in prewar days, so sometimes the new design is mixed with the old, making it a less compelling tourist city than Warsaw, Cracow, or Gdańsk. Of interest, however, is its imposing Gothic **Town Hall** (Ratusz), with a Renaissance spire on a Gothic tower, and the houses around it. Number 2, the **House of the Griffon**

(Dom pod Gryfami), with heraldic animals perched on its gables, is in the Flemish Renaissance style that appealed to its population in its Hapsburg days. And there are Hansel and Gretel houses (Jaś i Małgosia) beside a Baroque gate. (Wrocław's past has included years under Bohemian, Austrian, and Prussian rule — in Prussian days it was named Breslau.)

Off the Old Market Square on **Salt Market Square** (Rynek Solny) are other handsome patrician houses. Churches that merit a visit are the Gothic brick Church of St. Elizabeth (Kościół Św. Elźbiety), St. Mary Magdalene's (Kościół Św. Marii Magdaleny) with its Romanesque portal, the Cathedral of St. John the Baptist (Katedra Św. Jana Chrzciciela) with its two enormous red-brick towers on Cathedral Island (Ostrów Tumski), the Church of the Holy Cross (Kościół Św. Krzyża), and the Church of Our Lady on the Sand (Kościół N.P. Marii na Piasku), notable for its splendidly reconstructed vaulting.

ZAMOŚĆ

This Italian Renaissance town set down in Poland is sometimes referred to as "the Padua of the North," for its sixteenth-century architect Bernardo Morando was brought here from Padua to create it.

Classified today by UNESCO as of unusual international historic and artistic importance, it was the brainchild of Jan Zamoyski, the Italian-educated chancellor of Poland under King Stephen Batory and a resident of this area in his youth. When he achieved his governmental post, Zamoyski wished to create a perfect town, a center of both trade and culture set in a countryside of fields.

Though the years have taken their toll on the old buildings, a renovation project has been going on since the end of World War II and there are fine sights to be seen. Of particular interest is the enormous **Town Hall** (Ratusz) with its Baroque sweeping double staircase and tower — additions to the original Renaissance structure. Arcaded houses in blues, maroons, and pinks that were the homes of wealthy merchants surround the town square and are in varying states of repair, but the angels and lions of the past —

albeit a little the worse for wear — can still be seen in some alcoves.

Lying just off the square is the basilica that is the **Collegiate Church** where Jan Zamoyski is buried and where there are paintings said to have been done by Tintoretto's son.

GETTING THERE, SLEEPING, EATING, AND ENTERTAINMENT

The affinity between Poland and the United States goes back as far as the American Revolution when Tadeusz Kościuszko and Casimir Pulaski, staunch believers in the ideals of liberty, went to America to fight for the colonial cause. Pulaski died for those ideals in 1779 at the head of a cavalry attack on Savannah. Kościuszko returned safely to Poland to lead an ill-fated national uprising against the Austrians and Russians then occupying his country. America has remembered both these heroes with statues around the country and high praise in history books, and Poles have felt a camaraderie with Americans ever since.

Then, in the first quarter of this century, thousands of Poles emigrated to the United States, further strengthening the bond. (Chicago is said to be second only to Warsaw in its numbers of Poles.) As a result of all this, the visitor to Poland from the United States is welcomed with an enthusiasm that is found almost nowhere else in the world. Being warmly welcomed makes a guest feel comfortable, of course, but that is only one reason to visit Poland. There are also stunning churches, fairy-tale castles, soaring mountains, rushing rivers and evergreen forests where wild game thrives.

Even during the forty years of Communist rule, Poles somehow managed to maintain the spirit of independence for which they are renowned. In no other Eastern country did the black market thrive so openly, was the government the butt of so many jokes, and did the Christian religion hold its own so firmly against Communist atheism. More than 90 percent of Poles, even under communism, professed their faith, and in 1978, that faith was rewarded when Karol Wojtyla, the archbishop of Cracow, became the world's first Polish pope, as John Paul II. Though the number of Poles speaking English in out-of-the-way places is limited, there is hardly a Pole who does not have a relative or friend somewhere in the United States whom he will try to tell you about. This friendliness helps immeasurably to make a trip to Poland a journey to remember.

Both LOT, the Polish national airline, and Pan Am fly nonstop from New York to Warsaw. LOT also flies nonstop from Chicago. With a change of planes in their capital cities, most northern European airlines serving the United States also fly into Warsaw.

From Western Europe, there is international rail service from Vienna and Berlin. An East Pass, available for travel in Austria, Czechoslovakia, and Hungary, as well as Poland, allows five days of travel within those countries for $160 for a fifteen-day period or for ten days of travel within a month for $259. East Passes must, however, be purchased before departure in the United States. Further information about them is available from travel agents or by calling Rail Europe at 800-345-1990.

Although on such major runs as Warsaw-Cracow and Warsaw-Poznań, the Polish railway (PKP) has good express service, most rail travel in Poland is slow and uncertain, and trying to obtain information about schedules — even in Warsaw — is likely to be an ordeal. If you are planning to travel by rail, it would be best to make the arrangements through Orbis, the Polish tourist organization, at ulica Marszałkowska 142 (Tel. 27-36-73) or at ulica Bracka 16 (Tel. 26-02-71), where you are likely to find an English-speaking clerk. Orbis can also sell you a Polrail Pass that will enable you to avoid ticket-counter lines if you elect to use rail travel.

Bus travel in Poland is generally arduous.

It is also possible to rent Hertz, Avis, Budget, or National cars in many Polish cities, but making your reservation in the United States through one of these services or through Auto-Europe at Box 1097 in Camden, Maine 04843 (Tel. 800-223-5555) is generally less expensive and more certain than waiting until your arrival in Poland. Payment is by credit card or in Polish złotys (calculated from a dollar rate). Help on the road is provided by the PZM Automobile Tourism Office, whose main bureau is at aleje Jerozolimskie 63 in Warsaw (Tel. 286-251).

It is also possible to rent a car with a driver or to travel by taxi, but taxis — once cheap — are becoming increasingly expensive. Information about such services is available from Orbis in Warsaw or Orbis in New York at 500 Fifth Avenue, New York, New York 10110 (Tel. 212-391-0844). In the Midwest, the Polish National Tourist Office at 333 North Michigan Avenue, Chicago, Illinois 60601 (Tel. 312-236-9013), and in the East, Wegiel Tours, 1985 Main Street, Springfield, Massachusetts 01103 (Tel. 413-747-7702), can be of help.

Internal air travel on LOT is inexpensive and a possibility if you are in a hurry, but getting in and out of airports and through inspection, even going from city to city, can be tedious.

As is the case elsewhere in Eastern Europe, finding good accommodations and obtaining a table in a restaurant can be an ordeal in major cities and at tourist sites, although the situation is improving. Entry into churches and museums, unless you are accompanied by a Polish speaker, can also be difficult. For the past few years, ever since the theft of valuable historic church silver from Gniezno, only the entryways of some city churches have been open to worshippers, except at Sunday service times. To view the interior of a church otherwise may require finding the priest. You usually can find him, however — especially in smaller communities — and often the search itself will prove entertaining.

Although most Polish museums are open daily, except Monday, some close for lunch, while others open earlier and close later on certain days, so it is wise to check with a local tourist office (*biuro turystów*) or with Orbis in Warsaw for the hours.

It is also wise, particularly in the summer season, to make hotel reservations well in advance with a United States travel agent cognizant with Eastern Europe. On guided tours, of course, there is no need to worry about hotels, restaurants, or museum hours.

What will you eat in Poland? Polish cooking, like most Eastern European cooking, is heavy and filling. In general, breakfast is included in the hotel price, and it is likely to be a monumental meal — salami, cheese, ham, pickles, fruit and fruit juices, eggs, sausage (*kiełbasa*), dark and light breads, cake, tea or coffee.

Dinner — the midday meal — may begin with an appetizer (*przekęska*) like smoked fish (*ryby wędzone*), paté (*pasztety*), or smoked ham (*szynka*) and be followed by a soup (*zupa*). Soup is a favorite dish of hardworking Poles. Most popular is *barszcz*, made of beets, carrots, and meat stock, with or without sour cream. Served with it will be pastries stuffed with meat (*paszteciki*). Cabbage (*kapuśniak*), potato (*kartoflanka*), cauliflower (*kalafiorowa*), mushroom (*grzybowa*), or dill (*koperkona*) soups are also popular as are cold cucumber and fruit soups (*chłodnik*) — *of raspberries, strawberries, or cherries — with sour cream.*

Main dishes include bigos — sauerkraut with smoked meat, cabbage, and onions — and *pierogi* — filled dumplings. Duck (*kaczka*) and goose (*gęś*), roast pork (*pieczony schab*), and stuffed cabbage leaves (*gołąbki*), are favorites with the Poles but are not always easy to find. Around Cracow, trout (*pstrąg*) that has been flambéed is a specialty. Other fish dishes are pike with horseradish sauce (*szczupak w sosie chrzanowym*), carp in a sweet and sour jelly (*karp w galarecie*), and herring (*śledz*). Mushrooms (*grzyby*) in many forms are always a favorite, and fruits — fresh, stewed, or canned (*kompot*) — ice cream (*lody*), *kisiel,* a kind of blancmange, or crepes (*naleśniki*) are likely to end a meal.

Beer is the best drink to accompany all this, but since German and Danish beers are more expensive and not necessarily better, you should be sure to specify in restaurants that it is Polish beer you want — Żywiec and Okoćim are among the best. Poland's other popular drinks are its vodka and sweet, potent mead (*miód*), made from honey distilled with herbs and spices. Polish vodka is second to none, except Russian (and Poles will dispute that). It comes in the usual plain (*wyborowa*) variety, but also flavored with buffalo grass (*żubrówka*), with juniper berries (*myśliwska*), cherries, peppers, or plums. The nonalcoholic beverage of choice is *kompot* — a fruit-juice drink.

A milk bar (*bar mleczny*) is a good place for light, quick fare for travelers in a hurry. Milk bars are usually self-service, and vegetarian dishes are offered. In cafés (*kawiarnia*) tea or coffee (both served in a glass), along with your choice of cakes or ice cream, are served. Tea, on the whole, is a better bet than coffee in Poland.

There follows, in alphabetical order by town, a list of better hotels and restaurants. Bear in mind, however, that this is a rapidly changing country, and restaurants are opening and changing hands all the time.

CRACOW
HOTELS
Cracovia, aleje Puszkina (Tel. 286-66). This 427-room hotel is hardly cozy, but it is still good.

Forum, ulica Konopnickiej 28 (Tel. 669-500). This is a 280-room, new, centrally located hotel with a swimming pool, tennis courts, and sauna. The double room rate with continental breakfast is $142, single $120.

Francuski, ulica Pijarska 13 (Tel. 252-70). This centrally located pleasant hotel has been undergoing recent remodeling.

Grand Hotel, ulica Sławkówska 5 (Tel. 21-72-55). This 56-room hotel in the heart of the Old City is brand-new. A restaurant and coffee bar are almost ready.

Holiday Inn, ulica Koniewa 6 (Tel. 750-44). This is a very basic 308-room Holiday Inn, the first one built in Eastern Europe, but it is equipped with a pool and sauna. The double room rate is $80, single $60.

Pod Różą, ulica Floriańska 14 (Tel. 229-399). This is a small centrally located old hotel whose directors proudly claim the nineteenth-century French writer Honoré de Balzac among its guests. It has recently been renovated.

RESTAURANTS

Francuski, in the Francuski Hotel, ulica Pijarska 13. This is a pleasant hotel restaurant offering good fare.

Staropolska, ulica Sienna 4 (Tel. 22-58-21). Soups and vegetarian dishes like pancakes (*naleśniki*) with cottage cheese are particularly well prepared in this simple restaurant.

U Pani Staśi, ulica Mikołajska. Small and homey, this is a restaurant where you will almost certainly have to wait, but the home-cooked food is worth it.

U Wentzla, Rynek Główny 18. This is an elegant, centrally located restaurant. Reservations are essential.

Wierzynek, Rynek Główny 16 (Tel. 22-98-96). This is perhaps Poland's finest restaurant, and booking a day or more in advance is essential. Here in 1364, the city councilman for whom the restaurant is named entertained Casimir the Great, German emperor Charles IV, and King Louis I of Hungary. The restaurant tries to reflect that sort of elegance. Among the specialties on its extensive menu are many wild-game dishes and elegant desserts, among them a delicious poppy-seed cake.

CAFÉS

Jama Michalika, ulica Floriańska 45. The atmosphere and the Art Nouveau decoration make this famous old café a treat even if the service and the cake nowadays leave something to be desired.

Noworol, Old Cloth Hall, Rynek Główny. This is an elegant café in a pleasant setting on the Old Town Square.

Ratuszowa, Town Hall Tower basement, Rynek Główny: Meeting local residents isn't hard at all in this relaxed and comfortable place.

ENTERTAINMENT

There is good theater (for Polish-speakers) and fine music here, notably the Kraków Filharmonia. In August, annually, a Cracow Music Festival is held with concerts offered in palaces and churches throughout the city.

TOURIST INFORMATION
Centrum Informacji turystycznej, ulica Pawla 8 (Tel. 220-471).
There is also an Orbis office on Puszkina 1 (Tel. 222-885).

GDAŃSK

HOTELS

Grand, ulica Powstańców Warszawy 8-12, Sopot (Tel. 511-696).
Though this is a twenty-minute automobile ride or half-hour
train ride away from Gdańsk, the turn-of-the-century Grand
Hotel is one of the most atmospheric hotels in the neighborhood, situated as it is on the shore of the Baltic. It has recently
been remodeled and has added a popular nightclub.

Gdynia, ulica Lipca 22, Gdynia (Tel. 206-661). This modern hotel is a short train or car ride away from the center of Gdańsk
in sea-front Gdynia.

Hevelius, ulica Heweliusza 22 (Tel. 315-631). This 250-room
modern hotel's principal attraction is its central location.

Marina, ulica Jelitkowska 20 (Tel. 531-246). This is a modern
middle-sized hotel on the Baltic with a pool, tennis courts, and
good food among its attractions.

Novotel, ulica Pszenna 1 (Tel. 313-611). This motellike hotel is
satisfactory, but nothing more.

RESTAURANTS

Kaszubska, ulica Kartuska 76. Kashubian specialties like stuffed
pike and perch and eel are offered in this restaurant of the
northwestern lakes area.

Newska, ulica Grunwaldzka 99-101 (Tel. 41-46-46). Located on
the road to Sopot, there is a simple country air to this moderately priced restaurant.

Pod Łosośiem, ulica Szeroka 11. This is a first-class fish restaurant in the Old Town. Reservations are essential.

Pod Wieźa, ulica Piwna 51. Beef ragout is a specialty of this centrally located restaurant.

TOURIST INFORMATION
Orbis, Gorki plac 1 (Tel. 314-944). There is also an Orbis office
on ulica Heweliusza 22 (Tel. 314-544).

POZNAŃ

HOTELS

Merkury, ulica Roosevelta 15-20 (Tel. 408-01). This very modern 351-room hotel offers many amenities.

Novotel, ulica Warszawska 64-66 (Tel. 770-001), a new Orbis hotel is like a motel, and outside the city center.

Polonez, aleje Stalingradzka 56-68 (Tel. 699-141), is a new Orbis hotel.

Poznań, plac General H. Dąbrowskiego 1, is the newest Orbis hotel (Tel. 332-081).

RESTAURANT

Adria, ulica Głogowska 14 (Tel. 208-485). The trout is delicious at this upper-crusty restaurant and nightclub.

CAFÉ

Hortex, ulica Głogowska 29 (Tel. 66-07-14). Ice cream, cake, and coffee or tea here will fortify those not interested in a full meal.

TORÚN

HOTEL

Helios, ulica Kraszewskiego 1-3 (Tel. 250-33). This is an adequate, centrally located hotel with a fair dining room.

RESTAURANT

Zajazd Staropolski, ulica Żeglarska 12-14 (Tel. 260-61). There's an old-fashioned atmosphere and good food in this hotel restaurant on the Market Square.

WARSAW

HOTELS

Europejski, Krakowskie Przedmieśćie 13 (Tel. 255-051). The location of this older hotel is ideal, but it is noisy and distinctly in need of renovation — a fact its reasonable prices ($105 double, $71 single) reflect. Service is, at best, lackadaisical.

Forum, ulica Nowogrodzka 24-26 (Tel. 210-19). Sprawling, modern, and uninteresting, the Forum in the past has catered to large tour groups and businessmen.

Novotel, ulica 1-go Śierpnia 1 (Tel. 464-051). The location — out of town near the airport — of this moderately priced, adequately equipped hotel is, unfortunately, not in its favor.

Vera, ulica Wery Kostrzewy 16 (Tel. 227-421). This is a large, unimpressive, relatively inexpensive but adequate hotel, lacking in charm.

Victoria Intercontinental, ulica Królewska 11 (Tel. 279-291). This is a centrally located, generally well-managed large modern hotel where a double may be had for approximately $165 and a single for $140.

Warsaw Marriott, aleje Jerozolimskie 65 (Tel. 283-444). This ultramodern hotel of 525 rooms across from the central railway station has eleven restaurants (including a very American self-service snack bar and a fine Italian dining room), a health club, swimming pool, sauna, and businessmen's center. Doubles are about $190, singles $165.

Zajazd Napoleonski, ulica Płowiecka 83. It is because Napoleon is said to have slept here on his way to invade Russia that this small private inn with considerable charm gets its name.

RESTAURANTS

Ambassador, ulica Matejki 2. The decor makes this an attractive spot for a moderately priced meal.

Bar Mleczny, Pod Barbakanem. For inexpensive daytime dining (it closes at 8:00 P.M.), you would be hard-pressed to find anything cheaper and better in Warsaw. The menu is limited, however — largely to soups and noodle dishes — and no English is spoken.

Bazyliszek, Rynek Starego Miasta 7-9 (Tel. 31-18-41). This Old Town restaurant specializing in wild game is ever-popular with visitors. A dinner for one is likely to be $15 to $20 including wine. Reservations are essential.

Canaletto, in the Victoria Hotel, ulica Królewska 11 (Tel. 27-80-11). This is generally regarded as the finest restaurant in Warsaw. The decor is elegant, the service impeccable, and the dishes served prepared with care.

Cristal Budapest, ulica Marszałkowska 21 (Tel. 625-34-33). It hardly seems appropriate to eat Hungarian fare in Warsaw, but should you wish to, good, hearty Hungarian dishes are served here at reasonable prices.

Habana, ulica Piękna 28 (Tel. 21-37-16). The music is Cuban, but the fare is largely Polish, satisfying and moderate in price, with many pork dishes.

Kamienne Schodki, Rynek Starego Miasta 26 (Tel. 31-08-22). It would be hard to find duck better prepared anywhere outside of China. Duck roasted with apples is what this cozy little Old Town restaurant is all about. Dinner is $8 to $10, including a glass of wine.

Karczma Słupska, ulica Czerniakowska 127. A folk show accompanies dinner at this moderately priced restaurant.

Krokodyl, Rynek Starego Miasta 19 (Tel. 31-44-27). This is a centrally located favorite café-restaurant for young Poles. There's nothing dressy about it, but the food is good and after dinner (after 9:00 P.M.) there's likely to be music playing. If you get there then, there will be a charge over and above your dinner.

Kuźnia Królewska, ulica Wiernicza 24 (Tel. 42-31-71), is a pleasant country-style restaurant for lunch or dinner after a morning or afternoon of sightseeing at the Wilanów Palace.

Lers, ulica Długa 29 (Tel. 635-38-88). This is a moderately priced restaurant offering good food near the Old Town.

Pod Retmanem, ulica Bednarska 9 (Tel. 26-87-58). English is not a strong point at this restaurant off the beaten tourist track, but interesting local fare at reasonable prices is. The decor is of old Gdańsk.

Restaurant Soplica, Forum Hotel, ulica Nowogrodzka 24-26 (Tel. 21-02-71). Reservations are essential at this expensive hotel restaurant where wild game is among the specialties.

Świetoszek, ulica Jezuicka 6-8 (Tel. 31-56-34). There is fine food in this little Old Town restaurant with a medieval decor, but making a reservation before 11:00 A.M. on the day you would like to dine here is essential.

Wilanów Restaurant, ulica Wiernicza 27 (Tel. 42-18-52). Reservations are essential at this stylish restaurant near Wilanów Palace.

CAFÉS

Bombonierka, Rynek Nowega Miasta 1. Coffee and ice cream here can provide a pleasant respite from sightseeing.

Fukier, Rynek Starego Miasta 27 (Tel. 31-39-18). This 300-year-old wine cellar is ever popular with students for coffee or wine.

Gwiazdeczka, ulica Piwna 42. Students frequent this little café for coffee and cakes.

Telimena, Krakowskie Przedmieście 27. Artists and writers have long frequented this café.

There are exceptional pastry shop-cafés in both the Europejski Hotel at Krakowskie Przedmieście 13 and the Holiday Inn at ulica Złota 2.

ENTERTAINMENT

Akwarium, ulica Emilli Plater 49. This jazz hot spot is just across from the Palace of Culture and Science. Complete information on Warsaw jazz events is available from the Polish Jazz Association, Mazowiecka 11 (Tel. 27-79-04).

Chopin Society (Towarzystwo Chopina), ulica Okalnik. From time to time piano concerts are given here.

Łazienki Park. In the open air theater here, concerts are held every Sunday afternoon at noon and 4:00 P.M. from June through September.

National Philharmonic Orchestra (Filharmonia Narodowa), ulica Sienkiewicza 12 (Tel. 267-281). It is easiest to buy theater tickets of any kind through a hotel concierge or Orbis, but other possibilities are the ticket agency Kasy Teatralne, aleje Jerozolimskie 25, or, for the symphony, at the box office, half an hour before it begins. International Chopin competitions are held here and each fall there is a Festival of Modern Music.

Wielki Theater (Teatr Wielki), plac Teatralny. This is one of the largest stages in Europe for opera and ballet performances. Tickets may be bought at the box office.

TOURIST INFORMATION

Orbis, Krakowskie Przedmieście 13 (Tel. 261-667). There is also a tourist information bureau, Syrena, at ulica Krucza 16-25 (Tel. 257-201).

ZAKOPANE

HOTELS

Giewont, ulica Kościuszki 1 (Tel. 2011). This 52-room lodgelike hotel has a dining room that is reasonably good, though, in the way of most Polish hotel restaurants, smoky.

Kasprowy, Polana Szymoszkowa (Tel. 4011). This is a very modern, 300-room, resort-style hotel on the edge of town, with its own pool, sauna, ice-skating rink, mini-golf course, and restaurant. The double room rate, including breakfast, is $71.

RESTAURANTS

Obrochtówka, ulica Kraszewskiego 10A (Tel. 39-87). This is a small rustic restaurant, popular with Poles who enjoy the fresh trout and chicken shish kebab that are among its offerings.

Siedem Kotów. This rustic restaurant on the edge of town combines good food with attractive surroundings.

Jedruś, ulica Świerczewskiego. Good food and merriment (dancing until 2:00 A.M.) help to make this a popular night spot with young skiers.

Romania

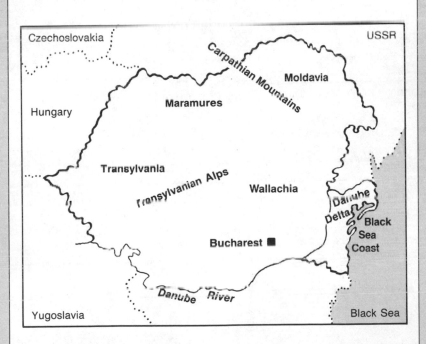

Czechoslovakia

USSR

Carpathian Mountains

Moldavia

Maramures

Hungary

Transylvania

Transylvanian Alps

Wallachia

Danube
Delta

Black
Sea
Coast

Bucharest ■

Danube River

Yugoslavia

Black Sea

$\mathcal{O}$f all the countries of Eastern Europe, it is Romania that offers the most virgin landscapes, the quaintest villages, the most picturesque scenes. Gooseherds in fur hats still tend their snowy flocks along the willow-lined roads. Dark-eyed Gypsy children tug at the tethers of pet lambs.

For the Romanian, of course, this picturesqueness has hardly been retained on purpose. Nicolae Ceauşescu's insistent demands for belt tightening to pay off the national debt and to support his grandiose building schemes for the capital city of Bucharest kept his country the poorest in the East. But in this lack of development lies much of Romania's charm for the traveler. There are no out-of-place modern structures on its swooping green hills; its snow-capped mountain peaks have yet to be scarred with ski lodges. In country restaurants, the starched white tablecloths are still decoratively strewn with rosebuds. Smiling nuns, not tip-hungry local entrepreneurs, proudly show off fifteenth- and sixteenth-century monasteries covered with painted Bible stories that have withstood the vagaries of climate through the centuries and — in the virtually carless countryside — have never had pollution to contend with. For the traveler intrigued by the macabre, Romania is, of course, the country of the legendary blood-sucking Count Dracula.

Although no united Romanian state existed until 1859, the shepherds and farmers, beekeepers and miners who were the forebears of today's Romanians occupied the land now called Romania as long ago as 514 B.C. About 100 B.C., the mountain shepherds, the Geto-Dacians, established a powerful and warlike kingdom. But it was not powerful or warlike enough to withstand a Roman onslaught under the emperor Trajan in A.D. 106. To celebrate his hard-won victory, Trajan had a monumental forum built in Rome; the triumphal column that was its centerpiece still stands there. A plaster cast of Trajan's Column is in Bucharest's Museum of History.

For the next 165 years, Rome ruled in Dacia. In the Roman way, roads, bridges, and fortifications were built, but the fortifications did not prove strong enough to stop Germanic and Slavic invaders from the north, and in A.D. 271 the Romans withdrew. Those years of colonization not only left their mark in intermarriage but in the language as well. Though surrounded on three sides by Slavic lands, Romanians speak a Romance tongue that is only slightly touched by Slavic words. Romance-language speakers like the French and Italians readily recognize phrases like *"Bună ziua"* — "Good day" — and *"Bună seara"* — "Good evening." While it may not be possible for an English-speaker to actually *read* a Romanian newspaper, it is not impossible to get the gist of what it says.

Both physically (Romanians tend to be dark-haired and dark-eyed) and emotionally (they are excitable and voluble but at the same time lackadaisical in matters of time and expenditure of energy), the Romanians tend to take after their Roman ancestors. In pre-Ceauşescu days, they enjoyed their wines and their food, which is embellished with Turkish and some Hungarian flourishes. They enjoyed Gypsy bands and, both then and now, sunny holidays on the golden sands of the Black Sea.

They are inordinately proud of those Roman days. Statues of Romulus and Remus with their wolf foster mother stand in Bucharest and Timişoara. Sadly, after the Romans came many less appreciated conquerors — Goths and Huns, Hungarians and Slavs, Turks and Austrians and Russians. By the thirteenth century, Transylvania was Hungarian; by the sixteenth century it was paying tribute to the Turks. The Austrians conquered it in the seventeenth century.

Meanwhile, in the thirteenth and fourteenth centuries, two feudal principalities — Moldavia in the east and Wallachia in the south — had been formed. Like Transylvania, they, too, eventually fell under Turkish dominion, with princes sent from Constantinople, largely to see that the two principalities paid their taxes to the Turks. The Orthodox religion they had adopted continued to be theirs, however. The Islamic faith was not imposed, and the Turks did not occupy.

But in those days of the "Turkish yoke," as it is always called, some of Romania's most valiant leaders were nurtured — Michael the Brave in Wallachia; Iancu of Hunedoara in Transylvania; Stephen the Great in Moldavia. This was the time, too, of Vlad Țepeș, prince of Wallachia, known as Vlad the Impaler for his habit of impaling his Turkish (and other) enemies and prototype for the legendary blood-sucking Dracula.

In 1829, after Russia won a war with the Turks, Moldavia and Wallachia became Russian protectorates for a while. Meanwhile, the Austrians continued to rule Transylvania. Not until 1859 did the future Romania, the United Principalities, formed by the union of Moldavia and Wallachia, come into being. But it was still not until 1877 and more fighting against the Turks that Romania, at last, threw off the detested "yoke." As for Transylvania, it was not until after the First World War and the defeat of the Austro-Hungarian Empire that it joined Moldavia and Wallachia in the Romanian kingdom. At the same time, it had altered its twentieth-century destiny by choosing a German prince, Karl of Hohenzollern (who changed his name to Carol) as its ruler.

Between the world wars, the new kingdom thrived. Crown Prince Carol, preferring love to duty, gave up his right to the throne, then changed his mind and returned as Carol II to establish a royal dictatorship.

With the arrival of the Second World War, when King Carol angered Hitler by not, at first, siding with the Axis, Hitler allowed Romanian lands in the northeast — Bessarabia and northern Bukovina — to go to the Russians, and, in the northwest, part of Transylvania to go to the Hungarians. Though Carol — Hohenzollern that he was — then shifted his support to Germany, the fascistic military organization called the Iron Guard forced him to abdicate in favor of his son, Michael, and Romania entered the war on the Axis side. But in phase two of the war, as the

Soviets reached the Romanian borders in 1944, the Fascists were ousted by the Resistance; King Michael arrested the leader of the Iron Guard and Romania joined the Allies.

At the war's end, a people's democracy came into being; the king abdicated, and in 1947, the Socialist Romanian People's Republic was established. In that same year, that part of Transylvania that Hungary had acquired was returned to Romania.

Romania had always been a rich agricultural land whose peasants had been devoted to nurturing their fields for generations, but the Communists brought industrialization and collective farming to it; neither improved the economy. Instead, in the Ceauşescu years that began in 1965, Romania grew poorer and poorer as the dictator, to make his nation solvent and important, sold the food and industrial goods Romania *did* produce to other nations so it would have money to pay off the national debt. (Too often, however, these were developing nations who thanked the dictator warmly — thereby satisfying his ego — but were unable to pay for what they got.) Always, Ceauşescu urged his people to be patriotic and wait a little longer, and all would be well. But shortages at home persisted, and the resultant anger led to his and his wife's Christmas Day 1989 execution.

History has not been kind to the descendants of the ancient Dacians, but each of the nations that has occupied their territory, and the nations that border it, have enriched the already rich Romanian tapestry. There are Roman mosaics, Turkish mosques, Teutonic castles, golden-yellow Austro-Hungarian and solid German villages. There are Gypsies whose dress brightens city streets and whose musicians fiddle charmingly.

While excitable, Romanians are also warm and welcoming. Children asked to pose for pictures, rather than demand coins in return, will shyly proffer Easter eggs that they have hand-painted or bouquets of flowers in thanks for the honor. Village householders will proudly show off their homes.

The Ceauşescu shadow remains in bullet-scarred buildings in Bucharest, blocks of unadorned high-rises where once apple trees and little houses stood, but in the farther reaches of the land where old women wind their wool on spindles in their yards and sleek horses gallop smartly home from fairs, it does not seem to linger.

BUCHAREST

Before World War II, this Romanian capital was often called "the Paris of the East." It was a city of high style; of outdoor cafés; wide, tree-lined boulevards and enormous squares; a triumphal arch; spacious houses with effulgent gardens and little churches

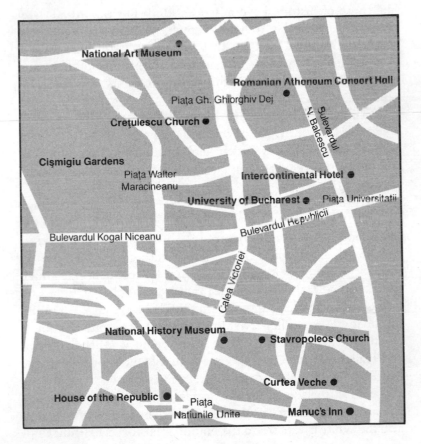

BUCHAREST

tucked in out-of-the-way corners. Nightlife thrived and Gypsy tunes — romantic, gay, wildly exuberant — were the entertainment in leafy garden restaurants.

Sadly, the war, Ceauşescu communism, revolution, and riots have left little of the lovely laziness that once characterized Bucharest. Good restaurants are gone. High style has long since disappeared. Many houses have given way to unimaginative, undecorated high-rise apartments erected to house factory workers brought in from the country when industrialization was seen as the route to prosperity. Bullet holes pockmark downtown buildings. Others are charred by firebombs. Contemporary events, like those of history, have not been kind. But the broad, tree-lined boulevards, the Arch of Triumph, the squares, the tucked-away churches, and shady parks for strolling still stand. There are monumental turn-of-the-century government buildings and more monumental ones of the dictator's years, and fine museums.

Bucharest, legend has it, had its beginnings in A.D. 800, when a shepherd, Bucur, came down the Dâmboviţa River that flows through Bucharest and settled here. But not until the fifteenth-century days of Vlad the Impaler, prince of Wallachia, is it mentioned by that name.

The principal places in Bucharest follow, in geographical order.

Victory Street (Calea Victoriei): This main shopping street stretches north to south from Victory Plaza (Piaţa Victoriei) to the Independence Embankment (Splaiul Independenţii). Though the cafés and fashion boutiques that once made it famous are gone, it remains the site of several notable buildings — the Baroque and Renaissance-style domed nineteenth-century Central Savings Bank (C.E.C.), the turn-of-the-century Atheneum Concert Hall, the Army Officers' Club (Clubul Ofiterilor), the Music Museum (Muzeul de Muzică — Casa Enescu), the National Art Museum in the former Royal Palace, the red-brick Creţulescu Church, the Museum of Natural History, the Hotel Athenée Palace, the White Church, and the National History Museum. Until the 1989 revolution the neoclassical Central University Library was a building of importance, but it was almost entirely destroyed by fire.

White Church (Biserica Albă): The diminutive White Church has long been the wedding church of the city.

Romanian Atheneum Concert Hall (Ateneul Român): Concerts are given regularly in this resplendent neoclassical 1880s building with its Greek facade and round cupola. It is the home of the George Enescu Philharmonic Orchestra, which honors the nineteenth-century Romanian violinist and composer who was also the teacher of Yehudi Menuhin.

Athenée Palace Hotel: This handsome old hotel was named for the Atheneum beside which it was built in the early twentieth century. In this Balkan city of intrigue it has often been a home away from home for spies and the foreign journalists reporting about the spying.

Creţulescu Church (Biserica Creţulescu): This richly decorated eighteenth century brick church, with its arcades, pillars, and lofty towers, is in Brîncoveanu style, the elaborate architecture of the reign in Wallachia of Prince Constantin Brîncoveanu. It was his son-in-law and daughter who provided the money for its construction.

Museum of Natural History (Muzeul de Istorie Naturală): The more than 89,000 brilliantly colored butterflies that are on display here make this one of the largest butterfly collections in all Europe.

National History Museum (Muzeul de Istorie Naţională): A plaster cast of Trajan's Column is a major attraction here, along with the rich collection of ancient golden jewelry and artifacts in the cellar. Among the most interesting of these are a 6,000-year-old Dacian figure with the head of an animal, the body of a fish, and the tail of a bird and the fifth-century Hen with the Golden Chickens, a twelve-piece treasure fashioned by the Goths. The work was found by four peasants in 1827 in a stone quarry near the village of Pietroasele, northeast of Bucharest. They cut the hen, a huge golden plate, into four pieces so each could have one.

It came into the hands of the government when the men betrayed each other. The museum is open from 10:00 A.M. to 6:00 P.M. daily, except Monday.

National Art Museum (Muzeul National de Arta): Housed in the northern wing of the former Royal Palace that was built in the 1930s, the art collection inside is considerably more impressive than the heavy, unimaginative exterior. (In recent years, the structure has served as the Palace of the Republic.) Richly embroidered silks and brocades of the boyars (the medieval nobles); icons, carpets, and sculptures by twentieth-century Constantin Brâncuşi; sixteenth-century frescoes; murals from the old Wallachian capital of Curtea de Argeş; historical works by nineteenth-century Theodor Aman (including the grisly *Bulgarians Massacring the Turks*); and portraits by turn-of-the-century Nicolae Grigorescu and nineteenth-century Gheorghe Tattarescu are highlights of the Romanian collection. The foreign paintings, many of them collected by King Carol I, include El Greco's *The Worshipping by the Shepherds,* Velázquez's *Philip IV,* and works of Titian, Tintoretto, Salvator Rosa, Delacroix, Rubens, Rembrandt, Memling, Lucas Cranach the Elder, Murillo, Monet, Veronese, Renoir, and the Breughels. Considerable damage was done to the museum during the December 1989 revolution, and, as this book went to press, it was still closed.

Running parallel to Calea Victoriei to the south is the Bulevardul Ana Ipătescu, where, at the Roman Square, Ceauşescu started a monument that was never finished. Today, candles burn for those who died in this area during the revolution. Then there is the Bulevardul Gen. Magheru and the Bulevardul N. Bălcescu, where airlines and Carpaţi travel offices are located. Farther south is the major intersection of the city at University Square (actually the Nicolae Bălcescu Square). It is the site of the Intercontinental Hotel, Bucharest University, and the Bucharest History Museum, which is housed in the early nineteenth-century Sutu Palace. Points of interest that are not on Calea Victoriei are listed below.

Arch of Triumph (Arcul de Triumf): Modeled after Paris's Arch of Triumph, this imposing structure was built in 1922 in celebration of victory in World War I and to honor Romania's war dead. Inside the arch are listed the Romanian victories in World War I.

Church of Mircea the Shepherd (Biserica lui Mircea Ciobanul): This sixteenth-century church in which rows of bricks alternate with rows of plaster and there are small niches under the cornices is the oldest structure still standing in Bucharest. Its founder, who had once sold sheep in Constantinople, was one of those "appointees" of the Turkish sultan sent as a prince to exact tribute from the newly acquired land in Wallachia.

Church of the Patriarchate (Biserica lui Patriarhia): The traveler visiting other parts of the country will find more interesting churches elsewhere than this seventeenth-century largely Byzantine structure, but the site above the city is a fine one, and the church is notable for having been the only one in the city whose towers have survived the earthquakes that, not infrequently, have devastated the capital.

Cişmigiu Gardens (Grădina Cişmigiu): A little zoo, a lake, and many pretty flowers make this nineteenth-century, 34-acre park a restful oasis in this city of heavy, oppressive buildings. The park is a short walk along the Bulevardul Republica and the Bulevardul Mihail Kogălniceanu from the university.

Curtea Veche: Southwest of the park gardens is this oldest part of the capital city, where, in the fifteenth century, Vlad the Impaler built himself a citadel. Warfare, earthquakes, and fires have left little of it, but there is a small museum in the cellars here, notable principally for the skulls of two boyars beheaded by one of the rulers who lived here — some say by Vlad the Impaler himself. The museum is open Tuesday through Sunday from 9:00 A.M. to 5:00 P.M.

Feudal Arts Museum (Muzeul de Arta Feudala): This eclectic collection of feudal weapons, tapestries, furniture, and stained glass from many lands was given to the state by Dr. Nicolae Minovici, the founder of Casualty Hospital. It is open Tuesday through Sunday from 9:00 A.M. to 5:00 P.M.

Herăstrău Park (Parcul Herăstrău): This 460-acre park surrounds the lake of the same name (the largest of Bucharest's dozen lakes). While it may not be a destination in itself for the foreign tourist, the visitor to the Village Museum will already be in it. It is popular with local residents on weekend afternoons and a fine place for people-watching. Children revel in its amusement park. In summer, **Rose Island** in the lake is bright with blossoms that perfume the air and strollers of all ages cross the little bridge that leads to it to admire them. The daring rent windsurfers, the more staid rowboats. There is an open air theater and several restaurants, the most popular of which is Pescarus, where there is a folk show.

House of the Republic (Casa Republîcu): Looking out on Revolutionary Boulevard is this sprawling 900-foot-long, 600-foot-wide palace that was to have been Nicolae Ceauşescu's answer to Louis XIV's Versailles. (Actually, it was the palace of North Korean President Kim Il Sung that he was hoping to outdo, so he dispatched architects to North Korea to see how to do it.) As for the site itself, he had thousands of homes and a number of historic monuments torn down to make way for the avenue, this monumental government palace, high-rise apartments, fountains, and gardens. Crystal chandeliers, carved marble pillars, inlaid pink-and-white marble floors, sweeping staircases, fourcarat industrial gold decoration, carpets that weigh as much as one ton — all are part of the decor of this eleven-story, 1,500-room building (with atom-bomb-proof cellars underneath). At the time of the dictator's death, 27,000 workers, many of them soldiers, were assigned to the construction. Still unfinished and with an uncertain future (no one knows for what *legitimate* purpose such a grandiose building could be used), it is now open to the public as a museum from 9:00 A.M. to 6:00 P.M. daily, except Monday.

Intercontinental Hotel, Bulevardul N. Bălcescu: What the Athenée Palace Hotel was to Bucharest in the first half of the twentieth century, this hotel has been since its erection in 1970. In its smoky, bustling lobby, the journalists of the world meet and mingle with government officials, revolutionaries, and spies. Black marketeers outside the door and prostitutes inside virtually became part of the hotel furnishings. Despite this, however, it remains one of the city's best-maintained and most comfortable hotels.

Manuc's Inn (Hanul lui Manuc): In the nineteenth century, when it was built by an Armenian merchant, Manuc-bey, Manuc's Inn was a caravansary for other visiting merchants. Today, recently refurbished, it houses a hotel and a garden restaurant and wine cellar. It is a two-tiered structure with wooden porches carved by craftsmen from Maramureş. A legend attached to it recounts how its founder, on a visit to Paris, stopped to see a fortune-teller, who, studying his hand, solemnly predicted the day of his death. Manuc-bey scoffed, but the fortune-teller made sure that her prediction did not fail. When she learned that he was planning a journey to Russia for the period during which she had predicted his death, she arranged to have him poisoned on his journey.

Museum of Popular Art (Muzeul de Arta Populară): Housed in the turreted Villa Minovici, built in 1905 by Dr. Nicolae Minovici in characteristic Romanian turn-of-the century style, are bright Transylvanian pottery, delicate Moldavian embroidery, carved wooden spoons, shepherds' pipes, icons painted on glass, and intricately painted Easter eggs. All were the private collection of the Minovici family, now given to the state. The museum is open Tuesday through Sunday from 9:00 A.M. to 5:00 P.M.

TV Compound (Studiou de Televiziune): Built in 1968, this is now a major landmark of the revolution of 1989. An intricate wooden cross carved in the style of northern Maramureş was erected here by its carver, Toader Bîrsan, as a monument to those who died defending the station.

Şoseaua Kiseleff: Stretching out at the north end of the city, this wide, chestnut-lined avenue leads from the Piaţa Victoriei to the Arch of Triumph, Herăstrău Lake and Park, the Village Museum, the State Publishing House (Casa Scinteii), and the Museums of Feudal and Popular Art before reaching the airport. It has a triumphal arch and is sometimes likened to the Champs-Elysées.

Stavropoleos Church (Biserica Stavropoleos): Elegant carving in both stone and wood make this pretty little eighteenth-century church designed in the style made famous in the days of Prince Constantin Brîncoveanu, the Wallachian builder-prince (*see* Crețulescu Church), a gem of Bucharest church architecture.

University of Bucharest (Universitatea București): Founded in 1856, the university — like all Romanian schools — retains a high quality of education. The exterior of its School of Architecture, richly decorated with twisted pillars and arches, is an example of the Brîncoveanu style that was popular in the seventeenth century and added Oriental and Venetian flourishes to the Dacian, Roman, and Byzantine architectural elements that had existed before.

University Square (Piața Universitații): In this square at the north-south city crossroads contemporary Romanian history was made. This was the scene of fierce fighting in the last days of the rule of Nicolae Ceaușescu. In the aftermath of his downfall and preceding the first free Romanian elections in more than four decades, crowds of those opposed to having former Communists in a new government camped out here for months, remaining even after the elections had been held. Their forced removal, with considerable bloodshed, by government-supporting miners said to have been brought in from far away at government expense, led to protests of human-rights violations from the United States and other Western countries.

Village Museum (Muzeul Satului): Three hundred structures — houses, farm buildings, windmills, churches — have been brought here, representing all parts of the country, and set among trees in Herăstrău Park. There are dark wooden houses from Maramureş in the north with elaborately carved gateways and roofs shingled like a dragon's scales; a church from Maramureş, decorated with Byzantine painting; a white fisherman's cottage from the Danube Delta; roofed well houses, mud-brick houses, and thatched-roof houses like miniature dwellings. For the traveler whose only stop in Romania is Bucharest, the Village Museum gives a glimpse of what the rest of the country is all about. For those who will travel farther, it offers a tempting foretaste. It is open 9:00 A.M. to 5:00 P.M. Tuesday through Sunday.

THE OUTSKIRTS OF BUCHAREST

Mogoşoaia Palace, Mogoşoaia: Ten miles northwest of Bucharest, the Wallachian prince Constantin Brîncoveanu, in 1702, erected this handsome lake-front palace in the woods. It is ornate in the way of the Brîncoveanu style with porches, loggias, arcades, and richly carved columns and is considered one of the finest examples of Romanian architecture. Unfortunately, earthquake damage prevents its being open to the public, but the gardens around it make a pleasant afternoon walk. The prince, who ruled Wallachia with great success from 1688 to 1714 and is responsible for the Byzantine-Venetian look of many of the old structures still standing in Bucharest, was a fierce fighter against the Turks. Captured by them, he, along with his four sons, was taken to Constantinople in 1714, and offered freedom if he became a Muslim. He refused, and his sons were then decapitated before his eyes. After the death of each, he was asked if he wished to reconsider, but each time he declined. Finally, he was beheaded himself and his property here confiscated.

Snagov Monastery (Mînâstirea Snagov), Snagov: Twenty-two miles to the north of the capital on a quiet little island in Lake Snagov is the monastery-church that Vlad the Impaler — the Dracula prototype — is said to have helped to build and where, legend has it, he lies buried beneath the altar. That way, each time the priest crosses his burial place during a service, he says a prayer for the wicked prince's soul. Defenders of the historical Dracula insist that, although he was harsh, he was also just. In this monastery he made his political prisoners kneel before an icon; while they were praying, a trapdoor would open and send them hurling into a ditch where stakes impaled them. In Ceauşescu days the birch and evergreen forest here and the little lake were reserved for use of the dictator and his family and friends alone. Now some of these private quarters have become hotels and restaurants open to the public.

MOLDAVIA

Tucked below the birch- and fir-clad hills of this northeasterly province bordering the Soviet Union are the painted monastery churches that are Romania's richest architectural treasure. Built in the fifteenth and sixteenth centuries and vividly painted inside and out with Bible stories, they have miraculously retained much of their color despite the winds, rains, and snows of as many as four centuries. Nowhere else in Europe is there anything quite like them. In Moldavia, too, monasteries fortified against the marauding Turks are hidden. The dramatic Bicaz Gorges and Mount Ceahlău's curious peaks and clusters of timber houses in mountain villages are other attractions to lure the traveler to this region. It's a long way from Bucharest, and the monasteries are most easily reached on guided tours, but for the stalwart traveler willing to rent a car, or a car and a driver, and simply explore in even more remote crannies, there are many wonders to be seen.

It was a Transylvanian prince, Bogdan Voda, who is credited with discovering this beautiful region — and naming it for his pet dog.

A great hunter, the prince — so the story goes — set off across the Carpathians one day in 1359 on a buffalo hunt. Hot in pursuit of a particularly impressive buffalo, Bogdan Vodă ventured deeper and deeper into the forests and valleys. Suddenly, Molda, his pet dog, racing ahead of her master, fell into the churning waters of a river, and was swept out of sight. The grieving prince named the river Moldova in honor of his canine friend and — not wanting to desert her (or perhaps to escape the Hungarian conquerors of his native Transylvania) — decided to stay forever in the new countryside.

He selected a site for a church and established a new feudal state which he called Moldavia after his dog and her river. That simple stone Romanesque church with arches that just begin to be pointed in a Gothic way and Byzantine-style painted pillars and walls still stands today in the town of Rădăuţi.

But it was a century later, in the Bukovina region of this sylvan setting, that the fifteenth-century warrior, builder, and prince Stephen the Great had the monasteries erected in gratitude for his successes in battle. Altogether, forty-four monasteries and churches were built by this Moldavian prince, who was dubbed the Athlete of Christ by the pope for his valiant efforts to protect Christendom from the infidel.

These monastery-churches borrow considerably from Byzantine art, with Gothic touches and such local Moldavian additions as the swooping, overhanging wooden roof that is a protection from the elements, the star-shaped central tower, and the snake-like bands of carved stone. Along with structures of the Brîncoveanu era, they are the most representative examples of Romanian architecture. But it is the frescoes, most of which Stephen's illegitimate son, Petru Rareş, had painted, that are most important.

How these frescoes, on outside as well as interior walls, and often compared with those at St. Mark's in Venice, have stayed bright through the brutal weather of five centuries remains a mystery. Chemical analysis has identified the sources of the colors — the red is from madder, the yellow from ochre, the black from charcoal and soot, the blue from indigo and lapis lazuli, the green from chromium oxide ore. The binders are cows' bile, egg yolk, vinegar, honey, and turpentine, but how they were combined to be of such a lasting quality no one knows. We do know, however, that the lime used for the walls before they were painted was kept in pits of water for three years before it was applied and was cleaned of impurities daily.

These brilliantly colored two-dimensional, Byzantine-style pictures of an inviting Heaven and a terrifying Hell, of the lives of the saints and Christ and the Virgin, of the fall of Christian Constantinople to the Turks, of curious beasts, fish, and birds were painted outside as well as inside the churches. Most of the time only the elite were allowed inside, but the peasants also needed to know the wages of sin and the rewards of good conduct that the Bible stories teach. These frescoes are now receiving UNESCO help in their restoration. The task, however, is an arduous one. Not only weather, but earthquakes, votive-candle smoke, battles, and today vandalism have ravaged the monasteries. Most churches remain unguarded with only a ticket seller at the monastery complex — often a sweet-faced nun in long skirts, with a scarf and a pillbox hat on her head. The monasteries are usually remote places, both an advantage and a disadvantage to those vandals who — less conscious than their ancestors of the debt one must pay for sin — scratch graffiti on the priceless art.

Nonetheless, five of the incomparable ecclesiastical buildings of Stephen the Great's period (and one that is later), situated in peaceful remote meadows, sheltered below rounded hills, or perched atop hills where shepherds in tall hats tend their flocks, are well worth the journey to see them. They are described below.

ARBORE

Green — blue-green, lime-green, dark forest green — is the color that predominates in the frescoes of this smallest of the Bukovina monastery-churches, constructed in 1503. Because it was built by one of Stephen's generals, Luca Arbore, not by a prince, it lacks a central tower, but the 1535 paintings by Dragoş Coman of Iaşi (Jassy) on the south and west exterior walls show perhaps the finest use of color at any of the churches. The scenes in good condition here include a Last Judgment and a Siege of Constantinople on the south exterior wall and tales from Genesis and the lives of the saints on the west wall. The interior of the church, where its founder is buried, is very dark, and it is difficult to make out the fresco pictures.

A curiosity here are the two stone slabs outside with indentations in them in which the artists are believed to have mixed their paints.

HUMOR

A high wooden wall surrounds this valley complex, but no fortification could have stopped the determined Turks who galloped through and laid waste to much of this monastery in the seventeenth century; after their departure, it was closed for eighty years. But today UNESCO experts have been cleaning away the votive-candle smoke on the interior frescoes with bread, and now the interior is the most worth seeing of any monastery's.

Like Arbore, Humor's church, built in 1535 by Theodor, chancellor to Stephen the Great's son, Petru Rareş, lacks a tower because its founder was only a nobleman, not a prince. It was Petru Rareş himself, however, who saw to its paintings. Rose is the predominant color.

One of the best-preserved frescoes here is the *Hymn to the Virgin* on the south exterior wall. Painted like a page of miniatures, one illustration shows the Mother of Christ offering help to the Christians of Constantinople when they were besieged by the Persians in 626. Hoping to nurture hatred of the Turks — the sixteenth-century enemies here — Toma, the painter of the frescoes, has garbed the attackers not as Persians but as Turks and painted a portrait of himself as a knight killing a Turkish official with a sword.

On the west wall is a Last Judgment. Those who look hard may be able to see that there is a fat old woman devil at Humor — in Romanian church lore seven evil women hold up Hell. (The female devil may be recognized not by her wings, but by the fact that she has no halo.)

Pretty flowers are painted over the doors here, and the UNESCO cleaning has brightened them as well as the draperies that decorate the lower third of the interior frescoes. No religious figures were painted at this level because, had they been, worshippers might have leaned or brushed up against them.

Also of interest in the interior is the elaborately carved wooden iconostasis, which, in an Orthodox church, separates the congregation from the sanctuary. For those with good eyesight, or accompanied by a guide with a flashlight, there is fine painting inside the dome of the narthex (the vestibule) to see.

MOLDOVIŢA

Built in a tranquil setting where sheep graze on the green hillsides, firs and spruce climb the mountains behind them, and fog spirals like smoke from mountain crevices, it is hard to see why outer stone walls twenty feet high would ever have been needed. A look, however, at the ferocious Turks the artist painted in the frescoes will tell why.

This 1557 structure was entirely constructed by Petru Rareş, who was prince of Moldavia when the Turks finally took it over. Here, the south wall, painted with much golden-yellow, depicts a Constantinople that is an assemblage of turrets and walls from which a group of Christian defenders fire crossbows at the Persian enemy of the seventh century, again dressed as if they were Turks. Meanwhile, other defenders parade an icon of the Virgin around the city. Taking even further artistic license than simply changing the Persians' clothes, this artist actually has the Christians routing the attackers rather than the other way around as it was historically. Also on the south wall, predominantly in a rich blue, is the twining Tree of Jesse, father of David, whose descendants, in this rendition, include the classical philosophers. The tree stops with Christ.

On the west porch there is a Last Judgment that lumps a Roman Catholic priest in with the pagan priests — an indication of what the Orthodox branch of Christendom thought of the Roman branch in those days after the eleventh-century split into an Eastern and Western rite. Inside, animals and flowers decorate the carved iconostasis and there is a picture of the church donor, Petru Rareş.

Because of the ill effects of candle smoke on this historic and artistic monument, and because there continues to be an active religious community here, a modern church has been constructed on a neighboring hill for today's worshippers. The visitor who arrives at service time will hear the *toaca* — the wooden board that hangs outside — being struck in the traditional way to call in the congregation. According to an ancient belief, the reverberating sound echoing in the hills is supposed to drive demons away.

PUTNA

Although this is not a white-plastered, painted monastery and has been rebuilt several times after fire, earthquakes, and battles, it is one of the most venerated Moldavian monasteries, for it was the first of those that Stephen built and it is here that he is buried. He is said to have selected the site by shooting an arrow from a neighboring hillside; where it fell, he would build the altar for his new church. It is a graceful stone structure with the characteristic swooping Romanian roof and is set inside ten-foot-high walls with towers at the corners.

Dandelions, daisies, and pansies brighten the grass around the church; the green velvet Carpathians rise outside. There is the tinkle of sheep bells, the rushing of a mountain stream. On a Saturday morning the visitor may happen on a wedding — priests intoning, wedding guests melodiously chanting. And outside the long spruce-lined approach to the monastery, in the village of Putna itself, a funeral procession, with an open coffin, followed again by singers, may be passing by the little gold-and-gray wooden houses behind picket fences. A boy with a stick may look up from tending his geese and his ducks in a dooryard.

SUCEVIŢA

If you look down on the monastery of Suceviţa from the fir-clad hills around it, you clearly see that it is a square-walled citadel with black guard towers at each corner and a boat-shaped, painted church as its centerpiece. The last and largest of the monasteries to be constructed, it is regarded by many as the finest and its frescoes have been classified as some of the best in the Byzantine world. Ieremia and Simion Movilă were the Moldavian noblemen who had it constructed in 1600. Twenty years later, it was painted in deep red and sea-green tones.

To enter it, you pass through a high arched gateway in the wall and enter a grassy courtyard. There, on the outside north wall of the church, the good seek to climb a ladder to Heaven with kindly angels offering them assistance and leering devils trying — and all too often succeeding — in hauling them from the ladder rungs. Under the cornice of the wall, priests and saints are ranged, dressed in robes decorated in the Byzantine way with patterns of crosses.

Under the arch of two buttresses there is a black carved woman's head, said to be a tribute to the farm wife who, for thirty years, hauled the stone for the monastery to this site in her ox cart.

On the southern wall, the graceful branches of the Tree of Jesse stretch heavenward. There the Virgin Mary, dazzlingly gowned as a Byzantine empress, sits beneath a large red veil held by angels and the philosophers of antiquity parade by on a frieze, with Plato bearing on his head an open coffin full of bones. Such a coffin was symbolic of the thoughts that living man should give to the death that lies ahead. The west wall is undecorated, for its painter is said to have fallen from the scaffolding to his death before it could be done.

Inside, around the apse, in teal blue and red and gold are angels, saints, and prophets. And there is a blazing river of fire in Hell.

In the quiet valley here, where the only sounds are singing birds and baaing sheep, it is easy to lose track of time contemplating these tapestrylike friezes.

Not far beyond Suceviţa in the village of Marginea, black pottery has been hand-made for generations, and it is worth stopping at almost any house, or at the cooperative, to look at the age-old forms in which it is still made and perhaps make a purchase. (The blackness here comes from smoking and polishing each piece before it is fired.)

VORONET

They call this painted church the Sistine Chapel of the Orient that Stephen the Great had built in just three months and three weeks in 1488. The remarkable blue of its frescoes, painted a few years later, has come to be known as Voronet blue.

The finest and best preserved of these is the ladder of the Last Judgment, a product of Romanian religious folklore, on the western exterior wall. There fish and animals — an octopus, a lion, an elephant — regurgitate the limbs of sinners they have consumed. Other sinners may be identified by their Turkish costumes. The coals of the fires of Hell burn at the feet of Jesus, and angels and devils are gleefully selecting the wicked and hurling them into Hell's flames while a crowd of good souls stampedes to get into Heaven, where the Virgin Mary waits to welcome them into a lovely garden.

On the outside southern wall there is a Tree of Jesse against a sky of brilliant blue. On the northern wall, but severely damaged by the weather, the Creation of the World — including the birth of the first child, Cain, to Eve — has been painted.

Inside are pictures of the life of Christ and of Stephen the Great and his family as well as a number of martyrdoms.

Artistically, the frescoes of Voronet are among the most imaginative and most human of any in Moldavia. The souls being carried to Heaven are wrapped in embroidered Moldavian towels. The angels in this sequence play the shepherd's *bucium* — the Romanian equivalent of the Swiss alpenhorn.

The easiest way to get to the monasteries is on a package air and bus tour booked through Carpați, the government tourist agency in Bucharest. There are also tours, offered from the city of **Suceava.**

Essential for the independent non-Romanian-speaking traveler who chooses to drive or be driven are a good road map and a list of gas stations. Reservations for all accommodations should be made in advance through Carpați in Bucharest.

In Suceava itself, a city of some 110,000 inhabitants, tourist sites are largely limited to the ruins of a fourteenth-century citadel in a pretty spot overlooking the verdant countryside. The sixteenth-century **Church of St. John the New,** with its multicolored tile roof (a Moldavian prince turned its original lead roof into bullets to fight invaders) and an impressive spire, is also worth a look, though it is far surpassed by the painted churches.

A few miles to the north, the seventeenth-century fortified **Monastery of Dragomirna,** though not painted, is remarkable for its slender Gothic lines, imposing carved stone ornamentation (architectural carving in both stone and wood are Romanian specialties) on its soaring tower, and the rare illuminated seventeenth-century manuscripts in its museum. Its founder, an ambitious patriarch of the church named Atanasie Crimca, is said to have insisted that the tower built for his church be twice as tall as any of Stephen the Great's church towers. Like the painted churches, this is in an exquisite setting among green forested hills.

In addition to Suceava, other possible monastery-touring centers with accommodations are **Cîmpulung Moldovenesc**, where there are some prettily decorated houses in the style of the Austro-Hungarian Empire of which it was once a part and a museum of wooden folk art and one of spoons; Gura Humorului; and Vatra Dornei, from which you can go to Lake Bicaz and the Bicaz Gorges or the villages of Bistriţa and Rădăuţi.

Gura Humorului is a pretty little town of golden-yellow houses, often with bulbous metal turrets. **Rădăuţi** is the site of Bogdan Vodă's stone church. There is also a restaurant in Rădăuţi — the Nordic — with a charming dining room for special guests — tourists included. Without a Romanian-speaker, it may be difficult to obtain a table, but if you succeed, you are likely to find the embroidered tablecloth flower-strewn in an old-fashioned way characteristic of the region, hot fresh bread, and simple well-prepared dishes. The appetizer might be stuffed grape leaves or sauerkraut; the soup, of potatoes and sour cream; the entree chicken roasted with onions. In 1990, such a dinner for three cost seven dollars.

The independent traveler who elects to rough it and go to the **Bistriţa** villages and the **Bicaz Gorges** might wish to visit the **Neamţ Monastery** outside **Tîrgu Neamţ** while in that area. Its main church is another built by Stephen with a characteristic Moldavian curved roof supporting an octagonal tower. Then there is Moldavia's capital city of **Iaşi** (Jassy), near the Russian border, site of another Moldavian architectural attraction — the seventeenth-century Gothic-Byzantine **Church of the Three Hierarchs** with its intricate stone lacework, Byzantine towers, and medieval arcading.

TRANSYLVANIA

Anyone who knows anything about Romania knows that it was among the "lofty steppes . . . the jagged rocks and painted crags" of the Carpathians that Count Dracula lured prey to his castle ruin. What they may not know is that the prototype for the long-toothed count, Vlad Ţepeş, was a fifteenth-century prince in the neighboring principality of Wallachia who destroyed his enemies by impaling them on spikes, or by having them boiled, roasted, strangled, or buried alive.

Although the real Dracula committed more of these grisly deeds in his own state across the soaring Carpathians than in Transylvania, the fourteenth-century Bran Castle here, with its turrets and parapets that dissolve in the mountain mists and then appear, has come to be known as his castle. And sometimes in Transylvania's remote mountain passes, there is eerie howling of wolves and the bold nighttime traveler may see wolf eyes gleaming in the dark.

But Transylvania is hospitable, too. Gold-and-pink Saxon villages established by traders who came from the West, four-towered medieval churches, haystacks swirled round sticks in green fields, and valleys white with apple blossoms in the spring and mountains where the snow glistens invitingly all welcome tourists. In Transylvania's fir forests, hunters find wild boar, deer, and bear. The Fǎgǎraş Mountains, with peaks more than 8,000 feet high, are the tallest mountains in Romania. There is a Swiss look to the landscape, but it has mellower touches.

In the far north, in the village of Maramureş, women sit on roadside benches, spinning wool on spindles. After a horse fair, long-legged, newly bought colts are trotted home beside hay wagons shaped like open boats. Dray horses sport red ribbons for luck. On city street corners, clusters of Gypsy women in flowered skirts sell celluloid toys and plastic glasses and a dark-eyed Gypsy child with a lamb may be kissing hands for a gift of coins. There are enormous hand-carved wooden gates outside Maramureş houses and the brightly painted carved crosses in the Merry Cemetery at Săpînţa dissipate the gloominess of death.

Transylvania, which was under Hungarian domination in the eleventh and twelfth centuries, and again from 1867 until 1918, and where Rhineland Germans were invited to settle by twelfth-century Hungarian king Géza II, reflects the influences of these peoples. Some say the monumental carving on doors and gates and houses for which Maramureş is renowned is of Hungarian origin; the pink-and-gold towns, the walled cities, and the onion domes are German and Austrian in origin. The geometric designs on the local pottery and embroidery and the painting on glass, however, are truly Romanian. But whereas Moldavia has an Eastern Byzantine look, Transylvania is more a land of the West.

Much of northern Transylvania has gone virtually untouched for centuries. Life in its villages, along its main roads shaded by chestnut trees and its muddy, rutted side roads, still revolves around hay and sheep and cows, ducks, and geese. Water comes from the wells housed in elaborate latticework well houses. Horses still pull the plows.

For all the tranquillity of the landscape, however, it cannot be said that Transylvania is without tensions. During the centuries of their rule, Hungarians oppressed the Romanians. Now in this period of Romanian rule, resentment of the Hungarian minority (there are about 1,800,000 Hungarians to 3,820,000 Romanians in Transylvania) is considerable. This is, in fact, the land of the city of Timişoara, where the revolution of December 1989 began, largely with the demands of the Hungarian minority.

But for the visitor, the beauty of the landscape, the ethnic diversity, and the old-fashioned ways overshadow these tensions.

Here are the major sites of a visit to Transylvania.

ALBA IULIA

It is almost as interesting to see Alba Iulia for its blocks of red-brick and stucco modern Ceauşescu apartment buildings with fountains and sunken garden areas and to imagine what they have replaced as to see what remains of the old city.

But most important of the old sites is the eighteenth-century red-brick **Citadel** that took 20,000 serfs twenty-four years to build. Erected in the star-shaped style of the French military engineer Sébastien Le Prestre, Marquis de Vauban, it is said to be the best Vauban-like fortification still standing in Europe. From the Citadel, you can look down on the winding Mureş River and onto the towers, roofs, and chestnut trees of the city and its surrounding green countryside. There have been fortifications on this site since Roman times when this was the capital of Roman Dacia. The grand seventeenth-century entrance to the fortress is a much-decorated, though now dilapidated, archway on which the eighteenth-century Hapsburg king Charles VI stands proudly with cowering Turks at his feet.

A less happy reminder of the rule of the Austro-Hungarian Empire is the **Monument to the Martyrs** of the 1784 Peasants' Revolt against Hapsburg taxes. After having been betrayed by their companions, two of the three leaders of the revolt were broken on the wheel, while the third saved himself from that fate by committing suicide.

Just a short walk from the Citadel, an enormous new Orthodox **Cathedral of Reunification** (Biserica Alba Julia) was erected in this century to celebrate the return of Transylvania to the kingdom of Romania when the Austro-Hungarian Empire was dismembered. It was also the 1914 coronation site for King Ferdinand I and his English-German queen, Marie. Before a crowd of 300,000, Ferdinand first crowned himself with an iron crown and then his wife with a four-pound diadem of emeralds, rubies, diamonds, turquoise, and moonstones.

At Catholic **St. Michael's Cathedral** (Biserica Sfîntul Mihai) across the street, Romanesque, Gothic, Renaissance, and Baroque architectural styles are united. Romanians and Hungarians alike make it something of a pilgrimage site as they come to visit the tomb of the fifteenth-century warrior-prince Ioan Hunedoara (in Hungarian, János Hunyadi), enemy of the Turks and father of Hungary's king in its Golden Age, Matthias Corvinus.

BRAN CASTLE (CASTELUL BRAN)

This formidable much-turreted castle perched high on a rock by a bubbling stream was built in 1378 by merchants who settled here and traveled back and forth through the Bran Pass to conduct their trade with the West. Its purpose was to protect the way to Wallachia. Later, tolls were exacted of travelers here. Set in its mountain fastness, and filled with nooks and secret crannies, dark corridors and winding stone stairs, Bran seems the perfect habitation for Bram Stokers's pale vampire count, Dracula. Historically, however, it is unlikely that the real Dracula — Prince Vlad Ţepeş — had much to do with Bran. One genuine resident was British-born Queen Marie of Romania, wife of Ferdinand I. The popular queen, a granddaughter of Queen Victoria and a castle collector, was given the castle as a gift by the citizens of Braşov and fell in love with it. She furnished it romantically with heavy, dark tables and chairs and enormous carved beds. This is the Bran that the tourist sees, along with old costumes, artifacts, and an outdoor museum of nineteenth-century peasant houses.

BRAŞOV

The **Old Town**, which is the nugget of Romania's second-largest city, is, happily, largely intact and well cared for. Built by the Saxon traders of medieval days, it was then called Kronstadt. According to one story, this was where the Pied Piper of Hamelin led the children he lured. With the opening of the doors to Western Europe, many Romanians of Saxon heritage have returned to the West, though there are still German-speaking residents here and German books in bookshops.

Braşov's Old Town has a fairy-tale look with its tipsy golden buildings edging the **Market Square**: the fifteenth-century **Town Hall** with its sprightly green-and-gold roof and Trumpeter's Tower from which alarms were sounded in times of danger; and the sixteenth-century **Merchants' Hall** that, in craft-guild days, was a trading center — now, as then, it houses shops along with a restaurant and an old-fashioned wine cellar.

But it is for the **Black Church** (Biserica Neagră), just behind the square, that Braşov is most renowned. Built between 1385 and 1477, architectural historians laud it as one of the finest German Gothic churches of Europe, and it is the largest between Vienna and Istanbul. Neither man nor nature has been kind to it, however. In 1421, when it was nearing completion, it was seriously damaged in a Turkish invasion; earthquakes have shaken it, and it gets its name from the 1689 fire the Austrians set in Braşov, which darkened its exterior walls with soot. But inside Oriental carpets that glow like gems decorate its walls. Legend has it that Braşov merchants heading for the Middle East promised God a rug if he would keep them safe on their journeys. As a result more than 100 Anatolian knotted rugs in jewel reds, blues, and golds hang from its walls. Its 400-pipe organ, on which there are concerts in summer and fall, is the largest mechanical organ in southeastern Europe, and there are charming primitive angels to be seen on the choir stalls.

Also to be viewed here is what remains of the fifteenth-century fortress erected around Braşov to keep out the Turks. It was erected with seven bastions, each to be guarded by a different guild. The best of these today is the **Weavers' Bastion** that now houses a museum recounting, in pictures and models, the days when attackers were at Braşov's walls. Among the attackers was Vlad the Impaler, who, in his usual fashion, left hundreds of captured townspeople stuck through with stakes on a hill on the outskirts of town. There is also a cable car up to Mount Tîmpa for a spectacular view.

Skiers who come here will find the modern resort of **Poiana Braşov,** eight miles away at the foot of 5,912-foot-high Mount Postavarul. The resort boasts a cable car, gondola, and numerous hotels and restaurants, both in the valley and on the slopes, where there is also a ski school. Skiing generally continues until May.

CLUJ-NAPOCA

It was in this former Austro-Hungarian city of golden-yellow and green houses frosted with white that Hungary's great Renaissance king and book collector Matyas (Matthias) Corvinus (*see* Hungary: Budapest) was born in 1448. His father was the heroic

medieval knight János Hunyadi (in Romanian, Ioan Hunedoara), victor against the Turks at the siege of Belgrade. The son
is remembered here by a monumental turn-of-the-century equestrian statue in the center of town on the Plaţa Libertaţii and by a
plaque on the house in which he was born at Matei Corvin 6, off
the main square.

Rising above the square is the fourteenth-century Catholic
Church of St. Michael (St. Mihail) with its 260-foot-high tower,
one of Romania's largest and finest Gothic churches. Also on the
square is the eighteenth-century Baroque Baniffy Palace, once
the home of Magyar nobility and now a museum of art and archeology (icons, weapons, carpets, and Transylvanian painting).
In early days, it was the Napoca of the Romans. Then, for many
centuries when Transylvania was an independent principality,
Cluj was its principal city and cultural center and sometimes its
capital. Later, from 1861 to 1918, it was either in Austrian or
Hungarian hands. In its Hungarian days in the 1890s, a school
of naturalistic, realistic painting developed here — called by the
Hungarians the Nagybanya School and by the Romanians the
Baia Mare. Samples of this style are exhibited in the palace museum.

Another site of interest here is the **Ethnographic Museum of
Transylvania** (Muzeul de Etnografie Transilvâniană) at Stradă 30
Decembrie 21 in the nineteenth-century Redoute building. In it
are pottery and costumes and one of Romania's most handsome
carpet collections. There is also a **Museum of the History of
Transylvania** at Stradă Emil Isac 2, and in **Hoia Forest** on the
edge of town, an open air museum of wooden houses and
churches.

On Stradă Republicii is the intriguing botanical garden of
Babeş-Bolyai University with trees and flowering plants from all
over Romania, plants used in industry, and a Japanese garden. In
Hungarian days the university, which is on Stradă Kogălniceanu,
was a leading Magyar educational institution.

Near it stands the fifteenth-century Gothic **Reformed Church**
with a statue of St. George and the Dragon, a copy of the one at
Hradčany Castle in Prague, in front of it, while at the end of the

street rises the only remaining tower of the city's fifteenth-century fortifications, the Tailor's Bastion.

In the same vicinity are the **Romanian National Theater** and **Opera** and the modern (1920s) Orthodox Byzantine **Cathedral,** built after Romania regained control of Cluj from Hungary after World War I.

A few dilapidated ruins of the old Citadel that protected the city rise above the Someş River. These are of interest primarily because of the fine view of the city and countryside they afford from the top.

HUNEDOARA

It is its extraordinary fortress-castle, **Corvin,** begun in the fourteenth century and added onto in the fifteenth, sixteenth, and seventeenth centuries, that is the reason to stop in this otherwise ordinary industrial town that is a major steel-making center.

Across a narrow bridge in the mountains outside of town, Corvin's red-roofed turrets and its parapets rise over its 100-foot-deep moat. In its inner courtyard are spiral staircases and rose-colored marble pillars, mullioned windows, and Gothic vaulting (a small replica of Corvin stands in Budapest in the City Park. See Hungary: Budapest). Exhibits in the museum inside recount how the castle was begun in 1421 by Iancu of Hunedoara. In time, it was passed down to the great medieval knight Ioan Hunedoara, who as ruler of Transylvania rebuilt it to make it almost as splendid as the Royal Castle in Buda. When Ioan Hunedoara died of the plague the day after his momentous defeat of the Turks at today's Belgrade, the castle went to his son, Matyas (Matthias) Corvinus, king of Hungary, who further reconstructed this castle. With the legendary Ioan Hunedoara a hero to (and claimed by) both Hungarians and Romanians, the castle was restored as a showplace in the 1960s.

MARAMUREŞ

Throughout this northernmost region of Transylvania near the border with the Soviet Union are picturesque villages of wooden houses with split shingle roofs and benches for sunning and peo-

17. In Maramureş, women sit on benches outside of their houses, spinning wool.

ple-viewing outside the high carved wooden gates. Ox and horse carts piled high with hay, wood, and peasants travel the roads. Here, women wear horizontally striped skirts on which yellow, red, or white stripes alternate with black; men carry their goods in twin checked cloth bags that drape over both shoulders. And tall-spired wooden churches with shingles like dragons' scales soar above streams and green churchyards and burial mounds. Among the best of the thirty-one of these wooden churches still standing (dating from the sixteenth and seventeenth centuries) are those at Şurdeşti, Plopiş, Naneşti, Deseşti, Şugatag, Sîrbi, Bogdan Vodă (birthplace also of Bogdan Vodă, who founded Moldavia), Bîrsana, Rozavlea, Poienile Izei (with terrifying pictures of the damned in Hell inside), Botiza, and Ieud.

At **Bîrsana,** one can watch Toader Bîrsan carving ornate wooden door posts and gates with flowers and animals outside his village house. (After the massacre at Timişoara, he and fellow Maramureş wood carvers carved and then carried a commemorative gate to Bucharest.)

It is wood carving, too, that makes **Săpînţa** one of the most charming communities of Transylvania. There, at the Merry Cemetery, Stan Ion Pĕtraş spent much of his lifetime carving and then gaily painting the crosses that stand in the graveyard. On each is a primitive picture of the deceased and a first-person mini-obituary in verse. If you can find a translator, you can learn, for example, "My name is Tite Anuta. As long as I lived, I liked just one thing, to work the whole day so I could offer my husband George turkey soup. Let God bless him and let him live longer than I do since I died when I was seventy." Above a painting of a farm wife with her cow, the obituary advises: "Who wants to get rich must get up early in the morning as I did all my life until I died when I was seventy-eight."

When Stan Pĕtraş himself died in 1977, the apprentice who has followed in his footsteps wryly wrote above his grave: "Many leaders of many countries used to come to see me, but when they come again they will not find me anymore."

It's a far cry from the macabre Transylvania of Vlad Ţepeş to the Merry Transylvania of the cemetery of Stan Pĕtraş.

SIBIU

Called Hermannstadt in German, this was the most important of the twelfth-century Saxon settlements in Transylvania and its industrious émigrés, primarily from the Rhineland, the Moselle valley, Flanders, and Saxony, erected walls around it for protection. The first wall was destroyed by invaders not long after its construction, but remains of a fifteenth-century brick wall still stand. (Because of the blood shed at its walls, the Turks, after an unsuccessful onslaught, called Sibiu "the Red City.") Built into the walls are defense towers that were assigned to particular guilds and medieval houses. You reach this labyrinth of arcaded medieval shops and houses down an old Passage of Stairs that descends from behind the immense **Evangelical Cathedral** on the old square — today the Piaţa Republicii. The cathedral, which took from the fourteenth to the fifteenth centuries to build, is of interest to Dracula aficionados because Vlad the Impaler's son, Mihnea the Bad, was assassinated while attending Mass here in its Catholic days in the sixteenth century and is buried in the crypt.

Also fronting on the old square are the Councillor's Tower, the Baroque Catholic church, and gay sixteenth- and seventeenth-century mauve, gold, and apricot houses. (These continue along the main walking street and are notable for the "eyes" — attic windows in their roofs — and their variety of color. Blue shutters may brighten a mauve house whose cornerstones are green.)

The handsome Baroque **Brukenthal Palace** on the square, which has been the Brukenthal Museum since 1817 and is one of the earliest museums of Europe, was built by art collector and, gossips say, lover of the Austrian empress Maria Teresa, Simon von Brukenthal, governor of Transylvania from 1777 to 1787. The palace was built as much, if not more, to show off his paintings to advantage as it was to be a dwelling place. Today, in addition to a fine folk-art collection that includes pottery, wood carving, costumes, and paintings on glass, it contains art from the workshops of Raphael, Andrea del Sarto, Correggio, Caravaggio, and Titian. An unsolved theft in 1968 depleted it of its original Van Eycks and Rubenses.

SIGIŞOARA

Vlad the Impaler, prince of Wallachia, was born here, in the hilltop **Old Town** of rose, gold, and gray Saxon houses. By the time he was five, his father, Vlad Dracul, had been enthroned as prince of Wallachia and the family had moved to Wallachia's Tîrgovişte, but a museum and restaurant are here in the house said to have been his birthplace.

Also worth seeing are the late Gothic Church on the Hill, the **Bergkirche**, reached by a climb up 175 steps, and the fourteenth-century **Clock Tower**, whose seven wooden marching figures that appear at midnight represent the seven days of the week. A soldier marches out on Tuesday (Mars Day). In Sigişoara's heyday, sixteen towers — some round, some hexagonal, some square, and each entrusted to a different guild — the tanners, the furriers, the butchers, the ropers, the tinsmiths — guarded the wall. Of these, nine remain, and the most interesting are the hexagonal Shoemakers' Tower and the Tinsmiths' Tower, where one floor is rectangular, others pentagonal, the top floor octagonal, and the roof hexagonal.

SZÉK

This village of thatched blue houses near Cluj is renowned for its Magyar folk music and the musicians who play and the Gypsies who dance to it at Saturday markets.

WALLACHIA

With the kind of pride an outsider might question, people here talk about the fifteenth-century ruler, Vlad Țepeș, who once impaled the wife of a peasant for shrinking his shirt when she washed it so it no longer covered his ankles. And they like to tell how the mason Manole, building the colorful, exotic monastery-church of Curtea de Argeș and finding its walls crumbling, walled his wife in alive when a dream vision told him that was the only way that the church would ever be done.

Although this is the land of the endless refineries and oil smells of Ploiești, it is also where the Danube River flows through the steep-walled Kazan Gorge (Cheila Cazane), one of the most dramatic spots of its 1,776-mile journey from Germany's Black Forest to this country's Black Sea. Here the extravagant royal summer castle at Sinaia captures the viewer's imagination the way Ludwig's castles do in Bavaria, and here the works of the shepherd boy Constantin Brâncuși, who became a sculptor, stand in a park by a river for all to freely view.

Wallachia has many sights to see.

COZIA

This oldest Wallachian monastery of alternating bands of red brick and stone was built by Vlad Țepeș's grandfather, the warrior Mircea the Old, in 1386, and he lies buried here. In the eighteenth century a vestibule was added by Prince Constantin Brîncoveanu, who introduced folk-art touches to the architectural style of this country. One of these is a belt, similar to a real one, called Brîncoveanu's Belt. A stone table at which the emperor Trajan is said to have dined is also of considerable historic interest. Though the highway is nearby, the dramatic gorges of the River Olt are below and blue-shadowed Mount Cozia rises to the east.

CURTEA DE ARGEȘ

The fanciful blue, green, and gold **Bishop's Church** here, grandly decorated with stone carvings and with two twisted and two octagonal towers, was built in the sixteenth century on orders from Prince Neagoe Basarab. Its admirers laud its vitality. Its detractors decry it as resembling an overfrosted cake. As noted above, this is the monastery-church within whose walls the mason Manole immured his wife to be sure the building would be completed.

Actually the story does not end there. The prince so admired his master mason's handiwork that he ordered Manole to build him another church. When Manole refused, fearful that without a wife to wall up in it, he would fail, the furious prince ordered him to throw himself from the church tower. Manole instead fashioned wings from some of the shingles on the roof and sought to fly off. Where he fell to his death, a spring spurted, known to this day as Manole's Well. Restored by a French architect in the last century, the monastery-church is now the mausoleum of some of Romania's royal family.

HOREZU

Most agree that this seventeenth-century monastery, with its serpentine columns, graceful sunny courtyards, intricately carved stone balustrades, pearwood stairways and iconostasis covered with carvings of animals and birds, and Byzantine-style frescoes, is the finest in Wallachia and one of the handsomest in all Romania. The town of Horezu itself, in pretty apple country, is known for its pottery decorated with birds and flowers.

CHEILE CAZONE (KAZAN GORGE)

The Danube River is at its most spectacular here at the border between Yugoslavia and Romania, where the 2,000-foot-high gray-rock sides of the gorge rise straight above the winding silver river and mist rises like smoke from rock crevices. You can drive through this impressive scenery from Orşova as far as the village of Moldova Nouă. Prior to the construction of the Iron Gates hydroelectric dam (the largest in Europe) just below the gorge in 1913, the most dangerous two miles of the Danube raced and roared over rocks in the narrow defile here.

POENARI

Only for Dracula fanciers are the remains of this fourteenth-century castle worth a visit; to reach it, there are 1,400 steps to climb, and though the view of purple mountains and verdant valleys is spectacular, the climb itself is exhausting. (To get the castle constructed, Vlad Ţepeş kidnapped the children of his nobles after an Easter Day party at Tîrgovişte and turned them into slave-laborers.) And from these heights, it is said that Vlad's wife flung herself to her death after receiving word that the castle was about to be taken by Turks. (First, of course, she dutifully warned her husband to flee.) Whether sorry about his wife's fate or not, Vlad took her advice. He escaped through a secret passage in the cellar and by shoeing his horse backward to elude his pursuers managed to make his way to Braşov.

SINAIA

This pearl of the Carpathians is nestled among fragrant pines in a narrow river valley around which mountain peaks soar to 7,000 feet. The air is crisp and clear summer and winter. Here, where skiers, hikers, and health seekers now gather, hermits from high in the mountains assembled in the Middle Ages for church services. In the seventeenth century, a Wallachian nobleman, Mihail Cantacuzino, was fleeing from enemies in the valley when he fell from his horse. He tried to escape along a streambed, and promised God that, were he saved, he would build a monastery here. Cantacuzino successfully eluded his pursuers and kept his promise, though not until he had completed a pilgrimage to the Holy Land. It was there he decided that the monastery he would construct here would resemble and be named for the one he had visited on Mount Sinai. Till the eighteenth century this remained a tranquil place. Then its fresh mountain air began to make it popular as a health resort, and in the 1870s the German-born Hohenzollern prince Carol I chose it for a summer palace and built the many-turreted Peleş Castle and two smaller palaces, Pelişor and Faison, here. The 160-room castle in the German neo-Renaissance style was fancifully decorated by his wife, Elizabeth, with carved woodwork, Swiss stained glass, and wall coverings of ebony and mother-of-pearl. Here, Carol II is said to have met his paramour, Magda Lupescu, a divorced woman, for love of whom he temporarily renounced his right to the throne. The castle has recently been reopened to the public and is worth seeing from the outside.

TÎRGOVIŞTE

Though today this former capital of Wallachia is principally a busy oil-producing city, it was here that Prince Vlad Ţepeş had his main residence. Though little remains of his palace but overgrown walls and the fifteenth-century Chindia Watchtower from which approaching enemies could be spotted, Dracula enthusiasts should certainly include it on their itinerary. Some of the approach from the direction of Bran Castle fifty miles away is through deep green valleys, where white-faced black cows graze and shepherds in black lambskin hats sell smoked sheep's milk cheese by the roadside. The red-roofed farmhouses have as their backdrop the snow-touched peaks of the Carpathians. Apple trees edge the roadsides and beehives perch on the hills.

At the Princely Court itself, if you can find someone who speaks English, you'll learn of the 500 noblemen whom the prince hospitably invited to a banquet. After they had enjoyed a satisfying dinner, he accused them of having plotted against his predecessors, took them outside, and impaled them on spikes beyond the city walls. You'll also hear of the beggars he similarly invited to dinner: when they had eaten and drunk their fill, he burned them alive, excusing himself with the remark that he had killed them "so they would be no further burden to the realm."

A happier site is the sixteenth-century **Princely Church** with its frescoed interior. Dracula's successors are painted in the entryway in their crowns and ermine robes.

TÎRGU JIU

The sculptor Constantin Brâncuşi was born in the village of **Hobiţa**, fourteen miles away from this industrial city. After he had achieved fame in Paris and America, he decided that the riverbank here would be the perfect setting for an outdoor museum of his work. Today you can view Brâncuşi's *Avenue of Seats, The Feast, The Endless Column, The Table of Silence, The Gate of the Kiss,* and other works and consider the success of the Romanian shepherd boy who died, an artist of renown, in 1957.

VATRA DORNEI

This spa is 2,625 feet above the Dorna River in forested mountains. In the winter it is a ski resort.

THE DANUBE DELTA

Northeastern Romania's 1,700 square miles of Danube Delta reeds and marshes, floating islands, and sand dunes is one of Europe's richest areas for bird life. More than 250 species of birds fly by here. Falcons from Mongolia, singing swans from Siberia, mandarin ducks from China, European reed nightingales, Iranian, Indian, and African birds pause on their journey north in the spring and south in the fall, for the delta lies almost halfway between the Equator and the North Pole and is on five major bird migration routes. In delta forests live wolves, foxes, and wildcats, owls and eagles. On floating reed islands wild boar forage. Mink, otter and ermine, muskrats and tortoises inhabit the delta, too, while sturgeon, pike, perch, carp, bream, and mackerel swim in the river and its estuaries, the sturgeon in spring laying the much-prized eggs that are black caviar.

The delta begins just beyond the port of Tulcea, where the river branches fan-shaped into three channels — Chilia, Sulina, and Sfîntu Gheorghe — before it reaches the Black Sea. Though the dedicated naturalist will not find its equal, exploring it can be difficult. Both hydrofoils and ferries make regular summertime trips from Tulcea down the central Sulina channel to the Black Sea, but it is really along the estuaries and in backwater lakes that wildlife may be seen. Reaching these areas is possible only with the help of a fisherman who has a canoe or rowboat.

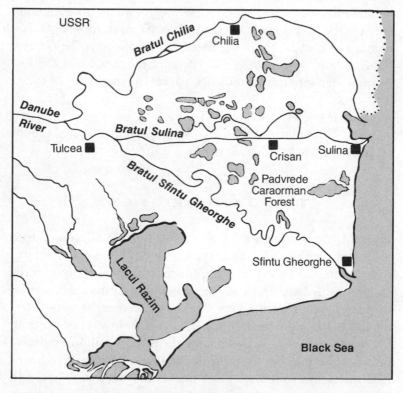

DANUBE DELTA

In the estuaries near Tulcea, 30-passenger boats do a little exploring, but the birds and animals, of course, tend to flee at the approach of a motorboat.

It is probably wisest either to book a tour with Carpaţi in Bucharest or at the Delta Hotel in Tulcea, but they are expensive, can only be paid for in dollars, and tend — when there are large boats used — to scare away the birds one has paid extravagantly to see. The alternative is to see if accommodations (which are limited) can be booked in Crişana, a ferry and hydrofoil stop on the Sulina channel, and from there try to make arrangements for a tour with a local fisherman.

But if you can arrange the trip, it is worth the effort. Along the narrow estuaries, willows dip into the green-gold waters, egrets stalk the banks, mallards skate by, and cormorants dive for fish. Tree trunks rise like sculpture in midchannel. Nets dry outside white fishermen's cottages on the estuary banks.

It is inadvisable, however, to go anywhere in the delta — on water or land — without a guide well informed in the ways of the wild. At Crişana the Hotel Lebăda is as good a hotel as one will find in the area. It has a Romanian first-class rating, but it may not live up to the usual Western expectations of first class.

That shouldn't matter. If you love the out-of-doors, you should see the delta, and the farther away from other tourists it is possible to go, the more you will see. Doing much of the fishing and guiding here are the Lipoveni people who fled through the *lipo* — linden forests — from the Ukraine in the seventeenth century, when Peter the Great was reforming the Russian Orthodox Church. They disapproved and settled here, making their living, then as now, as fishermen.

Often bearded and dressed in black cloaks, they are not hard to find once you are downriver. Communication, however, is likely to be a problem, but much can be accomplished with the help of a bottle of vodka.

If one manages to get off the much-traveled routes, there will be not only rare birds to see, but white-and-yellow water lilies as well as a multitude of other floating plants. And in fall, the reed cutters may be out, for delta reeds are used to make paper and cloth. (Rusty, floating dormitories to accommodate the reed cutters line the riverbank at Tulcea.)

There were plans in Ceauşescu days to farm much of the delta. Fortunately, little of this was done, and plans for future destruction of this rare environment have been canceled, but here and there along an estuary bank, you will still hear the rumbling of a tractor. Getting anything done in Romania — even putting a stop-work order into effect — can take a long time.

Since Tulcea is likely to be the point of entry for most delta visitors, a stop at the **Museum of the Delta** is a good introduction to what lies ahead.

THE BLACK SEA COAST

Golden sands where blue-gray olive trees toss in the wind, modern high-rise hotels and nightclubs, restaurants and discos, freshwater lakes and thermal springs, Roman ruins — and Romania's first nuclear-power station — are all part of Romania's Black Sea coast.

For the Romanian tourist, this is clearly *the* place to go in the heat of summer, and more than 1,500,000 people do. That may be a good reason *not* to come here at the height of summer, when hotels are crammed and sands a mass of sunners. But also along this coast and a little way inland are two notable sites of antiquity, Constanţa and Adamclisi.

CONSTANŢA

In ancient days, this was the city of Tomis, supposedly named for the pieces (*tomi*) of Medea's little brother, which she threw into the water to delay her father's pursuit as she fled from home with Jason and his Argonauts. Later, what is now Romania's largest port was given its present name in honor of the Byzantine emperor Constantine's sister. A big city today, Constanţa is spread out, but most of its historic and cultural sites are in the **Old City** (Oraşul Vechi), near the waterfront. The **Archeological Museum of the Dobruja** (Muzeul Archeologic Dobrogean) here is con-

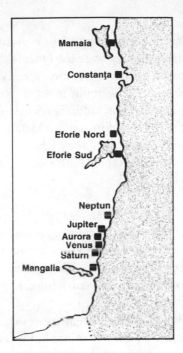

BLACK SEA COAST

sidered one of Europe's finest. Of particular interest are the 5000 to 4000 B.C. Hamangia-culture figures, *The Thinker* and *The Seated Woman,* and the second-century *Glykon Serpent* with its antelope head, serpent's body, and lion's tail. The originals of these (now at the National History Museum in Bucharest) and many other pieces in the museum were found in 1962 during excavations under the Constanța railroad station.

Also meriting a visit are the 1910 **Mahmudiye Mosque,** a colorful Roman mosaic that was originally probably part of a third- or fourth-century commercial building, and, for archeology buffs, the ruins of ancient Tomis.

The traveler here cannot help seeing the bronze statue of the Latin poet Ovid, who was exiled to this region by Caesar Augustus for playing a mysterious role in love intrigue in the imperial court. Here he revised his masterpiece, *Metamorphoses.*

ADAMCLISI

The original of the towering white stone monument near here that heralded Trajan's victory over the Dacians was built in A.D. 109. This 1977 reconstruction is, however, as close to the ancient monument as historians could make it. Recorded on it are the names of the 4,000 Roman soldiers who died in the ferocious fighting against the near indomitable Dacian king Decebalus, who committed suicide with his sons when he realized that the Roman conquest was inevitable. Battle scenes are also depicted on the monument's sides.

RESORTS

Mamaia: White sand and olive trees, glass-sided hotels (including a Club Med resort), and kidney-shaped swimming pools bring tourists by the thousands to this largest and best equipped of the Black Sea coast resorts. It is on a long, narrow strip of land between the sea and Lake Siutghiol.

Eforie Nord: This turn-of-the-century resort is more popular for the therapeutic mud baths of saline Lake Techirghiol behind it than for its swimming beach. But the setting, among pines and cypresses with red cliffs above the sea, is pretty.

Eforie Sud: Founded, like Eforie Nord, at the turn of the century, Eforie Sud was once called "Carmen Sylva" after Carol I's colorful queen, Elizabeth, who wrote poetry under that name.

Neptun: This is a considerably cozier resort than Mamaia, with its attractive garden going down to the sea and a yacht basin. The Ceauşescus had a villa here, now open to the public and a major tourist attraction.

Jupiter: Along with the beach, an artificial lake and a forest are among the attractions.

Venus: This is a smallish resort with man-made beaches.

Aurora: Pyramidlike hotels and a forest are the trademarks of Aurora.

Saturn: The forest is an appeal of this resort where horseback riding through the woods is offered.

Mangalia: Once upon a time, the ancient Greek city Kallatis was here, but since the 1950s this has been a resort lying between

the forest of Comorova, which is also behind Aurora and Saturn, and Lake Mangalia. One descends cliffs to the sea and the harbor, and there are a few Greek archeological remains here and an archeological museum.

Getting There, Sleeping, Eating, and Entertainment

Because of the beauty of the Romanian countryside, it's a pity to fly over it. Most main highways (Drum National or DN) are good, and there is virtually no traffic. (Drum Modernizat, however, are considerably better than Drum Nemodernizat.) Rental cars are now available in Bucharest through Carpaţi Bucureşti, the National Tourist Office at Bulevardul Magheru 7 in Bucharest, but dollars are needed to pay for them. It is, however, possible to reserve cars and prepay in the United States through Auto-Europe in Camden, Maine 04843 at 800-223-5555. Avis and Hertz also rent in Bucharest and the United States. The Romanian Automobile Club (ACR) at Stradă Nikos Beloianis 27 in Bucharest, which is affiliated with AAA, can provide a list of Peco (gas) stations. There is now considerably more gasoline available than in Ceauşescu days, but gas stations are in the cities rather than on the highways, so it is essential to know in advance where they are located. It is also wise to carry a little extra gasoline with you.

Along with information on gas stations, ACR can also give advice on repair stations around the country.

To buy gas, foreign visitors must prepay in hard currency for vouchers, which may be bought at Carpaţi offices, many hotels, at border-crossing points, and at Otopeni International and Kogălniceanu airports in Bucharest.

Taking a train is another good way to see the countryside, though it requires stamina, patience, and an adventurous spirit. It is, however, one way to get acquainted with Romanians, for rail is the most widely used form of transportation. The best trains to take are Rapid or Accelerat, as they make the fewest stops. Train schedules are posted in Railway *Câile Ferate Române* (CFR) stations with *Sosire* (SOS) indicating arrival times and *Plecare* (PL) departure hours. Both sleeping couchettes for long-distance overnight travel and reserved seats on the rapid trains are offered, but they should be booked in advance at a CFR agency (Agenţia CFR) or at Carpaţi's central office in Bucharest. Carpaţi is generally open from 7:30 A.M. to 3:30 P.M. Monday through Friday and from 8:30 A.M. to 1:30 P.M. on Saturday. There is usually someone who speaks English in the office.

Although there are buses that run between cities, it is generally inadvisable for any but the *most* adventurous to use them, for their schedules are subject to mysterious change. Local buses and trams, however, if you can find someone to tell you which one goes to your destination, run on a regular basis. Don't expect to see much out the windows, though. They never seem to get washed.

Tickets for trams and buses are bought at ITA kiosks or tobacco stores, and once you have boarded the bus or tram, it is your responsibility to punch your ticket in the ticket-punching machine. If you do not, you must pay a fine.

Air transportation from city to city is another option for the visitor, but unless you are accompanied by a Romanian companion, you may never find your way to the flight you are after. Tarom Airline's internal flights leave from Bucharest's Baneasa Airport. Reservations must be made in advance at Tarom's office at Stradă Mandeleev 11 or upstairs at Stradă Brezoianu 10 or with Carpaţi. Bear in mind that little English is spoken in either Tarom offices or at the airport, and finding the flight you are booked on and bucking the crowds of Romanians who are also booked on it will be virtually impossible without a native who knows something about it. Organization and orderliness are not Romanian strong points.

Tarom serves Bucharest from New York twice a week with a stop in Vienna. Other airlines with connecting service include Lufthansa and SwissAir. There is international rail service from Budapest and Belgrade.

Those wishing to explore the Danube Delta should also book well in advance for the spring, summer, or fall boat service there. If arrangements are not made with the Romanian Tourist Information office in the United States at 573 Third Avenue, New York, New York 10016 (212-697-6971), they should be made with NAVROM, the company that operates the boats, near the Gară de Nord in Bucharest on Bulevardul Dinicu Goescu, or with Carpaţi in Bucharest (Tel. 145-160). Again, in dealing with the boat line, remember that little English — if any — will be spoken.

Taking a package tour in Romania won't be anywhere near so much fun as doing it yourself, but it will surely be less frustrating. For complete information on U.S. tour operators with Romania on their itineraries, get in touch with the Romanian Tourist Information office in New York. Among the town operators are Litoral Travel, 124 East 40th Street, Suite 403, New York, New York 10016 (212-986-4210); ETS Tours, Inc., 450 Harmon Meadow Boulevard, Box 1568, Secaucus, New Jersey 07096-1568 (800-346-6314); Foreign Accent, Inc., 532 Third Street, No. 2, Ann Arbor, Michigan 48103, in conjunction with Unitours, 8 South Michigan Avenue, Chicago, Illinois 60603; and U.S. International Travel and Tours (800-759-7373). If you go by yourself, bear in mind that street names are changing daily.

However and whenever you choose to go, because of the limited number of accommodations of acceptable quality for foreigners, room reservations should be made in advance — ideally with a travel agent in the United States before departure; if not, with Carpaţi in Bucharest or local tourist offices (*inspectorat*) as soon as your itinerary has been planned. Visas may be obtained without photographs at any border crossing point.

As for dining in Romania, it, too, can be a problem for the independent traveler, as most restaurants that cater to foreign tourists cater to groups. As a result, travelers by themselves are likely to find all tables reserved. That is a little less true in hotel restaurants, but the service is bound to be slow.

Hotel dining rooms tend to be of two or three kinds — loud and smoky rooms where beer and food are served and more elegant dining rooms where wine, but no beer, is offered with meals, and private dining rooms where you eat alone.

Breakfasts (generally included in the hotel room rate) are substantial here. The choice is usually a cold ham and cheese plate or fried eggs and ham, both accompanied by white bread, thick jam, and strong Turkish-style coffee or tea. (Beware, the tea may be presweetened.)

Other meals begin with appetizers (*gustăre*). These can be salami (*salam dè Sibiu* is the best), goat cheese (*telemea*), and minced meat called *mititei* in sausage form strongly flavored with garlic and carraway seeds, or a pork or chicken aspic with a vegetable garnish (*piftie*).

Grilled meat — pork or veal — is the ubiquitous main-course offering. When there is chicken, it tends to be quite flavorful. Charcoal-grilled fish can also be good, as can stuffed cabbage, *sarmale,* but this is hard to come by. What is found virtually everywhere is a ground corn dish (*mămăliga*) that often is substituted for rice or potatoes. Soups either are thick and made with sour cream (*ciorbă*) or are meat broths (*supă*).

Beer (generally from Azuga in the Carpathians) and wine are good. The best of the wines are Grasa and Feteasca from Moldavia; and Riesling, Muscat, Cabernet Pinot Negru, and Chardonnay. *Ţuica* — plum brandy — is the strong drink available.

Pogăcsa (baking powder biscuits) are popular and filling.

Desserts invariably are overly sweet cakes and puddings, and bread is almost always white and uninteresting.

Hotels outside Bucharest — even when they have multistar ratings — are basic. Most lobbies are enormous, high-ceilinged, and smoky with only a handful of Naugahyde (or the Romanian equivalent) chairs generally occupied by "traders" of one sort or another. These may be black marketeers, salesmen of cheap goods brought in from other Eastern European countries, or prostitutes.

The bedrooms themselves, everywhere except in the very best hotels in the capital, generally need new mattresses, and the TV sets are more likely *not* to work than to work. Lamps throw faint light, heat is questionable, and toilets, sinks, and showers — like TVs — may work. Housekeeping, for the most part, is only adequate.

Below are a few acceptable hotels and restaurants at major tourist destinations.

BAIA MARE
HOTEL
Hotel Baia Mare, Blvd. Unirii 11 (Tel. 994-36660). For travelers planning visits to the wooden churches of the Iza Valley, this efficient, well-run modern hotel is the best bet. It isn't charming, but the food is good and more attention is paid to general upkeep than in most Romanian hotels.

BRAŞOV
HOTEL
Hotel Aro, Blvd. Gh. Gheorghiu-Dej 25 (Tel. 921-42840). This 312-room luxury hotel is equipped with a swimming pool and sauna, and a good restaurant.
RESTAURANTS
The Carpathian Stag (Cerbul Carpatin), Str. Republicii, is a cellar restaurant in an old merchant's house.
Cetatuia Fortress. Musicians from the Philharmonic Orchestra of Braşov often play at dinnertime here, or there may be operetta or dancing.

BUCHAREST
HOTELS
Ambassador, Blvd. Magheru 10 (Tel. 11-04-40). This is a centrally located first-class (as opposed to deluxe) hotel.
Athenée Palace, Str. Episcopeiei 1-3 (Tel. 14-08-99). This is an old-fashioned, centrally located hotel erected in 1914, but renovated. The price is $100–$125 for a double, including breakfast. Its dining room is fair, its fancy nightclub expensive.

Bucureşti, Calea Victoriei 63-81 (Tel. 15-45-80). This is Bucharest's newest and biggest hotel with indoor and outdoor pools, a sauna, and a health complex, but it has already been scheduled for renovation.

Intercontinental, Blvd. N. Bălcescu 406 (Tel. 14-04-40). Everyone who is anyone among foreign visitors stays nowadays at the Intercontinental, which is centrally located and has a nightclub, pool, health facilities, two restaurants (with good food in the twenty-first-floor restaurant), and a coffee shop. The price in season 1991 is about $170 double, including breakfast, and $140 single.

Lebăda, Blvd. Biruintei 3 (Tel. 24-30-10). Situated on Pantelimon Lake, eight miles outside the city, this is a pretty, new hotel that opened in 1988, but it is a stay-awhile sort of hotel, at which one can enjoy the lake, but it is not well situated for the tourist with little time who wishes to see Bucharest. The food is fair. The price is $100–$125 double.

Manuc's Inn, Str. 30 Decembrie 62 (Tel. 13-14-15). Once a genuine caravansary, the thirty rooms of this nineteenth-century hotel are situated around a central court. It has considerable charm, but it is Romanian first-class (not deluxe). Its location opposite the Princely Court is good. The double room rate is about $100, including breakfast.

RESTAURANTS

The Beer Cart (Carul cu Bere), Str. Stavropoleos 5. The spicy grilled little sausages called *mititei* are a specialty in this casual popular restaurant, and you are likely to be able to get other Romanian dishes here like *sarmale* (stuffed cabbage), *ghiveci* (a melange of fried vegetables), and the inevitable *mămăliga* served with beer.

Capsa, Calea Victoriei 54 (Tel. 13-44-82), an old-time literary café, is now a small restaurant serving good food well. In summer, however, it can be hot. Reservations are essential.

Casa Lido, Blvd. Magheru. There is good food in this new restaurant and good service. Reservations are essential, but the price is moderate.

Doina, Şoseaua Kiseleff 4. A Romanian-style restaurant with

Gypsy music. The restaurant is named for the melancholy folk songs of Maramureş that are part of the entertainment.

Manuc's Inn, Str. 30 Decembrie (Tel. 13-14-15), serves Romanian cuisine in the rooms adjoining the Old Inn. Reservations essential.

Parcul Privighetorilor in Pădurea Bâneasa. Typical Romanian restaurant cuisine. Reservations are essential.

Pescărus, Parcul Herăstrău (Tel. 79046-40). A pretty location and pleasant if not exceptional fish dishes. Reservations are essential.

ENTERTAINMENT

Cişmigiu Gardens (Gradina Cişmigiu). Open air concerts of the Ciprian Porumbescu Conservatory are performed here in summer.

Opera Romană, Blvd. Gheorghiu-Dej 70 (Tel. 13-18-57).

Opereta, Piaţa Natiunile Unite 1 (Tel. 14-80-11).

Romanian Atheneum (Ateneul Român), Str. Franklin 1, Piaţa Gheorghiu-Dej (Tel. 15-68-75). The George Enescu Philharmonic Orchestra gives its performances in this grandiose turn-of-the-century building.

Tăndărică Puppet Theater (Tăndărică Teatrul de Păpuşi), Calea Victoriei 50.

CONSTANŢA

HOTEL

Hotel Palas, Str. Opreanu 5-7 (Tel. 916-14696). The location of this recently renovated hotel above the sea and near the old port couldn't be better.

RESTAURANTS

Casa cu Lei (House of the Lions) is a pleasant restaurant with dining rooms done with Romanian, Spanish, and Venetian decor.

The Casino is a recently restored restaurant near the sea.

CRIŞANA

HOTEL

Hotel Lebăda (Tel. 915-14720), on the Sulina channel of the

Danube down the delta, is the only choice for travelers wishing to do delta exploring by small boat.

EFORIE NORD

HOTEL

Europa, Blvd. Republicii 19 (Tel. 917-42990). Overlooks the sea and offers either rooms in its high-rise section or villas by the water.

RESTAURANT

Nunta Zamfirei serves Romanian fare and offers a folklore show, but it is on the resort's outskirts.

MAMAIA

The Litoral National Tourist Office in the Hotel Bucharest here can provide information on Black Sea coast travel.

HOTEL

Hotel International (Tel. 918-31025). Though it isn't a new hotel, it is the only deluxe facility on the beach.

RESTAURANTS

Miorița serves Romanian food in an attractive lake setting.

Satul de Vacanta (Holiday Village) is a complex of small restaurants offering specialties of various parts of the country.

NEPTUN

HOTEL

Hotel Neptun (Tel. 91-31020). The lakeside location of this 126-room luxury hotel makes it especially attractive, and it is not far from the sea beach.

RESTAURANTS

Fish is the specialty at the **Insula** on an island in Lake Neptun while at the **Calul Balan** in the neighboring Comorova Forest, folklore shows are offered with dinner. The **Popasul Căprioarelor** is a pleasant garden restaurant where there are folklore shows.

OLIMP (ADJOINING NEPTUN)

HOTEL

Panoramic (Tel. 917-31356). This is an expensive hotel, but its location above the beach is a good one.

SIBIU
HOTEL
Hotel Imparatul Romanilor, Str. Nicolae Bălcescu 4 (Tel. 1-64-90). This ninety-six room, eighteenth-century hotel has been charmingly restored and, though the dining room service is slow, the food is better than average. There can, however, be large, noisy parties in the dining room.

SIGIŞOARA
RESTAURANT
The Citadel. Legend has it that this is where Vlad the Impaler — Dracula — was conceived and born. Under those circumstances, the quality of the fare is less important than the ambience.

SUCEAVA
HOTELS
Hotel Arcaşul, Str. Mihai Viteazul 4-6 (Tel. 1-09-44). This Romanian first-class hotel is distinctly second-class, with the same sorts of problems as the Bucovina. Its restaurant, however, serves fair food.

Hotel Bucovina, Blvd. Ana Ipătescu (Tel. 1 70-48). Don't expect the television to work or the beds to be anything but lumpy in this dark, down-at-the-heels, Romanian first-class but American second-class hotel, but Suceava has limited accommodations.

RESTAURANT (near Suceava)
Nordic, Piaţa Republicii 21 in the town of Rădăuţi (Tel. 989-62-803). Both food and service in the private dining room are charming. In season, try the raspberries. At any time, enjoy the roast chicken. The main dining room tends to be hot, crowded, and smoky, however.

TIMIŞOARA
RESTAURANT
Tourist Inn (Hanul Turistic Timis), Blvd. Calea Dorobantilor 94 (Tel. 961-32202). The ambience is nothing special, but the food is good.

TULCEA

Delta Hotel, Str. Isaccea 2 (Tel. 915-14720). This first-class hotel is adequate with a competent but unimpressive kitchen (though the grilled fish can be good). Its location directly above the Danube docks is a good one for those planning Danube Delta excursions.

INDEX